A Concise Dictionary of First Names

PATRICK HANKS
and FLAVIA HODGES

Oxford   New York

OXFORD UNIVERSITY PRESS

Oxford University Press, Walton Street, Oxford OX2 6DP
Oxford New York Toronto
Delhi Bombay Calcutta Madras Karachi
Kuala Lumpur Singapore Hong Kong Tokyo
Nairobi Dar es Salaam Cape Town
Melbourne Auckland Madrid
and associated companies in
Berlin Ibadan

Oxford is a trade mark of Oxford University Press

British Library Cataloguing in Publication Data
Data available

Library of Congress Cataloging in Publication Data
Hanks, Patrick.
A concise dictionary of first names / Patrick Hanks and Flavia Hodges.
p. cm.
1. Names, Personal—English—Dictionaries. I. Hodges. Flavia. II. Title.
929.4'4'03—dc20 CS2377.H35 1992 92-21005
ISBN 0-19-866190-8

3 5 7 9 10 8 6 4

Typeset by Wyvern Typesetting Ltd.
Printed in Great Britain by
Clays Ltd.
Bungay, Suffolk

Introduction

A person's given name is something very personal, but it is also a badge of cultural identity. It says something about the cultural group that he or she belongs to; in some cases even, something about the particular family which he or she comes from. Until recent years, cultural identity was closely associated with religious affiliation, but in the 20th century naming practices have become increasingly secular. Still, names such as *Aloysius, Ferdinand, Xavier*, and *Carmel* are strongly associated with the Roman Catholic Church, while *Calvin* and *Luther* are clearly Protestant. *Zipporah* is still clearly Jewish, *Siobhan* Irish, and *Rhodri* Welsh. Against this, other factors are at work. In the first place, there has been cultural seepage: *Rebecca, Deborah*, and *Judith* can no longer be regarded as even primarily Jewish names, nor *Alistair* and *Kenneth* as Scottish, nor *Shaun* and *Sheila* as Irish.

The process of augmenting the small stock of traditional names with new coinages has accelerated greatly since about 1960. Short forms, pet forms, nick-names, surnames, even placenames have been pressed into service. The film industry and the pop-music business have appeared, alongside hagiographies of Christian saints, as sources of names for children. This dictionary records all the traditional names of the English-speaking world – all those, in fact, which are well established or (at the very least) well on the way to becoming established. Altogether it contains over 3000 names, of which over 100 have never been recorded in any names dictionary before.

In some cultures, for example Arabic, names are just special uses of ordinary words. In such cultures, a name can be chosen on account of its meaning, as well as on grounds of its historical or religious associations or euphony. This is not the case with English; the 'meaning' of the vast majority of English names is to be sought in languages other than modern English, often ancient languages no longer spoken and only studied by specialists. Because of this, among English speakers there can rarely be any question of choosing a name for a child on the basis of its meaning. A name is chosen either on ornamental grounds – 'because it sounds nice' – or in honour of some close relative.

There are definite vogues for given names; they come into fashion and go out again for reasons that can sometimes be recorded: for example, a name may experience a sudden increase in use after it has been used for a character in a popular book, film, or television series. More seriously (but less noticeably), a particular set of names may be associated with a religious sect or cult, which will affect the popularity of those names. In other cases, the popularity of certain names seems to ebb and flow regularly with the generations.

Biblical Names

The most widespread of all given names are those taken from names of characters in the Bible. These are borne by Jews and Christians alike all over the world: names such as *Adam* and *Eve*; *Benjamin*, *Joseph*, and *Jacob*; *David*; *Sarah*, *Deborah*, *Rebecca*, and *Ruth*. Some of these names are rare now. Among non-Jews, names such as *Reuben* and Seth, *Zillah* and *Beulah* are associated particularly with Nonconformist sects of the 17th century and the Christian fundamentalists of the 19th. A few, especially female names such as *Abigail*, have survived or been revived in modern use, but others have once again dropped out of fashion. In general, Old Testament names are found among both Jews and Protestants, but are uncommon among Roman Catholics.

New Testament names are, of course, shared by Christians of all sects and persuasions. The most important names in the New Testament are those of the four evangelists, *Matthew*, *Mark*, *Luke*, and *John*, and the apostles, principally *Peter*, *James*, *Andrew*, *Thomas*, *Philip*, *Bartholomew*, *John*, *Matthew*, and *Simon*. *John* is trebly important: the name was borne by an apostle (the son of Zebedee), by the author of the fourth gospel, and by the forerunner of Christ, John the Baptist. The frequency of forms of *John* among early Christians ensured that it would be borne by some early saints, which further reinforced its popularity.

With the exception of Mary, the mother of Jesus, very few women play a major role in the gospels. This helps to explain why the set of conventional female Christian names is even smaller than that for males, and why *Mary* has been so enormously popular. The name *Mary* is borne by others in the New Testament – principally Mary Magdalene, a woman who 'had been healed of evil spirits and infirmities' (Luke 8), and who was identified in Christian tradition with the repentant sinner of Luke. Other important New Testament female names from the gospels are *Martha* and *Elizabeth*.

Saints' Names

A large number of names owe their importance to the fact that they were borne by early, famous, or canonized Christians, ranging from learned Church fathers (*Basil*, *Ambrose*, *Jerome*, *Augustine*, and *Gregory*) through innumerable martyrs (*Agatha*, *Agnes*, *Laurence*, *Sebastian*), mystics, ascetics, and visionaries (*Anthony*, *Simeon*, *Francis*, *Teresa*), founders of religious orders (*Benedict*, *Bernard*, *Dominic*), to the simple 19th-century French peasant girl (*Bernadette*), whose visions of the Virgin Mary led to the foundation of a healing shrine at Lourdes. What they all have in common is that at some time during the past two millennia a cult grew up around them. In some cases (*Christopher*, *George*) the legends of the cult have obscured any basis of historical fact that may once have existed.

Introduction

Christian sainthood is almost the only channel by which old Roman names have been transmitted to present-day use as given names. In spite of the pervasive use of Latin during most of the Christian era, Roman names that were not borne by early saints have almost entirely dropped out of use. This is because the early Church made repeated attempts to suppress classical literature and to obliterate all memory of pagan classical history. In the Christian era, therefore, there has been almost no tradition of naming children in honour of the great figures of classical antiquity. Where a Roman name such as *Antonius*, *Claudius*, *Julius*, or *Marcus* has yielded modern derivatives, we may look with confidence for an early saint or martyr somewhere along the road.

Royal and Aristocratic Names

A name that is borne by a member of a royal family, especially a successful and much-admired monarch, invariably rapidly increases its currency among his or her subjects. Thus, the popularity of the New Testament name *Elizabeth* was greatly enhanced by the fact that it was borne by the enlightened and skilful queen of England who reigned 1558–1603. It has remained popular, partly because of that association, ever since. Its popularity increased again in the 20th century, after it became apparent in 1936 that the Princess Elizabeth would succeed to the throne.

Elizabeth, like *James* and *John*, is a biblical name, firmly rooted in the Christian tradition. However, the majority of English royal and aristocratic names, for example *William*, *Henry*, *Richard*, and *Robert*, not to mention *Charles*, have their origin in a distant, pre-Christian Germanic past. Most of these names have been transmitted to us through Norman French. With the exception of *Edward*, most names of Old English derivation, even royal names, went out of use after the Norman Conquest. *Edward* survived, mainly because King Edward the Confessor was venerated by Normans and Saxons alike. Other names derived from Old English, such as *Alfred* and *Edwin*, *Audrey* and *Elfreda*, went out of use, but were revived in the Victorian period. Many of them now once again seem somewhat old-fashioned.

A few modern English first names reflect Old Norse personal names established in England before the Norman Conquest, such as *Harold*. However, the vast majority of royal and aristocratic English names are of Norman origin.

The Normans themselves spoke French, having abandoned their Norse language and pagan culture when they established themselves in northern France in the 10th century. Even more surprisingly, they abandoned most of their traditional Norse names. Within a few decades, they adopted the Christian religion, the French language, and French names. It so happens that although the French language is mainly derived from Latin, many of its names are derived from Germanic. These are survivals of the extremely ancient names that were used in the Germanic languages once spoken in France, in particular Frankish, the vernacular of the court of Charlemagne. Thus, *William* is from *wil* meaning 'will' plus *helm* meaning 'helmet'. Germanic names normally consist of two vocabulary elements, reflecting qualities that were prized in prehistoric Germanic society: they have meanings such as 'war', 'strife', 'battle'; 'protection', 'rule', 'counsel'; 'raven', 'wolf', and 'bear'.

Many, but not all of the most common male names of Germanic origin that are used in Britain today owe their importance to having been royal names: they were borne by one or more kings of England (or, as in the case of *Robert*, Scotland). But some, such as *Gerald*, *Hugh*, and *Roger*, were borne by members of the aristocracy rather than royalty.

Rather fewer Germanic female names, such as *Alice*, *Emma*, and *Matilda*, have survived into modern English. Generally, they are no less warlike in the meaning of their components than their male counterparts. The origins of these Germanic names owe nothing to Christianity, although in some cases, for example *Bernard*, their survival does: many such names were borne by people who became Christian saints, after whom children were named in succeeding generations.

The Celtic Tradition

After Christianity and Germanic royalty, the greatest influence on the stock of names in the English-speaking world has been the Celtic tradition. Many names are now used throughout the world by people who may be only vaguely aware, if at all, of their derivation from Irish or Scottish Gaelic or from Welsh. Examples are *Brian*, *Bridget*, *Donald*, *Duncan*, *Ian*, *Kenneth*, *Kevin*, *Neil*, and *Sheila* from Irish and Scottish Gaelic, and *Gareth*, *Gladys*, *Gwendolen*, and *Trevor* from Welsh. Other Celtic names exist in an Anglicized form, but are still used mainly by people conscious of their Celtic ancestry, for example *Brendan*, *Connor*, *Cormac*, *Declan*, and *Rory* from Gaelic and *Branwen*, *Dylan*, *Dilys*, *Gwyneth*, *Olwen*, and *Wyn* fom *Welsh*.

In Ireland, Gaelic names such as *Cathal*, *Caitlín*, and *Gráinne* have been widely revived since independence in their original form, unscrambling the garblings due to Anglicization. Increasingly now, the same is true of Scottish Gaelic names. Because of the differences in phonology and spelling, Gaelic names can look very different from English names, even when they are quite closely equivalent. For example, the Irish Gaelic form of *George* is *Seoirse*. Irish *Séamas* and Scottish *Seumas* are the Gaelic equivalents of English *James*.

A striking feature of the Gaelic naming tradition is the antiquity of its independence and folklore. *Meadhbh* (*Maeve*) recalls a 1st-century queen of Connacht, leader of the cattle raid of Cooley. The name *Deirdre* recalls the tragic story of a beautiful girl betrothed against her will to Conchobhar (*Connor*) and her elopement with her beloved Naoise, who is eventually caught and killed by Conchobhar.

In Scotland, where the Gaels settled from the 5th century onwards, particular names are sometimes associated with particular clans. So, for example, the name *Somerled* (*Somhairle* in Scottish Gaelic, Anglicized as *Sorley*) is traditionally associated with Clan Macdonald, the kindred of the Lords of the Isles. There was considerable interplay between Gaelic names and Norse names. Gaelic *Somhairle*, *Uisdean*, and *Raghnall* (*Ronald*) are from Norse, while Norse names such as *Njall* and *Birgit* are from Gaelic.

Welsh names are of similar antiquity, though there are fewer traditional names surviving in Welsh than in Gaelic. Many of the ancient names that are now in use or being revived are found in the *Mabinogi*, a medieval collection of traditional legends. These include *Branwen*, *Lleu*, *Geraint*, *Heilyn*, *Iorwerth*, *Rhiannon*, *Urien*, *Ynyr*, and *Pryderi*. Another group of traditional Welsh names commemorates heroes and princes who led resistance variously to the Romans (*Caradoc*), the Saxons (*Cadwaladr*), and the English (*Llewelyn*, *Glyndŵr*). Indeed, the most important Welsh source of names is the cycle of legends associated with the court of King Arthur, legendary defender of the Britons against the Saxon invaders. Names derived from this tradition include *Elaine*, *Enid*, *Gavin* (*Gawain*), *Guinevere*, *Lancelot*, *Merlin* (*Myrddin*), *Percival*, and *Tristan* (*Tristram*). The present century is witnessing not only a revival of traditional Welsh names but also an influx of new coinages. These are mainly from vocabulary elements (e.g. *Eirwen* 'snow-pure', *Glenda* 'clean-good'), but also from placenames such as *Trefor*.

The influence of literature, film, and popular culture

Works of literature have also had an influence on name choices. The names of some of Shakespeare's heroines have been used as given names, for example *Rosalind*, *Olivia*, *Portia*, *Perdita*, *Imogen*, *Juliet*, and *Cordelia*. However, on the whole, these have been less influential than might have been expected. Other writers have influenced particular names. Thus, *Pamela* and *Clarissa* probably owe much if not all of their popularity to Richardson; *Amelia* to Fielding; *Nicol* to Scott; *Justine* to Durrell; *Leila* to Byron and Lord Lytton; *Christabel* to Coleridge; *Maud* and *Vivien* to Tennyson; and *Pippa* to Browning. In the 19th century, the male given name *Shirley* changed sex, becoming a conventional female name after publication of Charlotte Brontë's novel *Shirley* (1849).

In the 20th century, films have had a considerable influence on the choice of names. *Tracy*, for example, underwent a great increase in popularity as a female name from the late 1950s onwards, after release of the 1956 film *High Society*, in which Grace Kelly played the character of Tracy Lord.

Not only fictional characters but also the actors who portray them can have an influence on the popularity of a name. *Greer, Cary,* and *Spencer,* for example, have been chosen as names in honour of the film stars Greer Garson, Cary Grant, and Spencer Tracy, and the popular status of *Clark* was clearly influenced by Gable, *Trevor* by Howard, *Jean* by Harlow, and *Marilyn* by Monroe.

Another characteristically 20th-century influence is that of rock and pop music: the rise of *Elvis, Kylie,* and *Madonna* is clearly traceable, but we can only guess how many present-day Johns and Pauls owe their name to Lennon and McCartney.

Surnames as Given Names

Throughout the English-speaking world a large number of surnames are now used as given names. Only those that have acquired conventional status are recorded here. Surnames had been sporadically used as first names for several centuries, mainly among landed families. In the 19th century this phenomenon became more frequent. In most cases it originated because of a connection between families. A bride from a rich and powerful family would christen her first-born with her own maiden surname; the conjunction of the two names would be taken as symbolic of the union between the two families. Some given names that were derived originally from surnames have become fully established as freely used first names in their own right (e.g. *Clifford, Dudley, Stanley*). In Britain such names are almost always borne by males, apart from a few conventionalized exceptions (e.g. *Shirley, Beverley, Kimberley*).

Other Sources of Given Names

There are many other sources from which a personal name may be derived. Some of them can be quite ephemeral. Since the 19th century, various types of vocabulary word have come to be used as given names: in particular, words denoting precious stones (*Beryl, Ruby*) and flowers (*Daisy, Primrose*). Sometimes a vocabulary word denoting a desirable quality for the life ahead is bestowed on a baby, as in the case of the names *Joy, Happy,* and *Felix*.

Occasionally, a placename will be found in use as a given name. Several of the Western Isles and other parts of Scotland have been used in this way, notably *Isla(y)* and *Iona*.

Nicknames rarely become established as personal names, but pet forms such as *Peggy* and *Bill* and short forms such as *Max* and *Kim* can take on a life of their own. Some short forms or pet forms are more commonly used than the more formal version, as in the case of *Reg*.

In the 20th century, the number of names used regularly has continued to grow apace. The use of vocabulary words as first names for women has increased, and the two categories (gemstones and flowers) have been expanded to include other precious and desirable things

(*Amber, Jade, Crystal*), plants (*Bryony, Fern, Poppy*), and birds (*Kestrel, Teale*). Names from other countries have been enthusiastically adopted, beginning in the early years of the century with Russian names introduced via France (*Vera, Tanya, Natasha*). A couple of decades later, there was a vogue for names of Scandinavian origin (*Ingrid, Astrid*). Currently, certain fanciful inventions, combinations, and respellings are gaining ground, a phenomenon associated particularly with America.

Cultural Variation

Black Names

In both America and Britain, the group of names typically borne by **Black** people differs noticeably from those of the White population. For example, it contains a much higher proportion of freely invented names such as *Floella, Laraine,* and *Latasha*. Characteristic Black names also include adopted European forms (*Antonio, Antoine, Anton*) and some surname forms that are much less common among the population as a whole (*Curtis, Leroy, Winston*).

The United States

The first European names to be established in **North America** were those brought by Puritan settlers to New England. Some of the more unusual Old Testament names remain in use, especially in rural areas, even though they are out of fashion elsewhere: for example *Jed* (*Jedidiah*), *Zeke* (*Ezekiel*), Hephzibah, and *Zillah*.

A characteristically American naming practice, now well established elsewhere is the adoption of a surname as a first name, not because of any family connection, but out of admiration for some famous contemporary or historical figure (e.g. *Bradford, Wesley, Winthrop*). A number of American presidents have been influential in this way, in particular *Washington* and *Lincoln*. Many first names derived from surnames are in America borne by women. A few are conventionalized in this use (*Brooke, Paige*), but many more are used equally for either sex, so that it is often not possible to determine the gender of a bearer from the name alone.

Another process of name creation well established in America is that of free invention. Formerly regarded as typical of the southern states, this has become more widespread. Most of the coined names are borne by women. Strategies include fanciful respelling (*Kathryn* (now the predominant form in America), *Madalynne, Ilayne*); the recombining of syllables from other names (*Jolene, Lolicia*); and elaborations with productive feminine suffixes (*-elle, -ette, -ice, -inda*).

Pet forms are more often used as first names in their own right in America than Britain, so that a *Pam* is not necessarily to be addressed more formally as *Pamela*, nor *Bobby* as *Robert*. In the same way some informal nicknames have come to be bestowed as official first names (*Bud, Ginger, Rusty*). Terms such as *Duke, Earl, Prince*, are also regularly used as first names.

Canada

First names in **Canada** are, for the most part, shared partly with those of Britain and partly with the United States. So, for example, in Canada more surnames are used as given names than in Britain, but fewer than in the United States. The Celtic tradition is also particularly important in Canada. There are a few names that are characteristically Canadian: for example *Lorne, Jaime,* and *Meaghan*.

Australia and New Zealand

Australia and New Zealand share the basic stock of English first names, but also have individual characteristics of their own. Irish influence is strong in Australia, so that, for example, use of *Kelly, Kerry,* and *Colleen* as given names is of Australian origin. *Barry, Bruce, Charlene, Darlene, Nolene,* and *Kylie* are examples of names which have particular associations with Australia.

A few New Zealand names of Maori origin have passed into more general use, and two in particular, *Ngaio* and *Nyree*, have achieved some currency in Britain as well as New Zealand.

Acknowledgements

Many of the entries here are derived from *A Dictionary of First Names*, a much larger work published in 1990 by Oxford University Press. The present book has benefited from the comments and suggestions made by various scholars for that work, in particular Professor Tomás de Bhaldraithe of the Royal Irish Academy, Mr Ronald Black of the Department of Celtic at Edinburgh University, Professor Gwynedd Pierce, formerly of the University of Wales College of Cardiff, and Dr Joseph A. Reif of Bar-Ilan University, Israel. Mr Black checked the Gaelic forms in this book. Katherine Barber of Oxford University Press, Canada, checked the North American entries. To all these scholars we express our appreciation. For any errors that remain, we alone are responsible.

PWH, FMH

Symbols used in the text

♂ male name
♀ female name
◊ see also (you will find more information at the name marked)

AARON ABBIE ABE ABEL ABIGAIL ABILENE
ABNER ABRAHAM ABRAM ADA ADAH AD
AM ADDISON ADELA ADELAIDE ADELE A
DELINE ADLAI ADRIAN ADRIANNE ADRIE
NNE AENGUS AFRICA AGATHA AGGIE AG
NES AIDAN AILEEN AILIE AILSA AIMEE AI

Aaron ♂

Biblical name, borne by the brother of
Moses, who was appointed by God to
be Moses' spokesman, and became the
first High Priest of the Israelites
(Exodus 4:14–16, 7:1–2). It is of
uncertain origin and meaning: most
probably, like ◊**Moses**, of Egyptian
rather than Hebrew origin. The
traditional derivation from Hebrew
har-on 'mountain of strength' is no
more than a folk etymology. The
name has been in regular use from
time immemorial as a Jewish name,
and was taken up by the
Nonconformists as a Christian name
in the 17th century.

Abbie ♀

Pet form of ◊**Abigail**.
Variants: **Abbey**, **Abby**.

Abe ♂

Short form of ◊**Abraham**.

Abel ♂

Biblical name, borne by the younger
son of Adam and Eve, who was
murdered for reasons of jealousy by
his brother Cain (Genesis 4:1–8). The
Hebrew form is *Hevel*, ostensibly
representing the vocabulary word
hevel 'breath', 'vapour', and so taken
to imply vanity or worthlessness. Abel
is considered by the Christian Church
to have been a pre-Christian martyr
(cf. Matthew 23:35), and is invoked as
a saint in the litany for the dying.
Nevertheless, his name has not been
much used either before or after its
brief vogue among the Puritans.

Abigail ♀

Biblical name (meaning 'father of
exaltation' in Hebrew), borne by one
of King David's wives, who had earlier
been married to Nabal (1 Samuel
25:3), and by the mother of Absalom's
captain Amasa (2 Samuel 1:25). The
name was popular in the 17th century
under Puritan influence. It was a
common name in literature for a
lady's maid, for example in Beaumont
and Fletcher's play *The Scornful Lady*
(1616). The biblical Abigail refers to
herself as 'thy servant'.
Pet forms: **Abbie, Abbey, Abby**.

Abilene ♀

U.S.: a comparatively rare name. In
the New Testament, Abilene is a
region of the Holy Land (Luke 3:1),
whose name is of uncertain origin, but
may be derived from a Hebrew word
meaning 'grass'. Several places in
America have been named from this
reference, notably a city in Kansas,
which was the boyhood home of
President Dwight D. Eisenhower. Its
adoption as a female given name was
encouraged partly by its resemblance
to ◊**Abbie** and partly by the fact that
-lene is a productive suffix of female
names (cf. e.g. ◊**Charlene**).

Abner ♂

Biblical name (meaning 'father of
light' in Hebrew), of a relative of King
Saul, who was in command of Saul's
army (1 Samuel 14:50; 26:5). It is not
common as a given name in England,
but has enjoyed a steady, modest
popularity in America, where it was

brought in at the time of the earliest Puritan settlements.

Abraham ♂

Biblical name, borne by the first of the Jewish patriarchs, with whom God made a covenant that his descendants should possess the land of Canaan. The Hebrew form is *Avraham*, and is of uncertain derivation. In Genesis 17:5 it is explained as 'father of a multitude (of nations)' (Hebrew *av hamon (goyim)*). It has always been a popular Jewish given name, and was also chosen by Christians, especially among 17th-century Puritans and other fundamentalists. Various early saints of the Eastern Roman Empire also bore this name. Its currency in the United States was greatly enhanced by the fame of President Abraham Lincoln (1809–65).
Short form: **Abe**.

Abram ♂

Biblical name, a variant of ◊**Abraham**. It was probably originally a distinct name (meaning 'high father' in Hebrew). According to Genesis 17:5, the patriarch's name was changed by divine command from *Abram* to *Abraham*. From the Middle Ages, however, if not before, it was taken to be a contracted version.

Ada ♀

Of uncertain origin, not in general use before the late 18th century. It may be a Latinate variant of the biblical name ◊**Adah**. However, it has also been explained as a pet form of ◊**Adele** and ◊**Adelaide**; it may go back to a Germanic female personal name, a short form from *adal* 'noble'. This was borne by a 7th-century abbess of Saint-Julien-des-Prés at Le Mans.

Adah ♀

Biblical name (meaning 'adornment' in Hebrew), borne by the wives of Lamech (Genesis 4:19) and of Esau (Genesis 36:2). See also ◊**Ada**.

Adam ♂

Biblical name of the first man (Genesis 2–3). It probably derives from Hebrew *adama* 'earth'; it is a common feature of creation legends that God or a god fashioned the first human beings from earth or clay and breathed life into them. The name was subsequently borne by a 7th-century Irish abbot of Fermo in Italy. It has been very popular in the English-speaking world since the 1960s. In Hebrew it is a generic term for 'man' (Genesis 5:2) and has never been considered a personal name, although *Hava* 'Eve' has enjoyed popularity as a Jewish name.

Addison ♂

Transferred use of the surname, which originated as a patronymic derived from *Addie* or *Adie*, a medieval (and occasional modern) pet form of ◊**Adam**. This is now a relatively popular given name in the United States.

Adela ♀

Latinate form of ◊**Adele**, especially popular in the late 19th century.

Adelaide ♀

Of Germanic origin (via French **Adélaïde**), from *adal* 'noble' + *heid* 'kind', 'sort'. It was borne in the 10th century by the wife of the Holy Roman Emperor Otto the Great. She became regent after his death and was revered as a saint. The given name increased in popularity in England during the 19th century, when it was borne by the wife of King William IV; she was the daughter of the ruler of the German duchy of Saxe-Meiningen. The Australian city of Adelaide was named in her honour.

Adele ♀

From French **Adèle**, an ancient name popular in medieval Europe because of the fame of a 7th-century saint, a daughter of the Frankish king Dagobert II. It is of Germanic origin, from *adal* 'noble' (a short form of a two-element name such as *Adelheid*; see ◊**Adelaide**). It was the name of William the Conqueror's youngest daughter (*c*.1062–1137), who became the wife of Stephen of Blois. However, it died out in England in the later Middle Ages. It was revived in the 19th century, being the name of a character in Johann Strauss's opera *Die Fledermaus*. Its popularity was further reinforced in the 1930s as the name of a character in the novels of Dornford Yates.

Adeline ♀

French diminutive of *Adèle* (see ◊**Adele**). The Latinate form **Adelina** is also found occasionally as an English name. Both enjoyed a brief vogue in the 19th century.

Adlai ♂

Biblical name, borne by a very minor character, the father of one of King David's herdsmen (1 Chronicles 27:29). It represents an Aramaic contracted form of the Hebrew name *Adaliah* 'God is just', and is one of a large crop of minor biblical names taken up by the Puritans in the 17th century. Many of them, including *Adlai*, were brought to New England by the early settlers and have survived in North America. *Adlai* is particularly associated with the American statesman and Democratic presidential candidate Adlai Stevenson (1900–65), in whose family the name was traditional: it was also borne by his grandfather (1835–1914), who was vice-president in 1893–7.

Adrian ♂

Usual English form of the Latin name *Hadriānus* 'man from Hadria'. Hadria was a town in northern Italy, which gave its name to the Adriatic Sea; it is of unknown derivation. The initial *H*- has always been very volatile. The name was borne by the Roman emperor Publius Aelius Hadrianus, during whose reign (AD 117–38)

Hadrian's Wall was built across northern England. The name was later taken by several early popes, including the only English pope, Nicholas Breakspeare (Adrian IV). It has been particularly popular in the English-speaking world during the past thirty years.

Adrianne ♀

Modern feminine form of ◊**Adrian**, less common than ◊**Adrienne**.
Variants: **Adrianna**, **Adriana**.

Adrienne ♀

French feminine form of ◊**Adrian**, now also used in the English-speaking world.

Aengus ♂

Usual Irish form of ◊**Angus**.

Africa ♀

Name adopted in the 20th century among American Blacks, conscious of their ancestral heritage in the continent of Africa.

Agatha ♀

Latinized version of the Greek name *Agathē*, from the feminine form of the adjective *agathos* 'good', 'honourable'. This was the name of a Christian saint popular in the Middle Ages; she was a Sicilian martyr of the 3rd century who suffered the fate of having her breasts cut off. According to the traditional iconography, she is depicted holding them on a platter. In some versions they look more like loaves, leading to the custom of blessing bread on her feast day (5 February). The name was revived in the 19th century, but has faded again since.
Pet form: **Aggie**.

Aggie ♀

Pet form of ◊**Agnes** and ◊**Agatha**.

Agnes ♀

Latinized version of the Greek name *Hagnē*, from the feminine form of the adjective *hagnos* 'pure', 'holy'. This was the name of a young Roman virgin martyred in the persecutions instigated by the Roman emperor Diocletian in AD 303. She became a very popular saint in the Middle Ages. Her name was early associated with Latin *agnus* 'lamb', leading to the consistent dropping of the initial *H*- and to her representation in art accompanied by a lamb. The name was revived in the 19th century, and has been especially popular in Scotland.

Pet form: **Aggie**.

Aidan ♂

Anglicized form of the Gaelic name **Áedán**, a diminutive of *Áed* (now written *Aodh*, pronounced '*ee*'), meaning 'fire'. This was borne by various early Irish saints, among them the 7th-century apostle of Northumbria. It has been revived in the 20th century, in particular during the past couple of decades, by parents conscious of their Irish ancestry.

Aileen ♀

Scottish variant spelling of ◊**Eileen**.

Ailie ♀

Scottish pet form of ◊**Aileen** or an Anglicized spelling of ◊**Eilidh**.

Ailsa ♀

Modern Scottish name derived from *Ailsa Craig*, name of a high rocky islet in the Clyde estuary off the Ayrshire coast, near the traditional estates of the Scottish Kennedys. This is actually from Old Norse *Alfsigesey* 'island of Alfsigr', a personal name derived from *alf* 'elf', 'supernatural being' + *sigi* 'victory'. However, use as a given name has been influenced by *Ealasaid*, the Gaelic form of ◊**Elizabeth**. Ailsa Craig is known in Gaelic as *Allasa*, but popularly as *Creag Ealasaid*.

Aimée ♀

French: originally a vernacular nickname meaning 'beloved', from the past participle of French *aimer* 'to love' (Latin *amāre*; cf. ◊**Amy**). It has

been in use in French since the Middle Ages, although it has never been very common. It is now also sometimes used, with or without the accent, as a given name in the English-speaking world.

Ainsley ♂, occasionally ♀

Transferred use of the Scottish surname also spelled *Ainslie*, which is borne by a powerful family long established in the Scottish borders. It was originally a local name, taken north from either *Annesley* in Nottinghamshire or *Ansley* in Warwickshire. The former gets its name from the genitive case of the Old English name *Ān* (a short form of any of various compounds containing the word *ān* 'one', 'only') + Old English *lēah* 'wood', 'clearing'. The latter is from Old English *ānsetl* 'hermitage' + *lēah*.

Variant: **Ainslee**.

Aisling ♀

Irish Gaelic: from the vocabulary word *aisling* 'dream', 'vision'. This was not in use as a given name during the Middle Ages, but was adopted as part of the Irish revival in the 20th century.

Variants: **Aislinn**; **Ashling** (Anglicized form).

Al ♂

Short form of any of the names beginning with this syllable.

Alan ♂

Of Celtic origin and uncertain derivation (possibly a diminutive of a word meaning 'rock'). It was introduced into England by Breton followers of William the Conqueror, most notably Alan, Earl of Brittany, who was rewarded for his services with vast estates in the newly conquered kingdom. In Britain the variants **Allan** and **Allen** are considerably less frequent, and generally represent transferred uses of surname forms, whereas in America

all three forms of the name are approximately equally common. See also ◊**Alun**.
Short form: **Al**.

Alana ♀
Latinate feminine form of ◊**Alan**, a comparatively recent coinage.
Variants: **Alanna**, ◊**Alannah**.

Alanda ♀
Recent coinage, a feminine form of ◊**Alan** influenced by ◊**Amanda**.

Alanna ♀
Variant of ◊**Alana**.

Alannah ♀
Variant spelling of ◊**Alanna**, possibly influenced by names of Hebrew origin such as ◊**Hannah** and ◊**Susannah** and by the Anglo-Irish term of endearment *alannah* (Gaelic *a leanbh* 'O child').

Alasdair ♂
Scottish Gaelic form of ◊**Alexander**, often Anglicized as ◊**Alistair**.
Variants: **Alastair**, **Alaster**.

Albert ♂
From an Old French name, *Albert*, of Germanic (Frankish) origin, derived from *adal* 'noble' + *berht* 'bright', 'famous'. This was adopted by the Normans and introduced by them to England, displacing the Old English cognate *Æþelbeorht*. The name is popular in a variety of forms in Western Europe, and has been traditional in a number of European princely families. Its popularity in England in the 19th century was largely in honour of Queen Victoria's consort, Prince Albert of Saxe-Coburg-Gotha.
Short forms: **Al**, **Bert**.
Pet form: **Bertie**.

Aldous ♂
Of uncertain origin; probably a medieval short form of any of various Norman names, such as *Aldebrand*, *Aldemund*, and *Alderan*, containing the Germanic word *ald* 'old'. It was relatively common in East Anglia

during the Middle Ages, but is now rare, known mainly as the given name of the novelist Aldous Huxley (1894–1963).

Alec ♂
English and Scottish short form of ◊**Alexander**, now somewhat less popular in England than ◊**Alex**, possibly because of the colloquial pejorative term *smart alec*.

Alethea ♀
A learned coinage, not found before the 17th century. It represents the Greek word *alētheia* 'truth', and seems to have arisen as a result of the Puritan enthusiasm for using terms for abstract virtues as female names. See also ◊**Althea**.

Alex ♂ ♀
Short form of ◊**Alexander**, ◊**Alexandra**, and ◊**Alexis**; also commonly used as a given name in its own right.
Variant: **Alix** ♀

Alexa ♀
Short form of ◊**Alexandra** or variant of ◊**Alexis** as a female name.

Alexander ♂
From the Latin form of the Greek name *Alexandros*, from *alexein* 'to defend' + *anēr* 'man', 'warrior' (genitive *andros*). The compound was probably coined originally as a title of the goddess Hera, consort of Zeus. It was also borne as a byname by the Trojan prince Paris. The name became extremely popular in the post-classical period, and was borne by several characters in the New Testament and some early Christian saints. Its use as a common given name throughout Europe, however, derives largely from the fame of Alexander the Great, King of Macedon (356–23 BC), around whom a large body of popular legend grew up in late antiquity, much of which came to be embodied in the medieval 'Alexander romances'.
Short forms: **Al**, **Alex**, **Alec**.
Pet form: **Sandy** (chiefly Scottish).

Alexandra ♀

Latinate feminine form of ◊**Alexander**. It was very little used in the English-speaking world before the 20th century, when it was brought in from Scandinavia and Eastern Europe. It owes its sudden rise in popularity in Britain at the end of the 19th century to Queen Alexandra, Danish wife of Edward VII.
Short forms: **Alex**, **Alexa**, **Sandra**.
Pet form: **Sandy** (chiefly Scottish).

Alexandria ♀

Variant of ◊**Alexandra**, influenced by the name of the city in Egypt, founded by Alexander the Great in 322 BC and named in his honour. This is now a relatively common given name in the United States, where it is also found as a placename, for example in Louisiana, Minnesota, and Virginia; the last was named in 1748 after a family of local landowners whose surname was *Alexander*.

Alexia ♀

Variant of ◊**Alexis** as a female name.

Alexis ♀ ♂

Variant (or female derivative) of *Alexius*, the Latin spelling of Greek *Alexios*, a short form of various compound personal names derived from *alexein* 'to defend'. St Alexius was a 5th-century saint of Edessa, venerated particularly in the Orthodox Church as a 'man of God'. *Alexis* was originally a male name, but is now more commonly given to girls.

Alfred ♂

From an Old English name derived from *ælf* 'elf', 'supernatural being' + *ræd* 'counsel'. It was a relatively common name before the Norman Conquest of Britain, being borne most notably by Alfred the Great (849–99), King of Wessex. After the Conquest it was adopted by the Normans in a variety of more or less radically altered forms (see ◊**Avery**), and provides a rare example (see also

◊**Edward**) of a distinctively Old English name that has spread widely on the Continent. It was strongly revived in the 19th century, along with other names of pre-Conquest historical figures, but has faded since.
Short forms: **Alf**, **Fred**.

Alger ♂

From an Old English name derived from *ælf* 'elf', 'supernatural being' + *gār* 'spear'; it is possible that this form may also have absorbed other names with the first elements *æþel* 'noble', *ēald* 'old', and *ēalh* 'temple'. The name was not common either before or after the Norman Conquest, but was revived in the 19th century, along with other Germanic names. It is relatively common in the United States.

Algernon ♂

Of Norman French origin, originally a byname meaning 'with a moustache' (from Old French *grenon*, *gernon* 'moustache'). The Normans were as a rule clean-shaven, and this formed a suitable distinguishing nickname when it was applied to William de Percy, a companion of William the Conqueror. In the 15th century it was revived, with a sense of family tradition, as a byname or second given name for his descendant Henry Percy (1478–1527), and thereafter regularly used in that family. It was subsequently adopted into other families connected by marriage with the Percys, and eventually became common property.
Pet forms: **Algy**, **Algie**.

Alice ♀

Originally a variant of ◊**Adelaide**, representing an Old French spelling of a greatly contracted version of Germanic *Adalheidis*. It was regarded as a distinct name when it was revived in the 19th century. It was the name of the child heroine of Lewis Carroll's *Alice's Adventures in Wonderland* (1865) and *Through the*

Looking Glass (1872), who was based on his child friend Alice Liddell, daughter of the Dean of Christ Church, Oxford.
Variant: **Alys**.

Alicia ♀
Modern Latinate form of ◊**Alice**.
Variants: **Alissa**, **Alyssa**.

Alick ♂
Variant of ◊**Alec**.

Alina ♀
Of uncertain origin. It is probably a variant of ◊**Aline**, but could also be of Arabic origin, from a word meaning 'noble' or 'illustrious'. In Scotland it has been used as a feminine form of ◊**Alistair**.

Alinda ♀
In the English-speaking world this name is of recent origin, apparently a blend of ◊**Alina** and ◊**Linda**. It is, however, also used in German-speaking countries, where it is derived from the ancient Germanic personal name *Adelinde*, from *adal* 'noble' + *lind* 'soft', 'tender'.

Aline ♀
In the Middle Ages this represented a contracted form of ◊**Adeline**. In modern use it is either a revival of this or a respelling of ◊**Aileen**. In Scotland and Ireland it has sometimes been chosen as representing an Anglicized spelling of the Gaelic vocabulary word *àlainn* (Scottish), *álainn* (Irish) 'lovely'.

Alison ♀
From a very common medieval name, a Norman French diminutive of ◊**Alice**. Despite its early popularity, it virtually died out in England in the 15th century. However, it survived in Scotland, with the result that until its revival in England in the 20th century it had a strongly Scottish flavour.
Variant: **Allison** (the usual North American spelling).
Pet forms: **Allie**, **Ally**.

Alissa ♀
Variant of ◊**Alicia**.

Alistair ♂
Scottish: altered spelling of Gaelic **Alasdair**, a form of ◊**Alexander**. Alexander has long been a popular name in Scotland, having been borne by three medieval kings of the country.
Variants: **Alisdair**, **Alastair**, **Alister**, **Al(l)aster**.
Pet form: **Aly**.

Alix ♀
Variant of ◊**Alex**, used only as a feminine name. Its formation has probably been influenced by ◊**Alice**.

Alizabeth ♀
Altered spelling of ◊**Elizabeth**.

Allan ♂
Variant spelling of ◊**Alan**.

Allaster ♂
Scottish: variant spelling of ◊**Alistair**. It is borne, for example, by a minstrel in Sir Walter Scott's *Rob Roy* (1818), which ensured its 19th-century popularity.

Allegra ♀
From the feminine form of the Italian adjective *allegro* 'gay', 'jaunty' (familiar in English as a musical tempo). It seems to have been an original coinage when it was given to Byron's illegitimate daughter (1817–22), but since then it has been taken up by parents in many English-speaking countries. It is not commonly used as a given name in Italy.

Allen ♂
Variant spelling of ◊**Alan**, in Britain generally found only as a surname, but in North America equally common as a given name.

Allie ♀
Pet form of ◊**Alison**.
Variant: ◊**Ally**.

Allison ♀

Variant spelling of ◊**Alison**.

Alma ♀

Relatively modern creation, of uncertain origin. It had a temporary vogue following the Battle of Alma (1854), which is named from the river in the Crimea by which it took place; similarly *Trafalgar* had occasionally been used as a female name earlier in the 19th century. Nevertheless, the historical event seems only to have increased the popularity of an existing, if rare, name. *Alma* is also the feminine form of the Latin adjective *almus* 'nourishing', 'kind' (cf. *alma mater* 'fostering mother', the cliché denoting an educational establishment). The name was borne by Alma Bennett (1889–1958), American vamp of the silent screen. In Tennessee Williams's play *Summer and Smoke* (1948), a bearer of the name explains that it is 'Spanish for soul', but this seems to be no more than coincidental.

Aloysius ♂

Of unknown origin, possibly a Latinized form of a Provençal version of ◊**Louis**. It was relatively common in Italy in the Middle Ages, and has subsequently enjoyed some popularity among Roman Catholics in honour of St Aloysius Gonzaga (1568–91), who was born in Lombardy.

Althea ♀

From Greek mythology. Although often considered to be a contracted form of ◊**Alethea**, it is actually a quite distinct name (Greek *Althaia*), of uncertain origin. It was borne in classical legend by the mother of Meleager, who was given a brand plucked from the fire at the instant of her son's birth, with the promise that his life would last as long as the brand did; some twenty years later she destroyed it in a fit of pique. The name was revived by the 17th-century poet Richard Lovelace, as a poetic pseudonym for his beloved.

Alun ♂

Welsh: possibly a cognate of ◊**Alan**. It is borne in the *Mabinogi* by Alun of Dyfed, a character mentioned in passing several times. It is also a river-name and a regional name in Wales, sometimes spelled *Alyn*. *Alun* was adopted as a bardic name by John Blackwell (1797–1840) and became popular as a result of his fame.

Alvar ♂

As a medieval name this was from the Old English personal name *Ælfhere*, from *ælf* 'elf', 'supernatural being' + *here* 'army', 'warrior'. In modern use it may be a revival of this, a transferred use of the surname derived from it, or an Anglicized form of Spanish *Álvaro*, a Visigothic personal name derived from Germanic *al* 'all' + *war* 'guard'.

Alvin ♂

From an Old English personal name derived from *ælf* 'elf', 'supernatural being' + *wine* 'friend'. This was not especially common in Britain either before or after the Norman Conquest, but it is popular in the United States. The reasons for this are not entirely clear; association with ◊**Calvin** may be a factor. A more plausible (though less elevated) explanation is that this was the name given to the naughty chipmunk in a popular television cartoon series of the 1960s.

Alys ♀

Variant spelling of ◊**Alice**.

Alyssa ♀

Variant spelling of ◊**Alissa**.

Amanda ♀

A 17th-century literary coinage from the Latin gerundive (feminine) *amanda* 'lovable', 'fit to be loved', from *amāre* 'to love'. This is evidently modelled on ◊**Miranda**. The masculine form *Amandus*, borne by various saints from the 4th to the 7th century,

seems not to have been the direct source of the feminine form. The female name has enjoyed considerable popularity in the mid-20th century.
Short form: **Manda**.
Pet form: ◊**Mandy**.

Amber ♀

From the vocabulary word for the gemstone *amber*, a word derived via Old French and Latin from Arabic *ambar*. This was first used as a given name at the end of the 19th century, but has become particularly popular in the past couple of decades. In part it owes its popularity to Kathleen Winsor's novel *Forever Amber* (1944).

Ambrose ♂

English form of the Late Latin name *Ambrosius*, from post-classical Greek *Ambrosios* 'immortal'. This was borne by various early saints, most notably a 4th-century bishop of Milan. The name has never been common in England, but has enjoyed considerably greater popularity in Roman Catholic Ireland, where the surname *Mac Ambrois* is Anglicized as *McCambridge*.

Amelia ♀

A blend of two medieval names: *Emilia* (which is of Latin origin: see ◊**Emily**) and the Latinized Germanic *Amalia* (a short form of various personal names containing the word *amal* 'work'). It was coined by Henry Fielding for the heroine of his novel *Amelia* (1751).

Amos ♂

Biblical name, borne by a Hebrew prophet of the 8th century BC, whose sayings are collected in the book of the Bible that bears his name. This is of uncertain derivation, but may be connected with the Hebrew verb *amos* 'to carry'. In some traditions it is assigned the meaning 'borne by God'. The name is used among Christians as well as Jews, and was popular among the Puritans. In Britain it survived

well into the 19th century, but is little used today.

Amy ♀

Anglicized form of Old French *Amee* 'beloved'. This originated in part as a vernacular nickname, in part as a form of Latin *Amāta*. The latter is ostensibly the feminine form of the past participle of *amāre* 'to love', but in fact it may have had a different, pre-Roman, origin; it was borne in classical mythology by the wife of King Latinus, whose daughter Lavinia married Aeneas and (according to the story in the *Aeneid*) became the mother of the Roman people.

Anastasia ♀

Russian: feminine form of the Greek male name *Anastasios* (a derivative of *anastasis* 'resurrection'). It has always been popular in Eastern Europe, in honour of a 4th-century saint who was martyred at Sirmium in Dalmatia. It was also used occasionally in medieval England. One of the daughters of the last tsar of Russia bore this name. She was probably murdered along with the rest of the family by the Bolsheviks in 1918, but in 1920 a woman claiming to be the Romanov princess Anastasia came to public notice in Germany, and a film was subsequently based on this story (1956).

André ♂

French form of ◊**Andrew**.

Andrea ♀

Of disputed origin. It has been in use since the 17th century, although never common. It is now generally taken as a feminine equivalent of ◊**Andreas**, and this probably represents its actual origin. However, it was not in use in the Middle Ages, and the suggestion has also been made that it represents a coinage in English from the Greek vocabulary word *andreia* 'manliness', 'virility'.

ANDREAS

Andreas ♂
The original New Testament Greek form of ◊**Andrew**, occasionally used in the English-speaking world as a learned variant.

Andrew ♂
English form of the Greek name *Andreas*, a short form of any of various compound names derived from *andr-* 'man', 'warrior'. In the New Testament this is the name of the first disciple to be called by Jesus. After the Resurrection, St Andrew preached in Asia Minor and Greece. He is traditionally believed to have been crucified at Patras in Achaia. He was one of the most popular saints of the Middle Ages and was adopted as the patron of Scotland, Russia, and Greece. The name has long been popular in Scotland; its popularity in England was further enhanced by its use as a British royal name for Prince Andrew (b. 1960), the Duke of York.
Short form: Scottish: **Drew**.
Pet form: **Andy**.

Aneirin ♂
Welsh: of uncertain derivation, possibly from an element cognate with Irish Gaelic *nár* 'noble', 'modest'. The original form of the name was *Neirin*; the initial *A*- was added in the 13th century. This was the name of the first known Welsh poet, who lived AD *c.*600. The 'Book of Aneirin' is a 13th-century manuscript which purports to preserve his work, including the *Gododdin*, a long work about the defeat of the Welsh by the Saxons.
Variant: **Aneurin** (a modern form).
Pet form: **Nye** (popularized as a result of the fame of the statesman Aneurin Bevan, 1897–1960).

Angel ♀, formerly also ♂
Originally a male name, as in the case of Angel Clare, the chief male character in Thomas Hardy's novel *Tess of the D'Urbervilles* (1891), and derived from the Church Latin name *Angelus*, from Greek *angelos*. This meant 'messenger' in classical Greek, but in New Testament Greek it had the specialized meaning 'messenger of God', i.e. an angel. It is now out of fashion as a male name in English, but is being increasingly bestowed as a female name, especially as an American Black name. The influence of the vocabulary word *angel* is obvious, in its use as an affectionate term of address for a good (or pretty) little girl.

Angela ♀
From Church Latin, a feminine form of the male name *Angelus* (see ◊**Angel**). It has been in use in Britain and America from the 18th century, since when it has increased greatly in popularity.
Pet form: **Angie**.

Angelica ♀
From Church Latin, from the feminine form of the Latin adjective *angelicus* 'angelic', or simply a Latinate elaboration of ◊**Angela**.

Angelina ♀
Latinate elaboration of ◊**Angela**.

Angharad ♀
Welsh: composed of the Old Celtic intensive prefix *an-* + the root *cār* 'love' + the noun suffix *-ad*. This was the name of the mother of the 12th-century chronicler Giraldus Cambrensis ('Gerald the Welshman'). In the *Mabinogi*, Angharad Golden Hand at first rejects Peredur's suit, but later falls in love with him when he comes back as the unknown Mute Knight. The name has been strongly revived in Wales since the 1940s, and is well known in connection with the actress Angharad Rees (b. 1949).

Angie ♀
Pet form of ◊**Angela**.

Angus ♂
Scottish: Anglicized form of the Gaelic name **Aonghus** or **Aonghas**

(pronounced 'een-yis'), from Celtic words meaning 'one' and 'choice'. This is the name of an ancient Celtic god, and is first recorded as a personal name in Adomnan's 'Life of St Columba', where it occurs in the form *Oinogus(s)ius* as the name of a man for whom the saint prophesied a long life and a peaceful death. This is also almost certainly the name of the 8th-century Pictish king variously recorded as *Onnust* and *Hungus*.
Usual Irish form: Aengus.
Short form: ◊**Gus**.
Pet forms: Angie (Scottish); Gaelic: *Angaidh*.

Anita ♀
Originally a Spanish pet form of *Ana*, the Spanish version of ◊**Anne**. It is now widely used in English-speaking countries with little awareness of its Spanish origin. In the 1950s it came to prominence as the name of the Swedish film actress Anita Ekberg (b. 1931).

Ann ♀
Variant spelling of ◊**Anne**. *Ann* was the more common of the two spellings in the 19th century, but is now losing ground to the form with final *-e*.
Pet form: Annie.

Anna ♀
Latinate variant of ◊**Anne**, in common use as a given name in most European languages. Among people with a classical education, it has from time to time been associated with Virgil's *Aeneid*, where it is borne by the sister of Dido, Queen of Carthage. This Phoenician name may ultimately be of Semitic origin, and thus cognate with the biblical *Anne*. However, the connection, if it exists, is indirect rather than direct.

Annabel ♀
Sometimes taken as an elaboration of ◊**Anna**, but more probably a dissimilated form of *Amabel*, an Old French name derived from Latin

amābilis 'lovable'. It has been common in Scotland since the 12th century and in the rest of the English-speaking world since the 1940s.
Variants: **Annabella** (Latinized); **Annabelle** (Gallicized, under the influence of ◊**Belle**).

Anne ♀
English form (via Old French, Latin, and Greek) of the Hebrew female name *Hanna* 'He (God) has favoured me (i.e. with a child)'. This is the name borne in the Bible by the mother of Samuel (see ◊**Hannah**), and according to non-biblical tradition also by the mother of the Virgin Mary. It is the widespread folk cult of the latter that has led to the great popularity of the name in various forms throughout Europe. The simplified form ◊**Ann** was in the 19th century very much more common, but the form with final *-e* has grown in popularity during the 20th century, partly perhaps due to the enormous popularity of L. M. Montgomery's story *Anne of Green Gables* (1908), and partly due to Princess Anne (b. 1950). See also ◊**Anna**.
Pet form: Annie.

Annette ♀
French pet form of ◊**Anne**, now also widely used in the English-speaking world.

Annie ♀
Pet form of ◊**Ann** or ◊**Anne**.

Anthea ♀
Latinized spelling of Greek *Antheia*, a personal name derived from the feminine of the adjective *antheios* 'flowery'. This was used in the classical period as a byname of the goddess Hera at Argos, but as a modern given name it was reinvented in the 17th century by English pastoral poets such as Robert Herrick.

Anthony ♂
The usual English form of the old Roman family name *Antōnius*, which

is of uncertain (probably Etruscan) origin. The spelling with -th- (not normally reflected in the pronunciation) represents a learned but erroneous attempt to associate it with Greek *anthos* 'flower'. In the post-classical period it was a common name, borne by various early saints, most notably a 3rd-century Egyptian hermit monk, who is regarded as the founder of Christian monasticism.
Variant: **Antony**.
Short form: **Tony**.

Antoine ♂
French form of ◊**Anthony**, now also used in the English-speaking world.

Antoinette ♀
French feminine diminutive of ◊**Antoine**, which has become very popular in the English-speaking world.
Short form: **Toinette**.

Anton ♂
German and Russian form of ◊**Anthony**, now also used in the English-speaking world.

Antonia ♀
Latin feminine form of ◊**Anthony**, unaltered since classical times, when it was a common Roman feminine family name.
Pet form: **Toni**.

Antonio ♂
Italian and Spanish form of ◊**Anthony**, from Latin *Antōnius*. It is now also used in parts of the English-speaking world.

Antony ♂
Variant spelling of ◊**Anthony**.

Aphra ♀
Of uncertain origin. It could be an altered spelling of a Late Latin name, *Afra*. This was originally an ethnic name for a woman from Africa (in Roman times meaning the area around Carthage). It was used in the post-classical period as a nickname for a dark person, and eventually became a given name, being borne, for example,

by saints martyred at Brescia under the Roman emperor Hadrian and at Augsburg under Diocletian. The respelling of the name may have been prompted by Micah 1:10 'in the house of Aphrah roll thyself in the dust', where *Aphrah* is often taken as a personal name, but is in fact a placename meaning 'dust'. As a given name it has never been frequent, and is known chiefly as the name of the writer Aphra Behn (1640–89).

Apollonia ♀
Latin feminine form of the Greek masculine name *Apollonios*, an adjectival derivative of the name of the sun god, *Apollo*. This is of uncertain origin, and may be pre-Greek. St Apollonia was an elderly deaconess martyred at Alexandria under the Emperor Decius in the mid-3rd century.

April ♀
From the month (Latin *(mensis) aprīlis*, probably a derivative of *aperīre* 'to open', as the month when buds open and flowers appear). It forms a series with the more common names ◊**May** and ◊**June**, all taken from months associated with the spring, a time of new birth and growth, and may originally have been intended as an English version of the supposedly French name ◊**Avril**.

Arabella ♀
Of Scottish origin and uncertain etymology. It probably represents an alteration of *An(n)abella* (see ◊**Annabel**).

Aranrhod ♀
Welsh: name borne in the *Mabinogi* by the mother of Dylan and Lleu Llaw Gyffes. It is apparently derived from Celtic elements meaning 'huge', 'round', or 'humped' + 'wheel'; the legendary heroine may originally have been a moon goddess. See also ◊**Arianrhod**.

Archibald ♂

Of Norman French origin, from a Germanic (Frankish) personal name derived from *ercan* 'genuine' + *bald* 'bold', 'brave'. It has long been associated with Scotland, where it is in regular use as the English equivalent of Gaelic *Gilleasbaig* (see ◊**Gillespie**).

Pet forms: **Archie, Archy; Baldie.**

Ariadne ♀

From classical mythology: the name of a daughter of the Cretan king Minos. She gave the Athenian hero Theseus a ball of wool to enable him to find his way out of the Labyrinth after killing the Minotaur. He took her with him when he sailed from Crete, but abandoned her on the island of Naxos on the way back to Athens. Greek lexicographers of the Hellenistic period claimed that the name was composed of the Cretan dialect elements *ari-* (an intensive prefix) + *adnos* 'holy'. The name survived in the Christian era because of St Ariadne (d. *c.*130), an early Phrygian martyr.

Derivatives: French: **Arianne.** Italian: **Arianna.** Both these forms are now also used in the English-speaking world, along with the simplified **Ariana.**

Arianrhod ♀

Welsh: altered form of ◊**Aranrhod**, made up of modern Welsh *arian* 'silver' + *rhod* 'wheel'.

Arianwen ♀

Welsh: from *arian* 'silver' + *(g)wen*, feminine of *gwyn* 'white', 'fair', 'blessed', 'holy'. The name was borne in the 5th century by one of the daughters of Brychan, a semi-legendary Welsh chieftain.

Ariel ♂ ♀

From the biblical placename *Ariel*, said to mean 'lion of God' in Hebrew. It is mentioned in the prophecies of Ezra (8:16) and Isaiah (29:1–2). This is relatively common as a male first name in modern Israel, but in the United States it is more frequently used as a female name.

Arielle ♀

Recent coinage, a distinctively female form of ◊**Ariel**, now quite common in the United States.

Variant: **Ariella.**

Arlene ♀

Modern coinage, especially common in North America. It is of unknown origin, probably a fanciful coinage based on ◊**Marlene** or ◊**Charlene**, or both. It became famous in the 1950s as the name of the American actress and beauty columnist Arlene Dahl (b. 1924).

Arlette ♀

Of ancient but uncertain origin. It is apparently a Norman French double diminutive, from Germanic *arn* 'eagle'. It was the name of the mistress of Duke Robert of Normandy in the 11th century; their son was William the Conqueror.

Arnold ♂

From an Old French name, *Arnald, Arnaud*, which is of Germanic (Frankish) origin, from *arn* 'eagle' + *wald* 'ruler'. It was adopted by the Normans and introduced to Britain by them. An early saint of this name, whose cult contributed to its popularity, was a musician at the court of Charlemagne. He is said to have been a Greek by birth; it is not clear when and how he acquired his Germanic name. It had died out in England by the end of the Middle Ages and was revived in the 19th century, along with a large number of other medieval Germanic names.

Short form: **Arn.**
Pet form: **Arnie.**

Art ♂

Now generally used as a short form of ◊**Arthur**. There is also a traditional Gaelic name of this form (from the vocabulary word *art* 'bear') which has generally been Anglicized as *Arthur* although it in fact has no connection with that name.

Artemas ♂

Of New Testament Greek origin, from a name representing a short form of various compound names containing that of the goddess ◊**Artemis** (for example, *Artemidoros* 'gift of Artemis' and *Artemisthenes* 'strength of Artemis'). It is borne in the Bible by a character mentioned briefly in St Paul's letter to Titus (3:12). The name enjoyed some popularity among the Puritans in the 17th century, but fell out of use again.

Variant: **Artemus** (Latinized).

Artemis ♀

From the name of the Greek goddess of the moon and of hunting, equivalent to the Latin ◊**Diana**. It is of uncertain derivation, and may well be pre-Greek. As a given name, it is rare, but is chosen occasionally by parents in search of something distinctive. It is borne by a granddaughter of Lady Diana Cooper, perhaps as an oblique tribute to the grandmother.

Artemus ♂

Variant of ◊**Artemas**.

Arthur ♂

Of Celtic origin. King Arthur was a British king of the 5th or 6th century, about whom virtually no historical facts are known. He ruled in Britain after the collapse of the Roman Empire and before the coming of the Germanic tribes, and a vast body of legends grew up around him in the literatures of medieval Western Europe. His name is first found in the Latinized form *Artorius* and is of obscure derivation. The spelling with -*th*-, now invariably reflected in the pronunciation of the English name, is not found before the 16th century, and seems to represent no more than an artificial embellishment. The name became particularly popular in Britain

in the 19th century, partly as a result of the fame of Arthur Wellesley (1769–1852), Duke of Wellington, partly because of the popularity of Tennyson's *Idylls of the King* (1859–85), and partly because of the enormous Victorian interest in things medieval in general and in Arthurian legend in particular.

Short form: ◊**Art**.

Asa ♂

Biblical name, borne by one of the early kings of Judah, who reigned for forty years, as recorded in 1 Kings and 2 Chronicles. It was originally a byname meaning 'doctor', 'healer' in Hebrew, and is still a common Jewish name. It was first used among English-speaking Christians by the Puritans in the 17th century, and although now far from common it has never completely dropped out of use. In the 20th century it is known as the given name of the historian Asa Briggs and the footballer Asa Hertford.

Asenath ♀

Biblical name, borne by Joseph's Egyptian wife (Genesis 41:45), who became the mother of Manasseh and Ephraim. The name is said to have meant 'she belongs to her father' in Ancient Egyptian.

Ashley ♀ ♂

An increasingly popular given name for girls, this is a transferred use of the surname, which comes from any of numerous places in England named with Old English *æsc* 'ash' + *lēah* 'wood'. Its use as a given name may have been first inspired by Anthony Ashley Cooper (1801–85), Earl of Shaftesbury, who was noted for his humanitarian work. It has recently become enormously popular in North America, where it was recorded in a 1989 survey as the second most common of all female given names bestowed in that year.

Variants: **Ashlea, Ashleigh, Ashlee, Ashlie, Ashly** (all ♀)

Ashling ♀
Irish: Anglicized form of ◊**Aisling**.

Ashlyn ♀
Altered form of ◊**Ashling**, or else a
combination of the first syllable of the
popular female name ◊**Ashley** with the
suffix *-lyn*.
Variants: **Ashlynn, Ashlynne**.

Ashton ♀ ♂
Mainly U.S.: transferred use of the
surname, itself in origin a local name
from any of the numerous places in
England named with Old English
æsc 'ash-tree' + *tūn* 'enclosure',
'settlement'. As a given name this is
predominantly female, partly, perhaps,
due to the vogue for ◊**Ashley**.

Aspen ♀
Mainly U.S.: from the name of the
tree, a type of poplar with delicately
quivering leaves. The word was
originally an adjective, derived from
the tree-name *asp* (Old English *æspe*),
but came to be used as a noun in the
16th century.

Astrid ♀
Scandinavian name, derived from Old
Norse *áss* 'god' + *fríðr* 'fair',
'beautiful'. It has become fairly
common in the English-speaking
world during the 20th century, in part
as a result of the fame of the Queen of
the Belgians (1905–35) who bore this
name.

Auberon ♂
From an Old French name of
Germanic (Frankish) origin. There is
some doubt about its origin; it may be
connected with ◊**Aubrey** or be derived
from *adal* 'noble' + *ber(n)* 'bear'.
Variant: **Oberon**.

Aubrey ♂ ♀
From a Norman French form of the
Germanic name *Alberic*, from *alb*
'elf', 'supernatural being' + *ric*
'power'. This was the name, according
to Germanic mythology, of the king of
the elves. The native Old English
form, *Ælfrīc*, borne by a 10th-century
archbishop of Canterbury, did not long
survive the Conquest. *Aubrey* was a
relatively common given name during
the Middle Ages, but later fell out of
favour. Its occurrence since the 19th
century may in part represent a
transferred use of the surname derived
from the Norman given name, as well
as a revival of the latter. In the United
States, this is mainly used as a female
given name, perhaps under the
influence of ◊**Audrey**.

Audra ♀
Modern variant of ◊**Audrey**, used
especially in the Southern United
States in forms such as **Audra Jo** and
Audra Rose.

Audrey ♀
Much altered form of the Old English
female name *Æðelþryð*, derived from
æðel 'noble' + *þryð* 'strength'. This
was the name of a 6th-century saint
(normally known by the Latinized
form of her name, *Etheldreda*), who
was a particular favourite in the
Middle Ages. According to tradition
she died from a tumour of the neck,
which she bore stoically as a divine
punishment for her youthful delight in
fine necklaces. The name went into a
decline at the end of the Middle Ages,
when it came to be considered vulgar,
being associated with *tawdry*, that is,
lace and other goods sold at fairs held
in her name (the word deriving from a
misdivision of *Saint Audrey*).
Shakespeare bestowed it on
Touchstone's comic sweetheart in *As
You Like It*. In the 20th century such
associations have largely been
forgotten and the name has revived,
partly due in the 1950s and 60s to the
popularity of the actress Audrey
Hepburn (1929–93).

Audrina ♀
Recent fanciful elaboration of
◊**Audrey**.

Augusta ♀

Latinate feminine form of ◊**Augustus**, which enjoyed a vogue in Britain towards the end of the 19th century.

Augustine ♂

English form of the Latin name *Augustīnus* (a derivative of ◊**Augustus**). Its most famous bearer is St Augustine of Hippo (354–430), perhaps the greatest of the Fathers of the Christian Church. He formulated the principles followed by the numerous medieval communities named after him as Austin canons, friars, and nuns. Also important in England was St Augustine of Canterbury, who brought Christianity to Kent in the 6th century. See also ◊**Austin**.

Augustus ♂

Latin name, from the adjective *augustus* 'great', 'magnificent' (from *augēre* 'to increase'). This word was adopted as a title by the Roman emperors, starting with Octavian (Caius Julius Caesar Octavianus), the adopted son of Julius Caesar, who assumed it in 27 BC and is now generally known as the Emperor Augustus. This name, together with ◊**Augusta**, was revived in England in the 18th century, but it has now again declined in popularity.
Short form: **Gus**.

Aurelia ♀

Feminine form of Latin *Aurēlius*, a family name derived from *aureus* 'golden'. The name was borne by several minor early saints, but its revival as a given name in the 17th century is probably due to its meaning rather than association with any of them.

Aurora ♀

From Latin *aurōra* 'dawn', also used in the classical period as the name of the personified goddess of the dawn. It was not used as a given name in the post-classical or medieval period, but is a reinvention of the Renaissance, and has generally been bestowed as a learned equivalent of ◊**Dawn**.

Austin ♂

A medieval contracted form of the Latin name *Augustīnus* (see ◊**Augustine**). The present-day use of this form as a given name is a reintroduction from its survival as a surname.
Variant: **Austen**.

Autumn ♀

Mainly U.S.: from the name of the season (Latin *autumnus*). This is now more popular as a given name than ◊**Summer**, in spite of its less sunny connotations and the fact that in American English *autumn* is felt to be a rather formal word for the season.

Ava ♀

Of uncertain origin, probably Germanic, from a short form of various female compound names containing the element *av* (of uncertain meaning). St Ava or Avia was a 9th-century abbess of Dinart in Hainault and a member of the Frankish royal family. Evidence for the existence of the name between the early Middle Ages and the mid-20th century is lacking, and it may well be a modern invention. Its popularity since the 1950s is largely due to the film actress Ava Gardner (b. 1922).

Avery ♂

Transferred use of the surname, which originated in the Middle Ages from a Norman French pronunciation of ◊**Alfred**.

Avril ♀

Although generally taken as the French form of the name of the fourth month (see ◊**April**), this also has been influenced by an Old English female personal name derived from *eofor* 'boar' + *hild* 'battle'.

Azalea ♀

Modern coinage from the name of the

flowering shrub, one of the most recent of the names taken from terms denoting flora from the 19th century onwards. The shrub was named in the 18th century with the feminine form of Greek *azaleos* 'dry', because it flourishes in dry soil.

Azalia ♀

Modern coinage, an altered spelling of ◊**Azalea**, perhaps influenced by ◊**Azania** or ◊**Azaria**. *Azaliah* is also a male name (meaning 'reserved by God' in Hebrew) borne by a minor biblical character (2 Kings 22:3).

Azania ♀

Modern coinage: *Azaniah* is a male name (meaning 'heard by God' in Hebrew) borne by a minor biblical character, but it seems more likely that this name is bestowed with reference to the African nationalist name for South Africa.

Azaria ♀

Modern coinage, apparently derived from the male biblical name *Azariah* (meaning 'helped by God' in Hebrew) borne by a biblical prophet who recalled King Asa to a proper observance of religion (2 Chronicles 15:1–8). The name is borne by a number of other minor characters in the Bible, all of them male.

Azelia ♀

Modern coinage, apparently a variant of ◊**Azalia**, possibly influenced by Greek *azēlos* 'not jealous'.

BABS BAILEY BALDIE BALDWIN BALTHASA
R BAPTIST BARBARA BARCLAY BARNABAS
BARNABY BARNEY BARRET BARRY BART B
ARTHOLOMEW BARTON BASIL BAXTER BA
YLIE BAZ BEA BEATRICE BEATRIX BEAU BEC
CA BECK BECKY BEE BELINDA BELLA BELLE B

Babs ♀
Informal pet form of ◊**Barbara**.

Bailey ♂ ♀
Transferred use of the surname, which has various origins. Most commonly it was an occupational name for a bailiff or administrative official; in other cases it was a local name for someone who lived near a bailey, i.e. a city fortification; in others it may be a local name from *Bailey* in Lancashire, which gets its name from Old English *bēg* 'berry' + *lēah* 'wood', 'clearing'. In the United States this is now more common as a female given name than a male one.
Variants: **Bailie, Baily, Bailee, Baileigh; Baylie, Baylee, Bayleigh**.

Baldie ♂
Scottish pet form of ◊**Archibald**.

Baldwin ♂
From an Old French name of Germanic (Frankish) origin, derived from *bald* 'bold', 'brave' + *wine* 'friend'. This was adopted by the Normans and introduced by them to Britain. In the Middle Ages it was a comparatively common name, which gave rise to a surname. It was borne by the Norman crusader Baldwin of Boulogne, who in 1100 was elected first king of Jerusalem, and by four further crusader kings of Jerusalem. In modern times, it normally represents a transferred use of the surname rather than a direct revival of the Norman given name.

Balthasar ♂
Name ascribed in medieval Christian tradition to one of the three wise men of the Orient who brought gifts to the infant Jesus. The name is a variant of that of the biblical king *Belshazzar* and means 'Baal protect the king'. It has never been a common given name in the English-speaking world.
Variant: **Balthazar**.

Baptist ♂
English form of Church Latin *baptista*, Greek *baptistēs* (a derivative of *baptein* 'to dip'), the epithet of the most popular of the numerous saints called ◊**John**. As an English name it is used mainly in the United States by members of evangelical sects.

Barbara ♀
From Latin, meaning 'foreign woman' (a feminine form of *barbarus* 'foreign', from Greek, referring originally to the unintelligible chatter of foreigners, which sounded to the Greek ear like no more than *bar-bar*). St Barbara has always been one of the most popular saints in the calendar, although there is some doubt whether she ever existed. According to legend, she was imprisoned in a tower and later murdered by her father, who was then struck down by a bolt of lightning; accordingly, she is the patron of architects, stonemasons, and fortifications, and of firework makers, artillerymen, and gunpowder magazines.
Variant: **Barbra** (a modern contracted spelling).
Short form: **Barb** (mainly North American, informal).
Pet forms: **Barbie, Babs**.

Barclay ♂

Transferred use of the Scottish surname, which was taken to Scotland in the 12th century by Walter de *Berchelai*, who became chamberlain of Scotland in 1165. His descendants became one of the most powerful families in Scotland. The surname is from *Berkeley* in Gloucestershire, which is named with Old English *beorc* 'birch-tree' + *lēah* 'wood', 'clearing'.

Barnabas ♂

From the New Testament, where *Barnabas* represents a Greek form of the name of a companion of St Paul. The Aramaic original meant 'son of consolation'.

Barnaby ♂

Variant of ◊**Barnabas**, from a medieval vernacular form.

Barney ♂

Pet form of ◊**Barnaby** or its learned equivalent ◊**Barnabas**.
Variant: **Barny**.

Barrett ♂

Transferred use of the surname, which is of obscure origin. It is probably a nickname from Middle English *baret* 'dispute', 'argument'. The transferred use as a given name is recent.

Barry ♂

Anglicized form of the Irish Gaelic name **Barra** (Old Irish *Bairre*), a short form of *Fionnb(h)arr* (see ◊**Finbar**). In the 20th century this name has become very popular throughout the English-speaking world, particularly in Australia.
Pet forms: **Baz**, **Bazza** (Australian informal).

Bart ♂

Short form of ◊**Barton** and ◊**Bartholomew**.

Bartholomew ♂

Of New Testament origin, the name of an apostle mentioned in all the synoptic gospels (Matthew, Mark, and Luke) and in the Acts of the Apostles. It is an Aramaic formation meaning 'son of Talmai', and has been assumed by many scholars to be a byname of the apostle ◊**Nathaniel**. *Talmai* is a Hebrew name, said to mean 'abounding in furrows' (Numbers 13:22).
Short form: **Bart**.

Barton ♂

Transferred use of the surname, originally a local name from any of the numerous places in England so called from Old English *bere* 'barley' + *tūn* 'enclosure', 'settlement'.
Short form: **Bart**.

Basil ♂

From the Greek name *Basileios* 'royal' (a derivative of *basileus* 'king'). This name was borne by St Basil the Great (*c.*330–379), bishop of Caesarea, a theologian regarded as one of the Fathers of the Eastern Church. It was also the name of several early saints martyred in the East.

Baxter ♂

Transferred use of the surname, which originated in the Middle Ages as an occupational name for a baker, Old English *bæcestre*. The *-estre* suffix was originally feminine, but by the Middle English period the gender difference had been lost; *Baxter* was merely a regional variant of *Baker*.

Baylie ♀

Mainly U.S.: variant spelling of ◊**Bailey**.
Variants: **Baylee**, **Bayleigh**.

Baz ♂

Mainly Australian: informal pet form of ◊**Barry**.
Variant: **Bazza**.

Bea ♀

Short form of ◊**Beatrice** or ◊**Beatrix**.

Beatrice ♀

Italian and French form of ◊**Beatrix**,

occasionally used in England during the Middle Ages, and strongly revived in the 19th century. It is most famous as the name of Dante's beloved.
Short forms: **Bea**, **Bee**.
Pet forms: **Beat(t)ie**.

Beatrix ♀

From a Late Latin personal name, which was borne by a saint executed in Rome, together with Faustinus and Simplicius, in the early 4th century. The original form of the name seems to have been *Viātrix*, a feminine version of *Viātōr* 'voyager (through life)', which was common among early Christians. This was then altered by association with Latin *Beātus* 'blessed' (*Via-* and *Bea-* sometimes being pronounced the same in Late Latin). See also ◊**Beatrice**.
Short forms: **Bea**, **Bee**.
Pet forms: **Beat(t)ie**.

Beau ♂

Recent coinage as a given name, originally a nickname meaning 'handsome', as borne by Beau Brummell (1778–1840), the dandy who was for a time a friend of the Prince Regent. The word was also used in the 19th century with the meaning 'admirer' or 'sweet-heart'. Its adoption as a given name seems to have been due to the hero of P. C. Wren's novel *Beau Geste* (1924) or to the character of Beau Wilks in Margaret Mitchell's *Gone with the Wind* (1936), which was made into an exceptionally popular film in 1939.

Becca ♀

Modern shortened form of ◊**Rebecca**.

Beck ♀

Modern informal short form of ◊**Rebecca**.

Becky ♀

Pet form of ◊**Rebecca**. It was especially popular in the 18th and 19th centuries.

Bee ♀

Variant spelling of ◊**Bea**.

Belinda ♀

Of uncertain origin. It was used by Sir John Vanbrugh for a character in his comedy *The Provok'd Wife* (1697), was taken up by Alexander Pope in *The Rape of the Lock* (1712), and has enjoyed a steady popularity ever since. It is not certain where Vanbrugh got the name from. The notion that it is Germanic (with a second element *lind* 'soft', 'tender', 'weak') is not well founded. In Italian literature it is the name ascribed to the wife of Orlando, vassal of Charlemagne, but this use is not supported in Germanic sources. The name may be an Italian coinage from *bella* 'beautiful' (see ◊**Bella**) + the feminine name suffix *-inda* (cf. e.g. ◊**Lucinda**).

Bella ♀

Shortened form of *Isabella*, the Italian version of ◊**Isabel**, but also associated with the Italian adjective *bella*, feminine of *bello* 'handsome', 'beautiful' (Late Latin *bellus*).

Belle ♀

Variant of ◊**Bella**, reflecting the French feminine adjective *belle* 'beautiful'.

Ben ♂

Short form of ◊**Benjamin**, or less commonly of ◊**Benedict** or ◊**Bennett**.
Pet forms: **Benny**, **Bennie**.

Benedict ♂

From Church Latin *Benedictus* 'blessed'. This was the name of the saint (*c.*480–*c.*550) who composed the Benedictine rule of Christian monastic life that is still followed in essence by all Western orders. He was born near Spoleto in Umbria, central Italy. After studying in Rome, he went to live as a hermit at Subiaco, and later organized groups of followers and imitators into monastic cells. In *c.*529 he moved to Monte Cassino, where he founded the great monastery that is still the centre of the Benedictine order. His rule is simple, restrained, and practical. The name is used mainly by Roman Catholics. See also ◊**Bennett**.

Benjamin ♂

Biblical name, borne by the youngest of the twelve sons of Jacob. His mother Rachel died in giving birth to him, and in her last moments she named him *Benoni*, meaning 'son of my sorrow'. His father, however, did not wish him to bear such an ill-omened name, and renamed him *Benyamin* (Genesis 35:16–18; 42:4). This means either 'son of the right hand' or more likely 'son of the south' (Hebrew *yamin* can also mean 'south'), since Benjamin was the only child of Jacob born in Canaan and not in Mesopotamia to the north. Another tradition is that the second element of the name is a variant of the Hebrew plural noun *yamim*, which means 'days' but is used idiomatically to mean 'year' or 'years'. The name would then mean 'son of (my) old age' and refer to the fact that Benjamin was Jacob's youngest child. In the Middle Ages the name was often given to sons whose mothers had died in childbirth. Today it has no such unfortunate associations, but is still mainly a Jewish name.
Short form: **Ben**.
Pet forms: **Benny**, **Bennie**, **Benji(e)**.

Bennett ♂

The normal medieval vernacular form of ◊**Benedict**, now sometimes used as an antiquarian revival, but more often it is a transferred use of the surname derived from the medieval given name.
Variants: **Benett**, **Bennet**, **Benet**.

Benson ♂

Transferred use of the surname, which originated in part as a patronymic from *Ben(n)*, a short form of ◊**Benedict**, and in part as a local name from *Benson* (formerly *Bensington*) in Oxfordshire.

Bentley ♂

Transferred use of the surname, which originated as a local name from any of the dozen or so places in England so called from Old English *beonet* 'bent grass' + *lēah* 'wood', 'clearing'.

Berenice ♀

From the Greek personal name *Berenikē*, which seems to have originated in the royal house of Macedon. It is almost certainly a Macedonian dialectal form of the Greek name *Pherenīkē* 'victory bringer'. It was introduced to the Egyptian royal house by the widow of one of Alexander the Great's officers, who married Ptolemy I. It was also borne by an early Christian woman mentioned in Acts 25, for which reason it was felt to be acceptable by the Puritans in the 17th century. It has now fallen out of fashion again. See also ◊**Bernice**.

Bernadette ♀

French feminine diminutive of ◊**Bernard**. Its use in Britain and Ireland is almost exclusively confined to Roman Catholics, who take it in honour of St Bernadette Soubirous (1844–79), a French peasant girl who had visions of the Virgin Mary and uncovered a spring near Lourdes where miraculous cures are still sought.
Variant: **Bernardette**.

Bernard ♂

From an Old French name of Germanic (Frankish) origin, derived from *ber(n)* 'bear' + *hard* 'hardy', 'brave', 'strong'. This was the name of three famous medieval churchmen: St Bernard of Menthon (923–1008), founder of a hospice on each of the Alpine passes named after him; the monastic reformer St Bernard of Clairvaux (1090–1153); and the scholastic philosopher Bernard of Chartres. It was adopted by the Normans and introduced by them to England. A native Old English form,

Beornheard, was superseded by the Norman form.
Pet form: **Bernie**.

Bernice ♀

Contracted form of ◊**Berenice**. This is the form that is used in the Authorized Version of the Bible, and it is now fairly popular in the English-speaking world.
Pet form: **Binnie**.

Berry ♀

From the vocabulary word (Old English *berie*). This is one of the less common of the names referring to flowers, fruit, and vegetation introduced as given names in the 20th century.

Bert ♂

Short form of any of the various names containing this syllable as a first or second element, for example ◊**Albert** and ◊**Bertram**. See also ◊**Burt**.
Pet form: **Bertie**.

Bertha ♀

Latinized version of a Continental Germanic name, a short form of various compound women's personal names derived from *berht* 'famous' (cognate with Modern English *bright*). It probably existed in England before the Conquest, and was certainly reinforced by Norman use, but fell out of use in the 15th century. It was reintroduced into the English-speaking world from Germany in the 19th century, but has once again gone out of fashion.

Bertram ♂

From an Old French name of Germanic (Frankish) origin, from *berht* 'bright', 'famous' + *hramn* 'raven'. Ravens were traditional symbols of wisdom in Germanic mythology; Odin was regularly accompanied by ravens called Hugin and Munin. This name was adopted by the Normans and introduced by them to Britain. See also ◊**Bertrand**.
Short form: **Bert**.

Bertrand ♂

Medieval French variant of ◊**Bertram**, imported to Britain by the Normans. In modern times it has been made famous by the English philosopher Bertrand Russell (1872–1970).

Beryl ♀

One of several women's names that are taken from gemstones and which came into fashion at the end of the 19th century. Beryl is a pale green semiprecious stone (of which emerald is a variety). Other colours are also found. The word is from Greek, and is ultimately of Indian origin.

Bess ♀

Short form of ◊**Elizabeth**, in common use in the days of Queen Elizabeth I, who was known as 'Good Queen Bess'.
Pet forms: **Bessie, Bessy**.

Bet ♀

Short form of ◊**Elizabeth**.
Pet form: **Betty**.

Beth ♀

Short form of ◊**Elizabeth**, not used before the 19th century, when it became popular in America and elsewhere after publication of Louisa M. Alcott's novel *Little Women* (1868), in which Beth March is one of the four sisters who are the central characters.

Bethan ♀

Originally a Welsh pet form of ◊**Beth**, now also popular elsewhere in the English-speaking world.

Bethany ♀

Of New Testament origin. In the New Testament it is a placename, that of the village just outside Jerusalem where Jesus stayed during Holy Week, before going on to Jerusalem and crucifixion (Matthew 21:17; Mark 11:1; Luke 19:29; John 12:1). Its Hebrew name may mean 'house of figs' (*beth te'ena* or *beth te'enim*). The given name is favoured mainly by

Roman Catholics, being bestowed in honour of Mary of Bethany, sister of Martha and Lazarus. She is sometimes identified with Mary Magdalene (see ◊**Madeleine**), although the grounds for this identification are very poor.

Betsy ♀
Pet form of ◊**Elizabeth**, a blend of *Betty* (see ◊**Bet**) and *Bessie* (see ◊**Bess**).

Bette ♀
Variant of ◊**Betty**, associated particularly with the film actress Bette Davis (1908–1992), born Ruth Elizabeth Davis.

Bettina ♀
Latinate elaboration of ◊**Betty**.

Betty ♀
Pet form of ◊**Elizabeth**, dating from the 18th century.
Variant: ◊**Bette**.

Beulah ♀
Biblical name: from the name (meaning 'married' in Hebrew) applied to the land of Israel by the prophet Isaiah (Isaiah 62:4). 'The land of Beulah' has sometimes been taken as a reference to heaven. It was taken up as a given name in England at the time of the Reformation and was popular among the Puritans in the 17th century. It was borne by the American actress Beulah Bondi (1899–1981), and was immortalized by Mae West's instruction to her maidservant: 'Beulah, peel me a grape.'

Beverley ♀, also ♂
Transferred use of the surname, which is from a place in Humberside named with Old English *beofor* 'beaver' + *lēac* 'stream'. The spelling **Beverly** is now used more or less exclusively for girls, and is the usual form of the female name in America. It is not clear why it should have become such a popular female name. In America, association with Beverly Hills in Los Angeles, the district where many film stars live, may have been an influencing factor.
Variant: **Beverly**.

Bianca ♀
Italian: from *bianca* 'white' (i.e. 'pure', but cf. ◊**Blanche**). The name was used by Shakespeare for characters in two of his plays that are supposed to take place in an Italian context: the mild-mannered sister of Katharina, the 'shrew' in *The Taming of the Shrew*, and a courtesan in *Othello*. It came to prominence in the 1970s as the name of Bianca Jagger, the Nicaraguan fashion model, peace worker, and diplomat, who was for a time married to the rock singer Mick Jagger.

Biddy ♀
Of Irish origin: pet form of ◊**Bride** or ◊**Bridget**. It was formerly quite common, but is now seldom used outside Ireland, partly perhaps because the informal expression 'an old biddy' in English has come to denote a tiresome old woman.

Bill ♂
Altered short form of ◊**William**, not used before the 19th century. The reason for the change in the initial consonant is not clear, but it conforms to the pattern regularly found when English words beginning with *w-* are borrowed into Gaelic. The nickname 'King Billy' for William of Orange is an early example from Ireland which may have influenced English usage.
Pet forms: **Billy**, ◊**Billie**.

Billie ♀ ♂
Variant of *Billy* (see ◊**Bill**), now mainly used for girls, and sometimes bestowed at baptism as a female equivalent of ◊**William**.

Binnie ♀
Pet form of ◊**Bernice**, associated particularly with the actress and singer Binnie Hale (1899–1984).

BLAIN

Blain ♂

Anglicized form of the Gaelic personal name *Bláán*, originally a byname representing a diminutive form of *blá* 'yellow'. This was the name of an early Celtic saint who lived in the 6th century.
Variants: **Blaine**, **Blane**.

Blair ♂ ♀

Transferred use of the Scottish surname, in origin a local name from any of various places named with Gaelic *blàr* 'plain', 'field'. In North America it is now widely used as a female given name.
Variant: **Blaire**.

Blaise ♂

French: the name (Latin *Blasius*, probably from *blaesus* 'lisping') of a saint popular throughout Europe in the Middle Ages but almost forgotten today. He was a bishop of Sebaste in Armenia, and was martyred in the early years of the 4th century; these bare facts were elaborated in a great number of legends that reached Europe from the East at the time of the Crusades.

Blake ♂

Transferred use of the surname, which has two quite distinct etymologies. It is both from Old English *blæc* 'black' and from Old English *blāc* 'pale', 'white'; it was thus originally a nickname given to someone with hair or skin that was either remarkably dark or remarkably light. It is now quite popular as a male given name.

Blanche ♀

Originally a nickname for a blonde, from *blanche*, feminine of Old French *blanc* 'white' (of Germanic origin). It came to be associated with the notion of whiteness as indicating purity, and was introduced into England as a given name by the Normans. A pale complexion combined with light hair has long been an ideal of beauty in Europe (cf. Modern English *fair*, which at first meant 'beautiful' and then, from the 16th century, 'light in colouring').

Blane ♂

Variant spelling of ◊**Blain**.

Blodwedd ♀

Welsh: name borne by a character in the *Mabinogi*. She was conjured up out of flowers as a bride for Lleu Llaw Gyffes, and was originally called *Blodeuedd*, a derivative of *blawd* 'flowers'. After she had treacherously had her husband killed she was transformed into an owl, and her name was changed to *Blodeuwedd* 'flower face', an allusion to the markings round the eyes of the owl.

Blodwen ♀

Welsh traditional name, derived from *blawd* 'flowers' + *(g)wen* 'white', feminine of *gwyn* 'white', 'fair', 'blessed', 'holy'. The name was relatively common in the Middle Ages and has recently been revived.

Blossom ♀

19th-century coinage, from the vocabulary word for flowers on a fruit tree or ornamental tree (Old English *blōstm*), used as an affectionate pet name for a young girl.

Boaz ♂

Biblical Hebrew name of uncertain origin, said by some to be from a word meaning 'swiftness'. In the Bible it is borne by a distant kinsman of Ruth, who treats her generously and eventually marries her. The given name was in occasional use in England in the 17th and 18th centuries but is now very rare. It is sometimes used in Jewish families.

Bob ♂

Altered short form of ◊**Robert**, a later development than the common medieval forms *Hob*, *Dob*, and *Nob*, all of which, unlike *Bob*, have given rise to English surnames.
Pet forms: **Bobby**, ◊**Bobbie**.

Bobbie ♀ ♂

Variant of *Bobby* (see ◊**Bob**), now mainly used as a female name, in part as a pet form of ◊**Roberta**.
Variant: **Bobbi**.

Bonita ♀

Coined in the United States in the 1940s from the feminine form of Spanish *bonito* 'pretty'. This is not used as a given name in Spanish-speaking countries. *Bonita* looks like the feminine form of a medieval Latin male name, *Bonītus* (from *bonus* 'good'), which was borne by an Italian saint of the 6th century and a Provençal saint of the 7th. However, no medieval record of the feminine form in use as a given name is known.
Pet form: ◊**Bonnie**.

Bonnie ♀

Chiefly North American: originally an affectionate nickname from the Scottish word *bonnie* 'fine', 'attractive', 'pretty'. However, it is not—or at any rate has not been until recently—used as a given name in Scotland. Its popularity may be attributed to the character of Scarlett O'Hara's infant daughter Bonnie in the film *Gone With the Wind* (1939), based on Margaret Mitchell's novel of the same name. (Bonnie's name was really Eugenie Victoria, but she had 'eyes as blue as the bonnie blue flag'.) A famous American bearer was Bonnie Parker, accomplice of the bank robber Clyde Barrow; their life together was the subject of the film *Bonnie and Clyde* (1967). The name has enjoyed a vogue in the second part of the 20th century, and has also been used as a pet form of ◊**Bonita**.

Boris ♂

Russian: from the Tartar nickname *Bogoris* 'small'. Later, however, it was taken to be a shortened form of the Russian name *Borislav*, from *bor* 'battle' + *slav* 'glory'. The name was borne in the 9th century by a ruler of Bulgaria who converted his kingdom to Christianity and sheltered disciples of Saints Cyril and Methodius when they were expelled from Moravia. The name was also borne by a 10th-century Russian saint, son of Prince Vladimir of Kiev and brother of St Gleb. It is as a result of his influence that *Boris* is one of the very few non-classical names that the Orthodox Church allows to be taken as a baptismal name (although the saint himself bore the baptismal name *Romanus*).

Brad ♂

Mainly North American: short form of ◊**Bradford** and ◊**Bradley**.

Braden ♂

Mainly U.S.: transferred use of the Irish surname, Gaelic *Ó Bradáin* 'descendant of Bradán'. The latter is a personal name meaning 'salmon'.

Bradford ♂

Mainly U.S.: transferred use of the surname, in origin a local name from any of the numerous places in England so called from Old English *brād* 'broad' + *ford* 'ford'. The surname was borne most famously by William Bradford (1590–1657), leader of the Pilgrim Fathers from 1621 and governor of Plymouth Colony for some 30 years. It was also the name of another William Bradford (1722–91), a printer who played an important part in the American Revolution.

Bradley ♂

Mainly North American: transferred use of the surname, in origin a local name from any of the numerous places in England so called from Old English *brād* 'broad' + *lēah* 'wood', 'clearing'. The most famous American bearer of this surname was General Omar N. Bradley (1893–1981).

Brady ♂ ♀

Mainly North American: transferred use of the surname, which is of Irish origin, from Gaelic *Ó Brádaigh* 'descendant of Brádach'. *Brádach* is an old Irish byname of uncertain origin, possibly a contracted form of *brághadach* 'large-chested', from *brágha* 'chest'.

Brandon ♂

Mainly North American: transferred use of the surname, in origin a local name from any of various places so called, most of which get their name from Old English *brōm* 'broom', 'gorse' + *dūn* 'hill'. In some cases it may be an altered form of ◊**Brendan**. There has perhaps also been some influence from the surname of the Italian American actor Marlon Brando (b. 1924).

Brandy ♀

Mainly U.S.: ostensibly from the vocabulary word for the type of liquor (earlier known as *brandy wine* or *brand(e)wine*, from Dutch *brandewijn* 'distilled wine'), but probably invented as a feminine form of ◊**Brandon**.
Variants: **Brandie**, **Brandi**.

Brant ♂

Mainly U.S.: probably a variant of the rather more common ◊**Brent**. The English surname *Brant* is a relatively infrequent variant of *Brand*, derived from the Old Norse personal name *Brandr*, meaning 'sword' (cf. ◊**Brenda**).

Branton ♂

Mainly U.S.: variant of ◊**Brandon** or transferred use of the surname *Branton*. This is a local name from places in Northumbria and West Yorkshire so named from Old English *brōm* 'broom', 'gorse' + *tūn* 'enclosure', 'settlement'.

Branwen ♀

Welsh traditional name, apparently from *brân* 'raven' + *(g)wen*, feminine of *gwyn* 'white', 'fair', 'blessed', 'holy', but more probably a variant of ◊**Bronwen**. The story of Branwen, daughter of Llŷr, forms the second chapter or 'branch' of the *Mabinogi*: it tells of her beauty and of the conflict on her account between her brother Bran, King of the 'Island of the Mighty' (i.e. Britain), and her husband Matholwch, King of Ireland.
Variant: **Brangwen**.

Breanna ♀

Mainly U.S.: variant spelling of ◊**Brianna**.
Variant: **Breanne**.

Breda ♀

Irish: Anglicized form of Gaelic *Bríd* (see ◊**Bride**).
Variant: **Breeda**.

Brenda ♀

A very popular name, of uncertain derivation. Until the 20th century it was confined mainly to Scotland and Ireland. It is probably of Scandinavian rather than Celtic origin, however: a short form of any of the various compound names derived from Old Norse *brand* 'sword'. Its popularity in Gaelic-speaking countries has no doubt been influenced by its similarity to ◊**Brendan**.

Brendan ♂

Irish: from the old Irish personal name *Bréanainn*, derived from a Celtic word meaning 'prince'. This was the name of two 6th-century Irish saints, Brendan the Voyager and Brendan of Birr. According to Irish legend, the former was the first European to set foot on North American soil. The modern Irish Gaelic form **Breandán** and the Anglicized *Brendan* are based on the medieval Latin form *Brendanus*.

Brenna ♀

Mainly U.S.: modern coinage, apparently created as a feminine form of ◊**Brennan**, but perhaps also influenced by ◊**Brianna**.

Brennan ♀

Mainly U.S.: transferred use of the Irish surname, Gaelic *Ó Braonáin* 'descendant of Braonán'. The latter is a personal name derived from a

diminutive of *braon* 'moisture', 'drop'.
It may also be taken as a contracted
form of ◊**Brendan**.

Brent ♂

Transferred use of the surname, which
is derived from any of several places
in Devon and Somerset which are on
or near prominent hills, and were
named with a Celtic or Old English
term for a hill. The given name has
enjoyed considerable popularity in
Britain and the United States in the
1970s and 1980s, and may have been
influenced by ◊**Brett**, which has
experienced a similar vogue, starting
somewhat earlier.

Brenton ♂

Mainly U.S.: transferred use of the
surname, in origin a local name from
a place near Exminster in Devon, so
called from Old English *Brȳningtūn*
'settlement associated with Brȳni'.
The latter is a personal name derived
from *bryne* 'fire', 'flame'. The modern
given name may also be a variant of
◊**Branton**.

Brett ♂

Transferred use of the surname, which
originated in the Middle Ages as an
ethnic name for one of the Bretons
who arrived in England in the wake of
the Norman Conquest; it is most
common in East Anglia, where Breton
settlement was particularly
concentrated. As a given name, it has
enjoyed something of a vogue in the
latter half of the 20th century.

Brewster ♂

Mainly U.S.: transferred use of the
surname, in origin an occupational
name for a brewer, Middle English
brēowestre. The *-estre* suffix was
originally feminine, but by the Middle
English period this grammatical
distinction had been lost (cf. ◊**Baxter**).

Brian ♂

Originally Irish: perhaps from an Old
Celtic word meaning 'high' or 'noble'.
The name has been perennially

popular in Ireland, largely on account
of the fame of Brian Boru (Gaelic
Brian Bóroimhe), a 10th-century high
king of Ireland. In the Middle Ages it
was relatively common in East Anglia,
to which it was introduced by Breton
settlers, and in north-west England, to
which it was introduced by
Scandinavians from Ireland. In Gaelic
Scotland it was at first borne
exclusively by members of certain
professional families of Irish origin.
Variant: **Bryan**.

Brianna ♀

Recent coinage to create a female
equivalent of ◊**Brian**.
Variant: **Brianne**. See also ◊**Breanna**.

Briar ♀

20th-century coinage from the
vocabulary word *briar* or *brier* (Old
English *brær*), denoting a thorny bush
of wild roses ('sweet briar') or
brambles.

Brice ♂

The name of a saint who was a
disciple and successor of St Martin of
Tours. His name is found in the
Latinized forms *Bri(c)tius* and *Bricius*
and is probably of Gaulish origin,
possibly derived from a word meaning
'speckled' (cf. Welsh *brych*).

Bride ♀

Irish: Anglicized form of *Bríd*, the
modern Gaelic contracted form of
Brighid (see ◊**Bridget**).
Pet form: **Bridie**.

Bridget ♀

Anglicized form of the Gaelic name
Brighid (now pronounced 'breed'). This
was the name of an ancient Celtic
goddess, which in Gaulish would have
been *Brigindos*, meaning 'the Exalted
One'. St Brigid of Kildare (c.450–c.525)
is one of the patron saints of Ireland.
Very few facts are known about her
life. She founded a religious house for
women at Kildare, and is said to have
been buried at Downpatrick, where St
Patrick and St Columba were also

buried. Many of the stories of miracles told about St Brigid seem to be Christianized versions of pagan legends concerning the goddess.
Variants: **Brigid**, **Brigit**, ◊**Brigitte**, **Bride**, **Breda**.
Pet forms: ◊**Biddy**, **Bridie**.

Brigham ♂

Mainly U.S.: name adopted in honour of the early Mormon leader, Brigham Young (1801–77). It was originally a surname, a local name from places in Cumbria and North Yorkshire so called from Old English *brycg* 'bridge' + *hām* 'homestead', 'settlement'. It is not known why the Mormon leader received this given name; he was the son of John and Abigail Young of Whitingham, Vermont.

Brigitte ♀

French form of ◊**Bridget**, associated particularly with the French film star of the 1950s Brigitte Bardot (born in 1933 as Camille Javal).

Briony ♀

Variant spelling of ◊**Bryony**.

Britt ♀

Swedish: contracted form of *Birgit*, the Swedish version of ◊**Bridget**, made famous in the English-speaking world by the Swedish actress Britt Ekland (b. 1924; her surname was originally Eklund).

Brittany ♀

Mainly North American: modern coinage, taken from the traditionally Celtic-speaking region of north-west France, known in medieval Latin as *Britannia*, because it was settled by refugees from Cornwall and Devon following the establishment of the Anglo-Saxon kingdom of Wessex. Its adoption as a given name has also been influenced by ◊**Britt**, of which it is sometimes regarded as the full form. In recent years it has rapidly established itself as a very popular name in North America: in one 1989 survey it was the most commonly

bestowed of all female given names in the United States.

Brock ♂

Transferred use of the surname, in origin a nickname for someone resembling a badger (Middle English *broc(k)*, Old English *brocc*, of Celtic origin).

Bronwen ♀

Welsh: from *bron* 'breast' + *(g)wen*, feminine of *gwyn* 'white', 'fair', 'blessed', 'holy'.

Brooke ♀

Mainly U.S.: transferred use of the surname, originally a local name for someone who lived near a brook or stream (Old English *bróc*). It has been borne by two American film actresses: Brooke Adams (b. 1949) and Brooke Shields (b. 1965).

Bruce ♂

Transferred use of the Scottish surname, now used as a given name throughout the English-speaking world, but in recent years particularly popular in Australia. The surname was originally a Norman baronial name, but a precise identification of the place from which it was derived has not been made (there are a large number of possible candidates). The Bruces were an influential Norman family in Scottish affairs in the early Middle Ages; its most famous member was Robert 'the Bruce' (1274–1329), who is said to have drawn inspiration after his defeat at Methven from the perseverance of a spider in repeatedly climbing up again after being knocked down. He ruled Scotland as King Robert I from 1306 to 1329.

Bruno ♂

From the Germanic word *brun* 'brown'. This was in use as a name in many of the ruling families of Germany during the Middle Ages. It was borne by a 10th-century saint, son of the Emperor Henry the Fowler, and by the Saxon duke who gave his name to Brunswick (German *Braunschweig*, i.e. 'Bruno's settlement'). Its use in the English-speaking world, which dates from the end of the 19th century, may have been partly influenced by Lewis Carroll's *Sylvie and Bruno* (1889), but more probably it was first used by settlers of German ancestry in the United States.

Bryan ♂
Variant of ◊**Brian**, influenced by the usual spelling of the associated surname.

Bryant ♂
Transferred use of the surname, which is derived from the given name ◊**Brian**. The final *-t* seems to have arisen as a result of a mishearing by English speakers of the devoicing of the *-n* in Gaelic, reinforced by association with names such as ◊**Constant**.

Bryce ♂, sometimes ♀
Mainly North American: variant of ◊**Brice**, now fairly commonly used as a given name, originating as a transferred use of the Scottish surname derived from the medieval given name.

Bryn ♂
Welsh: 20th-century coinage from the Welsh topographical term *bryn* 'hill', in part as a short form of ◊**Brynmor**. See also ◊**Brynn**.

Brynmor ♂
Welsh: 20th-century coinage from the name of a place in Gwynedd, named with *bryn* 'hill' + *mawr* 'large'.

Brynn ♂ ♀
Variant spelling of ◊**Bryn**. In the United States this is now used predominantly as a female name, perhaps by association with names such as ◊**Lynn**.

Bryony ♀
From the name of the plant (Greek *bryonia*). This is one of the names coined in the 20th century from vocabulary words denoting flowers. *Variant*: **Briony**.

Bryson ♂
Mainly U.S.: transferred use of the surname, which has a double origin. In part it represents a patronymic derived from the given name ◊**Brice** or ◊**Bryce**, in part it is an Anglicized form of the Irish Gaelic surname *Ó Briosáin*, an altered form of *Ó Muirgheasáin* 'descendant of Muirgheasán'. The latter is a personal name perhaps derived from *muir* 'sea' + *gus* 'vigour' + the diminutive suffix *-an*. The Ó Muirgheasáins were hereditary poets (and keepers of the relics of St Columba) in Donegal and Scotland.

Buck ♂
Mainly U.S.: from the nickname *Buck*, denoting a robust and spirited young man, from the vocabulary word for a male deer (Old English *bucc*) or a he-goat (Old English *bucca*).

Bud ♂
Mainly U.S.: originally a short form of the nickname or vocabulary word *buddy* 'friend', which may be an alteration, perhaps a nursery form, of *brother* or else derived from the Scottish Gaelic vocative case *a bhodaich* 'old man'. *Variant*: **Buddy**.

Buffy ♀
Informal pet form of ◊**Elizabeth**, based on a child's unsuccessful attempts to pronounce the name.

Bunty ♀
Nickname and occasional baptismal name, relatively popular in the early 20th century, but of uncertain derivation. It seems most likely that it derives from what was originally a dialectal pet name for a lamb, from the verb to *bunt* 'to butt gently'.

Burgess ♂
Transferred use of the surname, in

origin a status name from the Old French word *burgeis* 'freeman of a borough' (a derivative of *burg* 'town', of Germanic origin).

Burt ♂
Mainly U.S.: of various origins. In the case of the film actor Burt Lancaster (b. 1913) it is a short form of ◊**Burton**, but it has also been used as a variant spelling of ◊**Bert**. The pianist and composer Burt Bacharach (b. 1928) was the son of a Bert Bacharach, and his given name is presumably simply a variation of his father's.

Burton ♂
Transferred use of the surname, in origin a local name from any of the numerous places in England so called. In most cases the placename is derived from Old English *burh*

'fortress', 'fortified place' + *tūn* 'enclosure', 'settlement'.

Buster ♂
Mainly U.S.: originally a nickname from the slang term of address *buster* 'smasher', 'breaker', a derivative of the verb *bust* (altered form of *burst*). It was the nickname of the silent movie comedian Joseph Francis 'Buster' Keaton (1895–1966).

Byron ♂
Transferred use of the surname, first bestowed as a given name in honour of the poet Lord Byron (George Gordon, 6th Baron Byron, 1784–1824). The surname derives from the Old English phrase *æt ðǽm bȳrum* 'at the byres or cattlesheds', and denoted someone who lived there because it was his job to look after cattle.

CADE CADELL CADOGAN CAESAR CAILE C
AILEIGH CAITLIN CAITRIN CALE CALEB CA
LEIGH CALLY CALUM CALVIN CAMERON C
AMILLA CAMPBELL CANDACE CANDICE C
ANDIDA CANDY CARA CARADOC CAREEN
CAREY CARINA CARISSA CARL CARLA CARL

Cade ♂

Transferred use of the surname, which originated as a nickname from a word denoting something round and lumpish. It is one of several given names that owe their origin to their use for a character in Margaret Mitchell's novel *Gone with the Wind* (1936).

Cadell ♂

Welsh traditional name, derived from *cad* 'battle' + the diminutive suffix *-ell*.

Cadogan ♂

Anglicized form of the Old Welsh personal name *Cadwgan* or *Cadwgawn*, derived from *cad* 'battle' + *gwogawn* 'glory', 'distinction', or 'honour'. The name was borne by several Welsh princes in the early Middle Ages, and is mentioned as the name of two characters in the *Mabinogi*. It was revived in the 19th century, perhaps in part as a transferred use of the surname derived from it.

Caesar ♂

Mainly U.S.: Anglicized form of Italian *Cesare* or French *César*, or a direct adoption of the Roman imperial family name *Caesar*, of uncertain meaning. It has been connected with Latin *caesaries* 'head of hair', but this is no more than folk etymology; the name may be of Etruscan origin. Its most notable bearer was Gaius Julius Caesar (?102–44 BC) and it also formed part of the full name of his relative Augustus (Gaius Julius Caesar Octavianus Augustus). Subsequently it was used as an imperial title and eventually became a vocabulary word for an emperor (leading to German *Kaiser* and Russian *tsar*).

Caile ♂

Variant spelling of ◊**Cale**.

Caileigh ♀

See ◊**Kayley**.

Caitlín ♀

Irish Gaelic form of ◊**Katherine**, pronounced 'kat-*leen*'. It is being increasingly widely used in the English-speaking world, generally without the accent and with the pronunciation '*kate*-lin'.

Caitrín ♀

Irish Gaelic form of ◊**Katherine**.

Cale ♂

Mainly U.S.: of uncertain origin; perhaps a short form of ◊**Caleb** or a transferred use of a surname.
Variants: **Caile**, **Cayle**, **Kale**, **Kail(e)**, **Kayle**.

Caleb ♂

Biblical name, borne by an early Israelite, one of only two of those who set out with Moses from Egypt to live long enough to enter the promised land (Numbers 26:65). The name, which is apparently derived from the word for 'dog' in Hebrew, is said in some traditions to symbolize his devotion to God. It was popular among the Puritans and was introduced by them to America, where it is still in use.

Caleigh ♀

See ◊**Kayley**.

Cally ♀

Mainly U.S. It probably originated as a
variant of ◊**Kelly**, since none of the
women's names beginning with the
syllable *Cal-* (e.g. *Calliope* and
Callista) has ever been common.
Variant: **Callie**.

Calum ♂

Scottish Gaelic form of the Late Latin
personal name *Columba* 'dove'. This
was popular among early Christians
because the dove was a symbol of
gentleness, purity, peace, and the Holy
Spirit. St Columba was one of the
most influential of all the early Celtic
saints. He was born in Donegal in 521
into a noble family, and was trained
for the priesthood from early in life.
He founded monastery schools at
Durrow, Derry, and Kells, and then, in
563, sailed with twelve companions to
Scotland, to convert the people there
to Christianity. He established a
monastery on the island of Iona, and
from there converted the Pictish and
Irish inhabitants of Scotland. He
died in 597 and was buried at
Downpatrick.

Calvin ♂

Especially North American: from the
French surname, used as a given name
among Nonconformists in honour of
the French Protestant theologian Jean
Calvin (1509–64). The surname meant
originally 'little bald one', from a
diminutive of *calve*, a Norman and
Picard form of French *chauve* 'bald'.
(The theologian was born in Noyon,
Picardy.)

Cameron ♂ ♀

Transferred use of the Scottish
surname, which is borne by one of the
great Highland clans. Their name is
popularly derived from an ancestor
with a crooked nose (Gaelic *cam
sròn*). There were also Camerons in
the Lowlands, apparently the result of
an assimilation to this name of a
Norman baronial name derived from
Cambernon in Normandy. It is
common in North America and in the
United States is well established as a
female given name.

Camilla ♀

Feminine form of the old Roman
family name *Camillus*, of obscure and
presumably non-Roman origin.
According to tradition, recorded by the
Roman poet Virgil, Camilla was the
name of a warrior maiden, Queen of
the Volscians, who fought in the army
of Aeneas (*Aeneid* 7:803–17).

Campbell ♂

Transferred use of the Scottish
surname, borne by one of the great
Highland clans, whose head is the
Duke of Argyll. The name is popularly
derived from an ancestor with a
crooked mouth (Gaelic *cam beul*).

Candace ♀

The hereditary name of a long line of
queens of Ethiopia. One of them is
mentioned in the Bible, when the
apostle Philip baptizes 'a man of
Ethiopia, an eunuch of great authority
under Candace queen of the
Ethiopians, who had the charge of all
her treasure' (Acts 8:27). This form is
much less common than ◊**Candice**.

Candice ♀

Apparently a respelling of ◊**Candace**,
perhaps influenced by ◊**Clarice** or by a
folk etymology deriving the name
from Late Latin *canditia* 'whiteness'.
The name is best known as that of the
American actress Candice Bergen (b.
1946).

Candida ♀

From Late Latin, meaning 'white'. The
colour was associated in Christian
imagery with purity and salvation (cf.
Revelation 3:4 'thou hast a few names
even in Sardis which have not defiled
their garments; and they shall walk
with me in white: for they are
worthy'). This was the name of several
early saints, including a woman
supposedly cured by St Peter himself.

Candy ♀

Especially North American: from an affectionate nickname derived from the vocabulary word *candy* 'confectionery'. The word *candy* is from French *sucre candi* 'candied sugar', i.e. sugar boiled to make a crystalline sweet. The French word is derived from Arabic *qandi*, which is in turn of Indian origin. *Candy* is also found as a short form of ◊**Candice**.

Cara ♀

20th-century coinage, from the Italian term of endearment *cara* 'beloved' or the Irish Gaelic vocabulary word *cara* 'friend'.

Caradoc ♂

Welsh: respelling of *Caradog*, an ancient Celtic name apparently derived from the root *cār* 'love'. A form of this name was borne by the British chieftain recorded under the Latinized version *Caractacus*, son of Cunobelinos. He rebelled against Roman rule in the 1st century AD, and although the rebellion was swiftly put down he is recorded by the Roman historian Tacitus as having impressed the Emperor Claudius by his proud bearing in captivity.

Careen ♀

Of recent origin and uncertain derivation. Its first appearance seems to have been in Margaret Mitchell's novel *Gone with the Wind* (1936), where it is borne by one of the sisters of Scarlett O'Hara. The name may represent a combination of ◊**Cara** with the diminutive suffix *-een* (of Irish origin; cf. ◊**Maureen**), or it may be an altered form of ◊**Corinne** or ◊**Carina**.

Carey ♀

Variant spelling of ◊**Cary**, used mainly as a female name, under the influence of ◊**Carrie**.

Carina ♀

Late 19th-century coinage, apparently representing a Latinate elaboration of the feminine adjective *cara* 'beloved'; in part it may also have been inspired by ◊**Karin**.

Carissa ♀

Apparently a simplified spelling of ◊**Charissa**, or an elaborated form of ◊**Carys**.

Carl ♂

From an old-fashioned German spelling variant of *Karl*, the German version of ◊**Charles**. It is now increasingly used in the English-speaking world, and for some reason is particularly popular in Wales.

Carla ♀

Feminine form of ◊**Carl**.

Carlotta ♀

Italian form of ◊**Charlotte**, occasionally used in the English-speaking world.

Carlton ♂

Transferred use of the surname, a local name from any of various places (in Beds., Cambs., Co. Durham, Leics., Lincs., Northants, Notts., Suffolk, and Yorks.) named with Old English *carl* '(free) peasant' + *tūn* 'settlement', i.e. 'settlement of the free peasants'. This is the same name as ◊**Charlton**, *Ch*-representing the southern (Anglo-Saxon) pronunciation, while *C*-represents the northern (Anglo-Scandinavian) version.

Carly ♀

Pet form or variant of ◊**Carla**.
Variant: **Carlie**.

Carmel ♀

Of early Christian origin, referring to 'Our Lady of Carmel', a title of the Virgin Mary. *Carmel* is the name (meaning 'garden' or 'orchard' in Hebrew) of a mountain in the Holy Land near modern Haifa, which was populated from very early Christian times by hermits. They were later organized into the Carmelite order of monks. The name is used mainly by Roman Catholics.
Variant: **Carmela**.

Carmen ♀
Spanish form of ◊**Carmel**, altered by
folk etymology to the form of the
Latin word *carmen* 'song'. It is now
sometimes found as a given name in
the English-speaking world, in spite
of, or perhaps because of, its
association with the tragic romantic
heroine of Bizet's opera *Carmen*
(1875), based on a short story by
Prosper Mérimée.

Carol ♀, originally ♂
Anglicized form of *Carolus* (see
◊**Charles**), or of its feminine derivative
Carola. It has never been common as a
male name, and has become even less
so since its growth in popularity as a
female name. This seems to be of
relatively recent origin (not being
found much before the end of the 19th
century). It probably originated as a
short form of ◊**Caroline**.

Carole ♀
French form of ◊**Carol**, formerly quite
commonly used in the English-
speaking world. In the 1930s it was
associated particularly with the film
star Carole Lombard (1908–42). Now
that *Carol* is used almost exclusively
for girls, the form *Carole* has become
rather less frequent.

Caroline ♀
From the French form of Latin or
Italian **Carolina**, a feminine derivative
of *Carolus* (see ◊**Charles**).
Short forms: **Caro**; ◊**Carrie**.

Carolyn ♀
Altered form of ◊**Caroline**.

Carrie ♀
Pet form of ◊**Caroline** or occasionally
of other girls' names beginning with
the syllable *Car-*.

Carson ♂
Transferred use of the mainly Scottish
surname, which is of uncertain
derivation. The first known bearer is a
certain Robert *de Carsan* (or *de
Acarson*), recorded in 1276; the 'de'

suggests derivation from a placename,
but no suitable place has been
identified. Among Protestants in
Northern Ireland, it is sometimes
bestowed in honour of Edward Carson
(1854–1935), the Dublin barrister and
politician who was a violent opponent
of Home Rule for Ireland. In America
the popularity of the name may have
been affected by the legendary
Missouri frontiersman Kit Carson
(1809–68).

Carter ♂
Transferred use of the surname, which
originated as an occupational name for
someone who transported goods in a
cart.

Cary ♂, sometimes ♀
Transferred use of the surname, which
comes from one of the places in
Devon or Somerset so called from an
old Celtic river name. *Cary* became
popular as a given name in the middle
of the 20th century, due to the fame
of the film actor Cary Grant
(1904–89), who was born in Bristol
and made his first theatrical
appearances under his original name
of Archie Leach.
Variant: ◊**Carey**.

Caryl ♀, occasionally ♂
Of uncertain origin, probably a variant
of ◊**Carol**.

Carys ♀
Welsh: modern coinage, from *cār*
'love' + the ending *-ys*, derived by
analogy with names such as ◊**Gladys**.

Casey ♂ ♀
Especially North American: bestowed
originally in honour of the American
engine driver and folk hero 'Casey'
Jones (1863–1900), who saved the lives
of passengers on the 'Cannonball
Express' at the expense of his own. He
was baptized Johnathan Luther Jones
in Cayce, Kentucky, and acquired his
nickname from his birthplace. As a

female name it is probably a variant of ◊**Cassie**.
Variant: **Casy**.

Caspar ♂

Dutch form of ◊**Jasper**, also found as an occasional variant in English. According to legend, this was the name of one of the three Magi or 'wise men' who brought gifts to the infant Christ. The magi are not named in the Bible, but early Christian tradition assigned them the names *Caspar*, *Balthasar*, and *Melchior*.
Variant: **Casper**.

Cass ♀

Medieval and modern short form of ◊**Cassandra**.

Cassandra ♀

From Greek legend. Cassandra was a Trojan princess blessed with the gift of prophecy but cursed with the fate that nobody would ever believe her. She was brought back to Greece as a captive concubine by Agamemnon, but met her death at the hands of his jealous wife Clytemnestra. This was a popular female name in the Middle Ages, and has recently been revived by parents looking to the pages of classical mythology for distinctive names.

Cassidy ♀ ♂

Especially North American: from the Irish Gaelic surname *Ó Caiside*. Its use as a female name may be due to the *-y* ending, coupled with the fact that it could be taken as an expanded form of ◊**Cass**.

Cassie ♀

Pet form of ◊**Cass**.
Variant: **Cassy**.

Casy ♂ ♀

Variant spelling of ◊**Casey**.

Cath ♀

Short form of ◊**Catherine** and *Catharine*.

Cathal ♂

Irish Gaelic name, pronounced '*ko-hal*'. It is derived from the Old Celtic words *cath* 'battle' + *val* 'rule'. It was borne by a 7th-century saint who served as head of the monastic school at Lismore, Co. Waterford, before being appointed bishop of Taranto in south Italy.
Variant: **Cal** (in Ulster).

Catherine ♀

Variant spelling of ◊**Katherine**. This form of the name is also used in France.
Variant: **Catharine** (English only).
Short form: **Cath**.
Pet form: **Cathy**.

Cathleen ♀

Variant spelling of ◊**Kathleen**.

Cathy ♀

Pet form of ◊**Catherine** and *Catharine*.

Catrin ♀

Welsh form of ◊**Katherine**.

Catrina ♀

Simplified spelling of ◊**Catriona**.

Catriona ♀

Anglicized form of the Gaelic names **Ca(i)triona** (Scottish) and **Caitríona** (Irish), which are themselves forms of ◊**Katherine**. As the accents show, it is stressed on the second *i*. The name is now also used elsewhere in the English-speaking world, although it is still especially popular among people of Scottish ancestry. It attracted wider attention as the title of Robert Louis Stevenson's novel *Catriona* (1893), sequel to *Kidnapped*.

Cayle ♂

Variant spelling of ◊**Cale**.

Cayleigh ♀

See ◊**Kayley**.

Cecil ♂

Transferred use of the surname of a great noble family, which rose to prominence in England during the

16th century. The Cecils were of Welsh origin, and their surname represents an Anglicized form of the Welsh given name *Seissylt*, apparently a Brittonic or Old Welsh form of the Latin name *Sextilius*, from *Sextus* 'sixth'. In the Middle Ages *Cecil* was occasionally used as an English form of Latin *Caecilius* (an old Roman family name derived from the byname *Caecus* 'blind'), borne by a minor saint of the 3rd century, a friend of St Cyprian.

Cecilia ♀
From the Latin name *Caecilia*, feminine of *Caecilius* (see ◊**Cecil**). This was a good deal more common than the masculine form, largely due to the fame of the 2nd- or 3rd-century virgin martyr whose name is still mentioned daily in the Roman Catholic Canon of the Mass. She is regarded as the patron saint of music and has inspired works such as Purcell's 'Ode on St Cecilia's Day', although the reasons for this association are not clear.

Cecily ♀
From the medieval vernacular form of ◊**Cecilia**.
Variant: **Cicely**.
Pet forms: **Sessy, Sissy**.

Cedric ♂
Coined by Sir Walter Scott for the character Cedric of Rotherwood in *Ivanhoe* (1819). It seems to be a metathesized form of *Cerdic*, the name of the traditional founder of the kingdom of Wessex. Cerdic was a Saxon (Scott's novel also has a Saxon setting), and his name is presumably of Germanic origin, but the formation is not clear. The name has acquired something of a 'sissy' image, partly on account of Cedric Errol Fauntleroy, the long-haired, velvet-suited boy hero of Frances Hodgson Burnett's *Little Lord Fauntleroy* (1886). A well-know bearer was the film actor Sir Cedric Hardwicke (1893–1964).

Ceinwen ♀
Welsh traditional name, from *cain* 'fair', 'lovely' + *(g)wen* 'white', 'blessed', 'holy'. It was borne by a 5th-century saint, daughter of the chieftain Brychan, about whom little is known.

Céleste ♀
French, now also quite common in the English-speaking world (usually without the accent): from Latin *Caelestis* 'heavenly', a popular name among early Christians.

Celia ♀
From Latin *Caelia*, feminine form of the old Roman family name *Caelius* (of uncertain origin, probably a derivative of *caelum* 'heaven'). The name was not used in the Middle Ages, but was introduced to the English-speaking world as the name of a character in Shakespeare's *As You Like It*. It was popularized in the 1940s by the actress Celia Johnson (1908–82). This name is sometimes taken as a short form of ◊**Cecilia**.

Ceri ♀
Welsh: of uncertain origin, probably a short form of ◊**Ceridwen**.

Ceridwen ♀
Welsh: name in Celtic mythology of the goddess of poetic inspiration. This is apparently derived from *cerdd* 'poetry' + *(g)wen* feminine of *gwyn* 'white', 'fair', 'blessed', 'holy'. It is said to have been the name of the mother of the legendary 6th-century Welsh hero Taliesin, but it is not clear whether in fact it represents a personal name or whether Taliesin is to be regarded as the son of the goddess of poetry.

Cerise ♀
Modern coinage, apparently from French *cerise* 'cherry' (cf. ◊**Cherry**) or the English word for the colour (which is borrowed from the French term). However, it may be simply a

combination of elements, e.g. from
◊**Ceri** and ◊**Louise**.

Chad ♂
Modern spelling of the Old English
name *Ceadda*, the name of a 7th-
century saint who was Archbishop of
York. His name is of uncertain
derivation.

Chadwick ♂
Mainly U.S.: transferred use of the
surname, in origin a local name from
any of the various places in England
named as the 'dairy farm (Old English
wīc) of Ceadda (see ◊**Chad**) or Ceadel'.
In modern use, this name is
sometimes taken, wrongly, as a full
form of *Chad*.

Chance ♂
Mainly U.S.: transferred use of the
surname, in origin a nickname for an
inveterate gambler, or perhaps for
someone who had survived an
accident by a remarkable piece of
luck, from Anglo-Norman *chea(u)nce*
(good) fortune.

Chandler ♂
Transferred use of the surname, which
originated as an occupational name for
someone who made and sold candles
(an agent noun from Old French
chandele 'candle'). The extended sense
'retail dealer' arose in the 16th
century.

Chanel ♀
Mainly U.S.: transferred use of the
French surname *Chanel*, borne most
notably by Gabrielle 'Coco' Chanel
(1883–1971), who founded a famous
Parisian fashion house.
Variant: **Chanelle**.

Chantal ♀
French name sometimes used in the
English-speaking world. It was
originally bestowed as a given name in
honour of St Jeanne-Françoise Frémiot
(1572–1641), who in 1592 married the
Baron de Chantal (a place in Saône-et-
Loire, so called from a dialect form of

Old Provençal *cantal* 'stone',
'boulder'). After his death she became
an associate of St Francis of Sales and
founded a new order of nuns.

Chantel ♀
Altered form of ◊**Chantal**.
Variants: **Chantelle**, **Shantell**.

Chapman ♂
Transferred use of the surname, which
originated in the Middle Ages as an
occupational name for a merchant or
pedlar, from Old English *cēapmann* (a
compound of *cēapan* 'to buy', 'sell',
'trade' + *mann* 'man').

Charis ♀
From Greek *kharis* 'grace'. This was a
key word in early Christian thought,
but was not used as a name in the
early centuries after Christ or in the
Middle Ages. As a given name it is a
17th-century innovation, probably
chosen to express the Christian
concept of charity. In later use it may
sometimes have been selected as a
classical reference to the three Graces
(Greek *kharites*).

Charissa ♀
Apparently a recent elaboration of
◊**Charis**, perhaps as a result of crossing
with ◊**Clarissa**.

Charity ♀
From the vocabulary word, denoting
originally the Christian's love for his
fellow man (Latin *caritās*, from *carus*
'dear'). In spite of St Paul's words 'and
now abideth faith, hope, charity, these
three; but the greatest of these is
charity' (1 Corinthians 13:13), *Charity*
is now rarely used as a given name in
comparison with the shorter ◊**Faith**
and ◊**Hope**.

Charlene ♀
Chiefly Australian and North
American: 20th-century coinage, from
Charles + the feminine name-suffix
-ene. It may have been influenced by
the older but much rarer French name

Charline, a feminine diminutive of ◊**Charles**.

Charles ♂

From a Germanic word meaning 'free man', cognate with Old English *ceorl* 'man'. (The modern English words *churl* and *churlish* are derived from this, and their unpleasant overtones are a much later accretion.) The name originally owed its popularity in Europe to the Frankish leader Charlemagne (?742–814), who in 800 established himself as Holy Roman Emperor. His name (Latin *Carolus Magnus*) means 'Charles the Great'. *Charles* or *Karl* (the German form) was a common name among Frankish leaders, including Charlemagne's grandfather Charles Martel (688–741). It was introduced to Britain by Mary Queen of Scots (1542–87), who had been brought up in France. She chose the names *Charles James* for her son (1566–1625), who became King James VI of Scotland and, from 1603, James I of England. His son and grandson both reigned as King Charles, and the name thus became established in the 17th century both in the Stuart royal house and among English and Scottish supporters of the monarchy. In the 19th century its popularity was further increased by romanticization of the story of 'Bonnie Prince Charlie', leader of the 1745 rebellion. This popularity continued in the 20th century following the baptism in 1948 of the heir to the British throne as Prince Charles.
Pet form: **Charlie**.

Charlie ♂ ♀

Pet form of ◊**Charles** and sometimes of ◊**Charlotte**.

Charlotte ♀

French feminine diminutive of ◊**Charles**, used in England since the 17th century, but most popular in the 18th and 19th centuries, in part due to the influence of firstly Queen Charlotte (1744–1818), wife of George III, and secondly the novelist Charlotte Brontë (1816–55).
Pet forms: **Lottie**, **Tottie**, **Charlie**.

Charlton ♂

Transferred use of the surname, used as a given name largely as a result of the fame of the film actor Charlton Heston (b. 1924; *Charlton* was his mother's maiden name). The surname was originally a local name from any of numerous places, mainly in southern England, named in Old English as the 'settlement of the free peasants', Old English *ceorlatun* (compare ◊**Carlton**). The first element of the placename is ultimately connected with the name ◊**Charles**.

Charmaine ♀

Possibly a variant of ◊**Charmian**, influenced by names such as ◊**Germaine**, but more probably an invented name based on the vocabulary word *charm* + *-aine* as in ◊**Lorraine**. It is not found before 1920, but enjoyed some popularity in the 1960s due to The Bachelors' hit song of this name.

Charmian ♀

From the Late Greek name *Kharmion* (a diminutive of *kharma* 'delight'). The name was used by Shakespeare in *Antony and Cleopatra* for one of the attendants of the Egyptian queen; he took it from Sir Thomas North's translation of Plutarch's *Parallel Lives*.

Chase ♂

Especially U.S.: transferred use of the surname, which originated in the Middle Ages as a nickname for a huntsman, from Anglo-Norman *chase* 'chase', 'hunt'.

Chasity ♀

Mainly U.S.: a simplified form of ◊**Chastity** or a blend of that name with ◊**Charity**.

Chastity ♀

Mainly U.S.: from the vocabulary

word for the quality (from Late Latin *castitās*, a derivative of *castus*, 'pure', 'undefiled'). This name became known when it was given by the singer and actress Cher Bono to her daughter.

Chauncey ♂

U.S. coinage from a well-known New England surname. It was first chosen as a given name in honour of the Harvard College president Charles Chauncy (1592–1672), the New England clergyman Charles Chauncy (1705–87), or the naval officer Isaac Chauncey (1772–1840). These three men were descended from a single family; the surname is found in England in the Middle Ages, and probably has a Norman baronial origin, but is now extinct in Britain.
Variant: **Chauncy**.

Chaz ♂

Pet form of ◊**Charles**, derived in part from the use of **Chas** as a written abbreviation for that name.

Chelle ♀

Informal short form of ◊**Michelle**. See also ◊**Shell**.

Chelsea ♀

A 20th-century coinage enjoying a certain vogue. Ostensibly it is from the district of south-west London, which became known as the hub of the Swinging Sixties. (It was named in Old English as the 'chalk landing place', *cealc hȳð*). It is also the name of several places in North America, the earliest of which, in Maryland, was named in 1739. Another influence on the coinage may have been the given name ◊**Kelsey**.
Variants: **Chelsey, Chelsie**.

Cherelle ♀

Apparently a respelling of ◊**Cheryl**, influenced by the popular name ending *-elle* (originally a French feminine diminutive suffix).

Cherene ♀

Chiefly U.S.: modern coinage, a combination of *Cher-* (cf. the many names following) with the feminine ending *-ene*.

Cherida ♀

Modern coinage, a blend of ◊**Cheryl** and ◊**Phillida**. It has also been influenced by the Spanish vocabulary word *querida* 'darling' (cf. ◊**Cherie**).

Chérie ♀

Modern coinage from the French vocabulary word *chérie* 'darling'.
Variant: **Cheri**.

Cherish ♀

Modern coinage, apparently an alteration of ◊**Cheryth** to match the vocabulary word *cherish* 'to treasure', 'care for' (borrowed in the Middle Ages from Old French *cherir*, a derivative of *cher* 'dear').

Cherry ♀

19th-century coinage, probably taken from the vocabulary word denoting the fruit (Middle English *cheri(e)*, from Old French *cherise*). However, Dickens used it as a pet form of ◊**Charity**: in *Martin Chuzzlewit* (1844) Mr Pecksniff's daughters Charity and Mercy are known as Cherry and Merry. In modern usage it is perhaps to be regarded in some cases as an Anglicization of ◊**Cherie**.

Cheryl ♀

Not found before the 1920s, and not common until the 1940s, but increasingly popular since, being borne, for example, by the American actress Cheryl Ladd (b. 1951). It appears to be a blend of ◊**Cherry** and ◊**Beryl**.

Cheryth ♀

Apparently the result of a crossing of ◊**Cherry** with ◊**Gwyneth**.

Chester ♂

Transferred use of the surname, in origin a local name from the town of *Chester*, so called from an Old English form of Latin *castra* 'legionary camp'.

Use as a given name has become quite common in the 20th century.

Chevonne ♀
Anglicized spelling of ◊Siobhán.

Chiara ♀
Italian form of ◊Clara, now also occasionally used in the English-speaking world. The name has always been particularly popular in Italy and has been borne by several Italian saints, notably Clare of Assisi (c.1193–1253), an associate of Francis of Assisi and founder of the order of nuns known as the Poor Clares. See also ◊Ciara.

Chloe ♀
From the Late Greek name Khloē, originally used in the classical period as an epithet of the fertility goddess Demeter. It may be indirectly connected with ◊Chloris. A person of this name receives a fleeting mention in the New Testament (1 Corinthians 1:11), but its use as a given name in the English-speaking world almost certainly derives from this reference, leading to its adoption in the 17th century among the Puritans. It has fared better since than many of the minor biblical names taken up at that time.

Chloris ♀
From Greek mythology. Khlōris was a minor goddess of vegetation; her name derives from Greek khlōros 'green'. It was used by the Roman poet Horace for one of his loves (cf. ◊Lalage), and was taken up by Augustan poets of the 17th and 18th centuries.

Chris ♂ ♀
Short form of ◊Christopher, and of ◊Christine and the group of related female names.

Chriselda ♀
Elaboration of ◊Chris, apparently on the model of ◊Griselda.

Chrissie ♀
Pet form of ◊Christine and the group

of related female names. It is especially common in Scotland.
Variant: **Chrissy**.

Christa ♀
Latinate short form of ◊Christine and ◊Christina. It seems to have originated in Germany, but is now also well established in the English-speaking world.

Christabel ♀
19th-century coinage from the first syllable of ◊Christine, combined with the productive suffix *-bel* (see ◊Belle). The combination was apparently first made by Samuel Taylor Coleridge (1772–1834) in a poem called *Christabel* (1816). The name was borne by the suffragette Christabel Pankhurst (1880–1958), in whose honour it is now sometimes bestowed.
Variants: **Christabelle**, **Christabella**.

Christelle ♀
French: altered form of ◊Christine, derived by replacement of the feminine diminutive suffix *-ine* with the equally feminine suffix *-elle*. The name is now also used in the English-speaking world, where its popularity has been enhanced by its resemblance to ◊Crystal, of which it may in some cases be a variant.

Christene ♀
Variant of ◊Christine, influenced by the productive feminine name suffix *-ene*.
Variant: **Christeen**.

Christian ♂, occasionally ♀
From Latin Christiānus 'follower of Christ', in use as a given name during the Middle Ages, and sporadically ever since. The name Christ itself (Greek Khristos) is a translation of the Hebrew term Messiah 'anointed'.

Christiana ♀
Medieval learned feminine form of ◊Christian. As a recent revival it represents an elaborated form of ◊Christina. It is also sometimes

spelled **Christianna**, under the influence of the name ◊**Anna**.

Christie ♀ ♂
Pet form of ◊**Christine** or, particularly in Scotland and Ireland, of ◊**Christopher**.
Variant: **Christy**.

Christina ♀
Simplified form of Latin *Christiāna*, feminine of *Christiānus* (see ◊**Christian**), or a Latinized form of Middle English *Christin* 'Christian' (Old English *christen*, from Latin).

Christine ♀
French form of ◊**Christina**, not much used in Britain until the end of the 19th century. Until fairly recently it was principally associated with Scotland, but now it is very popular in all parts of the English-speaking world.
Short form: **Chris**.
Pet forms: **Chrissie**, **Chrissy**, **Christie**, **Christy**, ◊**Kirstie**.

Christmas ♂
From the festival celebrating the birth of Christ (so called from *Christ* (see ◊**Christian**) + *mass* festival). It is sometimes given to a boy born on Christmas Day. See also ◊**Noël** and ◊**Natalie**.

Christopher ♂
From the Greek name *Khristophoros*, derived from *Khristos* 'Christ' + *pherein* 'to bear'. This was popular among early Christians, conscious of the fact that they were metaphorically bearing Christ in their hearts. A later, over-literal interpretation of the name gave rise to the legend of a saint who actually bore the Christ-child over a stream; he is regarded as the patron of travellers.
Short form: **Chris**.
Pet forms: **Kit**. Scottish, Irish: **Christie**, **Christy**.

Christy ♂ ♀
Variant spelling of ◊**Christie**.

Chrystal ♀
Rare variant spelling of ◊**Crystal**, apparently influenced by Greek *khrysos* 'gold'.
Variant: **Chrystalla** (Latinate).

Chuck ♂
Mainly North American: now usually taken as a pet form of ◊**Charles**. It was originally a nickname, from an English term of endearment (as in Shakespeare's phrase 'dearest chuck'), probably from Middle English *chukken* 'to cluck'.
Pet form: **Chuckie**.

Cian ♂
Irish: traditional Gaelic name, pronounced '*kee*-an', derived from the Irish vocabulary word meaning 'ancient'. It was borne by a son-in-law of Brian Boru, who played a leading role in the battle of Clontarf (1014).
Anglicized forms: **Kean(e)**.

Ciara ♀
Irish, pronounced '*kee*-a-ra': modern coinage, created as a feminine form of ◊**Ciarán**.

Ciarán ♂
Irish Gaelic name, pronounced '*kee*-a-rawn' and often Anglicized as ◊**Kieran**. It was originally a byname, a diminutive form of *ciar* 'black'. It was borne by two Irish saints, of the 5th and 6th centuries.

Cicely ♀
Variant of ◊**Cecily**. This was a common form of the name in the Middle Ages, and was well known between the wars as the name of the British actress and singer Cicely Courtneidge.
Pet form: ◊**Sissy**.

Cillian ♂
Irish Gaelic name often Anglicized as ◊**Killian**. It was originally a byname representing a diminutive form of Gaelic *ceallach* 'strife', or possibly derived from Gaelic *ceall* 'monastery', 'church' (cf. ◊**Kelly**), and was borne by

various early Irish saints, including the 7th-century author of a life of St Bridget and missionaries to Artois and Franconia.

Cindy ♀

Pet form of ◊Cynthia or, less often, of ◊Lucinda, now very commonly used as a given name, especially in North America. It has sometimes been taken as a short form of the name of the fairy-tale heroine *Cinderella*, which is in fact unrelated (being from French *Cendrillon*, a derivative of *cendre* 'cinders').

Claire ♀

French form of ◊Clara. It was introduced to Britain by the Normans, but subsequently abandoned. This spelling was revived in the 19th century as a variant of ◊Clare.
Variant: **Clair**.

Clancy ♂

Mainly U.S.: transferred use of the Irish surname, Gaelic *Mac Fhlannchaidh* 'son of Flannchadh'. The latter is an ancient Irish personal name, probably composed of elements meaning 'red warrior'.
Variant: **Clancey**.

Clara ♀

Post-classical Latin name, from the feminine form of the adjective *clārus* 'famous'. In the modern English-speaking world it represents a re-Latinization of the regular English form ◊Clare. It was made famous in the 1920s by the silent film actress Clara Bow (1905–65), known as the 'it' girl (because, whatever 'it' was, she had it).

Clare ♀

The normal English vernacular form of ◊Clara during the Middle Ages and since.

Clarence ♂

In use from the mid-19th century, but now rare. It was first used in honour of the popular elder son of Edward VII,

who was created Duke of Clarence in 1890, but died in 1892. His title (*Dux Clarentiae* in Latin) originated with a son of Edward III, who in the 14th century was married to the heiress of Clare in Suffolk (which is so called from a Celtic river name and has no connection with the given name ◊Clare). The title has been held by various British royal princes at different periods in history. In the United States the name was borne most notably by the American defence lawyer Clarence Darrow (1857–1938), played in various films by Orson Welles, Spencer Tracey, and Henry Fonda.

Clarette ♀

Rare elaborated form of ◊Clare, with the French feminine diminutive suffix *-ette*. The formation may have been influenced by the wine *claret* (Medieval Latin *(vīnum) clārātum* 'clarified wine').

Clarice ♀

Medieval English and French form of the Latin name *Claritia*. This may have meant 'fame' (an abstract derivative of *clārus* 'famous'), but as a given name it may have been no more than an arbitrary elaboration of ◊Clara. It was borne by a character who features in some versions of the medieval romances of Roland and the other paladins of Charlemagne.

Clarinda ♀

Elaboration of ◊Clara with the suffix *-inda* (cf. ◊Belinda and ◊Lucinda). *Clarinda* first appears in Spenser's *Faerie Queene* (1596). The formation was influenced by *Clorinda*, which occurs in Torquato Tasso's *Gerusalemme Liberata* (1580). This is itself an arbitrary elaboration of ◊Chloris. Robert Burns (1759–96) wrote four poems *To Clarinda*.

Clarissa ♀

Latinate form of ◊Clarice occasionally found in medieval documents. It was revived by Samuel Richardson as the name of the central character in his novel *Clarissa* (1748).

Clark ♂

Transferred use of the surname, which originated as an occupational name denoting a clerk (Latin *clēricus*, in the Middle Ages a man in minor holy orders who earned his living by his ability to read and write). Since the 1930s, when it was associated particularly with the film star Clark Gable (1901–60), it has been widely used as a given name, especially in North America.

Variant: **Clarke**.

Clarrie ♂ ♀

Pet form of ◊**Clarence**, also of ◊**Clara** and various similar women's names. It is now quite rare.

Claud ♂

Anglicized spelling of ◊**Claude**.

Claude ♂

French: from the Latin name *Claudius*, an old Roman family name derived from the byname *Claudus* 'lame'. It was borne by various early saints, but its popularity in France is largely due to the fame of the 7th-century St Claude of Besançon. In France, *Claude* also occasionally occurs as a female name.

Claudette ♀

French: feminine diminutive form of ◊**Claude**, now also occasionally used in the English-speaking world. It gained considerable prominence in the 1930s as the name of the French film star Claudette Colbert (1905–), a Hollywood favourite for many years. Her original name was Lily Claudette Chauchoin.

Claudia ♀

From the Latin female name, a feminine form of *Claudius* (see ◊**Claude**). The name is mentioned in one of St Paul's letters to Timothy (2, 4:21 'Eubulus greeteth thee, and Pudens, and Linus, and Claudia, and all the brethren'), as a result of which it was taken up in the 16th century.

Claudine ♀

French: feminine diminutive form of ◊**Claude**. It was made popular at the beginning of the 20th century as the name of the heroine of a series of novels by the French writer Colette (1873–1954), and is now also occasionally used in the English-speaking world.

Claus ♂

German form of ◊**Nicholas**, representing a shortened form of *Niclaus* or *Niklaus*. In America this name tends to be associated with the figure of *Santa Claus* (originally *Sankt Niklaus*), which inhibits serious use of it.

Clay ♂

Either a shortened form of ◊**Clayton** or a transferred use of the surname *Clay*, a local name for someone who lived on a patch of land whose soil was predominantly clay (Old English *clæg*).

Clayton ♂

Especially U.S.: transferred use of the surname, originally a local name from any of the several places in England (for example, in Lancs., Staffs., Sussex, and W. Yorks.) named with Old English *clæg* 'clay' + *tūn* 'enclosure', 'settlement'.

Cledwyn ♂

Welsh traditional name, apparently derived from *caled* 'hard', 'rough' + *(g)wyn* 'white', 'fair', 'blessed', 'holy'.

Clem ♂ ♀

Short form of the male name ◊**Clement** and of female names such as ◊**Clemence**.

Pet form: **Clemmie** ♀

Clematis ♀

From the name of the flower (so named in the 16th century from Greek *klēmatis* 'climbing plant'), perhaps under the influence of names

such as ◊**Clemence**, with the ending
-*is* found in names such as ◊**Phyllis**.

Clemence ♀

Medieval French and English form of
Latin *Clēmentia*, a derivative of
Clēmens (see ◊**Clement**) or an abstract
noun meaning 'mercy'. It has never
been particularly common, but is still
occasionally used.

Clemency ♀

Rare variant of ◊**Clemence** or a direct
use of the abstract noun, on the model
of ◊**Charity**, ◊**Faith**, ◊**Mercy**, etc.

Clement ♂

From the Late Latin name *Clēmens*
(genitive *Clēmentis*) meaning
'merciful'. This was borne by several
early saints, notably the fourth pope
and the early Christian theologian
Clement of Alexandria (Titus Flavius
Clemens, AD ?150–?215).

Clementine ♀

Feminine form of ◊**Clement**, created
with the French feminine diminutive
suffix -*ine*. The name was first used in
the 19th century, and for a time it was
very popular. It is now largely
associated with the popular song with
this title. The Latinate form
Clementina is also found.

Clemmie ♀ ♂

Pet form of ◊**Clem**, borne more often
by girls than by boys.

Cleo ♀

Short form of ◊**Cleopatra**. See also
◊**Clio**.

Cleopatra ♀

From the Greek name *Kleopatra*,
derived from *kleos* 'glory' + *patēr*
'father'. This was borne by a large
number of women in the Ptolemaic
royal family of Egypt. The most
famous (?69–30 BC) was the lover of
Mark Antony, and has always figured
largely in both literature and the
popular imagination as a model of a
passionate woman of unsurpassed
beauty, who 'gave all for love' and in

the process destroyed the man she
loved. She had previously been the
mistress of Julius Caesar.

Cliff ♂

Short form of ◊**Clifford**, now also
sometimes of ◊**Clifton**. It is commonly
used as a given name, especially since
the advent in the 1950s of the pop
singer Cliff Richard (real name Harry
Webb). It has sometimes also been
associated with ◊**Clive**.

Clifford ♂

Transferred use of the surname, in
origin a local name from any of
several places (Gloucs., Herefords.,
Yorks.) named with Old English *clif*
'cliff', 'slope', 'riverbank' + *ford* 'ford'.

Clifton ♂

Transferred use of the surname, a
local name from any of the numerous
places named with Old English *clif*
'cliff', 'slope', 'riverbank' + *tūn*
'enclosure', 'settlement'. Use of this as
a given name is more recent than that
of ◊**Clifford**. It may in some cases
have been adopted as an expanded
form of ◊**Cliff**.

Clint ♂

Short form of the surname **Clinton**,
made famous by the actor Clint
Eastwood (b. 1930). It was apparently
originally used as a given name in
America in honour of the Clinton
family, whose members included the
statesman George Clinton
(1739–1812), governor of New York,
and his nephew De Witt Clinton
(1769–1828), who was responsible for
overseeing the construction of the Erie
Canal. It was also borne by Sir Henry
Clinton (1735–95), British
commander-in-chief in America
during the Revolution.

Clio ♀

From Greek *Kleio*, the name borne in
classical mythology both by one of the
nymphs and by one of the Muses. It is
probably ultimately connected with

45

the word *kleos* 'glory'; cf. ◊**Cleopatra**. The name is now sometimes used as a variant of ◊**Cleo**.

Clitus ♂
Mainly U.S.: Latinized form of Greek *Kleitos*, the name of one of Alexander the Great's generals. This name is probably ultimately connected with *Kleio* (see ◊**Clio**).

Clive ♂
Transferred use of the surname, in origin a local name from any of the various places (in e.g. Cheshire, Shropshire) so called from Old English *clif* 'cliff', 'slope'. As a given name it seems to have been originally chosen in honour of 'Clive of India' (Robert Clive, created Baron Clive of Plassey in 1760).

Clodagh ♀
Irish: of recent origin. It is the name of a river in Tipperary, and seems to have been arbitrarily transferred to use as a given name. There may be some association in the minds of givers with the Latin name *Clōdia* (borne by the mistress of the Roman poet Catullus), a variant of ◊**Claudia**.

Clover ♀
Modern coinage taken from word denoting the plant (Old English *clāfre*).

Clyde ♂
Mainly North American: from the name of river in south-west Scotland that runs through Glasgow, perhaps by way of a surname derived from the river name, although for many Scottish emigrants it was the point of departure from Scotland. The given name gained some currency, especially in the American South. The bank robber Clyde Barrow became something of a cult figure, especially after the film *Bonnie and Clyde* (1967), in which he was played by Warren Beatty.

Cody ♂♀
Mainly U.S. and Australian:

transferred use of the Irish surname, an Anglicized form of Gaelic Ó *Cuidighthigh* 'descendant of Cuidightheach' (originally a byname for a helpful person) or of *Mac Óda* 'son of Óda' (a personal name of uncertain origin). Use as a given name has been at least in part inspired by William Frederick Cody (1846–1917), better known as 'Buffalo Bill', the showman of the Wild West.
Variants: **Codi**, **Codie**, **Codee** (all ♀)

Colbert ♂
Transferred use of the surname, derived from an Old French given name of Germanic (Frankish) origin, from *col* (of uncertain meaning) + *berht* 'bright', 'famous'. This was introduced to Britain by the Normans, but its use as a given name soon died out.

Colby ♂
Mainly U.S.: transferred use of the surname, in origin a local name from places in Norfolk and Cumbria, so called from the Old Norse personal name *Koli* (a byname for a swarthy person, from *kol* 'charcoal') + Old Norse *bý́r* 'settlement'. Use as a given name seems to have been influenced by the 1980s television serial *The Colbys*, a spinoff from *Dynasty*.

Cole ♂
Transferred use of the surname, itself derived from a medieval given name of uncertain origin. It may represent a survival into Middle English of the Old English byname *Cola* 'swarthy', 'coal-black', from *col* 'charcoal'. As a given name, it is associated with the songwriter Cole Porter (1893–1964).

Coleman ♂
Variant of ◊**Colman**. In part it also represents a transferred use of the surname, which derives in most cases from the Gaelic personal name *Colmán*, but in others may be an occupational term for a charcoal burner.

Colette ♀
French feminine diminutive form of the medieval name *Col(le)*, a short form of ◊**Nicholas**. It was given particular currency from the 1920s onwards by the fame of the French novelist Colette (1873–1954).

Colin ♂
Diminutive form of the medieval name *Col(le)*, a short form of ◊**Nicholas**. In Scotland it has been used as an Anglicized form of the Gaelic name *Cailean*, particularly favoured among the Campbells and the MacKenzies. *Cailean* relates to St Columba (see ◊**Calum**) as *Crìsdean* does to Christ and *Moirean* to Mary.

Coll ♂
From a medieval short form of ◊**Nicholas**. It use as a modern given name in part represents a transferred use of the surname derived from the given name in the Middle Ages. In Scotland it has been used as an Anglicized form of the Gaelic name *Colla*, perhaps from an Old Celtic root meaning 'high'.

Colleen ♀
Mainly North American and Australian: from the Anglo-Irish vocabulary word *colleen* 'girl', 'wench' (Gaelic *cailín*). It became established as a name in the inter-War years in North America, and was associated with the star of the silent screen Colleen Moore (1901–88), whose original name was Kathleen Morrison. It is not used as a given name in Ireland. It is sometimes taken as a feminine of ◊**Colin** or a variant of ◊**Colette**.

Collette ♀
Variant spelling of ◊**Colette**.

Colm ♂
Irish Gaelic form of Latin *Columba*; see ◊**Calum**.

Colman ♂
Irish: Anglicized form of the Gaelic name **Colmán**, from Late Latin *Columbānus*, a derivative of *Columba* (see ◊**Calum**). The name was borne by a large number of early Irish saints, including Colman of Armagh, a 5th-century disciple of St Patrick. See also ◊**Coleman**.

Colton ♂
Mainly U.S.: transferred use of the surname, in origin a local name from any of various places in England so called. The placename is of varied origin: in most cases it derives from the Old English personal name *Cola*, a byname for a swarthy person (from *col* 'charcoal') + Old English *tūn* 'enclosure', 'settlement', and so is a doublet of ◊**Colby**.

Columbine ♀
From Italian *Colombina*, a diminutive of *Colomba* 'dove'. In the tradition of the *commedia dell'arte* this is the name of Harlequin's sweetheart. The modern name, however, was coined independently as one of the many female names taken in the 19th century from vocabulary words denoting flowers. The columbine gets its name from the fact that its petals are supposed to resemble five doves clustered together.

Conall ♂
Irish and Scottish Gaelic name, composed of Old Celtic words meaning 'wolf' and 'strong'. This name was borne by many early chieftains and warriors of Ireland, including the Ulster hero Conall Cearnach.

Conan ♂
Irish: Anglicized form of the Gaelic name *Cónán*, originally a byname representing a diminutive of *cú* 'hound'. The name was borne by a 7th-century saint, bishop of the Isle of Man. Sir Arthur Conan Doyle (1859–1930), creator of the fictional detective Sherlock Holmes, was of Irish stock.

Conn ♂
Irish Gaelic name meaning 'chief'. It is now also used as a short form of ◊Connor and of various non-Irish names beginning with the syllable Con-.

Connie ♀
Pet form of ◊Constance.

Connor ♂
Irish: Anglicized form of the Gaelic name Conchobhar, possibly meaning 'lover of hounds'. Conchobhar is a legendary Irish king said to have been an exact contemporary of Christ.

Conrad ♂
The usual English spelling of Konrad, a Germanic personal name derived from kuon 'bold' + rad 'counsel'. It was used occasionally in Britain in the Middle Ages in honour of a 10th-century bishop of Constance, but modern use in the English-speaking world is a reimportation from Germany dating mainly from the 19th century.

Constance ♀
Medieval form of the Late Latin name Constantia, which is either a feminine derivative of Constans (see ◊Constant), or an abstract noun meaning 'constancy'. This was a popular name among the Normans, and was borne by, amongst others, the formidable Constance of Sicily (1158–98), wife of the Emperor Henry VI.
Pet form: Connie.

Constant ♂
Medieval form of the Late Latin name Constans 'steadfast' (genitive Constantis). This was not a common name in the Middle Ages. It was taken up by the Puritans because of its transparent meaning, as an expression of their determination to 'resist stedfast in the faith' (1 Peter 5:9).

Cora ♀
Name apparently coined by James Fenimore Cooper for one of the characters in The Last of the Mohicans (1826). It could represent a Latinized form of Greek Korē 'maiden'. In classical mythology this was a euphemistic name of the goddess of the underworld, Persephone, and would not have been a well-omened name to take.

Coral ♀
Late 19th-century coinage. This is one of the group of female names taken from the vocabulary of gemstones. Coral is a pink calcareous material found in warm seas; it actually consists of the skeletons of millions of tiny sea creatures. The word is from Late Latin corallium and is probably ultimately of Semitic origin.

Coralie ♀
Apparently an elaboration of ◊Cora or ◊Coral on the model of ◊Rosalie.

Corbin ♂
Mainly U.S.: of uncertain derivation, perhaps a short form of the rare given name ◊Corbinian, or a transferred use of the surname, in origin a nickname from a diminutive form of Anglo-Norman corb 'crow'.

Corbinian ♂
The name of a Frankish saint (?670–770) who evangelized Bavaria from a base at Freising, near Munich. His name was presumably originally Frankish, but in the form in which it has been handed down it appears to be an adjectival derivative of Latin corvus 'crow', 'raven', which had a Late Latin variant corbus. This may represent a translation of the Germanic personal name Hraban.

Cordelia ♀
Name used by Shakespeare for King Lear's one virtuous daughter. It is not clear where he got it from; it does not seem to have a genuine Celtic origin. It may be a fanciful elaboration of Latin cor 'heart' (genitive cordis).

Cordula ♀

Apparently a Late Latin diminutive form of *cor* 'heart' (genitive *cordis*). A saint of this name was, according to legend, one of Ursula's eleven thousand companions.

Coretta ♀

Elaborated form of ◊**Cora**, with the addition of the productive feminine suffix *-etta* (originally an Italian diminutive form). This is the name of the widow of the American civil rights campaigner Martin Luther King.

Corey ♂

Mainly North American, especially common as a Black name. The reasons for its popularity are not clear. It may well be a transferred use of the English surname *Corey*, which is derived from the Old Norse personal name *Kori*.
Variants: **Cory**, **Corie**.

Corin ♂

From Latin *Quirīnus*, the name of an ancient Roman divinity partly associated with the legendary figure of Romulus. It is of uncertain origin, probably connected with the Sabine word *quiris* or *curis* 'spear'. In the early Christian period the name was borne by several saints martyred for the faith. The name is occasionally also used in the English-speaking world (where it is often regarded as a male equivalent of ◊**Corinna**), notably by the actor Corin Redgrave (b. 1939).

Corinna ♀

From the Greek name *Korinna* (probably a derivative of *Korē*; cf. ◊**Cora**), borne by a Boeotian poetess of uncertain date, whose works survive in fragmentary form. The name was also used by the Roman poet Ovid for the woman addressed in his love poetry.

Corinne ♀

French form of ◊**Corinna**, also used in the English-speaking world.

Cormac ♂

Irish Gaelic traditional name, of uncertain origin, apparently from *corb* 'defilement' + *mac* 'son'. This has been a very popular name in Ireland from the earliest times. Cormac Ó Cuilleannáin, a 10th-century king and bishop, was the author of a dictionary of the Irish language.

Cornelia ♀

From the Latin feminine form of the old Roman family name ◊**Cornelius**. It was borne in the 2nd century BC by the mother of the revolutionary reformers Tiberius and Gaius Sempronius Gracchus, and is still occasionally bestowed in her honour.

Cornelius ♂

From an old Roman family name, *Cornēlius*, which is of uncertain origin, possibly a derivative of Latin *cornu* 'horn'. This was the name of a 3rd-century pope who is venerated as a saint.

Cornell ♂

Medieval vernacular form of ◊**Cornelius**. In modern use it normally represents a transferred use of the surname, which is of very varied origin.

Cory ♂

Variant spelling of ◊**Corey**.

Cosima ♀

Feminine form of ◊**Cosmo**, occasionally used in the English-speaking world. The name was borne by Cosima Wagner (1837–1930), daughter of Franz Liszt and devoted wife of Richard Wagner.

Cosmo ♂

Italian form (also found as **Cosimo**) of the Greek name *Kosmas* (a short form of various names containing the word *kosmos* 'order', 'beauty'). This was borne by a Christian saint martyred, together with his brother Damian, at Aegea in Cilicia in the early 4th century. It was first brought to Britain in the 18th century by the Scottish dukes of Gordon, who had connections with the ducal house of Tuscany. The name was traditional in that family, having been borne most famously by Cosimo de' Medici (1389–1464), its founder and one of the chief patrons of the Italian Renaissance.

Coty ♂
Mainly U.S.: transferred use of the rare surname, apparently in origin a local name from a diminutive form of French *côte* 'riverbank'. Use as a given name has probably been influenced by its resemblance to ◊**Cody**.

Courtney ♂ ♀
Mainly North American: transferred use of the surname, originally a Norman baronial name from any of various places in Northern France called *Courtenay* 'domain of Curtius'. However, from an early period it was wrongly taken as a nickname derived from Old French *court nez* 'short nose'.

Coy ♂
Mainly U.S.: of uncertain origin. It is hardly likely to be from the modern English vocabulary word, which has both feminine and pejorative connotations. It probably represents a transferred use of the surname *Coy* or perhaps *McCoy*, a variant of *McKay*, meaning 'son of Aodh' (see ◊**Aidan**).

Craig ♂
From a nickname from the Gaelic word *creag* 'rock', or in some case a transferred use of the Scottish surname derived as a local name from this word. The given name is now fashionable throughout the English-speaking world, and is chosen by many people who have no connection with Scotland.

Creighton ♂
Transferred use of the Scottish surname, in origin a local name from *Crichton* in Midlothian, so called from

Gaelic *crìoch* 'border', 'boundary' + Middle English *tune* 'settlement' (Old English *tūn*).

Cressa ♀
Modern name, apparently originating as a contracted short form of ◊**Cressida**.

Cressida ♀
From a medieval legend, told by Chaucer and Shakespeare among others, set in ancient Troy. Cressida is a Trojan princess, daughter of Calchas, a priest who has defected to the Greeks. When she is restored to her father, she jilts her Trojan lover Troilus in favour of the Greek Diomedes. The story is not found in classical sources. Chaucer used the name in the form *Criseyde*, getting it from Boccaccio's *Criseida*. This in turn is ultimately based on Greek *Khryseis* (a derivative of *khrysos* 'gold'), the name of a Trojan girl who is mentioned briefly as a prisoner of the Greeks at the beginning of Homer's *Iliad*. Chaucer's version of the name was Latinized by Shakespeare as *Cressida*. In spite of the unhappy associations of the story, the name has enjoyed some popularity in the 20th century.

Crispin ♂
From Latin *Crispīnus*, a derivative of the old Roman family name *Crispus* 'curly(-headed)'. St Crispin was martyred with his brother Crispinian in *c*.285, and the pair were popular saints in the Middle Ages.

Cristina ♀
Italian, Spanish, and Portuguese form of ◊**Christina**, sometimes also used in the English-speaking world.

Crystal ♀
19th-century coinage. This is one of the group of names taken from or suggestive of gemstones. The word *crystal*, denoting high-quality cut glass, is derived from Greek *krystallos* 'ice'. As a male name, *Crystal*

originated as a Scottish pet form of
♢**Christopher**, but it is rarely used
today.

Variant: **Krystle**.

Curt ♂

Originally an Anglicized spelling of
the German name *Kurt* (contracted
form of *Konrad*; see ♢**Conrad**), but
now also used as a short form of
♢**Curtis**.

Curtis ♂

Transferred use of the surname, which
originated in the Middle Ages as a
nickname for someone who was
'courteous' (Old French *curteis*). At an
early date, however, it came to be
associated with Middle English *curt*
'short' + *hose* 'leggings'; cf.
♢**Courtney**.

Cuthbert ♂

From an Old English personal name
derived from *cūð* 'known' + *beorht*
'bright', 'famous'. This was borne by
two pre-Conquest English saints: a
7th-century bishop of Lindisfarne and
an 8th-century archbishop of
Canterbury who corresponded with St
Boniface.

Cy ♂

Short form of ♢**Cyrus**.

Cynthia ♀

From Greek *Kynthia*, an epithet
applied to the goddess Artemis, who
was supposed to have been born on
Mount *Kynthos* on the island of
Delos. The mountain name is of pre-
Greek origin. *Cynthia* was later used
by the Roman poet Propertius as the
name of the woman to whom he
addressed his love poetry. The English
given name was not used in the
Middle Ages, but dates from the

classical revival of the 17th and 18th
centuries.

Cyprian ♂

From the Late Latin family name
Cypriānus 'native of Cyprus', borne by
one of the leading figures in the
history of the Western Church. A 3rd-
century bishop of Carthage, he wrote
widely on theological themes and did
much to further the unity of the
Church.

Cyril ♂

From the post-classical Greek name
Kyrillos, a derivative of *kyrios* 'lord'. It
was borne by a large number of early
saints, most notably the theologians
Cyril of Alexandria and Cyril of
Jerusalem. It was also the name of one
of the Greek evangelists who brought
Christianity to the Slavonic regions of
Eastern Europe; in order to provide
written translations of the gospels for
their converts, they devised the
alphabet still known as Cyrillic.

Cyrille ♂ ♀

French form of ♢**Cyril**, now also
occasionally used in the English-
speaking world, sometimes as an
elaborated spelling variant and
sometimes as a feminine form.

Cyrus ♂

Mainly U.S.: from the Greek form
(*Kyros*) of the name of several kings of
Persia, most notably Cyrus the Great
(d. 529 BC). The origin of the name is
not known, but in the early Christian
period it was associated with Greek
kyrios 'lord', and borne by various
saints, including an Egyptian martyr
and a bishop of Carthage.

Short form: **Cy**.

DAFFODIL DAFYD DAGMAR DAHLIA DAI
DAISY DALE DALEY DALIA DALLAS DALTO
N DALY DALYA DAMARIS DAMIAN DAMO
N DAN DANA DANE DANIEL DANIELA DA
NIELLE DANNY DAPHNE DARBY DARCY D
ARELL DAREN DARIA DARIEN DARIN DARI

Daffodil ♀

One of the rarer flower names, which perhaps originated as an expanded version of ◊**Daffy**. The flower got its name in the 14th century from a run-together form of Dutch *de affodil* 'the asphodel'.

Dafydd ♂

Welsh form of ◊**David**; see also ◊**Dewi**. This form of the name was in widespread use during the Middle Ages. Later it was largely replaced by the English form *David*, but from the late 19th century it has come into its own again.

Dagmar ♀

Scandinavian: of uncertain origin. It is apparently from Old Norse *dag* 'day' + *mār* 'maid'. *Dag* is a male name in its own right in Swedish and Norwegian. Alternatively, *Dagmar* may represent a reworking of the Slavonic name *Dragomira*, which is from *dorog* 'dear' + *meri* 'great', 'famous'. It is now occasionally used also in the English-speaking world.

Dahlia ♀

From the name of the flower, which was so called in the 19th century in honour of the pioneering Swedish botanist Anders Dahl (1751–89). His surname represents a cognate of English ◊**Dale**.

Dai ♂

Welsh: now used as a Welsh pet form of ◊**David**, but originally of distinct origin, probably from an Old Celtic word *dei* 'to shine'.

Daisy ♀

From the word denoting the flower, Old English *dægesēage* 'day's eye', so called because it uncovers the yellow disc of its centre in the morning and closes its petals over it again at the end of the day. The name was used early on as a punning pet form of ◊**Margaret**, by association with French *Marguerite*, which is both a version of that name and the word for the flower. It was not widespread until taken up at the end of the 19th century as part of the general vogue for flower names.

Dale ♂ ♀

Transferred use of the surname, originally a local name for someone who lived in a *dale* or valley. It is now fairly commonly used as a given name, especially in North America, along with other monosyllabic surnames of topographical origin (cf. e.g. ◊**Dell** and ◊**Hale**).

Daley ♂

From the Irish surname, the Gaelic form of which is *Ó Dálaigh* 'descendant of Dálach'. The latter is a personal name derived from *dál* 'assembly', 'gathering'.
Variant: **Daly**.

Dalia ♀

In part a simplified spelling of ◊**Dahlia**, in part a Jewish name derived from Modern Hebrew *dalia* 'flowering branch'.
Variant: **Daliah** (associated especially with the Israeli film actress Daliah Lavi, b. 1940).

Dallas ♂

Mainly U.S.: transferred use of the surname, adopted in honour of George Mifflin Dallas, Vice-President 1845–9, after whom the city in Texas is named. The surname is of Scottish origin, derived from the village of Dallas in Morayshire, named in Gaelic as *Dalfhas* 'meadow stance', i.e. a meadow traditionally used as a night's resting place by cattle droves.

Dalton ♂

Mainly North American: transferred use of the surname, in origin a local name from any of various places named in Old English as 'the settlement in the valley', from *dæl* 'valley' + *tūn* 'enclosure', 'settlement'.

Daly ♂

Variant spelling of ◊**Daley**.

Dalya ♀

Variant spelling of ◊**Dalia**, influenced by Russian names such as *Katya* and *Tanya*.

Damaris ♀

New Testament: name of a woman mentioned as being converted to Christianity by St Paul (Acts 17:34). Its origin is not clear, but it is probably Greek, perhaps a late form of *Damalis* 'calf'. It was taken up in the 17th century, along with the names of other characters fleetingly mentioned in the New Testament, and has been occasionally used ever since.

Damian ♂

From Greek *Damianos*, the name of the brother of Cosmas (see ◊**Cosmo**). The two brothers were martyred together at Aegea in Cilicia in the early 4th century. The origin of the name is not certain, but it is probably akin to ◊**Damon**.

Damon ♂

From a classical Greek name, a derivative of *damān* 'to tame', 'to subdue' (often a euphemism for 'kill').

This was made famous in antiquity by the story of Damon and Pythias. In the early 4th century BC Pythias was condemned to death by Dionysius, ruler of Syracuse. His friend Damon offered to stand surety for him, and took his place in the condemned cell while Pythias put his affairs in order. When Pythias duly returned to be executed, rather than absconding and leaving his friend to his fate, Dionysius was so impressed by the trust and friendship of the two young men that he pardoned both of them. The name was not used in the early centuries of the Christian era or during the Middle Ages. Its modern use dates from the 1930s and is due at least in part to the fame of the American short-story writer Damon Runyon (1884–1946). It is sometimes taken as a variant of ◊**Damian**.

Dan ♂

In modern use this is taken as a short form of ◊**Daniel**, but it is also an independent biblical name, meaning 'he judged' in Hebrew, borne by one of Jacob's twelve sons (Genesis 30:6). *Pet form*: **Danny**.

Dana ♂ ♀

Mainly North American: transferred use of a surname that is fairly common in the United States, of unknown origin. Use as a given name began in honour of Richard Dana (1815–82), author of *Two Years before the Mast*. A lawyer by profession, he supported the rights of fugitive slaves, and lent his backing to the Union during the Civil War. Its popularity as a given name in the mid-20th century was increased by the fame of the film star Dana Andrews (b. 1909). *Dana* is also sometimes used as a feminine form of ◊**Dan** or ◊**Dane**.

Dane ♂

Transferred use of the surname, in origin a local name representing a dialect variant of ◊**Dean** that was common in south-east England, rather than an ethnic name for someone from Denmark. The latter sense may be behind the given name in some cases.

Daniel ♂

Biblical name (meaning 'God is my judge' in Hebrew), borne by the prophet whose story is told in the Book of Daniel. He was an Israelite slave of the Assyrian king Nebuchadnezzar, who obtained great favour through his skill in interpreting dreams and the 'writing on the wall' at the feast held by Nebuchadnezzar's son Belshazzar. His enemies managed to get him cast into a lions' den, but he was saved by God. This was a favourite tale in the Middle Ages, often represented in miracle plays.

Daniela ♀

Latinate feminine form of ◊Daniel, occasionally used in the English-speaking world.

Danielle ♀

French feminine form of ◊Daniel, occasionally used also in the English-speaking world.

Danny ♂

Pet form of ◊Dan.

Daphne ♀

Name borne in Greek mythology by a nymph who was changed into a laurel by her father, a river god, to enable her to escape the attentions of Apollo. The name means 'laurel' in Greek. According to the myth the nymph gave her name to the shrub, but in fact of course it was the other way about: her name was taken from the vocabulary word (which is probably of pre-Greek origin). The name came into use in England at the end of the 19th century, when it was adopted as part of the vogue for flower names at that time.

Darby ♂

Transferred use of the surname, in origin a local name from the city of

Derby or the district of West Derby near Liverpool. These are so called from Old Norse *diur* 'deer' + *býr* 'settlement'. In Ireland this name has been used as an Anglicized form of Gaelic *Diarmaid* (see ◊Dermot).

Darcy ♂ ♀

Transferred use of the Irish surname, originally a Norman baronial name (*d'Arcy*) borne by a family who came from *Arcy* in northern France. It has always retained a somewhat aristocratic flavour, which has enhanced its popularity as a given name. It is the surname of the hero of Jane Austen's novel *Pride and Prejudice* (1813). Use as a female name is confined mainly to North America.

Darell ♂

Especially U.S.: variant spelling of ◊Darrell.

Daren ♂

Variant spelling of ◊Darren.

Daria ♀

Feminine form of the much rarer male name ◊Darius. St Daria (d. 283) was a Greek woman married to an Egyptian Christian called Chrysanthus; they both lived at Rome and were martyred under the joint emperors Numerian and Carinus.

Darien ♂

Mainly U.S.: of uncertain origin, perhaps a cross between ◊Darren and ◊Darius. Its identity in form with a region of Panama and Colombia seems to be merely coincidental.

Darin ♂

Mainly U.S.: variant of ◊Darren, associated with the singer Bobby Darin (1936–73), who was originally called Walden Robert Cassotto. He chose the name that he made famous from the list of surnames in a telephone directory.
Variant: **Darrin**.

Darius ♂
Especially U.S.: from Greek *Dareios*,
originally a transliterated version of
the name of various ancient Persian
kings. The original form of the name
is said to have been *Darayavahush*,
from *daraya(miy)* 'possess' or
'maintain' + *vahu* 'well', 'good'. An
obscure saint of this name was
martyred at Nicaea with three
companions at an uncertain date.

Darlene ♀
Especially Australian and North
American: modern coinage, an
alteration of the affectionate term of
address *Darling*, by fusion with the
suffix *-lene*, found as an ending in
other female given names.
Variant: **Darleen**.

Darnell ♂
Mainly U.S.: of uncertain derivation.
It may represent a transferred use of a
surname, or it may be a variant of
◊**Darrell**, influenced by the plant name
darnel.

Darrell ♂
Especially North American:
transferred use of the surname,
originally a Norman baronial name
(*d'Airelle*) borne by a family who
came from *Airelle* in Calvados. It was
first used as a given name towards the
end of the 19th century, and has
enjoyed a considerable vogue in the
latter part of the 20th century.
Variants: **Darrel**, **Darell**.

Darren ♂
20th-century coinage, of uncertain
derivation. It may be a transferred
used of a surname (itself of obscure
origin). It seems to have been first
borne by the American actor Darren
McGavin (b. 1922). It came to public
notice as the name of a character in
the popular American television
comedy series *Bewitched*, made in the
1960s.
Variant: **Daren**.

Darrene ♀
Feminine form of ◊**Darren**, formed by
fusion with the productive feminine
suffix *-ene*.

Darryl ♂, occasionally ♀
Variant of ◊**Darrell**. Like its variant
Daryl, it is occasionally borne by
women, no doubt by analogy with
names such as ◊**Cheryl**. A recent
influence on the female name is the
actress Daryl Hannah.

Dassah ♀
Jewish: shortened form of ◊**Hadassah**,
as a result of erroneous association of
the first syllable with the Hebrew
definite article *ha*.

Dave ♂
Informal short form of ◊**David**.

David ♂
Biblical name, borne by the greatest of
all the kings of Israel, whose history is
recounted with great vividness in the
first and second books of Samuel and
elsewhere. As a boy he killed the giant
Philistine Goliath with his slingshot.
As king of Judah, and later of all
Israel, he expanded the power of the
Israelites and established the security
of their kingdom. He was also noted
as a poet, many of the Psalms being
attributed to him. The Hebrew
derivation of the name is uncertain; it
is said by some to represent a nursery
word meaning 'darling'. It is a very
popular Jewish name, but is almost
equally common among Gentiles in
the English-speaking world. It is
particularly common in Wales and
Scotland, having been borne by the
patron saint of Wales (see ◊**Dewi**) and
by two medieval kings of Scotland.
Short form: **Dave**.
Pet forms: Scottish: **Davy**, **Davey**, **Davie**.
Welsh: ◊**Dai**.

Davina ♀
Latinate feminine form of ◊**David**. The
name seems to have originated in
Scotland, and is occasionally

elaborated to **Davinia**, on the model of
◊**Lavinia**.

Davis ♂

Mainly U.S.: transferred use of the
surname, in origin a patronymic from
the given name ◊**Davy**. Use as a given
name is often in honour of Jefferson
Davis (1808–89), President of the
Confederate States during the Civil
War.
Variant: **Davies**.

Davy ♂

Pet form of ◊**David**.
Variants: **Davey**, **Davie**.

Dawn ♀

From the vocabulary word for
daybreak, originally bestowed as a
given name in the 1920s, no doubt
because of the connotations of
freshness and purity of this time of
day. It may have originated as a
translation of ◊**Aurora**. Twin girls are
sometimes given the names *Dawn* and
◊**Eve**, although the latter name does
not in fact have anything to do with
the time of day. The name is also
associated with the actress Dawn
Addams (b. 1930).

Dean ♂

Transferred use of the surname, which
has a double origin. In part it is a local
name for someone who lived in a
valley (Middle English *dene*, Old
English *denu*), in part an occupational
name for someone who served as a
dean, i.e. ecclesiastical supervisor
(Latin *decanus*). The given name also
sometimes represents Italian *Dino*
(short form of names such as
Bernardino), as in the case of the
American actor and singer Dean
Martin (b. 1917).
Variants: **Deane**, **Dene**.

Deanna ♀

Variant of ◊**Diana**, coined in 1936 by
the film star and singer Deanna
Durbin (b. 1921), whose original given
names were *Edna May*. It is now

sometimes used as a feminine form of
◊**Dean**.

Deborah ♀

Biblical name (meaning 'bee' in
Hebrew), borne by the nurse of
Rebecca (Genesis 35:8) and by a
woman judge and prophet (Judges 4–5),
who led the Israelites to victory over
the Canaanites. It has always been
popular as a Jewish name, and was
taken up among Christians by the
Puritans in the 17th century, in part
because the bee was a symbol of
industriousness. It has steadily
increased in popularity ever since.
Among other famous bearers is the
actress Deborah Kerr (b. 1921).
Variants: **Debora**, **Debra**.
Short form: **Deb**.
Pet forms: **Debbie**, **Debbi**, **Debi**, **Debs**.

Declan ♂

Irish: Anglicized form of Gaelic
Deaglán, of uncertain derivation. It
was borne by a 5th-century disciple of
St Colman, who became a bishop in
the district of Ardmore, Co.
Waterford. In recent years the name
has been strongly revived in Ireland.

Dee ♀ ♂

Pet form of any of the given names
beginning with the letter *D*- (cf. ◊**Kay**),
especially ◊**Dorothy**. It is also used as
an independent name, and may in
some cases be associated with the
River Dee (cf. ◊**Clyde**).

Deforest ♂

Mainly U.S.: transferred use of the
surname, apparently adopted in
honour of John DeForest (1826–1906),
the author of several novels, mostly
set during the American Civil War,
which enjoyed great popularity at the
end of the 19th century.
Variant: **Deforrest**.

Deiniol ♂

Welsh: apparently a form of ◊**Daniel**.
The name was borne by a 6th-century
Welsh saint.

Deirdre ♀

Name borne in Celtic legend by a tragic heroine, sometimes referred to as 'Deirdre of the Sorrows'. The story goes that she was betrothed to Conchobhar, King of Ulster, but instead eloped with her beloved Naoise. Eventually, however, the jilted king murdered Naoise and his brothers, and Deirdre herself died of a broken heart. She is sometimes taken as symbolic of the fate of Ireland under English rule, but this has not stopped her name's being used by English parents with no Celtic blood in them. It became popular in Ireland and elsewhere in the Edwardian era, following retellings of the legend by both the poet W. B. Yeats (1907) and the playwright J. M. Synge (1910). The name itself is of uncertain derivation; the earliest Celtic forms are very variable.

Del ♂

British colloquial pet form of ◊Derek, with alteration of the exposed -r of the short form to -l (cf. ◊Sal and ◊Tel).

Delia ♀

From a classical Greek epithet of the goddess Artemis, referring to her birth on the island of *Delos* (cf. ◊Cynthia). It was taken up by the pastoral poets of the 17th century, and has been moderately popular ever since.

Delicia ♀

Feminine form of the Late Latin name *Delicius*, a derivative of *deliciae* 'delight'. Use as a given name seems to be a modern phenomenon; it is not found in the Middle Ages.

Delilah ♀

Biblical name (of uncertain origin), borne by Samson's mistress, who wheedled him into revealing that the secret of his strength was in his hair, and then cut it off while he was asleep and betrayed him to the Philistines (Judges 16:4–20). Although the biblical Delilah was deceitful and treacherous,

the name was taken up enthusiastically by the Puritans in the 17th century, perhaps because she was also beautiful and clever. The name fell out of use in the 18th century, but has been occasionally revived as an exotic name.
Variant: **Delila**.

Dell ♂

Transferred use of the surname, originally a local name for someone who lived in a *dell* or hollow.

Della ♀

Name which first appeared in the 1870s and has continued to grow steadily in popularity ever since. Its derivation is not clear; if it is not simply an arbitrary creation, it may be an altered form of ◊Delia or ◊Delilah, or a short form of ◊Adela. In modern use it is sometimes taken as a feminine form of ◊Dell.

Delores ♀

Variant of ◊Dolores, quite common in the United States.
Variant: **Deloris**.

Delphine ♀

French: from Latin *Delphīna* 'woman from Delphi'. The Blessed Delphina (1283–1358) was a Provençal nun, who was probably named in honour of the 4th-century St Delphinus of Bordeaux. In modern times the name may sometimes be chosen for its association with the *delphinium* flower.

Delwyn ♀

Welsh: modern name composed of the words *del* 'pretty', 'neat' + *(g)wyn* 'white', 'fair', 'blessed', 'holy'.

Delyth ♀

Welsh: modern name composed of the vocabulary word *del* 'pretty', 'neat' + the ending -*yth*, formed on the analogy of names such as ◊Gwenyth.

Demelza ♀

Modern Cornish name, which has no history as a Celtic personal name but is derived from a placename in the parish of St Columb Major. The given name began to be used in the 1950s and was given a boost by the serialization on British television of the 'Poldark' novels by Winston Graham, in which it is the name of the heroine.

Den ♂
Short form of ◊Dennis.
Pet form: **Denny**.

Dena ♀
Modern coinage, representing either a respelling of ◊Dina, or else a form created as a feminine version of ◊Dean.

Dene ♂
Variant spelling of ◊Dean.

Denice ♀
Altered form of ◊Denise.

Denis ♂
Variant spelling of ◊Dennis, the usual French form of the name.

Denise ♀
French feminine form of ◊Denis, now also widely used in the English-speaking world.

Dennis ♂
Medieval vernacular form of the Greek name *Dionysios*, which was borne by several early Christian saints, including St Denis, a 3rd-century evangelist who converted the Gauls and became a patron saint of Paris. It was on his account that the name was popular in France and was adopted by the Normans. In classical times, the word originally denoted a devotee of the god *Dionysos*. This deity was a relatively late introduction to the classical pantheon; his orgiastic cult seems to have originated in Persia or elsewhere in Asia. His name is of uncertain derivation, although the first part seems to be related to the name of the supreme god *Zeus*.
Variant: **Denis**.

Short form: **Den**.
Pet form: **Denny**.

Denton ♂
Transferred use of the surname, originally a local name from any of the numerous places named in Old English as 'the settlement in the valley', from *denu* 'valley' + *tūn* 'enclosure', 'settlement'.

Denzil ♂
From the Cornish surname, the original spelling of which was *Denzell*, a local name from a place in Cornwall. It came to be used as a given name in the Hollis family in the 16th century, when the Hollis family and the Denzell family became connected by marriage, and spread from there into more general use.

Deon ♂
Variant spelling of ◊Dion.

Deonne ♀
Feminine form of ◊Deon.

Derek ♂
From a Low German form of *Theodoric* (see ◊Terry), introduced to Britain during the Middle Ages by Flemish settlers connected with the cloth trades.
Variants: **Dereck**, **Der(r)ick**.
Pet form: **Del**.

Dermot ♂
Irish: Anglicized form of the Gaelic name *Diarmaid*, earlier *Diarm(u)it*. The derivation is uncertain; it has been suggested that it is composed of the words *dí* 'without' + *airmit* 'injunction' or *airmait* 'envy'.

Derrick ♂
Variant spelling of ◊Derek. This is the usual American spelling of the given name, but in Britain it is more common as a surname than as a given name.

Derry ♂
Of uncertain origin, perhaps a cross between ◊Derek and ◊Terry.

Dervla ♀
Irish: Anglicized form of the Gaelic name *Deirbhile* (pronounced '*djair-veel-a*'), from *der* 'daughter' + *file* 'poet'.

Desdemona ♀
Name occasionally chosen by parents in search of an unusual name, who are no doubt attracted by the sweet nature and innocence of Shakespeare's character and not deterred by her tragic fate. She was murdered by her husband Othello in an ill-founded jealous rage, and her name is in fact particularly appropriate to her destiny, as it probably represents a Latinized form of Greek *dysdaimōn* 'ill-starred'.

Desirée ♀
French (now also used in the English-speaking world, usually without the accent): from Latin *Desiderāta* 'desired'. This name was given by early Christians to a longed-for child, but the French form is now often taken as suggesting that the bearer will grow up into a desirable woman.

Desmond ♂
Of Irish origin: from the Gaelic by-name *Deas-Mhumhan* '(man from) south Munster'.
Short form: **Des**.

Destiny ♀
Mainly U.S.: from the vocabulary word denoting the power of fate (Old French *destinee*, from Late Latin *destināta*). This has recently become established as a given name, with variant spellings such as **Destinie**, **Destiney**, and **Destinee**.

Devereux ♂
Especially U.S.: transferred use of a surname, which was originally a Norman baronial name derived (with fused preposition *de*) from *Evreux* in Eure. It was the family name of the 16th-century earls of Essex: Robert Devereux, the 2nd earl, was a favourite of Queen Elizabeth I, later disgraced and executed for treason.

Devin ♂
Mainly U.S.: transferred use of the Irish surname, Gaelic *Ó Damháin* 'descendant of Damhán'. The latter is a byname meaning 'fawn' (see ◊**Dymphna**).

Devon ♀ ♂
Mainly North American: from the name of the English county, either directly or as a transferred use of the surname. It derives from a British tribal name, said to mean 'worshippers of the god Dumnōnos'.
Variant: **Devonne** ♀

Dewey ♂
Mainly U.S.: of uncertain origin, perhaps a respelling of ◊**Dewi**.
Variant: **Dewy**.

Dewi ♂
A Welsh form (earlier *Dewydd*) of ◊**David**, traditionally associated with the patron saint of Wales. This form of the given name was little used during the Middle Ages, but during the 20th century it has become quite common in Wales, though rare elsewhere. St Dewi was born in South Wales in the 5th century and became the first bishop of Menevia, the tiny cathedral city now known as St Davids.

Dewy ♂
Mainly U.S.: variant spelling of ◊**Dewey**.

Dexter ♂
Mainly U.S.: transferred use of the surname. Although this is now a male given name, the word that gave rise to the surname originally denoted a female dyer, from Old English *dēag* 'dye' + *-estre*, feminine ending of agent nouns. However, the distinction of gender was already lost in Middle English. The name coincides in form with Latin *dexter* 'right-handed', 'auspicious', and may sometimes have been chosen because of this.
Short form: **Dex**.

Pet form: **Dexy** (as in the name of the rock band Dexy's Midnight Runners).

Di ♀
Short form of ◊**Diana** and ◊**Diane**.

Diahann ♀
Elaborated variant of ◊**Diane**, associated particularly with the American actress Diahann Carol (b. 1935).

Diamond ♀
One of the most recent of the female given names adopted from the vocabulary of gemstones, this enjoys some currency in the United States.

Diana ♀
Name borne in Roman mythology by the goddess of the moon and of hunting, equivalent to the Greek Artemis. In mythology she is characterized as both beautiful and chaste. Her name is of ancient and uncertain derivation. It probably contains a first element that is also found in the name of the Greek god *Dionysos* (see ◊**Dennis**) and the Latin name of the supreme god *Jupiter*. It was adopted in Britain during the Tudor period as a learned name, a borrowing from Latin influenced by the French form ◊**Diane**. Although it was much used by Elizabethan poets celebrating the virgin goddess and alluding to the virgin queen, it was not particularly popular as a given name until the end of the 19th century. In earlier centuries some clergymen were reluctant to baptize girls with this pagan name, mindful of the riots against St Paul stirred up by worshippers of Diana of the Ephesians (Acts 19:24–41).
Short form: **Di**.

Diane ♀
French form of ◊**Diana**, now also used in the English-speaking world. It was especially popular among the Renaissance aristocracy, who loved hunting and were therefore proud to name their daughters after the classical goddess of the chase.
Variants: **Dianne** (by association with ◊**Anne**); **Dyan** (U.S.).
Short form: **Di**.

Dick ♂
Short form of ◊**Richard**. The alteration of the initial consonant is supposed to result from the difficulty that English speakers in the Middle Ages had in pronouncing the trilled Norman *R-*.

Dickie ♂
Pet form of ◊**Dick**, with the originally Scottish and northern English diminutive suffix *-ie*. This has more or less completely replaced the medieval diminutive *Dickon*, with the Old French suffix *-on*.

Digby ♂
Transferred use of the surname, in origin a local name from a place in Lincolnshire, so called from Old Norse *díki* 'ditch' + *býr* 'settlement'.

Dillon ♂
Variant spelling of ◊**Dylan**, based on an English surname of different origin. The surname *Dillon* or *Dyllon* derives in part from a now extinct Norman French personal name of Germanic origin; in part it is a local name from *Dilwyn* in Hereford.

Dilly ♀
Pet form of ◊**Dilys** and ◊**Dilwen**, now sometimes used as an independent given name.

Dilwen ♀
Welsh: modern name, from *Dil-* (see ◊**Dilys**) + *(g)wen*, feminine form of *gwyn* 'white', 'fair', 'blessed', 'holy'.

Dilys ♀
Welsh: of modern origin, from the vocabulary word *dilys* 'genuine', 'steadfast', 'true'.

Dina ♀
In part a variant spelling of ◊**Dinah**, with which it often shares the same pronunciation. In part, however, it

derives from the Italian name *Dina*, a short form of diminutives such as *Bernardina*.

Dinah ♀

Biblical name (a feminine form derived from Hebrew *din* 'judgement'), borne by a daughter of Jacob. She was raped by Shechem but avenged by her brothers Simeon and Levi (Genesis 34). In modern times it is generally taken as a variant of the much more common ◊Diana.

Dion ♂

French: from Latin *Dio* (genitive *Diōnis*), a short form of the various names of Greek origin containing as their first element *Dio-* 'Zeus'. Examples include *Diodoros* 'gift of Zeus' and *Diogenēs* 'born of Zeus'. It is also used in the English-speaking world, especially as a Black name.

Dionne ♀

Feminine form of ◊Dion.

Dirk ♂

Flemish and Dutch form of ◊Derek. Its use in the English-speaking world since the 1960s is largely due to the fame of the actor Dirk Bogarde (b. 1921; originally Derek Niven van den Bogaerde). He is of Dutch descent, although he was actually born in Scotland. The manly image of the name has been reinforced by its coincidence in form with the Scottish vocabulary word *dirk* 'dagger' (from Gaelic *durc*).

Dixie ♀

Mainly U.S.: name chosen as symbolic of the American South. The nickname is of uncertain origin. It is said to be from the ten-dollar bills printed in New Orleans, named in the Cajun dialect from French *dix* 'ten'.

Dodie ♀

Pet form of ◊Dorothy, derived from a child's unsuccessful attempts to pronounce the name.

Dolly

♀, in Scotland occasionally ♂
Originally (from the 16th century onwards) a pet form of ◊Dorothy; now also a pet form of ◊Dolores. It is also found as an independent given name (taken as being from the vocabulary word *doll*, which was in fact derived in the 17th century from the pet name for *Dorothy*). In Gaelic areas of Scotland it is found as a pet form of the male name ◊Donald.

Dolores ♀

Spanish: from *Maria de los Dolores* 'Mary of the Sorrows', a reference to the Seven Sorrows of the Virgin Mary. The feast of Our Lady's Dolours was established in 1423. The name is now also borne in the English-speaking world, mainly by Roman Catholics. In part, it was popularized by the film star Dolores Del Rio (1905–83), born in Mexico as Dolores Asunsolo.
Variants: **Delores**, **Deloris**.
Pet forms: **Lola**, **Lolita**, **Dolly**.

Dominic ♂

From the Late Latin name *Dominicus*, a derivative of *dominus* 'lord'. It is used mainly by Roman Catholics, in honour of St Dominic (1170–1221), founder of the Dominican order of monks.
Variant: **Dominick** (an old spelling, still in occasional use).

Dominique ♀

Feminine form of ◊Dominic, from a French form that is used as both a female and a male name.

Don ♂

Short form of ◊Donald. It is also a variant of the Irish name ◊Donn.
Pet forms: **Donny**, **Donnie**.

Donal ♂

Irish: Anglicized form of the Gaelic name *Dónal*, a simplified form of *Domhnall* (see ◊Donald).
Variant: **Donall**.

Donald ♂

Scottish: Anglicized form of the
Gaelic name *Domhnall*, from Old
Celtic *dubno* 'world' + *val* 'rule'. The
final *-d* of the Anglicized form derives
partly from misinterpretation by
English speakers of the Gaelic
pronunciation, and partly from
association with Germanic-origin
names such as ◊**Ronald**. This name is
strongly associated with clan
Macdonald, the clan of the medieval
Lords of the Isles. *Donald* is now also
quite commonly used by families with
no Scottish connections.
Short form: **Don**.
Pet forms: **Donny**, **Donnie**; **Dolly** (in
Gaelic Scotland).

Donall ♂

Variant spelling of ◊**Donal**.

Donn ♂

Irish: ancient Gaelic byname meaning
either 'brown' or 'king', in use from
the earliest times until the 19th
century. In Irish mythology this is the
name of the king of the underworld.

Donna ♀

Of recent origin (not found before the
1920s). It is derived from the Italian
vocabulary word *donna* 'lady' (cf.
◊**Madonna**), but it has also been used
as a feminine form of ◊**Donald**.

Donnell ♂

Transferred use of the Scottish and
Irish surname, derived in the Middle
Ages from the given name ◊**Donald**.

Donny ♂

Pet form of ◊**Donald**.
Variant: **Donnie**.

Donovan ♂

Transferred use of the Irish surname,
Gaelic *Ó Donndubháin* 'descendant of
Donndubhán'. The latter is a personal
name from *donn* 'brown' + *dubh*
'black', 'dark' + the diminutive suffix
-án. Its use as a given name dates
from the early 1900s. The folk-rock
singer Donovan may have had some

influence on its increase in popularity
in the 1960s.

Dora ♀

19th-century coinage, representing a
short form of ◊**Isidora**, ◊**Theodora**,
◊**Dorothy**, and any other name
containing the Greek word *dōron*
'gift'. Wordsworth's daughter (b. 1804),
christened Dorothy, was always
known in adult life as Dora. The
name's popularity was enhanced by
the character of Dora Spenlow in
Dickens's novel *David Copperfield*
(1850).

Dorcas ♀

From Greek *dorkas* 'doe', 'gazelle'. It
was not used as a personal name by
the ancient Greeks, but is offered in
the Bible as an interpretation of the
Aramaic name ◊**Tabitha** (Acts 9:36),
and was taken up by the early
Christians. It was much used among
the Puritans in the 16th century, and
has remained in occasional use ever
since.

Dorean ♀

Irish: Anglicized form of the Gaelic
name *Doireann*, possibly from Gaelic
der 'daughter' + the name of the
legendary hero ◊**Finn**. This has been
revived as a given name in the 20th
century, and has become very popular,
perhaps influenced to some extent by
◊**Doreen**.

Doreen ♀

Derivative of ◊**Dora**, with the addition
of the productive suffix *-een* (in origin
an Irish diminutive). The name came
into use at the beginning of the 20th
century, when there was a particular
vogue for such names. See also
◊**Dorean**.
Variants: **Dorene**, **Dorine**.

Doria ♀

Of uncertain origin, probably a back-
formation from ◊**Dorian** or else an
elaboration of ◊**Dora** on the model of
the numerous women's given names
ending in *-ia*.

Dorian ♂

Early 20th-century coinage, apparently invented by Oscar Wilde, as no evidence has been found of its existence before he used it for the central character in *The Portrait of Dorian Gray* (1891). Dorian Gray is a dissolute rake who retains unblemished youthful good looks; in the attic of his home is a portrait which does his ageing for him, gradually acquiring all the outward marks of his depravity. This macabre background has not deterred parents from occasionally bestowing the name on their children. Wilde probably took the name from Late Latin *Dōriānus*, from Greek *Dōrieus*, member of the Greek-speaking people who settled in the Peloponnese in pre-classical times. *Dorian* would thus be a masculine version of ◊**Doris**. It may have been selected occasionally by admirers of ancient Sparta and its militaristic institutions, since the Spartans were of Dorian stock.
Variant: **Dorien**.

Dorinda ♀

Artificial elaboration of ◊**Dora**, with the suffix -*inda* (cf. ◊**Clarinda**). The name was coined in the 18th century, and has undergone a modest revival of interest in the 20th.

Doris ♀

From the classical Greek ethnic name meaning 'Dorian woman'. The Dorians were one of the tribes of Greece; their name was traditionally derived from an ancestor, *Dōros* (son of Hellen, who gave his name to the Hellenes), but it is more likely that Doros (whose name could be from *dōron* 'gift') was invented to account for a tribal name of obscure origin. In Greek mythology, Doris was a minor goddess of the sea, the consort of Nereus and the mother of his daughters, the Nereids or sea-nymphs, who numbered fifty (in some versions, more). The name was especially popular from about 1880 to about 1930, and was borne by the American film star Doris Day (b. 1924 as Doris Kappelhoff), among others.

Dorothea ♀

Latinate form of a post-classical Greek name, from *dōron* 'gift' + *theos* 'god' (the same elements as in ◊**Theodora**, but in reverse order). The masculine form *Dōrotheus* was borne by several early Christian saints, the feminine only by two minor ones, but only the female name has survived. In modern use in the English-speaking world it represents either a 19th-century Latinization of ◊**Dorothy** or a learned reborrowing.

Dorothy ♀

Usual English form of ◊**Dorothea**. The name was not used in the Middle Ages, but was taken up in the 16th century and became common thereafter. It was borne by the American film star Dorothy Lamour (b. 1914).
Short form: **Dot**.
Pet forms: **Dottie, Dotty, Dodie, Dolly**.

Doug ♂

Short form of ◊**Douglas**.

Dougal ♂

Scottish: Anglicized form of the Gaelic name *Dubhghall* or *Dùghall*, from *dubh* 'black', 'dark' + *gall* 'stranger'. This was a byname applied to Danes, in contrast to the fairer Norwegians and Icelanders (see ◊**Fingal**).
Variants: **Dugal(d)**.
Pet form: **Dougie**.

Douglas ♂

Transferred use of the surname borne by one of the most powerful families in Scotland, the earls of Douglas and of Angus, also notorious in earlier times as Border reivers. Their surname is derived from the place in the Southern Uplands of Scotland where they had their stronghold, named with

the Gaelic words *dubh* 'black' + *glas* 'stream'.
Short form: **Doug**.

Dreda ♀

Shortened form of ◊**Etheldreda**, quite commonly used as an independent given name in the 19th century, when the longer form was also in fashion. It has survived slightly better than the four-syllable original, but is nevertheless now rare.

Drew ♂

Scottish short form of ◊**Andrew**, often used as an independent name in Scotland, and in recent years increasingly popular elsewhere in the English-speaking world.

Drusilla ♀

From a Late Latin name, a feminine diminutive of the old Roman family name *Dr(a)usus*, which was first taken by a certain Livius, who had killed in single combat a Gaul of this name and, according to a custom of the time, took his victim's name as a cognomen. Of the several women in the Roman imperial family who were called Livia Drusilla, the most notorious was Caligula's sister and mistress. The name is borne in the Bible by a Jewish woman, wife of the Roman citizen Felix, who was converted to Christianity by St Paul (Acts 24:24). In England it was taken up as a given name in the 17th century as a result of the biblical mention.

Drystan ♂

Welsh variant of ◊**Tristan**. Drystan son of Tallwch is fleetingly mentioned in the *Mabinogi* as one of the members of King Arthur's council of advisers.

Duald ♂

Irish: Anglicized form of the Gaelic name *Dubhaltach* (pronounced 'doo-al-tah'), which probably means 'black-haired' (Gaelic *dubh-fholtach*).

Duane ♂

Irish: Anglicized form of the Gaelic name *Dubhán* (pronounced 'doo-vain'). This was originally a byname, a diminutive of Gaelic *dubh* 'dark', 'black'. In modern use it may be derived from the surname *Ó Dubháin* 'descendant of Dubhán'. Its popularity in the mid-1950s was influenced by the guitarist Duane Eddy.
Variants: **Dwane**, **Dwayne**.

Dudley ♂

Transferred use of the surname of a noble family, who came originally from Dudley in the West Midlands, named in Old English as the 'wood or clearing of Dudda'. Their most famous member was Robert Dudley, Earl of Leicester (?1532–88), who came closer than any other man to marrying Queen Elizabeth I. This given name is much less common in North America than in England.
Short form: **Dud**.

Duff ♂

Scottish: from the Gaelic nickname *dubh* 'black', i.e. 'dark-haired one'. In modern use it is in part a transferred use of the surname *Duff*, derived from the nickname.

Dugald ♂

Scottish: variant of ◊**Dougal**. The final consonant may be due to the devoicing of the final *-ll* of the Gaelic form, suggesting to English ears that a *d* or *t* followed.

Duke ♂

In modern use this normally represents a coinage parallel to ◊**Earl** and ◊**King**, but it is also a short form of ◊**Marmaduke**. It is especially popular in the United States.

Dulcie ♀

Learned re-creation in the 19th century of the medieval name *Dowse*, Late Latin *Dulcia*, a derivative of *dulcis* 'sweet'.

Duncan ♂

Scottish: Anglicized form of the Gaelic name *Donnchadh*, from *donn* 'brown' + *cadh* or *cádh* 'chief', 'noble'. This was the name of a 7th-century Scottish saint (abbot of Iona), a 10th-century Irish saint (abbot of Clonmacnoise), and two medieval kings of Scotland. The final *n* in the Anglicized form seems to be the result of confusion with the Gaelic word *ceann* 'head', due to the Latinized form *Duncanus*. In Ireland, *Donnchadh* is now often spelled *Donncha*; it was formerly sometimes Anglicized as ◊**Dennis**.

Dunstan ♂

From an Old English personal name derived from *dun* 'dark' + *stān* 'stone', borne most notably by a 10th-century saint who was archbishop of Canterbury. The name is now used mainly by Roman Catholics.

Dustin ♂

Transferred use of the surname, which is of uncertain origin, probably a Norman form of the Old Norse personal name *Þórsteinn*, composed of elements meaning 'Thor's stone'. It is now used fairly regularly as a given name, largely as a result of the fame of the film actor Dustin Hoffman (b. 1937), who is said to have been named in honour of the less well-known silent film actor Dustin Farman (1870–1929).

Dusty ♂ ♀

Apparently a pet form, or in some cases a feminine form, of ◊**Dustin**. As a female name it was made familiar in the 1960s by the singer Dusty Springfield.

Dwane ♂

Variant spelling of ◊**Duane**.
Variant: **Dwayne**.

Dwight ♂

Transferred use of the surname, which probably comes from the medieval English female name *Diot*, a pet form of *Dionysia* (see ◊**Dennis**). It is especially common in North America, where its increase in popularity since the Second World War is mainly a result of the fame of the American general and president Dwight D. Eisenhower (1890–1969). He was named in honour of the New England philosopher Timothy Dwight (1752–1817) and his brother Theodore Dwight (1764–1846).

Dyan ♀

Modern variant spelling of ◊**Diane**, especially popular in the United States.

Dylan ♂

Welsh: of uncertain origin, probably connected with a Celtic word meaning 'sea'. In the *Mabinogi* it is the name of the miraculously born son of Arianrhod, who became a minor divinity of the sea. In the second half of the 20th century the name has become fairly popular outside Wales as a result of the fame of the Welsh poet Dylan Thomas (1914–53) and the American singer Bob Dylan (b. 1941), who changed his surname from Zimmerman as a tribute to the poet.

Dymphna ♀

Irish: Anglicized form of the Gaelic name *Damhnait* (pronounced 'dav-nit'). This originated as a feminine diminutive of *damh* 'stag'. Little is known of the saint of this name, beyond the fact that she is regarded as the protector of lunatics. Her relics are preserved at Gheel, near Antwerp in Belgium.
Variant: **Dympna**.

EAMON EARL EARLA EARNEST EARNESTIN
E EBENEZER EBONY ED EDAN EDDIE EDEN
EDGAR EDIE EDITH EDMOND EDMUND E
DNA EDOM EDSEL EDWARD EDWIN EDWI
NA EFFIE EGAN EGBERT EGLANTINE EIDD
WEN EILEEN EILIDH EIRA EIREEN EIRLYS EI

Eamon ♂

Irish name, pronounced 'ay-mon': from the Gaelic form of ◊**Edmund**. The normal Gaelic spellings are *Éamon(n)* or *Éaman(n)*. Éamon de Valera (1882–1973) was president of Ireland 1959–73.

Earl ♂

North American: from the rank of the peerage, originally a nickname parallel to ◊**Duke**, ◊**King**, etc. The title was used in England in Norman times as an equivalent of the French *comte* 'count'; it is from Old English *eorl* 'warrior', 'nobleman', 'prince'. In some cases the given name may have been taken from the surname *Earl*, which was originally either a nickname or a term denoting someone who worked in the household of an earl.
Variants: **Earle**, **Erle**.

Earla ♀

Mainly U.S.: coined as a feminine form of *Earl*.
Elaborated forms: **Earlina**, **Earline**, **Earlene**, **Earleen**.

Earnest ♂

Mainly North American variant spelling of ◊**Ernest**.

Earnestine ♀

Especially U.S.: variant spelling of ◊**Ernestine**.

Ebenezer ♂

Biblical term, originally a placename (meaning 'stone of help' in Hebrew). This was the site of the battle where the Israelites were defeated by the Philistines (1 Samuel 4:1). After they took their revenge, Samuel set up a memorial stone bearing this name (1 Samuel 7:12). It was taken up as a given name by the Puritans in the 17th century, possibly after being misread in the Bible as a personal name, or else because of its favourable etymological connotations. It now has unfavourable connotations because of the miserly character of Ebenezer Scrooge in Charles Dickens's *A Christmas Carol* (1843).

Ebony ♀

From the name of the deeply black wood (Late Latin *ebenius*, from Greek *ebenos*, ultimately of Egyptian origin). This name has been adopted recently (since the 1970s) by Blacks as a symbol of pride in their colour.

Ed ♂

Short form of the various male names with the first syllable *Ed-*, especially ◊**Edward**.

Edan ♂

Scottish and Irish: variant of ◊**Aidan**. St Edan was an Irish disciple of St David of Wales who later became bishop of Ferns.

Eddie ♂

Pet form of ◊**Ed**.

Eden ♀ ♂

Mainly U.S.: of uncertain origin. It probably refers to the biblical 'Garden of Eden', so named from Hebrew *ayinēden* 'place of pleasure'. As a male name it may also represent a variant of ◊**Edan** or a transferred use of a surname, itself derived in the Middle Ages from a given name *Edun* or

Edon. This is of Old English origin, from *ēad* 'prosperity', 'riches' + *hūn* 'bear cub'.

Edgar ♂

From an Old English personal name derived from *ēad* 'prosperity', 'riches' + *gār* 'spear'. This was the name of an English king and saint, Edgar the Peaceful (d. 975), and of Edgar Atheling (?1060–?1125), the young prince who was chosen by the English to succeed Harold as king in 1066, but who was supplanted by the Normans.

Edie ♀

Pet form of ◊**Edith**.

Edith ♀

From an Old English female personal name derived from *ēad* 'prosperity', 'riches' + *gӯð* 'strife'. This was borne by a daughter (961–84) of Edgar the Peaceful (she was named in accordance with the common Old English practice of repeating name elements within a family). She spent her short life in a convent, and is regarded as a saint.
Pet form: **Edie**.

Edmond ♂

French form of ◊**Edmund**, also occasionally used in the English-speaking world.

Edmund ♂

From an Old English personal name derived from *ēad* 'prosperity', 'riches' + *mund* 'protector'. It was borne by several early royal and saintly figures, including a 9th-century king of East Anglia killed by invading Danes, allegedly for his adherence to Christianity.

Edna ♀

In Ireland this has been used as an Anglicized form of ◊**Eithne**. The name occurs in the apocryphal Book of Tobit, where it is the name of the mother of Sarah and stepmother of Tobias. This is said to be from Hebrew *ayinednah* 'pleasure', 'delight', and if so it is connected with the name of the Garden of ◊**Eden**. The earliest known uses of the given name in England are in the 18th century, when it was probably imported from Ireland, rather than taken from the Bible.

Edom ♂

Biblical name (meaning 'red' in Hebrew), which was the byname of Esau. It was given to him because he sold his birthright for a bowl of red lentil soup. This was frequently used as a given name in medieval Scotland, where it was taken to represent a variant of ◊**Adam**. It is occasionally bestowed in modern times by parents with Scottish connections.

Edsel ♂

In Germanic mythology this name is a variant of *Etzel*, apparently derived from *adal* 'noble', or else from the nickname *Atta* 'father'. In modern times its best-known bearer was Edsel Ford, son of Henry Ford, founder of the Ford Motor Corporation. The family was partly of Dutch or Flemish descent, but the reason for the choice of given name is not known.

Edward ♂

From an Old English personal name derived from *ēad* 'prosperity', 'riches' + *weard* 'guard'. This has been one of the most successful of all Old English names, surviving from before the Conquest to the present day, and even being exported into other European languages. It was the name of three Anglo-Saxon kings and has been borne by eight kings of England since the Norman Conquest. It is also the name of the youngest son of Queen Elizabeth II. The most influential early bearer was King Edward the Confessor (?1002–66; ruled 1042–66). In a troubled period of English history, he contrived to rule fairly and (for a time at any rate) firmly. But in the latter part of his reign he paid more attention to his religion than to his

kingdom. He died childless, and his death sparked off conflicting claims to his throne, which were resolved by the victory of William the Conqueror at the Battle of Hastings. His memory was honoured by Normans and English alike, for his fairness and his piety. Edward's mother was Norman; he had spent part of his youth in Normandy; and William claimed to have been nominated by Edward as his successor. Edward was canonized in the 12th century, and came to be venerated throughout Europe as a model of a Christian king.
Short forms: **Ed**, **Ned**, **Ted**.
Pet form: **Eddie**.

Edwin ♂
19th-century revival of an Old English personal name derived from *ēad* 'prosperity', 'riches' + *wine* 'friend'. It was borne by a 7th-century king of Northumbria, who was converted to Christianity by St Paulinus and was killed in battle against pagan forces, a combination of circumstances which led to his being venerated as a martyr.

Edwina ♀
19th-century coinage, representing a Latinate feminine form of ◊**Edwin** or, in at least one case, of ◊**Edward**. Edwina Ashley, a descendant of Lord Shaftesbury who became the wife of Earl Mountbatten, was so named in honour of Edward VII; the king had originally wished her to be called *Edwardina*.

Effie ♀
Pet form of ◊**Euphemia**, now as rarely used as the full form, but popular in the 19th century.

Egan ♂
Irish: Anglicized form of the Gaelic name *Aogán*, earlier *Aodhagán*, a double diminutive of *Aodh* (see ◊**Aidan**). In some cases it may be a transferred use of the surname, which has the same origin.

Egbert ♂
From an Old English personal name derived from *ecg* 'edge (of a sword)' + *beorht* 'bright', 'famous'. It was borne by two English saints of the 8th century and by a 9th-century king of Wessex. It survived for a while after the Conquest, but fell out of use by the 14th century. It was briefly revived in the 19th century, but is now again completely out of fashion.

Eglantine ♀
Flower name, used as a nickname by Chaucer, and occasionally as a given name in the 19th century, but not at present in use. It is from an alternative name for the sweetbrier, derived in the 14th century from Old French *aiglent*, ultimately a derivative of Latin *acus* 'needle', referring to the prickly stem of the plant.

Eiddwen ♀
Welsh: modern coinage, apparently derived from *eiddun* 'desirous', 'fond', with the feminine names suffix *(g)wen*, from *gwyn* 'white', 'fair', 'blessed', 'holy'.

Eileen ♀
Anglicized form of the Irish Gaelic name spelt *Eibhlín*, *Eilín*, or *Aibhilín*. This is derived from Norman French *Aveline*, a derivative of ◊**Ava**. *bh* is normally pronounced as 'v' in Gaelic, but is sometimes silent, whence the Anglicized form. This name became extremely popular in many parts of the English-speaking world in the early part of the 20th century.
Variant: **Aileen** (esp. Scottish).

Eilidh ♀
Scottish Gaelic name, pronounced 'ay-lee', a comparatively recent coinage on the basis of English *Ellie*.
Variant: **Ailie** (an Anglicized spelling).

Eira ♀
Welsh: modern coinage from the vocabulary word *eira* 'snow'.

Eireen ♀
Of recent origin, a respelling of ◊**Irene**
under the influence of ◊**Eileen**.

Eirlys ♀
Welsh: modern coinage from the
vocabulary word for the snowdrop.

Eirwen ♀
Welsh: modern coinage, from *eira*
'snow' + *(g)wen*, feminine form of
gwyn 'white', 'fair', 'blessed', 'holy'.

Eithne ♀
Irish Gaelic: traditional name,
apparently from the vocabulary word
eithne 'kernel', which was used as a
term of praise in bardic poetry. The
name has been Anglicized variously as
◊**Edna**, ◊**Ena**, **Et(h)na**, and **Ethenia**. St
Ethenia was a daughter of King
Laoghaire and one of St Patrick's first
converts, together with her sister
Fidelma.

Elaine ♀
Originally an Old French form of
◊**Helen**, but now generally regarded as
an independent name. The Greek and
Latin forms of the name had a long
vowel in the second syllable, which
produced this form (as opposed to
◊**Ellen**) in Old French. In Arthurian
legend, Elaine is the name of one of
the women who fell in love with
Lancelot. The name occurs in this
form in the 15th-century English
Morte D'Arthur of Thomas Malory. In
the 19th century it was popularized in
one of Tennyson's *Idylls of the King*
(1859). Most of the characters in
Arthurian legend have names that are
Celtic in origin, although subjected to
heavy French influence, and it has
therefore been suggested that *Elaine*
may actually be derived from a Welsh
word meaning 'hind' or 'fawn'.

Eldon ♂
Transferred use of the surname, in
origin a local name from a place in
Co. Durham, so called from the Old
English male personal name *Ella* +
Old English *dūn* 'hill'.

Eleanor ♀
From an Old French respelling of the
Old Provençal name *Alienor*. This has
sometimes been taken as a derivative
of ◊**Helen**, but it is more probably of
Germanic derivation (the first element
being *ali* 'other', 'foreign'; the second
is obscure). The name was introduced
to England by Eleanor of Aquitaine
(1122–1204), who came from south-
west France to be the wife of King
Henry II. It was also borne by Eleanor
of Provence, the wife of Henry III, and
Eleanor of Castile, wife of Edward I.
Variants: **Ellenor**, **Elinor**.

Elen ♀
Welsh form of ◊**Helen**. It is identical
with the Welsh vocabulary word *elen*
'nymph', but this is unlikely to be the
origin. It is found in Welsh texts from
an early period as an equivalent of
Helen, for example as the name of the
mother of Constantine, finder of the
True Cross.
Variant: **Elin**.

Elena ♀
Italian and Spanish form of ◊**Helen**,
now sometimes also used in the
English-speaking world.

Eleonora ♀
Italian form of ◊**Eleanor**, now
sometimes also used in the English-
speaking world.

Eleri ♀
Welsh: ancient name of uncertain
origin. It was borne in the 5th century
by a daughter of the semi-legendary
chieftain Brychan. *Eleri* is also a
Welsh river name, and here it is
probably derived from *alar* 'surfeit'. It
is not clear whether there is a
connection between the personal
name and the river name.

Elfreda ♀
19th-century revival of a Latinized
form of the Old English female
personal name *Ælfþrýð*, from *ælf* 'elf',
'supernatural being' + *þrýð* 'strength'.
This form may also have absorbed the

Old English name Æðelþryð, which was originally distinct (see ◊**Audrey**). *Short form*: Freda.

Eli ♂
Biblical name, from a Hebrew word meaning 'height'. This was borne by the priest and judge who brought up the future prophet Samuel (1 Samuel 4). It was especially popular among Puritans in the 17th century.

Elias ♂
Biblical name, from the Greek form (used in the New Testament) of the name of the prophet ◊**Elijah**. See also ◊**Ellis**.

Elijah ♂
Biblical name (meaning 'Yahweh is God' in Hebrew), borne by an Israelite prophet whose exploits are recounted in the First and Second Book of Kings. Elijah's victory over the prophets of Baal on Mount Carmel played an important part in maintaining the Jewish religion, recognizing just one God. This story, and other stories in which he figures, including his conflicts with Ahab's queen, Jezebel, and his prophecies of doom, are among the most vivid in the Bible. For some reason it has not been much used as a given name by Christians, although it is found among the early Puritan settlers in New England. More recently, it has been adopted among Black Muslims.

Elin ♀
Welsh: variant of ◊**Elen**.

Elinor ♀
Variant spelling of ◊**Eleanor**.

Eliot ♂
Variant spelling of ◊**Elliot**. *Variant*: Eliott.

Elisabeth ♀
The spelling of ◊**Elizabeth** used in the Authorized Version of the New Testament, and in most modern European languages. This was the name of the mother of John the Baptist (Luke 1:60). Etymologically, the name means 'God is my oath', and is therefore identical with *Elisheba*, the name of the wife of Aaron according to the genealogy at Exodus 6:23. The final element seems to have been altered by association with Hebrew *shabbāth* 'Sabbath'.

Élise ♀
French: short form of ◊**Elisabeth**. The name was introduced into the English-speaking world (where it is often written without the accent) in the late 19th century.

Eliza ♀
Short form of ◊**Elizabeth**, first used in the 16th century, and popular in the 18th and 19th centuries. It was used by George Bernard Shaw for the main female character, Eliza Dolittle, in his play *Pygmalion* (1913), which was the basis for the musical and film *My Fair Lady*.

Elizabeth ♀
The usual spelling of ◊**Elisabeth** in English. It was first made popular by being borne by Queen Elizabeth I of England (1533–1603). In the 20th century it became extremely fashionable, partly because it was the name of Elizabeth Bowes-Lyon (b. 1900), who in 1936 became Queen Elizabeth as the wife of King George VI; even more influentially, it is the name of her daughter Queen Elizabeth II (b. 1926).
Variant: **Elisabeth**. See also ◊**Elspeth** and ◊**Isabel**.
Short forms: **Eliza, Elsa, Liza, Lisa, Liz; Beth, Bet, Bess; Lisbet**.
Pet forms: **Elsie, Bessie, Bessy, Betty, Betsy, Tetty, Libby, Lizzie, Lizzy, Buffy**.

Ella ♀
Of Germanic origin, introduced to Britain by the Normans. It was originally a short form of any of various compound names containing *ali* 'other', 'foreign' (cf. ◊**Eleanor**). It is

now often taken to be a variant or pet form of ◊**Ellen**.

Ellen ♀
Originally a variant of ◊**Helen**, although now no longer associated with that name. Initial *H-* tended to be added and dropped rather capriciously, leading to many doublets (cf. e.g. ◊**Esther** and *Hester*).
Pet form: ◊**Nell**.

Ellenor ♀
Variant spelling of ◊**Eleanor**, the result of blending with ◊**Ellen**.

Ellie ♀
Pet form of any of the numerous female names beginning with the syllable *El-*, in particular ◊**Eleanor**.

Elliot ♂
Transferred use of the surname, itself derived from a medieval (Norman French) masculine given name. This was a diminutive of *Elie*, the Old French version of ◊**Elias**.
Variants: **Elliott**, **Eliot(t)**.

Ellis ♂
Transferred use of the surname, which is derived from the usual medieval vernacular form of ◊**Elias**. In Wales it is now often taken as an Anglicized form of the Old Welsh name *Elisud*, a derivative of *elus* 'kind', 'benevolent'.

Elmer ♂
Transferred use of the surname, itself derived from an Old English personal name derived from *æðel* 'noble' + *mǣr* 'famous'. This has been used as a given name in the United States since the 19th century, in honour of the brothers Ebenezer and Jonathan Elmer, leading activists in the American Revolution. It is also found in Canada.

Elroy ♂
Variant of ◊**Leroy**. The initial syllable seems to be the result of simple transposition of the first two letters; it may also have been influenced by the Spanish definite article *el*.

Elsa ♀
Shortened form of ◊**Elisabeth** or ◊**Elizabeth**. The name was borne by the English-born film actress Elsa Lanchester (1902–86). Elsa Belton was a character in Angela Thirkell's once widely read *Barsetshire Chronicles*. The name is now also associated with the lioness named Elsa featured in the book *Born Free*, by Joy Adamson, which was made into a film.

Elsdon ♂
Mainly U.S.: transferred use of the surname, in origin a local name from a place in Northumbria. The placename is recorded in the 13th century in the forms *Eledene*, *Hellesden*, *Elisden*, and *Ellesden*; it is probably named as 'Elli's valley' (Old English *denu*)'.

Elsie ♀
Scottish simplified form of *Elspie*, a pet form of ◊**Elspeth**. This came to be used as an independent name, and in the early 20th century proved more popular than *Elspeth*.

Elspeth ♀
Scottish contracted form of ◊**Elizabeth**.

Elton ♂
Transferred use of the surname, in origin a local name from any of numerous places in England so called (mostly from the Old English masculine personal name *Ella* + Old English *tūn* 'enclosure', 'settlement'). In England it is largely associated with the singer-songwriter Elton John; born Reginald Dwight, he adopted the given name by which he is famous in honour of the saxophonist Elton Dean.

Eluned ♀
Welsh: apparently a revival of the older Welsh name *Luned*, *Lunet*. *Lunete* is the form of the name used by the French writer Chrétien de Troyes. Cf. ◊**Lynette**.

Elvira ♀
Spanish name of Germanic

(Visigothic) origin, very common in the Middle Ages and enjoying a minor revival today. The original form and meaning of the elements of which it is composed are uncertain (probably *ali* 'other', 'foreign' + *wēr* 'true'). The name was not used in the English-speaking world until the 19th century, when it was made familiar as the name of the long-suffering wife of Don Juan, both in Mozart's opera *Don Giovanni* (1789) and Byron's satirical epic poem *Don Juan* (1819–24). It is the name of the heroine of the Swedish film *Elvira Madigan* (1967), directed by Bo Widerberg, a romantic tragedy about a pair of lovers who would rather die than be separated.

Elvis ♂
Of obscure derivation, made famous by the American rock singer Elvis Presley (1935–77). It may be a transferred use of a surname, or it may have been made up, but it was certainly not chosen for the singer in anticipation of a career in show business, for his father's name was Vernon Elvis Presley. A shadowy Irish St Elvis, of the 6th century, is also known as *Elwyn*, *Elwin*, *Elian*, and *Allan*.

Elwyn ♂
Welsh and Irish: of uncertain origin. In the modern Welsh name the influence of the word *(g)wyn* 'white', 'fair', 'blessed', 'holy' is apparent (see ◊**Delwyn**). However, this is also one of the forms used for the name of a 6th-century Irish saint; it may be no more than a variant of ◊**Alan**.

Elyse ♀
Altered spelling of ◊**Élise**.

Emanuel ♂
See ◊**Emmanuel**.

Emer ♀
Irish Gaelic: traditional name of uncertain derivation. This was the name of Cú Chulainn's beloved, a woman of many talents who was blessed with the gifts of beauty, voice, sweet speech, needlework, wisdom, and chastity. It has been revived as a given name in the 20th century. It is familiar in Scotland in the spelling *Eimhir* through the 'Poems to Eimhir' of Sorley MacLean (b. 1911).

Emerald ♀
From the name of the gemstone, representing a vernacular form of ◊**Esmeralda**.

Emily ♀
From a medieval form of the Latin name *Aemilia*, the feminine version of the old Roman family name *Aemilius* (probably from *aemulus* 'rival'). It was not common in the Middle Ages, but was revived in the 19th century and is very popular today. Its best-known 19th century bearer was probably the novelist and poet Emily Brontë (1818–48).

Emlyn ♂
Welsh: of uncertain origin, possibly from Latin *Aemiliānus* (a derivative of the old Roman family name *Aemilius*; see ◊**Emily**). On the other hand, it may have a Celtic origin; there are Breton and Irish saints recorded as *Aemilianus*, which may be a Latinized form of a lost Celtic name.

Emma ♀
Old French name, of Germanic (Frankish) origin, originally a short form of compound names such as ◊**Ermintrude**, containing the word *erm(en)*, *irm(en)* 'entire'. It was adopted by the Normans and introduced by them to Britain, but its popularity in medieval England was greatly enhanced by the fact that it had been borne by the mother of Edward the Confessor, herself a Norman.

Emmanuel ♂
Biblical name (meaning 'God is with us' in Hebrew) used for the promised Messiah, as prophesied by Isaiah (7:14; referred to in Matthew 1:23). The

Authorized Version of the Bible uses the Hebrew form *Immanuel* in the Old Testament, *Emmanuel* in the New.
Variant: **Emmanuel**.

Emmarald ♀
Variant of ◊**Emerald**, influenced by the given name ◊**Emma**.

Emmeline ♀
Old French name of Germanic (Frankish) origin, introduced to Britain by the Normans. In origin it seems to have been a derivative of ◊**Emma**, but when it was revived in the 19th century there was some confusion with ◊**Emily**. A famous bearer was the suffragette Emmeline Pankhurst (1858–1928), mother of Christabel and Sylvia.

Emmet ♂
Transferred use of the surname, itself derived from the medieval female given name *Emmet*, a diminutive form of ◊**Emma**. It may sometimes be used by parents with Irish connections, in honour of the rebel Robert Emmet (1778–1803), who led a disastrous attempt at rebellion against the English.
Variant: **Emmett**

Emmy ♀
Pet form of ◊**Emma**, ◊**Emily**, and related names. It is sometimes found in the southern United States in combinations such as **Emmy Jane** and **Emmy Sue**.

Emrys ♂
Welsh form of ◊**Ambrose**, very common in families of Welsh origin in the 20th century.

Emyr ♂
Welsh: originally a byname meaning 'ruler, king, lord'. The name was borne by a 6th-century Breton saint who settled in Cornwall.

Ena ♀
One of several Anglicized forms of the Gaelic name ◊**Eithne**. In the case of Queen Victoria's granddaughter Princess Ena (Victoria Eugénie Julia Ena, 1887–1969) it had a different origin: it was a misreading by the minister who baptized her of a handwritten note of the originally intended name ◊**Eva**. In England, the name is remembered principally as that of the fearsome Ena Sharples in the television soap opera *Coronation Street*.

Enfys ♀
Welsh: modern name, taken from the vocabulary word meaning 'rainbow'.

Enid ♀
Celtic name of uncertain derivation, borne by a virtuous character in the Arthurian romances, the long-suffering wife of Geraint. The name was revived in the second half of the 19th century, following Tennyson's *Idylls of the King* (1859), which contains the story of Geraint and Enid, in which Enid recovers her husband's trust by patience and loyalty after he has suspected her, wrongly, of infidelity.

Enoch ♂
Biblical name (possibly meaning 'experienced' in Hebrew), borne by the son of Cain (Genesis 4:16–22) and father of Methuselah (Genesis 5:18–24). The latter is said to have lived for 365 years. The apocryphal 'Books of Enoch' are attributed to him.

Enola ♀
20th-century coinage of uncertain derivation. One theory is that it originated as a reversal in spelling of the word *alone*, but this may be no more than coincidental.

Enos ♂
Biblical name (meaning 'mankind' in Hebrew), borne by a son of Seth and grandson of Adam (Genesis 4:26), who allegedly lived for 905 years.

Ephraim ♂
Biblical name, borne by one of the sons of Joseph and hence one of the

tribes of Israel. The name probably
means 'fruitful' in Hebrew; it is so
explained in the Bible (Genesis 41:52
'and the name of the second called he
Ephraim: For God hath caused me to
be fruitful in the land of my
affliction'). Unlike many Old
Testament names, this was not
particularly popular with the Puritans,
and was used more in the 18th and
19th centuries than the 17th. It is still
a common Jewish given name.

Erasmus ♂
Latinized form of Greek *Erasmos*, a
derivative of *erān* 'to love'. St Erasmus
(d. 303) was a bishop of Formiae in
Campania, martyred under Diocletian;
he is numbered among the Fourteen
Holy Helpers and is a patron of
sailors. This is a fairly rare given
name in the English-speaking world. It
is sometimes bestowed in honour of
the great Dutch humanist scholar and
teacher Erasmus Rotterodamus
(?1466–1536).

Eric ♂
Of Old Norse origin, from *ei* 'ever',
'always' (or *einn* 'one', 'alone') + *ríkr*
'ruler'. It was introduced into Britain
by Scandinavian settlers before the
Norman Conquest. As a modern given
name, it was revived in the mid-19th
century and has remained in use
since.

Erica ♀
Latinate feminine form of ◊**Eric**,
coined towards the end of the 18th
century. It has also been reinforced by
the fact that *erica* is the Latin word
for 'heather'.

Erin ♀
From Irish Gaelic *Éirinn*, dative case
of *Éire* 'Ireland'. *Erin* has been used as
a poetic name for Ireland for centuries,
and in recent years this has become a
popular given name, especially in
North America, even among people
with no Irish ancestry.

Erla ♂
Variant spelling of ◊**Earla**.

Erle ♀
Variant spelling of ◊**Earl**.

Ermintrude ♀
Of Germanic origin, adopted from Old
French by the Normans and
introduced by them to Britain. It is
derived from *erm(en)*, *irm(en)* 'entire'
+ *traut* 'beloved'. It did not survive
long into the Middle Ages, but was
occasionally revived in the 18th and
19th centuries. It is now completely
out of fashion.

Ern ♂
Short form of ◊**Ernest**.
Pet form: **Ernie**.

Erna ♀
Simplified version of *Ernesta*, created
as a feminine form of ◊**Ernest**.

Ernan ♂
Irish: Anglicized form of the Gaelic
name *Earnán*, possibly a derivative of
iarn 'iron'. St Earnán is the patron
saint of Tory Island.

Ernest ♂
Of Germanic origin, derived from the
Old High German vocabulary word
eornost 'serious business', 'battle to
the death'. The name was introduced
into England in the 18th century by
followers of the Elector of Hanover,
who became George I of England. A
variant spelling, **Earnest**, has arisen by
association with the modern English
adjective *earnest*, which is, however,
only distantly connected with the
name.
Short form: **Ern**.
Pet form: **Ernie**.

Ernestine ♀
Elaborated feminine form of ◊**Ernest**,
created in the 19th century.

Errol ♂
Transferred use of the Scottish
surname, which derives from a
placename. It has been made famous

by the film actor Errol Flynn (1909–59), noted for his 'swashbuckling' roles. He was born in Australia, but spent most of his career in Hollywood. It is now very popular as a Black name, influenced by such figures as the jazz pianist Erroll Garner.
Variant: **Erroll**.

Erskine ♂

Transferred use of the Scottish surname, which derives from the name of a place near Glasgow. The surname has also been taken to Ireland by Scottish settlers, and was first brought to public attention as a given name by the half-Irish writer and political activist Erskine Childers (1870–1922).

Esmeralda ♀

From the Spanish vocabulary word *esmeralda* 'emerald'. Its occasional modern use as a given name dates from Victor Hugo's *Notre Dame de Paris* (1831), in which it is the nickname of the gypsy girl loved by the hunchback Quasimodo; she was given the name because she wore an amulet containing an artificial emerald.
Variant: **Esmerelda**.

Esmond ♂

From an Old English personal name derived from *ēast* 'grace', 'beauty' + *mund* 'protection'. A Norman French form is found, reflecting a Continental Germanic original. However, it was not used in Britain as a given name between the 14th century and the late 19th century, when it was revived.

Esta ♀

Latinate respelling of ◊**Esther**.

Estelle ♀

Old French name meaning 'star' (Latin ◊**Stella**), comparatively rarely used during the Middle Ages. It was revived in the 19th century, together with the Latinate form **Estella**, which was used by Dickens for the ward of Miss Havisham in *Great Expectations* (1861).

Esther ♀

Biblical name, borne in the Bible by a Jewish captive who became the wife of the Persian king Ahasuerus. According to the book of the Bible that bears her name, she managed, by her perception and persuasion, to save large numbers of the Jews from the evil machinations of the royal counsellor Haman. Her Hebrew name was *Hadassah* 'myrtle', and the form *Esther* is said to be a Persian translation of this, although others derive it from Persian *stara* 'star'. It may also be a Hebrew form of the name of the Persian goddess *Ishtar*.

Ethan ♂

Biblical name (meaning 'firmness' or 'long-lived' in Hebrew) of an obscure figure, Ethan the Ezrahite, mentioned as a wise man whom Solomon surpassed in wisdom (1 Kings 4:31). The name was sparingly used even among the Puritans, but became famous in the United States since it was borne by Ethan Allen (1738–89), leader of the 'Green Mountain Boys', a group of Vermont patriots who fought in the American Revolution.

Ethel ♀

19th-century revival of an Old English name, a short form of various female personal names containing *ethel* 'noble' as a first element, for example ◊**Etheldreda**. The name enjoyed great popularity for a period at the beginning of the 20th century. It is at present out of fashion.

Etheldreda ♀

Latinized form of the Old English female personal name *Æðelþryð* (see ◊**Audrey**). It was taken up as a given name in the 19th century, but is now rare.

Ethna ♀

Irish: Anglicized form of ◊**Eithne**.
Variant: **Etna**.

Etta ♀
Short form of the various names such as *Rosetta* and *Henrietta* ending in this element, originally an Italian feminine diminutive suffix.

Euan ♂
Scottish: Anglicized form of Gaelic *Eóghan*, currently much in fashion. *Eóghan* is a name of great antiquity and disputed derivation: it has been suggested that it may be composed of Old Celtic words meaning 'yew' and 'born', i.e. 'born of the yew'.

Eudora ♀
Ostensibly a Greek name, from *eu* 'well', 'good' + a derivative of *dōron* 'gift'. However, there is no saint of this name, and it is more probably a 19th-century learned coinage, made up of elements which are common in other given names.

Eugene ♂
From the Old French form of the Greek name *Eugenios* (from *eugenēs* 'well-born', 'noble'). This name was borne by various early saints, notably a 5th-century bishop of Carthage, a 7th-century bishop of Toledo, and four popes.
Short form: **Gene**.

Eugenia ♀
Feminine form of Greek *Eugenios* or Latin *Eugenius*; see ◊**Eugene**.

Eugénie ♀
French form of ◊**Eugenia**. The name was introduced to England as the name of the Empress Eugénie (Eugenia María de Montijo de Guzmán, 1826–1920), wife of Napoleon III, and has since been occasionally used (sometimes without the accent) in the English-speaking world.

Euna ♀
Scottish: Anglicized form of the Gaelic name *Ùna* (see ◊**Úna**).

Eunan ♂
Irish and Scottish: Anglicized form of the Gaelic name *Ádhamhnán*, traditionally said to be a diminutive form of *Ádhamh*, the Gaelic version of ◊**Adam**. However, it is more likely to be a diminutive of *adomnae* 'great fear', i.e. 'little horror'. The name was borne by a 7th-century saint, abbot of Iona and biographer of St Columba.

Eunice ♀
From a Late Greek name, derived from *eu* 'well', 'good' + *nikē* 'victory'. This is mentioned in the New Testament as the name of the mother of Timothy, who introduced him to Christianity (2 Timothy 1:5). This reference led to the name being taken up by the Puritans in the 17th century.

Euphemia ♀
Latin form of a Late Greek name derived from *eu* 'well', 'good' + *phēnai* 'to speak'. This was the name of various early saints, notably a virgin martyr said to have been burnt at the stake at Chalcedon in 307. It was particularly popular in England in the Victorian period, especially in the pet form ◊**Effie**.

Eustace ♂
From the Old French form of the Late Greek names *Eustakhios* and *Eustathios*. These were evidently of separate origin, the former derived from *eu* 'well', 'good' + *stakhys* 'grapes', the latter from *eu* + *stēnai* 'to stand'. However, the tradition is very confused. The name was introduced in this form to Britain by the Normans, among whom it was popular as a result of the fame of St Eustace, who was said to have been converted to Christianity by the vision of a crucifix between the antlers of the stag he was hunting.

Eva ♀
Latinate form of ◊**Eve**.

Evadne ♀
From a Greek personal name derived
from *eu* 'well', 'good' + another
element, of uncertain meaning. The
name was borne by a minor figure in
classical legend, who threw herself on
to the funeral pyre of her husband,
and was therefore regarded as an
example of wifely piety. The modern
spelling and pronunciation are the
result of transmission through Latin
sources. The name has never been
common. It is associated with the
character of Dr Evadne Hinge in the
British comedy television series *Hinge
and Bracket*.

Evan ♂
As a Welsh name this represents an
Anglicized form of *Iefan*, a later
development of ◊**Ieuan**. As a Scottish
name it is a variant of ◊**Euan**.

Evander ♂
Classical name used in the Scottish
Highlands as an Anglicized form of
Gaelic *Ìomhair* (see ◊**Ivor**). In classical
legend, *Evander* is the name of an
Arcadian hero who founded a city in
Italy where Rome was later built. It is
a Latin form of Greek *Euandros*,
derived from *eu* 'good' + *anēr* 'man'
(genitive *andros*).

Evangeline ♀
Fanciful name derived from Latin
evangelium 'gospel' (Greek
euangelion, from *eu* 'good' + *angelma*
'tidings') + the suffix *-ine* (in origin a
French feminine diminutive).
Evangeline is the title of a narrative
poem (1848) by the American poet
Henry Wadsworth Longfellow, in
which the central character is called
Evangeline Bellefontaine.

Eve ♀
English vernacular form of the name
borne in the Bible by the first woman,
created from one of Adam's ribs
(Genesis 2:22). It derives, via Latin
Ēva, from Hebrew *Havva*, which is
considered to be a variant of the

vocabulary word *hayya* 'living' or
'animal'. Adam gave names to all the
animals (Genesis 2:19–20) and then to
his wife, who was 'the mother of all
living' (Genesis 3:20).
Pet form: **Evie**.

Evelina ♀
Latinate form of the female name
◊**Evelyn**, or combination of ◊**Eve** with
the suffix *-lina*.

Evelyn ♂ ♀
Modern use of this as both a male and
a female given name derives from a
transferred use of an English surname,
from the Norman female name
Aveline, an elaborated form of ◊**Ava**.
Variants: **Evelyne**, **Eveline** ♀

Everard ♂
From an Old English personal name
derived from *eofor* 'boar' + *heard*
'hardy', 'brave', 'strong'. This was
reinforced at the time of the Norman
Conquest by a Continental Germanic
cognate introduced by the Normans.
The modern given name may be a
transferred use of the surname, but it
was in regular use in the Digby family
of Rutland from the 15th to the 17th
centuries, probably as a survival of the
Norman name. It alternated in this
family with ◊**Kenelm**.

Everett ♂
Transferred use of the surname, a
variant of ◊**Everard**.

Evette ♀
Altered form of ◊**Yvette**, influenced by
◊**Eve**.

Evie ♀
Pet form of ◊**Eve** or ◊**Eva**, occasionally
also of ◊**Evelyn** as a female name.

Evonne ♀
Altered form of ◊**Yvonne**, influenced
by ◊**Eve**.

Ewan ♂
The usual Anglicized form in Scotland
of Gaelic *Eóghan* (see ◊**Euan**).
Variant: **Ewen**.

Ewart ♂
Transferred use of the Scottish
surname, probably first used as a given
name in honour of the Victorian
statesman William Ewart Gladstone
(1809–98). The surname has several
possible origins: it may represent a
Norman form of ◊**Edward**, an

occupational name for a ewe-herd, or a
local name from a place in
Northumbria.

Ezekiel ♂
Biblical name (meaning 'God
strengthens' in Hebrew), borne by
one of the major prophets. The book
of the Bible that bears his name is
known for its vision of a field of dry
bones, which Ezekiel prophesies
will live again (chapter 37). His
prophecies were addressed to the
Jews in Babylonian exile, after
Nebuchadnezzar had seized Jerusalem
in 597 BC.
Short form: **Zeke**.

Fabia ♀

Latin feminine form of the old Roman family name *Fabius*, said to be a derivative of *faba* 'bean'.

Fabian ♂

From the Late Latin name *Fabiānus*, a derivative of the old Roman family name *Fabius* (see ◊**Fabia**). It was borne by an early pope (236–50), who was martyred under the Emperor Decius. The name was introduced into Britain by the Normans, but it has never been much used in the English-speaking world.

Fabiola ♀

Late Latin feminine diminutive form of the old Roman family name *Fabius* (see ◊**Fabia**). St Fabiola (d. *c.*400) was a Roman widow who founded the first Western hospital, originally a hostel to accommodate the flood of pilgrims who flocked to Rome, in which she tended the sick as well as accommodating the healthy.

Fae ♀

Variant spelling of ◊**Fay**.

Faith ♀

From the abstract noun denoting the quality of believing and trusting in God. The name began to be used in the 16th century, and was very popular among the Puritans of the 17th.

Fanny ♀

Pet form of ◊**Frances**, very popular in the 18th and 19th centuries, but now much rarer.

Fay ♀

Late 19th century coinage, from the archaic word *fay* 'fairy'. It was to some extent influenced by the revival of interest in Arthurian legend, in which Morgan le Fay is King Arthur's half-sister, a mysterious sorceress who both attempts to destroy Arthur and tends his wounds in Avalon after his last battle. She is sometimes identified with the 'Lady of the Lake'. Between the wars the name came to prominence as that of the British actress Fay Compton (1894–1979).
Variants: ◊**Faye**, **Fae**.

Faye ♀

Variant of ◊**Fay**, associated particularly with the American actress Faye Dunaway (b. 1941).

Felicia ♀

Latinate feminine form of ◊**Felix**, of medieval origin.

Felicity ♀

From the abstract noun denoting luck or good fortune (via Old French from Latin *felicitās*; cf. ◊**Felix**). The English vocabulary word was first used as a given name in the 17th century. It also represents the English form of the Late Latin personal name *Felicitas*, which was borne by several early saints, notably a slave who was martyred in 203 together with her mistress Perpetua and several other companions.
Pet form: **Flick**.

Felix ♂

Latin name meaning 'lucky', which has from time to time been popular as a given name in Britain and elsewhere because of its auspicious omen. It was in use as a byname in Latin, being applied for example to the dictator Sulla (138–78 BC). It was very popular among the early Christians, being borne by a large number of early saints.

Fenella ♀
Scottish: Anglicized form of the old Gaelic name *Fionnghuala* (see ◊**Fionnuala**).
Variants: **Finella, Fi(o)nola**.

Fenn ♂
Mainly U.S.: transferred use of the surname, in origin a local name for someone who lived in a low-lying marshy area, from Old English *fenn* 'marsh', 'fen'. It is also found as a short form of ◊**Fenton**.

Fenton ♂
Transferred use of the surname, in origin a local name from any of the various places (for example, in Cumbria, Lincs., Northumbria, Notts., Staffs., and W. Yorks.) so called from Old English *fenn* 'marsh', 'fen' + *tūn* 'enclosure', 'settlement'.

Ferdinand ♂
From a Spanish name, originally *Ferdinando* (now *Hernán*), which is of Germanic (Visigothic) origin, derived from *farð* 'journey' (or possibly an altered form of *frið* 'peace') + *nand* 'ready', 'prepared'. This was a traditional name in the royal families of Spain from an early date. It appeared in Britain in the 16th century, having been introduced by Roman Catholic supporters of Queen Mary I, who married Philip II of Spain in 1554.
Pet form: **Ferdi**.

Fergal ♂
Irish: Anglicized form of the Gaelic name *Fearghal*, derived from *fear* 'man' + *gal* 'valour'.

Fergus ♂
Scottish and Irish: Anglicized form of the Gaelic name *Fearghas*, derived from *fear* 'man' + *gus* 'vigour'. This was the name of a shadowy hero in Irish mythology, also of the grandfather of St Columba. It is still used mainly in Scotland and Ireland and by those who remain conscious of their Gaelic ancestry.
Pet form: **Fergie**.

Fern ♀
From the vocabulary word denoting the plant (Old English *fearn*). Use of this word as a given name is of comparatively recent origin: it is one of several words denoting flowers and plants that have been pressed into service during the past hundred years. Its popularity is steadily increasing.

Fife ♂
Transferred use of the Scottish surname, which originated in the Middle Ages as a local name for someone from the Kingdom (now region) of Fife. In Gaelic legend this is said to get its name from the legendary Pictish hero *Fib*, one of the seven sons of Cruithne.
Variant: **Fyfe**.

Fifi ♀
French nursery form of ◊**Joséphine**. In the English-speaking world it now has definite connotations of frivolity.

Finbar ♂
Irish: Anglicized form of the Gaelic name *Fionnb(h)arr*, derived from *fionn* 'white', 'fair' + *barr* 'head'. This was the name of at least three early Irish saints, one of whom became the first bishop of Cork in the 6th century. He is the subject of many legends, for example that he crossed the Irish Sea on horseback. The Isle of Barra in Scotland is said to be named after him.

Finella ♀
Scottish: variant of ◊**Fenella**.

Fingal ♂

Scottish: Anglicized form of the Gaelic name *Fionnghall*, derived from *fionn* 'white', 'fair' + *gall* 'stranger'. It was originally a byname applied to Norse settlers (cf. ◊**Dougal**), and was used by James Macpherson (1736–96), author of the Ossianic poems, to render the name of the Gaelic hero *Fionn mac Cumhaill* (see ◊**Finn**).

Variant: **Fingall**.

Finlay ♂

Scottish: Anglicized form of the Gaelic name *Fionnlagh*, derived from *fionn* 'white', 'fair' + *laogh* 'warrior' or 'calf'.

Variant: **Finley**.

Finn ♂

Irish: traditional Gaelic name meaning 'white', 'fair' (the modern Gaelic form is **Fionn**). The mythological Irish hero Finn MacCool (*Finn mac Cumaill* in early Irish) was noted for his wisdom and fairness. He was leader of the Fenians or *Fianna*, a band of warriors about whom many stories are told. There may be a basis of fact behind the legends, in that Finn may be identified with an early Irish leader who defended Ireland against Norse raiders.

Finnian ♂

Irish: Anglicized form of Gaelic *Finnén*, a derivative of Old Irish *finn* 'white', 'fair'. This name was borne by two 6th-century Irish bishops.

Variant: **Finian**.

Finola ♀

Irish and Scottish: Anglicized form of ◊**Fionnuala**.

Fiona ♀

Scottish: Latinate derivative of the Gaelic word *fionn* 'white', 'fair'. It was first used by James Macpherson (1736–96), author of the Ossianic poems, which were supposedly translations from ancient Gaelic. It was subsequently used as a pen-name by William Sharp (1855–1905), who produced many romantic works under the name of Fiona Macleod. It has since become popular throughout the English-speaking world.

Fionnuala ♀

Irish Gaelic name, pronounced 'fyun-noo-a-la': the modern form of *Fionnguala*, a traditional name derived from *fionn* 'white', 'fair' + *guala* 'shoulder'.

Short form: **Nuala**.

Fionola ♀

Scottish: variant of ◊**Finella** and ◊**Finola**. In the English-speaking world it is now sometimes taken as an elaboration of ◊**Fiona**.

Flann ♂

Irish Gaelic: from a nickname meaning 'red' or 'ruddy'.

Flannan ♂

Irish: Anglicized form of the Gaelic name *Flannán*, originally a diminutive of Gaelic *flann* 'red', 'ruddy'. St Flannan is the patron of the diocese of Killaloe in Co. Clare, and this is still a popular given name in that area.

Flavia ♀

Feminine form of the old Roman family name *Flāvius* (from *flāvus* 'yellow(-haired)'). This was the name of at least five minor early saints.

Fletcher ♂

Transferred use of the surname, in origin an occupational name for a maker of arrows, from Old French *flech(i)er*, an agent derivative of *fleche* (of Germanic origin). An early bearer of this as a given name was Fletcher Christian, leader of the mutiny on the *Bounty* in 1789.

Fleur ♀

From an Old French name meaning 'flower', occasionally used in the Middle Ages. Modern use, however, seems to derive mainly from the character of this name in John Galsworthy's *The Forsyte Saga* (1922).

Flick ♀
Informal pet form based on ◊**Felicity**.

Flo ♀
Short form of ◊**Florence** and ◊**Flora**, common in the early part of the 20th century, but now widely considered somewhat old-fashioned.

Floella ♀
Recent coinage, in Britain especially popular as a Black name. It is evidently a compound of ◊**Flo** and ◊**Ella**.

Flora ♀
Name borne in Roman mythology by the goddess of flowers and the spring (a derivative of Latin *flōs* 'flower', genitive *flōris*). It is also the feminine form of the old Roman family name *Flōrus*, likewise derived from *flōs*. *Flora* was little used in England before the 18th century, when it was imported from Scotland. In 1746 Flora Macdonald (1722–90), daughter of Ranald Macdonald of Milton in South Uist, helped Bonnie Prince Charlie to escape from there to the Island of Skye, disguised as a woman, after his defeat at Culloden. In fact, *Flora* was merely an Anglicized form of her Gaelic name, *Fionnaghal*, a variant of *Fionnghuala* (see ◊**Fenella**). However, her fame made the name *Flora* popular in the Highlands and elsewhere.
Short form: **Flo**.
Pet form: Scottish: **Florrie** (Gaelic *Flòraidh*).

Florence ♀, formerly also ♂
Medieval form of the Latin masculine name *Florentius* (a derivative of *florens* blossoming, flourishing) and its feminine form *Florentia*. In the Middle Ages the name was commonly borne by men (as, for example, the historian Florence of Worcester), but it is now exclusively a female name. This was revived in the second half of the 19th century, being given in honour of Florence Nightingale (1820–1910), the founder of modern

nursing, who organized a group of nurses to serve in the Crimean War. She herself received the name because she was born in the Italian city of Florence (Latin *Florentia*, Italian *Firenze*).
Short form: **Flo**.
Pet form: **Flossie**.

Florrie ♀
Scottish pet form of ◊**Flora**, now little used except in the Highlands.

Flossie ♀
Pet form from a contraction of ◊**Florence**, common in the 19th century, but no longer much used. The popularity of the name was perhaps enhanced by association with the soft downy material known as *floss*.

Flower ♀
From the vocabulary word (from Old French; cf. ◊**Fleur**), which is also sometimes used as a term of endearment.

Floyd ♂
Transferred use of the Welsh surname, in origin a variant of ◊**Lloyd**. This form of the name results from an attempt to represent the sound of the Welsh initial *Ll-* using traditional English pronunciation and orthography. In the 20th century it has been particularly common in the southern United States.

Forbes ♂
Transferred use of the Scottish surname, in origin a local name from the lands of Forbes in Aberdeenshire. These are named from the Gaelic word *forba* 'field', 'district' + the locative suffix *-ais*. In Scotland this name was traditionally pronounced in two syllables, but a monosyllabic pronunciation is now the norm.

Ford ♂
Transferred use of the common surname, in origin a local name for someone who lived near a place where

a river could be crossed by wading through it (Old English *ford*).

Forrest ♂

Transferred use of the surname, in origin a local name for someone who lived in or by an enclosed wood, Old French *forest*.
Variant: **Forest**. Cf. ◊**Deforest**.

Foster ♂

Transferred use of the surname, an occupational name with at least four possible derivations: from Middle English *foster* 'foster parent', *for(e)ster* 'forester', *fors(e)ter* 'shearer', or *fu(y)ster* 'saddle-tree maker'.

Fran ♀♂

Short form of ◊**Frances**, or less commonly of ◊**Francis**.

France ♂♀

Mainly U.S.: short form of ◊**Francis** or ◊**Frances** or bestowed with reference to the country.

Francene ♀

Variant spelling of ◊**Francine**.
Variant: **Franceen**.

Frances ♀

Feminine form of ◊**Francis**. In the 16th century the two spellings were used indiscriminately for both sexes, the distinction in spelling not being established until the 17th century.
Short form: **Fran**.
Pet form: **Fanny**.

Francesca ♀

Italian form of ◊**Frances**. Originally a vocabulary word meaning 'French', it was bestowed from the 13th century onwards in honour of St Francis of Assisi. It has also been used independently as an English name. Its most famous bearer was Francesca di Rimini, daughter of Giovanni da Polenta, Count of Ravenna. A legendary beauty, she was betrothed by her father to the misshapen Giovanni Malatesta, Lord of Rimini, in return for military support. Malatesta's good-looking younger

brother, Paolo, acted as his proxy in the betrothal, but Francesca and he fell in love. They were discovered, and put to death by Malatesta in 1289. Their tragedy is enshrined in the Fifth Canto of Dante's *Inferno*, as well as in several other works of literature and in a symphonic fantasy by Tchaikovsky.

Francine ♀

From a French diminutive pet form of *Françoise*, the French form of ◊**Frances**.
Variants: **Francene**, **Franceen**.

Francis ♂

English form of Italian *Francesco*, originally a vocabulary word meaning 'French' or 'Frenchman' (Late Latin *Franciscus*; cf. ◊**Frank**). This was a nickname given to St Francis of Assisi (1181–1226) because of his wealthy father's business connections with France. His baptismal name was *Giovanni*, the Italian form of *John*. He had a pleasant, ordinary life as a child and young man, but after two serious illnesses, a period of military service, and a year as a prisoner of war in Perugia, he turned from the world and devoted himself to caring for the poor and sick. He was joined by groups of disciples, calling themselves 'minor friars' (*friari minores*). The main features of the Franciscan rule are humility, poverty, and love for all living creatures. The given name was introduced into England in the early 16th century, when there was a surge of admiration for, and imitation of, Italian Renaissance culture.
Short forms: ◊**Frank**, **Fran**, **France**.

Frank ♂

Of Germanic origin. The name referred originally to a member of the tribe of the Franks, who are said to have got the name from a characteristic type of spear that they used. When the Franks migrated into Gaul in the 4th century, the country received its modern name of France

(Late Latin *Francia*) and the tribal term Frank came to mean 'Frenchman'. The name is now quite often taken as a short form of ◊**Francis**.

Frankie ♂ ♀
Pet form of ◊**Frank**, also sometimes of ◊**Frances**, ◊**Francesca**, or ◊**Francine**. As a female name, it is perhaps most familiar as the name of the heroine of *The Ballad of Frankie and Johnny*.

Franklin ♂
Transferred use of the surname, derived from Middle English *frankeleyn* 'freeman', denoting a member of a class of men who were not of noble birth but who were nevertheless freeholders. The vocabulary word is derived from Old French *franc*, meaning both 'free' and 'Frankish'. The connection between freemen and Franks is reflected in the Late Latin term *francālia*, originally denoting lands held by Franks, which came to mean lands not subject to taxes. The given name is now quite common, especially in the United States, where it is often bestowed in honour of the statesman and scientist Benjamin Franklin (1706–90). A more recent influence was President Franklin D. Roosevelt (1882–1945).

Fraser ♂
Scottish: transferred use of the surname of a leading Scottish family. The surname is of Norman origin, but its exact derivation is uncertain. The earliest forms recorded are *de Frisselle* and *de Fresel(iere)*, but it was altered, possibly by association with Old French *fraise* 'strawberry'.
Variants: **Frazer**, **Frazier**.

Fred ♂
Short form of ◊**Frederick** or, occasionally, of ◊**Alfred**.
Pet forms: **Freddie**, **Freddy**.

Freda ♀
Short form of various names such as

◊**Elfreda** and ◊**Winifred**, also occasionally of ◊**Frederica**.
Pet form: **Freddie**.

Freddie ♂ ♀
Pet form of ◊**Fred** and ◊**Freda**.
Variant: **Freddy** (mostly ♂)

Frederica ♀
Latinate feminine form of ◊**Frederick**.
Short forms: **Freda**.

Frederick ♂
From an Old French name of Germanic origin, from *fred*, *frid* 'peace' + *rīc* 'power', 'ruler'. It was adopted by the Normans and introduced into Britain by them, but did not survive long. Modern use in Britain dates from its reintroduction in the 18th century by followers of the Elector of Hanover, who in 1714 became George I of England. It was reinforced by the vogue for Germanic names in Victorian times.
Variants: **Frederic**, **Fredric**.
Short form: **Fred**.
Pet forms: **Freddy**, **Freddie**.

Freya ♀
Scottish: of Old Norse origin. *Freya* or *Fröja* was the goddess of love in Scandinavian mythology, and her name seems to be derived from a cognate of Old High German *frouwa* 'lady', 'mistress'. The name has for long been a traditional one in Shetland, and it is still used in Scotland. A notable modern bearer is the explorer and writer Freya Stark.

Fulk ♂
Of Germanic origin, introduced to Britain by the Normans. The name originally represented a short form of various compound names containing the word *volk* 'people, tribe' (cf. modern English *folk*). It has gradually died out of general use, but is still used in certain families, such as the Grevilles. Fulke Greville, 1st Baron Brooke, was a leading figure at the

court of Elizabeth I.
Variant: **Fulke**.

Fulton ♂

Transferred use of the Scottish surname, which seems to have been originally a local name from a lost place in Ayrshire. Robert Fulton (1765–1815) was the American engineer who designed the first commercially successful steamboat.

Fulvia ♀

From the feminine form of the old Roman family name *Fulvius*, a derivative of Latin *fulvus* 'dusky', 'tawny' (ultimately akin to *flāvus*; cf. ♀**Flavia**). The name does not seem to have been much used among early Christians, and there are no saints Fulvia or Fulvius. In classical times its most famous bearer was the wife of Mark Antony, who opposed Octavian by force on her husband's behalf while he was in Egypt.

Fyfe ♂

Scottish: variant spelling of ♂**Fife**.

GABRIEL GABRIELA GABRIELLE GAE GAENO
R GAIL GALE GALEN GARETH GARFIELD GA
RRET GARRICK GARRISON GARRY GARTH
GARY GAVIN GAY GAYLE GAYLORD GAYNO
R GAZ GED GEMMA GENE GENETTE GENEV
A GENEVIEVE GEOFF GEOFFREY GEORDIE G

Gabriel ♂

Biblical name (meaning 'man of God' in Hebrew), borne by one of the archangels. Gabriel appeared to Daniel in the Old Testament (Daniel 8:16; 9:21), and in the New Testament to Zacharias (Luke 1:19; 26:27) and, most famously, to Mary to announce the impending birth of Christ (Luke 1:2). *Gabriel* has occasionally been used as a given name in the English-speaking world, mainly as a result of Continental European influence.

Gabriela ♀

Latinate feminine form of ◊**Gabriel**.

Gabrielle ♀

French feminine form of ◊**Gabriel**.

Gae ♀

Variant spelling of ◊**Gay**.

Gaenor ♀

Welsh: apparently a form of ◊**Gaynor** adapted to Welsh orthography. It also may have been influenced by the name of the saint commemorated at *Llangeinwyr* in Glamorgan, known popularly as *Llangeinor*. Her name is derived from Welsh *cain* 'beautiful' + *(g)wyry(f)* 'maiden'.

Gail ♀

Shortened form of ◊**Abigail**. It is now very common as an independent given name, but was not found before the middle of the 20th century.
Variants: **Gale**, **Gayle**.

Gale ♀

Variant spelling of ◊**Gail**.

Galen ♂

From the name of the Graeco-Roman medical writer Claudius *Galēnus* (AD ?130–?200). His name represents a Latinized form of a Greek name derived from *galēnē* 'calm'.

Gareth ♂

Apparently of Celtic origin, but uncertain derivation. It first occurs in Malory's *Morte D'Arthur* as the name of the lover of Eluned, and seems to have been heavily altered from its original form, whatever that may have been (possibly the same as ◊**Geraint**). It is now very popular in Wales. ◊**Gary**, which is actually an independent name, is often taken to be a pet form of it.

Garfield ♂

Transferred use of the surname, in origin a local name for someone who lived near a triangular field, from Old English *gār* 'triangular piece of land' + *feld* 'open country'.

Garret ♂

Transferred use of the surname, which is derived from the given names ◊**Gerald** and ◊**Gerard**. In Ireland it often represents a direct Anglicization of *Gearóid*, the Gaelic form of ◊**Gerald**, and is the name of the former taoiseach, Garret Fitzgerald (b. 1926).
Variant: **Garrett**.

Garrick ♂

Mainly U.S.: transferred use of the surname, in some cases perhaps adopted in honour of the English actor-manager David Garrick (1717–79). He was of Huguenot descent, the grandson of a certain David *de la Garrique*. This is a

Languedoc placename, from *garrigue*, denoting a stretch of open limestone country.

Garrison ♂

Mainly U.S.: transferred use of the surname, originally a local name from *Garriston* in North Yorkshire or else a patronymic for the son of someone called ◊**Garret**. William Lloyd Garrison (1805–79) was a prominent American anti-slavery campaigner: the given name may originally have been bestowed in honour of him. It is now sometimes given to the sons of fathers who are called ◊**Gary** or ◊**Garry**.

Garry ♂

Variant spelling of ◊**Gary**, influenced by ◊**Barry**.

Garth ♂

Transferred use of a surname, but often taken to be a contracted form of ◊**Gareth**. As a surname it originated in the north of England, as a local name for someone who lived near an enclosure of some sort (Old Norse *garðr*). In modern times its popularity has been influenced by the virile superhero of this name, main character in a long-running strip cartoon in the *Daily Mirror* newspaper.

Gary ♂

Transferred use of a surname, which is probably derived from a Norman personal name of Continental Germanic origin, a short form of any of the various compound names with *gar* 'spear' as a first element. One bearer of this surname was the American industrialist Elbert Henry Gary (1846–1927), who gave his name to the steel town of Gary, Indiana (chartered in 1906). In this town was born the theatrical agent Nan Collins, who suggested *Gary* as a stage name for her client Frank J. Cooper, who thus became Gary Cooper (1901–61). His film career caused the name to become enormously popular from the

1930s to the present day. Its popularity has been maintained by the cricketer Gary Sobers (b. 1936; in his case it is in fact a pet form of *Garfield*) and the pop singer Gary Glitter (real name Paul Gadd). It is now often taken as a pet form of ◊**Gareth**.
Variant: **Garry**.
Pet form: **Gaz** (informal).

Gavin ♂

Of Celtic origin, but uncertain ultimate derivation; it first appears in French sources as *Gauvain*. The name is borne in the Arthurian romances by one of the knights of the Round Table (more familiar in English versions as Sir *Gawain*). It died out in the 16th century except in Scotland, whence it has been reintroduced in the past couple of decades. It is now widely popular in England, Wales, and elsewhere in the English-speaking world.

Gay ♀ ♂

From the vocabulary word meaning 'blithe', 'cheerful' (from Old French, of Germanic origin), chosen as a given name because of its well-omened meaning. It was not used before the 20th century, and has fallen out of favour again since the 1960s, as the vocabulary word *gay* has acquired the meaning 'homosexual'. It was generally a female name, but has also been borne by men. In Ireland it has been used as a pet form of ◊**Gabriel**.
Variants: **Gaye**, **Gae** ♀

Gayle ♀

Variant spelling of ◊**Gail**. Its popularity has no doubt been increased by the fame of the American film actress Gayle Hunnicutt (b. 1942).

Gaylord ♂

Transferred use of a surname, which is a form, altered by folk etymology, of the Old French nickname *Gaillard* 'dandy'. In the past it may have been chosen as a given name because parents liked the idea of their son's living as a fine lord, but it now seems likely to suffer the same fate as ◊**Gay**.

Gaynor ♀

Medieval form of the name of Arthur's queen, *Guinevere*, recently undergoing a strong revival in popularity.

Gaz ♂

Informal pet form of ◊**Gary**.
Variant: **Gazza**.

Ged ♂

Short form of ◊**Gerald** or ◊**Gerard**.

Gemma ♀

From a medieval Italian nickname meaning 'gem', 'jewel'. It has been chosen in modern times mainly because of its transparent etymology. Among Roman Catholics it is sometimes chosen in honour of St Gemma Galgani (1878–1903), who was the subject of many extraordinary signs of grace, such as ecstasies and the appearance of the stigmata.
Variant: **Jemma**.

Gene ♂ ♀

Short form of ◊**Eugene**, now quite commonly used as a male given name, especially in North America. It has been made familiar by film actors such as Gene Autry, Gene Hackman, Gene Kelly, and Gene Wilder. It is also occasionally used as a female name, in which case it represents a respelling of ◊**Jean**.

Genette ♀

Variant spelling of ◊**Jeannette**.

Geneva ♀

Of recent origin and uncertain derivation: possibly a variant of ◊**Jennifer**. In form it coincides with the name of the city in Switzerland (cf. ◊**Florence** and ◊**Venetia**). It may alternatively have been intended as a short form of ◊**Geneviève**.

Geneviève ♀

The name of the patron saint of Paris,

a 5th-century Gallo-Roman nun who encouraged the people of Paris in the face of the occupation of the town by the Franks and threatened attacks by the Huns. Her name is probably derived from Celtic words meaning 'people, tribe' and 'woman', but if so it has been heavily altered during its transmission through French sources. The name was introduced to Britain from France in the 19th century and is now in steady use, often without the accent.

Geoff ♂

Short form of ◊**Geoffrey**. See also ◊**Jeff**.

Geoffrey ♂

Of Germanic (Frankish and Lombard) origin, introduced to Britain by the Normans. It was in regular use among the counts of Anjou, ancestors of the English royal house of Plantagenet, who were descended from Geoffrey Plantagenet, Count of Anjou (1113–51). It was a particularly popular name in England and France in the later Middle Ages; notable bearers in England include the poet Geoffrey Chaucer (c.1340–1400) and in Wales the chronicler Geoffrey of Monmouth (d. 1155). The original form and meaning of the elements of which the name is composed are disputed. According to one theory, the name is merely a variant of ◊**Godfrey**; others derive the first part from the Germanic word *gawia* 'territory', *walah* 'stranger', or *gisil* 'pledge'. Medieval forms can be found to support all these theories, and it is possible that several names have fallen together, or that the name was subjected to reanalysis by folk etymology at an early date.
Variant: ◊**Jeffrey**.

Geordie ♂

Pet form of ◊**George**, still used in Scotland and the north of England. It is from this name that the generic term *Geordie* for a Tynesider derives.

George ♂

Via Old French and Latin, from Greek *Georgios* (a derivative of *geōrgos* 'farmer', from *gē* 'earth' + *ergein* 'to work'). This was the name of several early saints, including the shadowy figure who is now the patron of England (as well as of Germany and Portugal). Gibbon identified him with a Cappadocian leader of this name, but this cannot be right. If the saint existed at all, he was perhaps martyred in Palestine in the persecutions instigated by the Emperor Diocletian at the beginning of the 4th century. The popular legend in which the hero slays a dragon is a medieval Italian invention. He was for a long time a more important saint in the Orthodox Church than in the West, and the name was not much used in England during the Middle Ages, even after St George came to be regarded as the patron of England in the 14th century. The real impulse for its popularity was the accession of the first king of England of this name, who came from Germany in 1714 and brought many German retainers with him. It has been one of the most popular English male names ever since.

Pet forms: **Georgie**, **Geordie**.

Georgene ♀

Altered form of ◊**Georgine**, by association with the productive suffix *-ene*.

Georgette ♀

French feminine diminutive of *Georges*, the French form of ◊**George**, now also used in the English-speaking world. The crêpe material so called derives its name from that of an early 20th-century French dressmaker, Mme Georgette de la Plante.

Georgia ♀

Latinate feminine form of ◊**George**. It was borne by a 5th-century saint who became a recluse near Clermont in the Auvergne.

Georgiana ♀

Elaborated Latinate form of ◊**Georgia** or ◊**Georgina**.

Georgie ♀ ♂

Occasionally used as a pet form of ◊**George**, but more commonly as a female name, a pet form of ◊**Georgia** or ◊**Georgina**.

Georgina ♀

Latinate feminine derivative of ◊**George**. This feminine form originated in Scotland in the 18th century, when *George* itself became common among anti-Jacobites.

Georgine ♀

French form of ◊**Georgina**, now also used in the English-speaking world.

Geraint ♂

Welsh: of uncertain origin, derived from a British name that first appears in a Greek inscription in the form *Gerontios*, possibly influenced by the Greek vocabulary word *gerōn* 'old man' (genitive *gerontos*). The story of Geraint (or *Gereint*), son of Erbin of Cornwall, is told in the *Mabinogi*. Geraint is one of the knights of Arthur's Round Table. He wins the love of Enid at a tournament, and marries her. He is infatuated with her to the point of neglecting all else, but comes to suspect her, wrongly, of infidelity. By her submissiveness and loyalty, she regains his trust. The story of Geraint and Enid was used by Tennyson in the *Idylls of the King* (1859). In recent years the name has become extremely popular in Wales.

Gerald ♂

From an Old French name of Germanic (Frankish) origin, derived from *gār*, *gēr* 'spear' + *wald* 'rule'. It was adopted by the Normans and introduced by them to Britain, where it soon became confused with ◊**Gerard**. It died out in England at the end of the 13th century. However, it continued in Ireland, where it had been brought in the 12th century at the time of Strongbow's invasion. It was revived in England in the 19th century, along with several other long-extinct names of Norman, Old English, and Celtic origin, and is now more common than *Gerard*, which survived all along as an English 'gentry' name.

Variant: **Jerrold**.

Short form: **Ged**.

Pet forms: **Gerry**, **Jerry**.

Geraldine ♀

Feminine derivative of ◊**Gerald**, invented in the 16th century by the English poet the Earl of Surrey, in a poem praising Lady Fitzgerald. It remained very little used until the 18th century, when it suddenly increased in popularity.

Pet form: **Gerry**.

Gerard ♂

Old French name of Germanic (Frankish) origin, introduced to Britain by the Normans. It is derived from *gār*, *gēr* 'spear' + *hard* 'brave', 'hardy', 'strong'. In the later Middle Ages this was a much more common name than ◊**Gerald**, with which it was sometimes confused. Nowadays it is less common, surviving mainly among Roman Catholics, in honour of the many saints of this name.

Variants: **Gerrard**, **Jerrard**.

Short form: **Ged**.

Pet forms: **Gerry**, **Jerry**.

Germaine ♀♂

Feminine form of the rarer French male name **Germain** (Late Latin *Germānus* 'brother'; the original reference may have been to the concept of Christian brotherhood). Germaine Cousin (*c*.1579–1601) was a Provençal saint, the daughter of a poor farmer. Her canonization in 1867 gave an additional impulse to the use of the name in Europe and the English-speaking world. This form of the name is now also used as a male name in the United States; see also ◊**Jermaine**.

Gerrard ♂

Variant spelling of ◊**Gerard**, in part from the surname derived from the given name in the Middle Ages.

Gerry ♂♀

Pet form of ◊**Gerald**, ◊**Gerard**, or ◊**Geraldine**; it is also sometimes used as a female name. See also ◊**Jerry**.

Gertrude ♀

From a Germanic woman's personal name, derived from *gār*, *gēr* 'spear' + *þrūþ* 'strength'. The name is not found in England immediately after the Conquest, but only in the later Middle English period: it was probably introduced by migrants from the Low Countries, who came to England in connection with the cloth trade. It was popular in the 19th century, at the time of the revival of many Germanic names, but has now fallen from favour again.

Short form: **Gert**.

Pet form: **Gertie**.

Gervaise ♂

Norman name of unknown origin. It has been suggested that it might be Germanic, with *gēr* 'spear' as the first element; if so, the second element is unknown. The given name is bestowed in honour of a certain St Gervasius, whose remains, together with those of Protasius, were discovered in Milan in the year 386. Nothing is known about their lives, but St Ambrose, who had ordered the search for their remains, declared that they were martyrs, and a cult soon grew up. Given these circumstances, we might expect their names to be Greek or Latin, but if they are, the origins are unknown. The name is in use mainly among Roman Catholics. *Protasius* has not survived as a given name. See also ◊**Jarvis**.

Variant: **Gervase**.

Ghislain ♀

Of recent origin, or at any rate a recent introduction to the English-

speaking world. It is evidently a revival of the Old French oblique case of ◊**Giselle**, in a spelling that suggests Low German, Dutch, or Flemish influence.
Variant: **Ghislaine**.

Gib ♂
Medieval and modern short form of ◊**Gilbert**.
Variant: **Gibb**.

Gideon ♂
Biblical name (meaning 'he who cuts down' in Hebrew), borne by an Israelite leader appointed to deliver his people from the Midianites (Judges 6:14). He did this by getting his army to creep up on them with their torches hidden in pitchers. The name was popular among the 17th-century Puritans, and is still occasionally used in the United States.

Gigi ♀
French pet form of ◊**Giselle**, made famous in the English-speaking world by Lerner and Loewe's immensely popular musical *Gigi* (1958), starring Leslie Caron in the title role.

Gilbert ♂
Old French name of Germanic (Frankish) origin, derived from *gisil* 'pledge' + *berht* 'bright', 'famous'. It was adopted by the Normans and introduced by them to Britain. This was the name of the founder of the only native British religious order (abolished at the Dissolution of the Monasteries), St Gilbert of Sempringham (?1083–1189), in whose honour it is still sometimes bestowed, especially among Roman Catholics. It gained a wider currency in the 19th century.
Short form: **Gib**.

Giles ♂
Much altered English vernacular form of the Late Latin name *Aegidius*, from Greek *Aigidios* (a derivative of *aigidion* 'kid', 'young goat'). The name was very popular in the Middle Ages,

as the result of the fame of the 8th-century St Giles. According to tradition, he was an Athenian citizen who fled to Provence because he could not cope with the fame and adulation caused by his power to work miracles, in particular by healing the lame and crippled.
Variant: **Gyles**.

Gill ♀
Short form of ◊**Gillian**, rather less frequent than ◊**Jill**.

Gillespie ♂
Scottish: Anglicized form of Gaelic *Gille Easbaig* 'bishop's servant'. See also ◊**Archibald**.

Gillian ♀
Variant of ◊**Julian**, from which it was differentiated in spelling only in the 17th century.
Variant: **Jillian**.
Short forms: **Gill**, **Jill**.
Pet form: **Gilly**.

Gilly ♀
Pet form of ◊**Gill**. There may have been some influence from the name of the *gilly-flower* (earlier *gilofre*, *girofle*, from Late Greek *karyophyllon*).

Gilroy ♂
Transferred use of the Irish and Scottish surname, perhaps influenced to some extent by ◊**Elroy** and ◊**Leroy**. The surname is of Gaelic origin, from *an giolla ruadh*, 'the red-haired lad'.

Gina ♀
Shortened form of ◊**Georgina**. As an Italian name it also represents a short form of *Giorgina* or *Luigina*, and was made famous by the actress Gina Lollobrigida (b. 1927).

Ginger ♂ ♀
Originally a nickname for someone with red hair, occasionally used as a given name in the 20th century. As a female name it sometimes also represents a pet form of ◊**Virginia**, as in the case of the film star Ginger

Rogers, born in 1911 as Virginia McMath.

Ginny ♀
Pet form of ◊**Virginia**.

Giselle ♀
French name of Frankish origin, from the Germanic word *gisil* 'pledge'. It was a common practice in medieval Europe to leave children as pledges for an alliance, to be brought up at a foreign court, and the name may be derived as a byname from this practice. This was the name by which the wife of Duke Rollo of Normandy (*c*.860–*c*.930) was known. On her account the name enjoyed considerable popularity in France from an early period. Use of the name in English-speaking countries is much more recent, and is due mainly to the ballet *Giselle* (first performed in 1841). *Pet form*: ◊**Gigi**.

Gladstone ♂
Transferred use of the Scottish surname, in origin a local name from *Gledstanes* in Biggar, so called from Old English *glæd* 'kite' + *stān* 'rock' (the final *-s* is a later addition). As a given name it has sometimes been bestowed in honour of the Victorian Liberal statesman William Ewart Gladstone (1809–98). It is now favoured by West Indians: the Warwickshire and England fast bowler Gladstone Small is of West Indian parentage.

Gladwin ♂
Transferred use of the surname, itself from a medieval given name derived from Old English *glæd* 'bright' + *wine* 'friend'.

Gladys ♀
From the Welsh name *Gwladus*, which is of uncertain derivation. It has been quite widely used outside Wales in the 20th century.

Glen ♂
From the Gaelic word *gleann* 'valley',

in some cases perhaps representing a transferred use of the surname derived from this word. In recent years it has been used far beyond Scotland as a given name. There has been some confusion with the Welsh name ◊**Glyn**, which has the same meaning. *Variant*: **Glenn**.

Glenda ♀
Welsh: modern coinage, composed of the vocabulary words *glân* 'clean', 'pure', 'holy' + *da* 'good'. It is associated particularly with the actress and politician Glenda Jackson (born 1937).

Glenn ♂ ♀
Variant spelling of ◊**Glen**, borne as a female name by the American actress Glenn Close.

Glenna ♀
Modern coinage, invented as a female form of ◊**Glen**.

Glenys ♀
Welsh: modern coinage from *glân* 'pure', 'holy' + the ending *-ys* by analogy with names such as ◊**Dilys** and ◊**Gladys**.

Gloria ♀
From the Latin word meaning 'glory', not used as a given name before the 20th century, but now very popular. It first occurs as the name of a character in George Bernard Shaw's play *You Never Can Tell* (1898).

Glory ♀
Anglicized form of ◊**Gloria**, now occasionally used as a given name.

Glyn ♂
Welsh: from the Welsh placename element *glyn* 'valley'. This has been adopted as a given name in the 20th century, as the result of a desire to bestow on Welsh children specifically Welsh names. *Variant*: **Glynn**.

Glyndwr ♂
Welsh: adopted in the 20th century in

honour of the medieval Welsh patriot Owain Glyndŵr (c.1359–1416; known in English as Owen Glendower). In his case it was a byname referring to the fact that he came from a place named with Welsh *glyn* 'valley' + *dŵr* 'water'.

Glynis ♀
Altered form of ◊**Glenys**.

Glynn ♂
Welsh: variant spelling of ◊**Glyn**.

Godfrey ♂
From the Old French name *Godefroy*, which is of Germanic (Frankish) origin, from *god* 'god' (or *gōd* 'good') + *fred*, *frid* 'peace'. This was adopted by the Normans, and introduced by them to Britain. It was a very popular name in the Middle Ages, and was borne by, among others, a Norman saint (c.1066–1115) who became bishop of Amiens. There has been considerable confusion with ◊**Geoffrey**.

Godwin ♂
From the Old English personal name *Godwine*, derived from *god* 'god' + *wine* 'friend'. This was borne in the 11th century by the Earl of Wessex, the most important man in England after the king. He was an influential adviser to successive kings of England, and father of the King Harold who was defeated at Hastings in 1066. The personal name continued in use after the Norman Conquest long enough to give rise to a surname. Modern use as a given name is probably a transferred use of the surname, rather than a revival of the Old English name.

Goldie ♀
From a nickname for a blonde, a girl with golden hair, as in the case of the actress Goldie Hawn (b. 1945).

Gomer ♂
Biblical name (meaning 'complete' in Hebrew), borne by a son of Japheth and grandson of Noah. It was taken up by the Puritans, and is still in occasional use in the United States. *Gomer* is also an English surname, and the given name may also be a transferrred use of this. It is derived from an Old English personal name derived from *gōd* 'good' + *mær* 'famous'.

Goodwin ♂
Transferred use of the surname, which is derived from the Old English personal name *Gōdwine*, from *gōd* 'good' + *wine* 'friend'. There has been considerable confusion with ◊**Godwin**.

Gordon ♂
Transferred use of the Scottish surname, which is derived from a placename. It is a matter of dispute whether it referred originally to the Gordon in Berwickshire or to a similarly named place in Normandy. As a given name it seems to have been taken up in honour of Charles George Gordon (1833–85), the British general who died at Khartoum.

Goronwy ♂
Welsh: of uncertain derivation, borne in the *Mabinogi* by Goronwy the Staunch, Lord of Penllyn. He became the lover of the flower-maiden Blodeuedd and murdered her husband Lleu Llaw Gyffes, but Lleu was later restored to life and definitively dispatched Goronwy.

Grace ♀
From the abstract noun (via Old French, from Latin *grātia*), first used as a given name by the Puritans in the 17th century. It has always been particularly popular in Scotland and northern England (borne, for example, by Grace Darling, the lighthouse keeper's daughter whose heroism in 1838, saving sailors in a storm, caught the popular imagination). In more recent times it was famous as the name of the actress Grace Kelly (1928–82), who became Princess Grace of Monaco. In Ireland it is used as an Anglicized form of ◊**Gráinne**.

Gracie ♀
Pet form of ◊**Grace**. It was made
famous by the Lancashire singer and
comedienne Gracie Fields (1898–1979),
whose original name was Grace
Stansfield.

Graham ♂
Transferred use of a Scottish surname,
in origin a local name from *Grantham*
in Lincolnshire. This is recorded in
Domesday Book not only in its
current form but also as *Grandham*,
Granham, and *Graham*; it was
apparently named as the 'gravelly
place', from Old English *grand* 'gravel'
+ *hām* 'home-stead'. The surname
was taken to Scotland in the 12th
century by Sir William de Graham,
founder of a famous clan. The earls of
Montrose were among his
descendants.
Variants: **Grahame**, **Graeme**.

Gráinne ♀
Irish Gaelic name, pronounced 'gron-
nya'. It is of uncertain origin, possibly
connected with *grán* 'grain', as the
name of an ancient corn goddess. In
Irish legend Gráinne was the daughter
of King Cormac; she was beloved by
the hero Finn, but eloped with Finn's
nephew Diarmait. Finn pursued them
over great distances, and eventually
brought about the death of Diarmait,
after which Gráinne killed herself.
Gráinne Uí Mháille, known in English
as Grace O'Malley, was a semi-
legendary commander of war galleys
on the Mayo coast in the late 16th
century, 'for forty years the stay of all
rebellions in the west'. The name is
sometimes Anglicized as ◊**Grace**.

Grania ♀
Latinized form of the Irish Gaelic
name ◊**Gráinne**.
Variant: **Granya**.

Grant ♂
Transferred use of the surname, very
common in Scotland, where it is the
name of a famous clan. It is derived

from a nickname meaning 'large'
(Anglo-Norman *grand*). In the United
States the name is sometimes
bestowed in honour of the Civil War
general and 18th president, Ulysses S.
Grant (1822–85).

Granville ♂
From one of the Norman baronial
names that subsequently became
aristocratic English surnames and are
now used intermittently as male given
names. This one derives from any of
several places in Normandy named
with Old French *grand* 'large' + *ville*
'settlement'.

Granya ♀
Variant spelling of ◊**Grania**, influenced
by Russian names such as ◊**Sonya** and
◊**Tanya**.

Greer ♀
Transferred use of the Scottish
surname, which originated in the
Middle Ages from a contracted form of
◊**Gregor**. It has become known as a
female name in the English-speaking
world through the fame of the actress
Greer Garson (b. 1908), whose
mother's maiden name it was.
Variant: **Grier**.

Greg ♂
Short form of ◊**Gregory** and ◊**Gregor**.
Variant: **Gregg**.

Gregor ♂
Scottish form of ◊**Gregory**. In part it
represents an Anglicized form of
Gaelic *Griogair*, which gave rise to the
Highland surname *MacGregor*.

Gregory ♂
Via Latin *Gregorius* from the post-
classical Greek name *Gregōrios*
'watchful' (a derivative of *gregōrein* 'to
watch', 'be vigilant'). The name was a
very popular one among the early
Christians, who were mindful of the
injunction 'be sober, be vigilant' (1
Peter 5:8). It was borne by a number
of early saints. The most important, in
honour of whom the name was often

bestowed from medieval times onwards, were Gregory of Nazianzen (c.329–90), Gregory of Nyssa (d. c.395), Gregory of Tours (538–94), and Pope Gregory the Great (c.540–604). A famous bearer of the name in modern times is the film star Gregory Peck (b. 1916). The name has traditionally been popular in Scotland, where it is often found in the form *Gregor*.
Short forms: **Greg(g)**.

Greta ♀
Short form of *Margareta*, a Latinate form of ◊**Margaret**. It became fairly popular in the English-speaking world as a result of the fame of the Swedish-born film actress Greta Garbo (1905–92; b. Greta Louisa Gustafsson).

Greville ♂
Transferred use of the surname, which is a Norman baronial name from *Gréville* in La Manche. The Greville family were earls of Warwick, and held Warwick Castle from the time of Queen Elizabeth I, who granted it to her favourite Fulke Greville (1554–1628).

Grier ♀
Variant spelling of ◊**Greer**.

Griff ♂
Welsh: informal short form of ◊**Griffith**.

Griffin ♂
Welsh: from a medieval Latinized form, *Griffinus*, of ◊**Griffith**.

Griffith ♂
Welsh: Anglicized form of *Gruffudd* or *Griffudd*, Old Welsh *Grip(p)iud*. The second element of this means 'lord, prince'; the first is of uncertain origin. Gruffydd ap Llewellyn (d. 1063) was one of the most able rulers of Wales in the Middle Ages, scoring some notable victories over the English until he was eventually defeated by King Harold in 1063.
Short form: **Griff**.

Griselda ♀
Of uncertain origin, possibly from a Germanic name derived from *gris* 'grey' + *hild* 'battle'. It became popular in the Middle Ages with reference to the tale of 'patient Griselda' (told by Boccaccio and Chaucer), who was taken as a model of the patient, long-suffering wife.

Grizel ♀
Medieval vernacular form of ◊**Griselda**, used particularly in Scotland. The name has now died out, no doubt in part because of its similarity to the vocabulary word *grizzle* meaning 'to grumble or whine'.

Grover ♂
Transferred use of the surname, in origin a local name for someone who lived near a grove of trees (Old English *grāf*). Use as a given name is partly due to the U.S. president (Stephen) Grover Cleveland (1837–1908).

Guinevere ♀
From the Old French form of the Welsh name *Gwen-hwyfar*, from *gwen* 'white', 'fair', 'blessed', 'holy' + *hwyfar* 'smooth', 'soft'. It is famous as the name of King Arthur's wife, who in most versions of the Arthurian legends is unfaithful to him, having fallen in love with Sir Lancelot. See also ◊**Gaynor** and ◊**Jennifer**.

Gus ♂
Short form of ◊**Augustus** or ◊**Angus**. In the case of Gus the Theatre Cat, a character in T. S. Eliot's *Old Possum's Book of Practical Cats* (1939), it is a short form of *Asparagus*!
Pet form: **Gussie**.

Guy ♂
From an Old French name, of Germanic (Frankish) origin, originally a short form of a compound name starting with *witu* 'wood' or *wīt* 'wide'. This was adopted by the Normans and introduced by them to England. In Old French initial *w-* regularly became *gu-*. The usual

Norman forms of the name were *Gy* or *Guido*. In medieval Latin the same name is found as *Wido*. It was a popular name among the Normans, enhanced no doubt by the romance of Guy of Warwick, recounting the exploits of a folk hero of the Crusades.

Gwen ♀
Welsh: short form of ◊**Gwendolen** or ◊**Gwenllian**, or an independent name from Welsh *gwen*, the feminine form of *gwyn* 'white', 'fair', 'blessed', 'holy' (see ◊**Gwyn**). It was borne by a 5th-century saint, aunt of St David and mother of the minor saints Cybi and Cadfan.

Gwenda ♀
Welsh: of modern origin, composed of the vocabulary words *gwen* 'white', 'fair', 'blessed', 'holy' (see ◊**Gwen**) + *da* 'good'.

Gwendolen ♀
Welsh: from *gwen* 'white', 'fair', 'blessed', 'holy' (see ◊**Gwyn**) + *dolen* 'ring', 'bow'. According to Geoffrey of Monmouth, this was the name of the wife of a mythical Welsh king Locrine, who abandoned her for a German princess called Estrildis. Gwendolen in revenge had Estrildis and her daughter Sabrina drowned in the River Severn. The name is borne by one of the principal characters in Oscar Wilde's play *The Importance of Being Earnest* (first performed in 1895).
Variants: **Gwendolin**, **Gwendolyn**; **Gwendoline** (formed under the influence of the many female given names ending in *-line*).

Gwenllian ♀
Welsh traditional name, derived from *gwen* 'white', 'fair', 'blessed', 'holy'

(see ◊**Gwyn**) + *lliant* 'flood', 'flow' (probably in the transferred sense 'foamy' or 'white', referring to a pale complexion).

Gwenyth ♀
Welsh: variant of ◊**Gwyneth**. It may alternatively be based on Welsh *gwenith* 'wheat', a word used in poetry to mean 'the favourite' or 'the pick of the bunch'.

Gwilym ♂
Welsh form of ◊**William**, in use since the Middle Ages.

Gwyn ♂
Welsh: originally a byname from Welsh *gwyn* 'white', 'fair', 'blessed', 'holy'. See also ◊**Wyn**.

Gwynedd ♂
Welsh name taken from a region of medieval North Wales (now resurrected as the name of a new composite county in Wales).

Gwyneth ♀
Welsh: altered form of ◊**Gwynedd**, used as a female name. Its popularity from the late 19th century, at first in Wales and then more widely in the English-speaking world, seems to have been due originally to the influence of the popular novelist Annie Harriet Hughes (1852–1910), who adopted the pen-name Gwyneth Vaughan.

Gwynfor ♂
Welsh: coined in the 20th century from *gwyn* 'white', 'fair', 'blessed', 'holy' + the mutated form of *mawr* 'great', 'large' (found in this form in a number of placenames).

Gyles ♂
Variant spelling of ◊**Giles**.

HADASSAH HAIDEE HAILEY HAL HALE HA
LEY HALL HAMILTON HAMISH HANK HA
NNAH HAPPY HARDING HARDY HARLA
N HARLEY HAROLD HARPER HARRIET HA
RRIETTE HARRISON HARRY HARTLEY HAR
VARD HARVEY HATTIE HAYDN HAYLEY H

Hadassah ♀

Hebrew form of *Esther*, which is the Persian form of the name. See Esther 2:7. This form is now sometimes chosen as a modern Jewish given name.

Short form: **Dassah**.

Haidee ♀

As the name of a character in Byron's poem *Don Juan* (1819–24), this may have been intended to be connected with the classical Greek adjective *aidoios* 'modest'. In modern use it is taken as a variant of ◊**Heidi**.

Hailey ♀

Variant spelling of ◊**Hayley**.

Variant: **Hailee**.

Hal ♂

Short form of ◊**Harry**, of medieval origin. It was used by Shakespeare in *King Henry IV* as the name of the king's son, the future Henry V. Similar substitution of *-l* for *-r* has occurred in derivatives of *Terry* (*Tel*), *Derek* (*Del*), and in girls' names such as *Sally* (from *Sarah*).

Hale ♂

Transferred use of the surname, in origin a local name for someone living in a nook or recess (Old English *halh*).

Haley ♀

Variant spelling of ◊**Hayley**.

Variant: **Haleigh**.

Hall ♂

Transferred use of the surname, which originated as a local name for someone, usually a servant or retainer, who lived at a manor house (Old English *heall*).

Hamilton ♂

Mainly North American: transferred use of the Scottish surname. This was brought to Scotland in or before the 13th century from a village (now deserted) called *Hamilton* or *Hameldune*, near Barkby in Leicestershire (named with Old English *hamel* 'blunt', 'flat-topped' + *dūn* 'hill'). It is the surname of an enormously widespread and influential family, who acquired many titles, including the dukedom of Hamilton. The town near Glasgow so called is named after the family, not vice versa. Use as a given name seems to have begun in the United States in honour of Alexander Hamilton (?1757–1804), who was Secretary of the Treasury under George Washington and did much to establish the political and financial system on which the industrial growth and prosperity of the United States came to be founded. He was killed in a duel with the irascible Aaron Burr.

Hamish ♂

Scottish: Anglicized spelling of the vocative case, *Sheumais*, of the Gaelic version of ◊**James**. It is now sometimes chosen by families with no Scottish connections.

Hank ♂

Originally a medieval back-formation from *Hankin*, which is composed of *Han* (a short form of *Jehan* ◊**John**) + the Middle English diminutive suffix *-kin*. However, the suffix was mistaken for the Anglo-Norman diminutive -in, hence the form *Hank*. *Hank* is now sometimes used as an independent given name in North America, where it is usually taken as a pet form of ◊**Henry**. It has more or less died out in Britain.

Hannah ♀
Biblical name, borne by the mother of the prophet Samuel (1 Samuel 1:2), Hebrew *Hanna*. It is derived from a Hebrew word meaning 'He (i.e. God) has favoured me (i.e. with a child)'. See also ◊**Anne**. This form of the name was taken up as a given name by the Puritans in the 16th and 17th centuries.

Happy ♀
From the vocabulary word (originally meaning 'prosperous', a derivative of *hap* 'chance', 'good luck', of Old Norse origin), occasionally used in the 20th century for the sake of the good omen of its meaning; cf. ◊**Merry** and ◊**Gay**.

Harding ♂
Especially U.S.: transferred use of the surname, which is derived from a medieval English given name. The Old English form was *Hearding*, a derivative (originally patronymic in form) of *Heard* 'hardy', 'brave', 'strong', a byname or short form of the various compound personal names containing this element. Use as a given name may have been influenced by the U.S. president Warren Gamaliel Harding (1865–1923).

Hardy ♂
Especially U.S.: transferred use of the surname, in origin a nickname for a brave or stouthearted man (from Middle English, Old French *hardi*, of Germanic origin). It may in part also be used as a pet form of ◊**Harding**.

Harlan ♂
Especially U.S.: transferred use of the surname, in origin a local name from any of various places in England called *Harland*, from Old English *hār* 'grey' or *hara* 'hare' + *land* cleared land. Use as a given name honours the American judge John Marshall Harlan (1833–1911), a conservative Republican who was nevertheless a pioneering supporter of civil rights in the Supreme Court. He was a descendant of the Quaker George Harland from Durham, England, who emigrated to Delaware in 1687, and became governor there in 1695. *Variant*: **Harland**.

Harley ♂
Especially U.S.: transferred use of the surname, in origin a local name from places in Shropshire and West Yorkshire, so called from Old English *hær* 'rock', 'heap of stones', or *hara* 'hare' + *lēah* 'wood', 'clearing'.

Harold ♂
From an Old English personal name derived from *here* 'army' + *weald* 'ruler', reinforced before the Norman Conquest by the Scandinavian cognate *Haraldr*, introduced by Norse settlers. The name was not common in the later Middle Ages, probably because it was associated with the unfortunate King Harold, killed at the Battle of Hastings in 1066. It was revived in the 19th century, along with a number of other Old English names.

Harper ♂ ♀
Mainly U.S.: transferred use of the surname, in origin an occupational name for someone who played the harp. As a female name it has been borne in particular by the southern American writer Harper Lee, author of *To Kill a Mockingbird* (1960).

Harriet ♀
Anglicized form of French *Henriette*, a feminine diminutive of ◊**Henry** (French *Henri*) coined in the 17th century. It was quite common in England in the 18th and early 19th centuries. *Pet form*: **Hattie**.

Harriette ♀

Variant of ◊**Harriet**, probably coined to
look more feminine, but it could be a
reconstructed form, blending ◊**Harriet**
with its source *Henriette*.

Harrison ♂

Especially U.S.: transferred use of the
surname, which originated as a
patronymic meaning 'son of Harry'.
Use as a given name may have been
influenced by the U.S. presidents
William Henry Harrison (1773–1841)
and his grandson Benjamin Harrison
(1833–1901). A more recent influence
is the actor Harrison Ford (b. 1942).

Harry ♂

Pet form of ◊**Henry**. This was the
usual English form of ◊**Henry** in the
Middle Ages and later. It was used by
Shakespeare, for example, as the
familiar name of the mature King
Henry V (compare ◊**Hal**).

Hartley ♂

Transferred use of the surname, in
origin a local name from any of the
numerous places so called. Most (for
example, those in Berkshire, Dorset,
Hampshire, and Kent) are so called
from Old English *heorot* 'hart', 'male
deer' + *lēah* 'wood', 'clearing'. One in
Northumbria is from *heorot* + *hlāw*
'hill', and one in Cumbria is probably
from *haraδ* 'wood' + *clā* 'claw', i.e.
river-fork.

Harvard ♂

Mainly U.S.: transferred use of the
surname, which is from an Old Norse
personal name derived from *herr*
'army' + *varþr* 'guardian' (a cognate of
Old English *Hereweard*). Use as a
given name has no doubt been
influenced by Harvard College in
Cambridge, Massachusetts. This takes
its name from John Harvard (1607–38),
who emigrated from London in 1637
and left half his wealth and the whole
of his library to support the newly
founded college.

Harvey ♂

Transferred use of the surname, which
is derived from a Breton personal
name composed of *haer* 'battle' + *vy*
'worthy'. It was introduced to Britain
by Bretons who settled in East Anglia
and elsewhere in the wake of the
Norman Conquest.
Short forms: Harv(e).

Hattie ♀

Pet form of ◊**Harriet**.

Haydn ♂

From the surname of the composer,
adopted in his honour particularly by
the music-loving Welsh. Josef Haydn
(1732–1809) was court composer and
kapellmeister to the powerful Count
Nicholas Esterhazy, and spent most of
his working life at the Esterhazy
palace near Vienna. His surname is a
respelling of the nickname *Heiden*
'heathen' (Middle High German
heiden, Old High German *heidano*).
Variants: **Hayden**, **Haydon**.

Hayley ♀

Transferred use of the surname, which
derives from a placename, probably
Hailey in Oxfordshire, which was
originally named from Old English *hēg*
'hay' + *lēah* 'clearing'. Use as a given
name began in the 1960s, inspired
perhaps by the actress Hayley Mills (b.
1946), daughter of Sir John Mills and
Mary Hayley Bell. It has enjoyed great
popularity since then.
Variants: **Haylee**, **Hailey**, **Hailee**, **Haley**,
Haleigh.

Hazel ♀

From the vocabulary word denoting
the tree (Old English *hæsel*), or its
light reddish-brown nuts. This is one
of the most successful of the names
coined in the 19th century from words
denoting plants. The fact that it also
denotes an eye colour may have been
a factor in its continuing popularity.

Heath ♂

Transferred use of the surname, in
origin a local name for someone who

lived on a patch of heathland (Old
English *hǣð*).

Heather ♀
From the vocabulary word denoting
the hardy, brightly coloured plant
(Middle English *hather*; the spelling
was altered in the 18th century as a
result of folk etymological association
with *heath*). The name was first used
in the late 19th century; it has been
particularly popular since about 1950.

Hebe ♀
pronounced '*hee*-bee': from a Greek
name, a feminine form of the adjective
hēbos 'young'. This was borne in
Greek mythology by a minor goddess
who was a personification of youth.
She was a daughter of Zeus and the
wife of Hephaistos; it was her duty to
act as cup-bearer to the gods. The
name was taken up in England in the
late 19th century, but it has fallen out
of fashion again.

Heber ♂
Irish: Anglicized form of the Gaelic
name *Éibhear* (pronounced '*ay*-ver').
This was borne in Irish legend by the
son of Míl, leader of the Gaelic race
that first conquered Ireland. *Hever* is
also a biblical name (meaning
'enclave' in Hebrew), borne by various
minor characters in the Bible.

Hector ♂
Name borne in classical legend by the
Trojan champion who was killed by
the Greek Achilles. His name (Greek
Hektōr) is probably an agent derivative
of Greek *ekhein* 'to restrain'.

Heddwyn ♂
Welsh: modern coinage, from *hedd*
'peace' + *(g)wyn* 'white', 'fair',
'blessed', 'holy'. Use as a given name
was popularized by the fame of the
poet Ellis Humphrey Evans, who
posthumously won the bardic chair at
the National Eisteddfod in 1917,
having been killed in the First World
War; his bardic name was *Hedd Wyn*.

Hedley ♂
Transferred use of the surname, in
origin a local name from one of
several places in Durham and
Northumbria so called from Old
English *hǣþ* 'heather' + *lēah* 'wood',
'clearing'.

Heidi ♀
Swiss pet form of *Adelheid*, the
German form of ◊**Adelaide**. The name
is now also popular in the English-
speaking world, largely due to Johanna
Spyri's children's classic *Heidi* (1881).

Heilyn ♂
Welsh traditional name, originally an
occupational byname for a steward or
wine-pourer, composed of the stem of
the verb *heilio* 'to prepare', 'wait on'
+ the diminutive suffix -*yn*. The
name is borne in the *Mabinogi* by two
characters: Heilyn the son of Gwynn
the Old, and Heilyn the Red, son of
Cadwgawn.

Heledd ♀
Welsh traditional name of uncertain
derivation. It was borne by a semi-
legendary princess of the 7th century,
in whose name a lament for her
brother's death was composed in the
9th century.

Helen ♀
English vernacular form of the name
(Greek *Hēlēnē*) borne in classical
legend by the famous beauty, wife of
Menelaus, whose seizure by the
Trojan prince Paris sparked off the
Trojan War. Her name is of uncertain
origin; it may be connected with a
word meaning 'ray' or 'sunbeam'; cf.
Greek *hēlios* 'sun'. It has sometimes
been taken as connected with the
Greek word meaning 'Greek', *Hellēn*,
but this is doubtful speculation. In the
early Christian period the name was
borne by the mother of the Emperor
Constantine, who is now usually
known by the Latin version of her
name, *Helena*. She is credited with
having found the True Cross in

Jerusalem. She was born in about 248, probably in Bithynia. However, in medieval England it was thought that she had been born in Britain, which greatly increased the popularity of the name there.

Helena ♀
Latinate form of ◊**Helen**.

Helga ♀
From an Old Norse woman's personal name, a derivative of the adjective *heilagr* 'prosperous', 'successful' (from *heill* 'hale', 'hearty', 'happy'). It was introduced to England before the Conquest, but did not survive long. It has been reintroduced to the English-speaking world in the 20th century from Scandinavia and Germany. See also ◊**Olga**.

Henrietta ♀
Latinate form of French *Henriette*, a feminine diminutive of *Henri*, the French form of ◊**Henry**. This form of the name enjoyed a vogue from the late 19th century until well into the 20th century. See also ◊**Harriet**.
Pet forms: **Hennie**, **Hettie**, **Hattie**.

Henry ♂
A perennially popular given name, of Continental Germanic origin, from *haim* 'home' + *rīc* 'power', 'ruler'. It was an Old French name, adopted by the Normans and introduced by them to Britain. It has been borne by eight kings of England. Not until the 17th century did the form *Henry* (as opposed to ◊**Harry**) became the standard vernacular form, mainly due to the influence of the Latin form *Henricus* and French *Henri*.
Pet forms: ◊**Hal**, ◊**Hank**, ◊**Harry**.

Hephzibah ♀
Biblical name (meaning 'my delight is in her' (i.e. a new-born daughter)), borne by the wife of Hezekiah, King of Judah; she was the mother of Manasseh (2 Kings 21). It is also used in the prophecies of Isaiah as an allusive name for the land of Israel (cf. ◊**Beulah**).
Variant: **Hepzibah**.

Herbert ♂
From an Old French name of Germanic (Frankish) origin, introduced to Britain by the Normans. It is derived from *heri*, *hari* 'army' + *berht* 'bright', 'famous'. An Old English form, *Herebeorht*, existed in England before the Conquest, but was superseded by the Norman form, which gave rise to an important surname. The family in question were earls of Pembroke in the 16th and 17th centuries; the poet George Herbert was a member of the family. By the end of the Middle Ages *Herbert* was little used as a given name, and its greater frequency in Britain from the 19th century onwards is due partly to the trend for the revival of medieval names of Germanic origin and partly to the trend for the transferred use of surnames.
Short form: **Herb**.
Pet form: **Herbie**.

Herman ♂
English form of *Hermann*, from a Germanic personal name derived from *heri*, *hari* 'army' + *man* 'man'. The name was in use among the Normans, but had died out by the 14th century. It enjoyed a limited revival in Britain in the 19th century, when it also became common in America, most probably as a result of the influence of German immigrants.

Hermia ♀
Latinate derivative of the name of the Greek god *Hermes* (cf. ◊**Hermione**). This was used by Shakespeare for the name of a character in *A Midsummer Night's Dream* (1595).

Hermione ♀
Name borne in classical mythology by a daughter of Helen and Menelaus, who grew up to marry her cousin Orestes. It is evidently a derivative of

Hermes, name of the messenger god, but the formation is not clear. The name was used by Shakespeare for one of the main characters in *A Winter's Tale*, and is still occasionally used in the 20th century.

Hesketh ♂
Transferred use of the surname, in origin a local name from any of the various places in northern England named with Old Norse *hestr* 'horse' + *skeiðr* 'racecourse'. Horse racing and horse fighting were favourite sports among the Scandinavian settlers in England.

Hester ♀
Variant of ◊**Esther**, of medieval origin. For a long while the two forms were interchangeable, the addition or dropping of *h*- being commonplace in a whole range of words, but now they are generally regarded as two distinct names.

Hettie ♀
Pet form of ◊**Henrietta** and occasionally also of ◊**Hester**.

Hewie ♂
Scottish and N. English: variant spelling of ◊**Hughie**.

Hilary ♀ ♂
From the medieval form of the (post-classical) Latin masculine name *Hilarius* (a derivative of *hilaris* 'cheerful') and its feminine form *Hilaria*. From the Middle Ages onwards, the name was borne principally by men (in honour of the 4th-century theologian St Hilarius of Poitiers). Now, however, it is more commonly given to girls.
Variant: **Hillary** (♀; the usual U.S. spelling).

Hilda ♀
Of Germanic origin, a Latinized short form of any of several female names derived from *hild* 'battle'. Many of these are found in both Continental Germanic and Old English forms. St

Hilda (614–80) was a Northumbrian princess who founded the abbey at Whitby and became its abbess. *Hilda* was a popular name in England both before and after the Norman Conquest. Its popularity waned in Tudor times, but it never quite died out, and was strongly revived in the 19th century.
Variant: **Hylda**.

Hillary ♀
Variant spelling of ◊**Hilary**, found mainly in North America.

Hiram ♂
Biblical name, borne by a king of Tyre who is repeatedly mentioned in the Bible (2 Samuel 2:11; 1 Kings 5; 9:11; 10:11; 1 Chronicles 14:1; 2 Chronicles 2:11) as supplying wood, craftsmen, and money to enable David and Solomon to construct various buildings. It was also the name of a craftsman of Tyre who worked in brass for Solomon (1 Kings 7:13). The name is presumably of Semitic origin, but is probably a Phoenician name; if it is Hebrew, it may be a shortened form of *Ahiram* 'brother of the exalted'. In England, the name was taken up by the Puritans in the 17th century, but soon dropped out of use again. It is still used in the United States.

Holly ♀
From the vocabulary word denoting the evergreen shrub or tree (Middle English *holi(n)*, Old English *holegn*). The name was first used at the beginning of the 20th century, and has been particularly popular since about 1960. It is bestowed especially on girls born around Christmas, when sprigs of holly are traditionally taken indoors to decorate rooms.
Variant: **Hollie**.

Homer ♂
English form of the name of the Greek epic poet *Homēros*, now regularly used as a given name in the United

States (cf. ◊**Virgil**). Many theories have been put forward to explain the name of the poet, but none is conclusive. It is identical in form with the Greek vocabulary word *homēros* 'hostage'.

Honesty ♀
Modern coinage, partly from the quality (via Old French, from Latin *honestās*, connected with *honor* 'honour') and partly from the flower named with this word.

Honey ♀
From the vocabulary word (Old English *huneg*). Honey was used throughout the Middle Ages in place of sugar (which was only introduced from the New World in the 16th century), and the word has long been used as a term of endearment. Modern use as a given name was prompted by a character in Margaret Mitchell's novel *Gone with the Wind* (1936), made into a film in 1939.

Honor ♀
Variant spelling of ◊**Honour**; the dominant spelling of both the vocabulary word and the given name in the United States today. This spelling of the name is also found in Britain, as in the case of the actress Honor Blackman (b. 1926).

Honora ♀
Latinate elaboration of ◊**Honor**, used mainly in Ireland.

Honour ♀
From the vocabulary word denoting the quality (via Old French, from Latin *honor*). The name was popular with the Puritans in the 17th century and has survived quietly to the present day.
Variant: **Honor**.

Hope ♀
From the vocabulary word (Old English *hopa*) denoting the quality, in particular the Christian quality of expectation in the resurrection and in eternal life. The name was created by the Puritans and has been one of their most successful coinages.

Hopkin ♂
Transferred use of the surname, now found mainly in Wales. It is derived from a medieval given name, a pet form (with the diminutive suffix *-kin*) of *Hob*, a short form of ◊**Robert** that probably had its origin through English mishearing of the Norman pronunciation of *R-*.

Horace ♂
From the old Roman family name ◊**Horatius**. The name was once widely used among admirers of the Roman poet Horace (Quintus Horatius Flaccus), but it is at present out of fashion. See also ◊**Horatio**.

Horatia ♀
Feminine form of Latin ◊**Horatius**. It has never been common in the English-speaking world, but was borne, for example, by the daughter of Horatio Nelson.

Horatio ♂
Variant of ◊**Horace**, influenced by the Latin form ◊**Horatius** and the Italian form *Orazio*. It is chiefly known as having been borne by Admiral Horatio Nelson (1758–1805), victor of many sea battles with the French during the Napoleonic Wars, culminating in the Battle of Trafalgar, in which he was killed.

Horatius ♂
An old Roman family name, which is of obscure, possibly Etruscan, origin. Its most famous bearer was the Roman poet Quintus Horatius Flaccus (65–8 BC), generally known in English as ◊**Horace**. From the mid-19th century, the name has occasionally been used by English speakers in its original Latin form. This probably owes more to the *Lays of Ancient Rome* (1842) by Thomas Babbington Macaulay than to the poet Horace. Macaulay relates, in verse that was once enormously popular, the exploit

of an early Roman hero, recounting 'How Horatius kept the bridge'.

Hortense ♀
French form of Latin *Hortensia*, the feminine version of the old Roman family name *Hortensius*. This is of uncertain origin, but may be derived from Latin *hortus* 'garden'. The given name began to be used in the English-speaking world in the 19th century, but is not common today.

Howard ♂
Transferred use of the surname of an English noble family. The surname has a large number of possible origins, but in the case of the noble family early forms often have the spelling *Haward*, and so it is probably from a Scandinavian personal name derived from *hā* 'high' + *ward* 'guardian'. (The traditional derivation from the Old English name *Hereweard* 'army guardian' is untenable.) It is now a widespread and popular given name.

Howell ♂
Anglicized form of the Welsh name ◊**Hywel**, or a transferred use of the surname derived from that name.

Hubert ♂
Old French name of Germanic (Frankish) origin, derived from *hug* 'heart', 'mind', 'spirit' + *berht* 'bright', 'famous'. It was popular among the Normans, who introduced it to Britain, where it was later reinforced by settlers from the Low Countries. An 8th-century St Hubert succeeded St Lambert as bishop of Maastricht and is regarded as the patron of hunters, since, like St Eustace, he is supposed to have seen a vision of Christ crucified between the antlers of a stag.

Hugh ♂
From an Old French name, *Hugues*, *Hugo*, of Germanic (Frankish) origin, derived from *hug* 'heart', 'mind', 'spirit'. It was originally a short form of various compound names containing this element. This was borne by the aristocracy of medieval France, adopted by the Normans, and introduced by them to Britain.

Hughie ♂
Pet form of ◊**Hugh**.
Variant: **Hewie**.

Hugo ♂
Latinized form of *Hugh*, used throughout the Middle Ages in official documents, and occasionally revived as a modern given name.

Hulda ♀
Biblical name (meaning 'weasel' in Hebrew), borne by a prophetess who foretold to Josiah the destruction of Jerusalem (2 Kings 22).
Variant: **Huldah**.

Humbert ♂
From an Old French name of Germanic (Frankish) origin, derived from *hun* 'bear-cub', 'warrior' + *berht* 'bright', 'famous'. It was adopted by the Normans and introduced by them to Britain. However, it was not common in Britain in the Middle Ages, and has always had a Continental flavour. It was used by Vladimir Nabokov for the name of the demented pederast, Humbert Humbert, who is the narrator in his novel *Lolita* (1955). This has no doubt contributed to its demise as a given name in the English-speaking world.

Humphrey ♂
From a Norman name, *Hunfrid*, of Germanic origin, derived from *hun* 'bear-cub', 'warrior' + *fred, frid* 'peace'. The Norman form absorbed the native Old English form, *Hunfrith*, which existed in England before the Conquest. The spelling with -*ph*- reflects classicizing influence. It has always enjoyed a modest popularity in England. Perhaps its best known bearer was the youngest son of King Henry IV, the Duke of Gloucester (1391–1447), known as 'Duke Humphrey'. He was noted as a patron

of literature, and founded what became the Bodleian Library at Oxford. In modern times, probably the most famous bearer has been the film star Humphrey Bogart (1899–1957).
Variants: **Humphry**, **Humfr(e)y**.

Hunter ♂
Transferred use of the surname, in origin an occupational name. The term was used not only of hunters on horseback of game such as stags and wild boars, which was in the Middle Ages a pursuit restricted to the ranks of the nobility, but also of much humbler bird catchers and poachers seeking food.

Huw ♂
Welsh form of ◊**Hugh**, now sometimes also used in other parts of the English-speaking world.

Hyacinth ♀
English form of the name (Greek *Hyakinthos*) borne in classical mythology by a beautiful youth who was accidentally killed by Apollo and from whose blood sprang a flower bearing his name (not the modern hyacinth, but a type of dark lily). The name was later borne by various early saints, principally one martyred in the 3rd century with his brother Protus. This encouraged its use as a male name in Christian Europe, including, occasionally, Britain. However, in Britain at the end of the 19th century there was a vogue for coining new female names from vocabulary words denoting plants and flowers (e.g. ◊**Daisy**, ◊**Ivy**). *Hyacinth* accordingly came to be regarded as an exclusively female name. It has never been common.

Hyam ♂
Jewish: from the Hebrew word *hayyim* 'life'. This is sometimes added to the existing given name of a seriously ill person during prayers for his recovery.

Hylda ♀
Variant spelling of ◊**Hilda**.

Hywel ♂
Welsh traditional name, originally a byname from a vocabulary word meaning 'eminent, conspicuous'. This name was common in the Middle Ages and lies behind the Anglicized surname *Howell*. In the 20th century it has been revived and now enjoys great popularity.
Variants: **Hywell**; **Howell** (Anglicized).

IAIN IAN IDA IDRIS IDWAL IEUAN IFOR IG
NATIUS IKE ILLTUD ILONA IMOGEN INA I
NDIA INES INGRAM INGRID INIGO INNES
IOLE IOLO IONA IONE IORWERTH IRA IRE
NE IRIS IRMA IRVIN IRVINE IRVING IRWIN
ISAAC ISABEL ISABELLE ISADORA ISIDORE I

Iain ♂
Distinctively Scottish variant of ◊**Ian**.
Iain is the normal Gaelic spelling.

Ian ♂
Scottish form of ◊**John**, now also
extensively used in the wider English-
speaking world.

Ida ♀
Originally a Norman name, of
Germanic origin, derived from *īd*
'work'. This died out during the later
Middle Ages. It was revived in the
19th century, influenced by its use in
Tennyson's *The Princess* (1847) for the
central character, who devotes herself
to the cause of women's rights and
women's education in a thoroughly
Victorian way. The name is also
associated with Mount Ida in Crete,
which was connected in classical
times with the worship of Zeus, king
of the gods, who was supposed to have
been brought up in a cave on the
mountainside. In the 1930s it became
famous as name of the film star Ida
Lupino (1914–).

Idris ♂
Welsh traditional name, derived from
iud 'lord' + *rīs* 'ardent', 'impulsive'. It
was common in the Middle Ages and
earlier, and has been strongly revived
since the late 19th century.

Idwal ♂
Welsh traditional name, derived from
iud 'lord', 'master' + *(g)wal* 'wall',
'rampart'.

Ieuan ♂
The original Welsh form of ◊**John**,
from Latin *Johannes*. Later forms are
Iefan and **Ifan**.

Ifor ♂
Welsh: traditional name of uncertain
derivation. It has sometimes been
Anglicized as ◊**Ivor**, but there is in
origin no connection between the two
names.

Ignatius ♂
Late Latin name, derived from the old
Roman family name *Egnatius* (of
uncertain origin, possibly Etruscan).
This was altered in the early Christian
period by association with Latin *ignis*
'fire'. It was borne by various early
saints, and more recently by St
Ignatius Loyola (1491–1556), who
founded the Society of Jesus (Jesuits).
In the modern English-speaking world
it is used mainly if not exclusively by
Roman Catholics.

Ike ♂
English: pet form of ◊**Isaac**. However,
it was made famous in the 20th
century as the nickname of the
American general and president
Dwight D. Eisenhower (1890–1969). In
this case, of course, it was based on
his surname.

Illtud ♂
Welsh traditional name, derived from
il, el 'multitude' + *tud* 'land', 'people'.
This was borne by a famous Welsh
saint (d. c.505) who founded the abbey
of Llantwit (originally *Llan-Illtut*
'church of Illtud').
Variant: **Illtyd** (a modern spelling).

Ilona ♀
Hungarian form of ◊**Helen**, now also

sometimes used in the English-speaking world.

Imogen ♀

The name owes its existence to a character in Shakespeare's *Cymbeline* (1609), but in earlier accounts of the events on which the play is based this character is named as *Innogen*. The modern form of the name is thus due to a misreading of these sources by Shakespeare, or of the play's text by his printer. The name *Innogen* is of Celtic origin, from Gaelic *inghean* 'girl', 'maiden'.

Ina ♀

Short form of any of the various female names ending in these two syllables (representing a Latinate feminine suffix), for example *Christina* and *Georgina*. See also ◊**Ena**.

India ♀

From the name of the subcontinent, used as the name of a character in Margaret Mitchell's novel *Gone with the Wind* (1936). In the case of India Hicks, Lord Mountbatten's granddaughter, the name was chosen because of her family's association with the subcontinent.

Inés ♀

Spanish form of ◊**Agnes**. The name is now also used, usually without the accent, in the English-speaking world.

Ingram ♂

Transferred use of the surname, which is derived from a medieval given name. This was probably a contracted form of the Norman name *Engelram*, composed of the Germanic ethnic name *Engel* 'Angle' + *hramn* 'raven'. It is also possible that in some cases the first element was the name of the Old Norse fertility god, *Ing*.

Ingrid ♀

From an Old Norse female personal name composed of the name of the fertility god *Ing* + *fríðr* 'fair',

'beautiful'. It was introduced into the English-speaking world from Scandinavia in the 20th century and became very popular, largely because of the fame of the Swedish film actress Ingrid Bergman (1915–82).

Inigo ♂

From the medieval Spanish given name *Íñigo*, a vernacular derivative of ◊**Ignatius**, apparently the result of crossing with a name recorded in the Middle Ages as *Ennecus*. This is of uncertain, possibly Basque, origin. *Íñigo* is now rarely used as a given name in Spain. In the English-speaking world it is mainly associated with the architect and stage designer Inigo Jones (1573–1652). The name had previously been borne by his father, a London clothmaker, who may well have received it at around the time of Queen Mary's marriage to Philip of Spain, when Spanish ways and Spanish names were fashionable, especially among devout Roman Catholics. The architect passed it on to his son, but later occurrences are rare.

Innes ♂ ♀

Scottish: Anglicized form based on the pronunciation of the Gaelic name *Aonghas* (see ◊**Angus**). It is also a surname, and use as a female name is in part the result of a regular trend (cf. e.g. ◊**Lesley**), but may have been influenced by adoption in the English-speaking world of the Spanish name ◊**Inés**.

Iole ♀

Name borne in classical mythology by a daughter of Eurytus of Oechalia; Herakles' infatuation with her led to his murder by his wife Deianeira. It represents the classical Greek vocabulary word meaning 'violet', and may in part have been chosen as a learned response to the 19th-century vogue for given names derived from words denoting flowers and plants.

Iolo ♂
Welsh: pet form of ◊**Iorwerth**.

Iona ♀
From the name of the tiny island in the Hebrides, off the west coast of Mull, where in 563 St Columba founded a monastery that became an important early centre of Christianity. It is said to result from a misreading of a Latin form of the island's name, *Ioua*, as *Iona*. Its Gaelic name is *Ì*, from Old Norse *ey* 'island'. The given name is most common in Scotland, but is also used elsewhere in the English-speaking world.

Ione ♀
19th-century coinage, apparently with reference to the glories of Ionian Greece in the 5th century BC. No such name exists in classical Greek.

Iorwerth ♂
Welsh traditional name, derived from *iōr* 'lord' + a mutated form of *berth* 'handsome'. It is borne in the *Mabinogi* by the jealous brother of Madawg, son of Maredudd. *Iorwerth* came to be regarded as a Welsh form of ◊**Edward**, but it has no actual connection with that name.
Variant: **Yorath**.
Pet form: **Iolo**.

Ira ♂
Biblical name (meaning 'watchful' in Hebrew), borne by a character mentioned very briefly in the Bible, one of the chief officers of King David (2 Samuel 20:26). It was taken up by the Puritans in the 17th century, and is still occasionally used, mainly in the United States.

Irene ♀
Name (from Greek *eirēnē* 'peace') borne in Greek mythology by a minor goddess who personified peace, and by a Byzantine empress (752–803). The name was taken up in the English-speaking world at the end of the 19th century, and became popular in the 20th, partly as a result of being used

as the name of a character in John Galsworthy's *The Forsyte Saga* (1922). It was formerly pronounced in three syllables, as in Greek, but is now thoroughly naturalized as an English name and usually pronounced as two syllables.

Iris ♀
Name (from Greek *iris* 'rainbow') borne in Greek mythology by a minor goddess, one of the messengers of the gods, who was so named because the rainbow was thought to be a sign from the gods to men. In English her name was used in the 16th century to denote both the flower and the coloured part of the eye, on account of their varied colours. In modern English use the name is often taken as being from the word for the flower, but it is also in use in Germany, where there is no such pattern of flower names.

Irma ♀
German: pet form of various female names of Germanic origin beginning with the element *irm(en)*, *erm(en)* 'whole', 'entire', for example *Irmgard* and *Irmtraud*. It was introduced to the English-speaking world at the end of the 19th century.

Irvin ♂
Mainly U.S.: variant of ◊**Irvine** or ◊**Irving**.

Irvine ♂
Mainly North American: transferred use of the Scottish surname, in origin a local name from a place in the former county of Ayrshire. The placename is probably derived from a Celtic river name, cognate with Welsh *ir*, *yr* 'green', 'fresh' + *afon* 'water'.

Irving ♂
Transferred use of the Scottish surname, in origin a local name from a place in the former county of Dumfriesshire, which has the same origin as ◊**Irvine**. In the case of the songwriter Irving Berlin (1888–1989),

the name was adopted: he was of Jewish origin, and was originally called Israel Baline. This is now a common given name, especially in North America. Among Jewish bearers, it is generally taken as an English equivalent of ◊Israel.

Irwin ♂
Transferred use of the surname, which is derived from the medieval given name *Erwin*, from Old English *eofor* 'boar' + *wine* 'friend'. There has also been some confusion with ◊Irving.

Isaac ♂
Biblical name, borne by the son of Abraham, who was nearly sacrificed by his father according to a command of God which was changed at the last moment. A ram, caught in a nearby thicket, was sacrificed instead (Genesis 22:1–13). Isaac lived on to marry Rebecca and become the father of Esau and Jacob. The derivation of the name is not certain; it has traditionally been connected with the Hebrew verb meaning 'to laugh'. In the Middle Ages it was borne only by Jews, but it was taken up by the Puritans in the 17th century and has continued in use since then among Christians in the English-speaking world, although it is still more common as a Jewish name.
Pet form: ◊Ike.

Isabel ♀
Originally a Spanish version of ◊Elizabeth, which was coined by deletion of the first syllable and alteration of the final consonant sound to one that can normally end a word in Spanish. The name was imported into France in the early Middle Ages, and thence into England. It was a royal name, and its popularity may have been enhanced by the fact that it was borne by a queen of England—Isabella (1296–1358), daughter of Philip IV of France—even though she led a turbulent life and

eventually had her husband, Edward II, murdered.
Variants: **Isobel**, **Isbel**.
Pet forms: **Izzy**, **Izzie**.

Isabella ♀
Latinate form of ◊Isabel, which became popular in England in the 18th century.

Isabelle ♀
French form of ◊Isabel, occasionally used in the English-speaking world.

Isadora ♀
Variant spelling of ◊Isidora, borne for example by the American dancer Isadora Duncan (1878–1927).

Isaiah ♂
Biblical name (meaning 'God is salvation' in Hebrew), borne by the most important of the major prophets. Rather surprisingly perhaps, the name has never been common in the English-speaking world, although it was occasionally used among the Puritans in the 17th century. It is well established as a Jewish name.

Isbel ♀
Scottish contracted form of ◊Isabel and ◊Isobel.

Isidora ♀
Feminine form of ◊Isidore. This name was little used in the Middle Ages, but has recently become modestly popular.
Pet forms: **Izzy**, **Izzie**.

Isidore ♂
English form (via Old French and Latin) of the Greek name *Isidōros*, composed of the name of the goddess *Isis* (of Egyptian origin) + Greek *dōron* 'gift'. In spite of its pagan connotations the name was a common one among early Christians, and was borne for example by the great encyclopedist St Isidore of Seville (c.560–636). By the late Middle Ages, however, it had come to be considered a typically Jewish name (although

originally adopted as a Christianized version of ◊Isaiah).
Pet forms: **Izzy, Izzie**.

Isla ♀
Scottish, pronounced '*eye*-la': of recent origin, from the usual pronunciation of the island name *Islay*.

Islwyn ♂
Welsh: taken from the name of a mountain in the county of Gwent, named with Welsh *is* 'below' + *llwyn* 'grove'.

Isobel ♀
Variant spelling of ◊Isabel, found mainly in Scotland.

Isolde ♀
The name of the tragic mistress of Tristan in the Arthurian romances. There are several versions of the story. The main features are that the beautiful Isolde, an Irish princess, is betrothed to the aged King Mark of Cornwall. However, through accidentally drinking a magic potion, she and the young Cornish knight Tristan fall in love, with tragic consequences. The story has exercised a powerful hold on the European imagination. The name was relatively common in Britain in the Middle Ages, but is much rarer today. The Welsh form **Esyllt** probably originally meant 'of fair aspect'.
Variant: **Isolda**.

Israel ♂
Biblical name: originally the byname (meaning 'he who strives with God' in Hebrew) given to Jacob after he had wrestled with an angel: 'Thy name shall be called no more Jacob, but Israel: for as a prince hast thou power with God and with men, and hast prevailed' (Genesis 32:28). The name was later applied to his descendants, the Children of Israel, and was chosen as the name of the modern Jewish state. The given name was used by the

Puritans in the 17th century, but is now once again almost exclusively a Jewish name.

Ita ♀
Irish: Anglicized form of the Gaelic name **Íde** (pronounced '*ee*-da', of uncertain origin (possibly connected with Old Irish *ítu* 'thirst'). This name was borne by a 6th-century saint who founded a convent in Limerick.

Ivan ♂
Russian form of ◊John, sometimes used in the English-speaking world in the 20th century.

Ivo ♂
Form of ◊Yves used in Germany and occasionally in the English-speaking world. It represents the nominative case of the Latinized form of the name.

Ivon ♂
Variant of ◊Ivo, derived from the oblique case of the name.

Ivor ♂
Of Scandinavian origin, from an Old Norse personal name derived from *ýr* 'yew', 'bow' + *herr* 'army'. In the 1920s and 30s it came to prominence as the name of the songwriter and actor Ivor Novello (1893–1951).
Variant: Scottish Gaelic: **Íomhar**.

Ivy ♀
From the vocabulary word denoting the plant (Old English *ífig*). This given name was adopted at the end of the 19th century together with a large number of other female names derived from words denoting flowers and plants. It is currently somewhat out of fashion.

Izzy ♀ ♂
Pet form of ◊Isabel, ◊Isidora, and, as a male name, ◊Isidore.
Variant: **Izzie**.

JACK JACKIE JACKLYN JACKSON JACKY JAC
LYN JACOB JACQUELINE JACQUETTA JACQ
UI ADE JAGO JAIME JAIMIE JAKE JAMES J
AMESINA JAMESON JAMIE JAMIESON JA
N ANCIS JANE JANELLE JANET JANETTE JA
N CE JANIE JANINE JANIS JANNA JARED J

Jack ♂

Originally a pet form of ◊**John**, but now well established as a given name in its own right. It is derived from Middle English *Jankin*, later altered to *Jackin*, from *Jan* (a contracted form of *Jehan* 'John') + the diminutive suffix *-kin*. This led to the back-formation *Jack*, as if the name had contained the Old French diminutive suffix *-in*. It is sometimes also used as an informal pet form of ◊**James**, perhaps influenced by the French form *Jacques*. See also ◊**Jock** and ◊**Jake**.

Jackie ♂ ♀

Originally a male name, a pet form of ◊**Jack**, but now also used as a female name, a pet form of ◊**Jacqueline**. *Variant*: **Jacky**.

Jacklyn ♀

Variant spelling of ◊**Jaclyn**, influenced by ◊**Jack**.

Jackson ♂

Transferred use of the surname, meaning originally 'son of Jack' and in modern times sometimes bestowed with precisely this meaning. In the United States it has also been used in honour of President Andrew Jackson (1767–1845) and the Confederate general Thomas 'Stonewall' Jackson (1824–63).

Jacky ♂ ♀

Variant spelling of ◊**Jackie**.

Jaclyn ♀

Simplified spelling of ◊**Jacquelyn**.

Jacob ♂

English form of the biblical Hebrew name *Yaakov*. This was borne by perhaps the most important of all the patriarchs in the Book of Genesis. Jacob was the father of twelve sons, who gave their names to the twelve tribes of Israel. He was the son of Isaac and Rebecca. According to the story in Genesis, he was the cunning younger twin, who persuaded his fractionally older brother Esau to part with his right to his inheritance in exchange for a bowl of soup ('a mess of pottage'). Later, he tricked his blind and dying father into blessing him in place of Esau. The derivation of the name has been much discussed. It is traditionally explained as being derived from Hebrew *akev* 'heel' and to have meant 'heel grabber', because when Jacob was born 'his hand took hold of Esau's heel' (Genesis 25:26). This is interpreted later in the Bible as 'supplanter'; Esau himself remarks, 'Is he not rightly named Jacob? for he has supplanted me these two times' (Genesis 27:36). As a given name, *Jacob* is especially common as a Jewish name, although it has also been used by Christians. Cf. ◊**James**.

Jacqueline ♀

Feminine diminutive form of *Jacques*, the French version of ◊**James**. In the 1960s it became very popular in the United States and elsewhere, influenced in part by the fame and stylish image of Jacqueline Bouvier Kennedy Onassis, whose family is of French extraction.

Pet forms: **Jackie, Jacky, Jacqui** (all now very common).

Jacquelyn ♀
Respelled form of ◊**Jacqueline**, influenced by the productive suffix -*lyn* (see ◊**Lynn**).
Variants: **Jac(k)lyn**.

Jacquetta ♀
Respelling (influenced by ◊**Jacqueline**) of the Italian name *Giachetta*, a feminine diminutive of *Giac(om)o*, the Italian version of ◊**James**.

Jacqui ♀
Pet form of ◊**Jacqueline**, once a modish spelling of what was normally written *Jackie*, but now well established.

Jade ♀
From the name of the precious stone, a word that reached English from Spanish *(piedra de) ijada*, which literally means '(stone of the) bowels'. It was so called because it was believed to have the magical power of providing protection against disorders of the intestines. The vogue for this word as a given name developed later than that for other gemstone names, possibly because it sounds the same as the vocabulary word denoting a broken-down old horse or a nagging woman. Its popular appeal received a considerable boost in the early 1970s when the daughter of the English rock singer Mick Jagger was so named.

Jago ♂
Cornish form of ◊**James**. It has increased in popularity recently, perhaps as a transferred use of the surname *Jago*, which itself derives from the Cornish given name.

Jaime ♂ ♀
This is the Spanish form of ◊**James**, but in the United States and Canada it has in recent years come to be used also as a female name, apparently a respelling of the female name ◊**Jamie**.

Jaimie ♀
Variant spelling of the female name ◊**Jamie**.
Variant: **Jaimee**.

Jake ♂
Variant of ◊**Jack**, of Middle English origin, which has now come back into fashion as an independent given name. It is also sometimes used as a short form of ◊**Jacob**.

James ♂
English form of the name borne in the New Testament by two of Christ's disciples, James son of Zebedee and James son of Alphaeus. This form comes from Late Latin *Iacomus*, a variant of *Iacobus*, Latin form of Greek *Iakobos*. This is the same name as Old Testament ◊**Jacob** (Hebrew *Yaakov*). For many centuries now it has been thought of in the English-speaking world and elsewhere as a distinct name. In Britain, *James* is a royal name that from the beginning of the 15th century onwards has been associated particularly with the Scottish house of Stewart: James I of Scotland (1394–1437; ruled 1424–37) was a patron of the arts and a noted poet, as well as an energetic ruler. King James VI of Scotland (1566–1625; reigned 1567–1625) succeeded to the throne of England in 1603. His grandson, James II of England (1633–1701; reigned 1685–8) was a Roman Catholic, deposed in 1688 in favour of his Protestant daughter Mary and her husband William of Orange. From then on he, his son (also called James), and his grandson Charles ('Bonnie Prince Charlie') made various unsuccessful attempts to recover the English throne. Their supporters were known as Jacobites (from Latin *Iacobus*), and the name James became for a while particularly associated with Roman Catholicism on the one hand, and Highland opposition to the English government on the other.

Short form: **Jim**.
Pet forms: **Jamey, Jamie, Jimmy, Jimmie**.

Jamesina ♀
Latinate feminine elaboration of
◊**James**, at one time regularly used in
Scotland, but now obsolete.

Jameson ♂
Transferred use of the surname, in
origin a patronymic meaning 'son of
James'.

Jamie ♂ ♀
Originally a male pet form of ◊**James**
and still so used, especially in
Scotland and Northumberland. In
North America it is now widely used
as a female given name, a feminine
equivalent of *James*.
Variants: **Jamey; Jamee, Jami** (female
only).

Jamieson ♂
Transferred use of the Northern
English and Scottish surname, in
origin a patronymic meaning 'son of
Jamie'.
Variant: **Jamieson**.

Jan ♂ ♀
As a male name this represents a
revival of Middle English *Jan*, a
byform of ◊**John**, or an adoption of the
common European form with this
spelling. As a female name it is a
short form of names such as ◊**Janet**
and ◊**Janice**.

Jancis ♀
Modern blend of ◊**Jan** and ◊**Frances**,
first used in the novel *Precious Bane*
(1924) by Mary Webb, for the
character of Jancis Beguildy, daughter
of Felix and Hephzibah.

Jane ♀
Originally a feminine form of ◊**John**,
from the Old French form *Je(h)anne*.
Since the 17th century it has proved
the most popular of the feminine
forms of *John*, ahead of ◊**Joan** and
◊**Jean**. It now also commonly occurs
as the second element in
combinations such as *Sarah-Jane*. In

Britain it is still one of the most
frequent of all female names, but in
the United States it barely scraped
into the top three hundred names
bestowed on baby girls in 1989. It is
not a royal name, but was borne by
the tragic Lady Jane Grey (1537–54),
who was unwillingly proclaimed
queen in 1553, deposed nine days
later, and executed the following year.
Seventy years earlier, the name had
come into prominence as that of Jane
Shore, mistress of King Edward IV and
subsequently of Thomas Grey, 1st
Marquess of Dorset, Lady Jane's
grandfather. Jane Shore's tribulations
in 1483 at the hands of Richard III,
Edward's brother and successor,
became the subject of popular ballads
and plays, which may well have
increased the currency of the name in
the 16th century. A 19th-century
influence was its use as the name of
the central character in Charlotte
Brontë's novel *Jane Eyre* (1847). In the
20th century it has been used
intermittently since the 1940s as the
name of a cheerful and scantily clad
beauty whose adventures are
chronicled in a strip cartoon in the
Daily Mirror, and in the 1940s was
borne by the statuesque American
film star Jane Russell (b. 1921).
Variant: **Jayne**. See also ◊**Jean**, ◊**Joan**, and
◊**Joanna**.
Pet forms: **Janey, Janie, Jaynie**.

Janelle ♀
Modern elaborated form of ◊**Jane**, with
the feminine ending *-elle* abstracted
from names such as ◊**Danielle**. In the
United States in 1989 this form was
far more commonly bestowed than the
simple *Jane*.
Variant: **Janella** (a Latinate form; for the
ending, cf. ◊**Prunella**).

Janet ♀
Originally a diminutive of ◊**Jane**,
already in common use in the Middle
English period. Towards the end of the
Middle Ages the name largely died out

except in Scotland. It was revived at the end of the 19th century to much more widespread use, while still retaining its popularity in Scotland.
Short form: ◊**Jan**.

Janette ♀
Either an elaborated version of ◊**Janet**, emphasizing the feminine form of the suffix, or a simplified form of ◊**Jeannette**.

Janey ♀
Pet form of ◊**Jane**.
Variants: **Janie**, **Jaynie**.

Janice ♀
Derivative of ◊**Jane**, with the addition of the suffix *-ice*, abstracted from female names such as ◊**Candice** and ◊**Bernice**. It seems to have been first used as the name of the heroine of the novel *Janice Meredith* by Paul Leicester Ford, published in 1899.
Variant: **Janis**.
Short form: **Jan**.

Janie ♀
Variant spelling of ◊**Janey**.

Janine ♀
Simplified form of ◊**Jeannine**.

Janis ♀
Variant spelling of ◊**Janice**, made popular in the 1960s and 70s by the American rock singer Janis Joplin (1943–70).

Janna ♀
Latinate elaboration of the female name ◊**Jan**.

Jared ♂
Biblical name (probably meaning 'descent' in Hebrew), borne by a descendant of Adam (Genesis 5:15). According to the Book of Genesis, he became the father of Enoch at the age of 162, and lived for a further eight hundred years. This name was occasionally used by the Puritans. It was briefly revived in the 1960s, for reasons that are not clear.

Jarlath ♂
Irish: Anglicized form of the Gaelic name *Iarlaith*, derived from *ior* (an element of uncertain meaning) + *flaith* 'prince', 'leader'. St Jarlath is the patron of the diocese of Tuam in Co. Galway, and *Jarlath* is still a popular given name in that area.

Jarrett ♂
Transferred use of the surname, in origin a variant of ◊**Garrett**. The popularity of the given name may also have been influenced by ◊**Jared**.

Jarvis ♂
Transferred use of the surname, which is from a Middle English form of the Norman given name ◊**Gervaise**. Modern use may in part represent an antiquarian revival of the medieval given name.

Jasmine ♀
From the vocabulary word denoting the climbing plant with its delicate, fragrant flowers (from Old French, ultimately from Persian *yasmin*).
Variants: **Jasmin**, ◊**Yasmin**.

Jason ♂
English form of the name (Greek *Iasōn*) borne in classical mythology by a hero, leader of the Argonauts, who sailed to Colchis in search of the Golden Fleece, enduring many hardships and adventures. The sorceress Medea fell in love with him and helped him to obtain the Fleece; they escaped together and should have lived happily ever after. However, Jason fell in love with another woman and deserted Medea. Medea took her revenge by killing her rival, but Jason himself survived to be killed in old age by one of the rotting timbers of his ship, the *Argo*, falling on his head. The classical Greek name *Iasōn* probably derives from the Greek vocabulary word *iasthai* 'to heal'. In New Testament Greek, the name probably represents a classicized form of ◊**Joshua**. It was borne by an early

Christian in Thessalonica, at whose house St Paul stayed (Acts 17:5-9; Romans 16:21). Probably for this reason, it enjoyed some popularity among the Puritans in the 17th century. In the mid-20th century it has enjoyed a considerable burst of popularity, although it has also been the subject of some rather surprising hostility. A 20th-century influence has been the film actor Jason Robards (b. 1920); his father, also a film actor, was likewise called Jason Robards. A more recent influence is the Australian actor Jason Donovan. The name has been used for various characters in films and television series.

Jasper ♂
The usual English form of the name assigned in Christian folklore to one of the three Magi or 'wise men', who brought gifts to the infant Christ at his birth (Matthew 2:1). The name does not appear in the Bible, and is first found in medieval tradition. It seems to be ultimately of Persian origin, from a word meaning 'treasurer'. There is probably no connection with the English vocabulary word *jasper* denoting a gemstone, which is of Semitic origin.

Jay ♂ ♀
Pet form of any of the given names beginning with the letter *J*- (cf. ◊**Dee** and ◊**Kay**); now also used as an independent given name.

Jayne ♀
Elaborated spelling of ◊**Jane**.

Jaynie ♀
Variant spelling of ◊**Janey**.

Jean ♀
Like ◊**Jane** and ◊**Joan**, a medieval variant of Old French *Je(h)anne*. Towards the end of the Middle Ages this form became largely confined to Scotland. In the 20th century it has been more widely used in the English-speaking world, but still retains a Scottish flavour.

Jeana ♀
Latinate elaboration of ◊**Jean**, common especially in the United States.

Jeane ♀
Variant spelling of ◊**Jean**, common especially in the United States.

Jeanette ♀
Variant spelling of ◊**Jeannette**, in the 1920s and 30s associated particularly with the singer and film star Jeanette MacDonald (1902-65).

Jeanie ♀
Pet form of ◊**Jean**.

Jeanine ♀
Variant spelling of ◊**Jeannine**.

Jeannette ♀
French diminutive form of *Jeanne*, feminine form of *Jean* 'John', now also commonly used in the English-speaking world.

Jeannie ♀
Variant spelling of ◊**Jeanie**.

Jeannine ♀
French diminutive form of *Jeanne*, feminine form of *Jean* 'John', now also sometimes used in the English-speaking world.

Jed ♂
Mainly U.S.: now generally used as an independent given name, this was originally a short form of the biblical name **Jedidiah**. This means 'beloved of God' in Hebrew, and was used as an alternative name of King Solomon (2 Samuel 12:25). It was a favourite with the Puritans, who considered themselves, too, to be loved by God, but the full form fell out of favour along with other rare or unwieldy Old Testament names. See also ◊**Ged**.

Jeff ♂
Short form of ◊**Jeffrey**, now also used as an independent given name, especially in North America.

Jefferson ♂
Transferred use of the surname,

originally a patronymic meaning 'son of Jeffrey'. The given name is still sometimes so used. In the United States it has often been bestowed in honour of the statesman Thomas Jefferson (1743–1826), principal author of the Declaration of Independence, who became the third president of the Union. He is also remembered as a scientist, architect, and writer.

Jeffrey ♂

Variant spelling of ◊**Geoffrey**, common in the Middle Ages (as reflected in surnames such as *Jefferson*). This is the usual spelling of the name in North America and is now becoming more common in Britain.
Variant: **Jeffery**.
Short form: **Jeff**.

Jem ♂

From a medieval vernacular form of ◊**James**. In modern use, however, it is often used as a short form of ◊**Jeremy**.

Jemima ♀

Biblical name (meaning 'dove' or 'bright as day' in Hebrew), borne by the eldest of the daughters of Job, born to him towards the end of his life when his prosperity had been restored (Job 42:14). The name was common in the first part of the 19th century, and has continued in modest use since then.

Jemma ♀

Variant spelling of ◊**Gemma**.

Jenessa ♀

Recent coinage, a blend of ◊**Jennifer** and ◊**Vanessa**.

Jenkin ♂

Transferred use of the surname, which is derived from the medieval given name *Jankin*. This was a pet form of the male name ◊**Jan**, with the diminutive suffix *-kin*. The modern given name is popular in Wales, where the surnames *Jenkin* and *Jenkins* are common.

Jenna ♀

Fanciful alteration of ◊**Jenny**, with the Latinate feminine ending *-a*.

Jenni ♀

Variant spelling of ◊**Jenny**, now commonly used for the sake of variety or stylishness (*-i* as an ending of female names being in vogue; cf. ◊**Jacqui**, ◊**Toni**).

Jennifer ♀

Of Celtic (Arthurian) origin. This represents a Cornish form of the name of King Arthur's unfaithful ◊**Guinevere**. At the beginning of the 20th century, the name was merely a Cornish curiosity, but since then it has become enormously popular all over the English-speaking world. One factor in its rise was probably Bernard Shaw's use of it for the character of Jennifer Dubedat in *The Doctor's Dilemma* (1905). See also ◊**Gaynor**.

Jenny ♀

Now universally taken as a short form of ◊**Jennifer**. In fact, this name existed during the Middle Ages as a pet form of ◊**Jean**.
Variants: **Jenni**, **Jenna**.

Jeremiah ♂

Biblical name (meaning 'appointed by God' in Hebrew), borne by a Hebrew prophet of the 7th–6th centuries BC, whose story, prophecies of judgement, and lamentations are recorded in the book of the Bible that bears his name. The Book of Lamentations is also attributed to him; it bewails the destruction of Jerusalem and the temple by the Babylonians in 587 BC. Despite the gloomy subject-matter of these texts, the name enjoyed some popularity among Puritans and Christian fundamentalists, partly perhaps because Jeremiah also preached reconciliation with God after his wrath was assuaged.

Jeremy ♂

Anglicized form, used in the Authorized Version of the New

Testament (Matthew 2:17; 27:9), of
the biblical name ◊**Jeremiah**.
Short form: **Jem**.
Pet form: **Jerry**.

Jermaine ♂
Variant spelling of ◊**Germaine**, now
quite common as a male name in the
United States.

Jerome ♂
Anglicized form of the Greek name
Hieronymos, derived from *hieros*
'holy' + *onoma* 'name'. St Jerome
(c.342–420) was a citizen of the
Eastern Roman Empire, who bore the
Greek names Eusebios Hieronymos
Sophronios; he was chiefly responsible
for the translation into Latin of the
Bible, the Vulgate. He also wrote
many works of commentary and
exposition on the Bible, and is
regarded as one of the Doctors of the
Church.
Pet form: **Jerry**.

Jerrard ♂
Rare variant of ◊**Gerard**.

Jerrold ♂
Rare variant of ◊**Gerald**, probably a
transferred use of the surname derived
from the given name in the Middle
Ages.

Jerry ♂ ♀
As a male name this is a pet form of
◊**Jeremy** or ◊**Gerald**, or occasionally of
◊**Gerard** and ◊**Jerome**. As a female
name it is a variant of ◊**Gerry**.

Jervaise ♂
Variant spelling of ◊**Gervaise**.

Jess ♀ ♂
Usually a female name, a short form
of ◊**Jessie** or ◊**Jessica**. As a male name,
it is a short form of ◊**Jesse**.

Jesse ♂
Biblical name (meaning 'gift' in
Hebrew), borne by the father of King
David (1 Samuel 16), from whose line
(according to the New Testament)
Jesus was ultimately descended. It was

popular among the Puritans, and is
still used fairly frequently in the
United States, more rarely in Britain.
Variant or short form: **Jess**.

Jessica ♀
Apparently of Shakespearian origin.
This was the name of the daughter of
Shylock in *The Merchant of Venice*
(1596). Shakespeare's source has not
been established, but he presumably
intended it to pass as a typically
Jewish name. It may be from a
biblical name that appeared, in the
translations available in Shakespeare's
day, as *Jesca* (Genesis 11:29; *Iscah* in
the Authorized Version). This occurs
in a somewhat obscure genealogical
passage; Iscah appears to have been
Abraham's niece.
Short form: **Jess**.

Jessie ♀
Pet form of ◊**Jessica**, also recorded in
Scotland from an early date as a pet
form of ◊**Jean**, although the derivation
is not clear. The Gaelic form is
Teasag. It is now quite often used in
Scotland and elsewhere as a given
name in its own right.
Short form: **Jess**.

Jethro ♂
Biblical name, borne by the father of
Moses's wife Zipporah (Exodus 3:1;
4:18). It seems to be a variant of the
Hebrew name *Ithra*, said to mean
'excellence', which is found at 2
Samuel 17:25. It was popular among
the Puritans, but then fell out of
general use. It was borne by the
agricultural reformer Jethro Tull
(1674–1741). In 1968 a 'progressive
rock' group in Britain adopted the
name Jethro Tull, and shortly
afterwards the given name *Jethro*
enjoyed a revival of popularity.

Jetta ♀
Comparatively recent coinage, a
Latinate derivative of the vocabulary
word denoting the mineral *jet*. This
word is derived from Old French *jaiet*,

from Latin *(lapis) gagātēs* 'stone from Gagai'. The latter is a town in Lycia, Asia Minor.

Jewel ♀
A recent adoption of the vocabulary word meaning 'gemstone' (from Old French *jouel*, diminutive of *jou* 'plaything', 'delight', Latin *iocus*). The given name may derive from its use as a term of affection, or may have been suggested by the vogue in the 19th century for creating given names from words denoting particular gemstones, e.g. ◊Beryl, ◊Ruby.

Jill ♀
Short form (respelled) of ◊Gillian, now often used as an given name in its own right. It was already used as a prototypical female name in the phrase 'Jack and Jill' in the 15th century.

Jillian ♀
Variant spelling of ◊Gillian.

Jim ♂
Short form of ◊James, already common in the Middle Ages.
Pet forms: Jimmy, Jimmie.

Jo ♀ ♂
Usually a female name, a short form of ◊Joanna, ◊Joanne, ◊Jody, or ◊Josephine, sometimes used in combination with other names, for example *Nancy Jo* and *Jo Anne* (see ◊Joanne). Occasionally it is a male name, a variant of ◊Joe.

Joachim ♂
Biblical name, probably from the Hebrew name *Johoiachin*, meaning 'established by God'. This was borne by a king of Judah who was defeated by Nebuchadnezzar and carried off into Babylonian exile (2 Kings 24). His father's name was *Jehoiakim*, and there has clearly been some confusion between the two forms in the derivation of the modern name. The reason for its great popularity in Christian Europe is that in medieval tradition it was the name commonly ascribed to the father of the Virgin Mary. He is not named at all in the Bible, but with the growth of the cult of Mary many legends grew up about her early life, and her parents came to be venerated as saints under the names Joachim and Anne.

Joan ♀
Contracted form of Old French *Jo(h)anne*, from Latin *Io(h)anna* (see ◊Joanna). In England this was the usual feminine form of ◊John from the Middle English period onwards, but in the 16th and 17th centuries it was largely superseded by ◊Jane. It was strongly revived in the first part of the 20th century, partly under the influence of George Bernard Shaw's play *St Joan* (1923), based on the life of Joan of Arc (1412–31). Claiming to be guided by the voices of the saints, she persuaded the French dauphin to defy the occupying English forces and have himself crowned, and she led the French army that raised the siege of Orleans in 1429. The following year she was captured by the Burgundians and sold to the English, and a year later she was burned at the stake for witchcraft at the age of 18 or 19. Her story has captured the imagination of many writers, and she is variously portrayed as a national and political hero, a model of apolitical straightforwardness and honesty, and a religious heroine. She was canonized in 1920.
Pet forms: Joanie, Joni.

Joanna ♀
From the Latin form, *Io(h)anna*, of Greek *Iōanna*, the feminine equivalent of *Iōannēs* (see ◊John). In the New Testament, this name is borne by a woman who was one of Jesus's followers (Luke 8:3; 24:10). She was the wife of the steward of the household of King Herod Antipas. The name was regularly used throughout the Middle Ages in most parts of

Europe as a feminine equivalent of ◊**John**, but in England it has only been in common use as a vernacular given name since the 19th century.
Short form: **Jo.**

Joanne ♀
From Old French *Jo(h)anne*, and so a doublet of ◊**Joan**. This too was revived as a given name in its own right in the first half of the 20th century. It has to some extent been influenced by the independently formed combination *Jo Anne*.
Short form: **Jo.**

Job ♂
Biblical name, borne by the eponymous hero of the Book of Job, a man of exemplary patience, whose faith was severely tested by God's apparently motive-less maltreatment of him. His name, appropriately enough, means 'persecuted' in Hebrew. His story was a favourite one in the Middle Ages and frequently formed the subject of miracle plays. The name was used among Puritans and Christian fundamentalists, but is currently out of favour.

Jocasta ♀
Name borne in classical legend by the mother of Oedipus, King of Thebes. As the result of a series of misunderstandings, she also became his wife and the mother of his children. The derivation of her name is not known. In spite of its tragic associations, the name has enjoyed a certain vogue in recent years.

Jocelyn ♀ ♂
Now normally a female name, but in earlier times more often given to boys. It represents a transferred use of the English surname, which in turn is derived from an Old French masculine personal name introduced to Britain by the Normans in the form *Joscelin*. This was originally a derivative, *Gautzelin*, of the name of a Germanic tribe, the *Gauts*. The spelling of the first syllable was altered because the name was taken as a double diminutive (with the Old French suffixes *-el* and *-in*) of *Josce* (see ◊**Joyce**).
Variant: **Josceline** ♀
Short form: **Joss.**

Jock ♂
Scottish: variant of ◊**Jack**, sometimes used as an archetypal nickname for a Scotsman.
Pet forms: **Jockie**, **Jockey.**

Jodene ♀
Recent fanciful coinage, formed from ◊**Jody** plus the productive suffix *-ene*.

Jody ♀ ♂
Of uncertain origin. It may have originated as a pet form of ◊**Judith** and ◊**Jude**, but if so the reason for the change in the vowel is not clear. Alternatively, it may be a playful elaboration of ◊**Jo** and ◊**Joe**, with *-d-* introduced for euphony before the diminutive suffix *-y*.
Variants: **Jodie** (associated particularly with the actress Jodie Foster, b. 1962); **Jodi.**

Joe ♂
Short form of ◊**Joseph**.
Variant: **Jo.**
Pet form: **Joey.**

Joel ♂
Biblical name, composed of two different Hebrew elements, *Yah(weh)* and *El*, both of which mean 'God'; the implication of the name is that the Hebrew God, *Yahweh*, is the only true god. This is a common name in the Bible, being borne by, among others, one of King David's 'mighty men' (1 Chronicles 11:38), and a minor prophet who lived in the 8th century BC. The name has been perennially popular as a Jewish name; it was also taken up by the Puritans and other Christian fundamentalists. It is still used in North America. In Britain, however, it is not at all common.

Joelle ♀

Borrowing of the fashionable French
name *Joëlle*, a feminine form of ◊**Joel**.
Its selection as a given name may also
have been influenced by the fact that
it can be taken as a combination of
◊**Jo** and the productive suffix *-elle*
(originally a French feminine
diminutive ending).

Joey ♂

Pet form of ◊**Joe**.

Johanna ♀

Latinate feminine form of *Johannes*
(see ◊**John**), a variant of ◊**Joanna**.

John ♂

English form of Latin *Io(h)annes*, New
Testament Greek *Iōannēs*, a
contracted form of the Hebrew name
Johanan 'God is gracious' (the name of
several different characters in the Old
Testament, including one of King
David's 'mighty men'). *John* is the
spelling used in the Authorized
Version of the New Testament. The
name is of great importance in early
Christianity: it was borne by John the
Baptist (the precursor of Christ
himself, who baptized sinners in the
River Jordan), by one of Christ's
disciples (John the Apostle, a
fisherman, brother of James), and by
the author of the fourth gospel (John
the Evangelist, identified in Christian
tradition with the apostle, but more
probably a Greek-speaking Jewish
Christian living over half a century
later). The name was also borne by
many saints and by twenty-three
popes, including John XXIII (Giuseppe
Roncalli, 1881–1963), whose
popularity was yet another factor
influencing people to choose this
given name. It was also a royal name,
being borne by eight Byzantine
emperors and by kings of Hungary,
Poland, Portugal, France, and
elsewhere. In its various forms in
different languages, it has been the
most perennially popular of all
Christian names.

Pet forms: **Johnny, Johnnie,** ◊**Jack,**
◊**Hank.**

Johnathan ♂

Respelled form of ◊**Jonathan**, as if a
combination of ◊**John** and ◊**Nathan**.

Johnny ♂ ♀

Pet form of ◊**John**. In the United
States it is occasionally also used as a
female name.
Variant: **Johnnie.**

Jolene ♀

Recent coinage, combining the short
form ◊**Jo** with the productive suffix
-lene, extracted from names such as
◊**Marlene**. It seems to have originated
in the United States in the 1940s. It
was made famous by a hit song with
this title, recorded by Dolly Parton in
1979.

Jolyon ♂

Medieval variant spelling of ◊**Julian**.
Its occasional use in modern Britain
derives from the name of a character
in John Galsworthy's sequence of
novels *The Forsyte Saga* (1922), which
was serialized on television in the late
1960s.

Jon ♂

Simplified spelling of ◊**John** or short
form of ◊**Jonathan**.

Jonah ♂

Biblical name (meaning 'dove' in
Hebrew), borne by a prophet whose
adventures are the subject of one of
the shorter books of the Bible. God
appeared to Jonah and ordered him to
go and preach in Nineveh. When
Jonah disobeyed, God caused a storm
to threaten the ship in which Jonah
was travelling. His shipmates,
realizing that Jonah was the cause of
their peril, threw him overboard,
whereupon the storm subsided. A
'great fish' swallowed Jonah and
delivered him, willy-nilly, to the
coasts of Nineveh. This story was
immensely popular in the Middle

Ages, and a favourite subject of miracle plays.

Jonas ♂
Variant of ◊Jonah, from the New Testament Greek form of the name.

Jonathan ♂
Biblical name, meaning 'God has given', composed of the same elements as those of ◊Matthew, but in reverse order. This is the name of several characters in the Bible, most notably a son of King Saul, who was a devoted friend and supporter of the young David, even when David and Saul were themselves at loggerheads (1 Samuel 31; 2 Samuel 1:19–26). The name is often taken as symbolic of steadfast friendship and loyalty.
Variants: **Jonathon, Johnathan**.
Short form: **Jon**.

Joni ♀
Modern respelling of *Joanie*, pet form of ◊Joan. It is particularly associated with the Canadian folk singer Joni Mitchell (b. 1943).

Jonquil ♀
From the name of the flower, which was taken into English from French *jonquille* (a diminutive of Spanish *junco*, Latin *juncus* 'reed'). This is one of the latest and rarest of the flower names, which enjoyed a brief vogue during the 1940s and 1950s.

Jordan ♂ ♀
Originally a name given to a child of either sex baptized in holy water that was, purportedly at least, brought from the River Jordan, whose Hebrew name, *ha-yarden*, means 'flowing down'. It was in this river that Christ was baptized by John the Baptist, and medieval pilgrims to the Holy Land usually tried to bring back a flask of its water with them. The modern given name is either a revival of this, or else a transferred use of the surname that was derived from the medieval given name.

Variants: **Jorden, Jordin, Jordon, Jordyn** (all mainly U.S.).

Jory ♀
Pet form of ◊Marjorie.

Josceline ♀
Variant of ◊Jocelyn as a female name.

Joseph ♂
English form of the biblical Hebrew name *Yosef*, meaning '(God) shall add (another son)'. This was borne by the favourite son of Jacob, whose brothers became jealous of him and sold him into slavery (Genesis 37). He was taken to Egypt, where he rose to become chief steward to Pharaoh, and was eventually reconciled to his brothers when they came to buy corn during a seven-year famine (Genesis 43–7). In the New Testament *Joseph* is the name of the husband of the Virgin Mary. It is also borne by a rich Jew, Joseph of Arimathea (Matthew 27:57; Mark 15:43; Luke 23:50; John 19:38), who took Jesus down from the Cross, wrapped him in a shroud, and buried him in a rock tomb. According to medieval legend, Joseph of Arimathea brought the Holy Grail to Britain.
Short forms: **Joe, Jo**.

Josephine ♀
From French *Joséphine*, a feminine equivalent of ◊Joseph formed with the diminutive suffix *-ine*. It is now widely used in the English-speaking world.
Short form: **Jo**.
Pet form: **Josie**.

Josette ♀
Modern French pet form of *Joséphine*, sometimes also used in the English-speaking world in the 20th century.

Josh ♂
Short form of ◊Joshua.

Joshua ♂
Biblical name (meaning 'God is salvation' in Hebrew), borne by the Israelite leader who took command of the children of Israel after the death of

Moses and led them, after many battles, to take possession of the promised land. The name is especially common as a Jewish name, and has also been favoured by Nonconformist Christians.

Josiah ♂
Biblical name (meaning 'God heals' in Hebrew), borne by a king of Judah, whose story is recounted in 2 Kings 22–3. This was fairly frequently used as a given name in the English-speaking world, especially among Dissenters, from the 18th to the early 20th century. The most famous English bearer is the potter Josiah Wedgwood (1730–95). In North America this was a recurrent name in the Quincy family of Massachusetts; the best-known Josiah Quincy (1744–75) was a pre-Revolutionary patriot, who died at the age of thirty-one while returning from arguing the cause of the American colonists in London.

Josie ♀
Pet form of ◊Josephine, now widely used as an independent given name.

Joss ♂ ♀
Short form of ◊Jocelyn, occasionally used as an independent given name. In part it may also be a revival of a medieval male name (see ◊Joyce).

Joy ♀
From the vocabulary word (Old French joie, Late Latin gaudia). Being 'joyful in the Lord' was a duty that the Puritans took seriously, so the name became popular in the 17th century under their influence. In modern times, it is generally bestowed with reference to the parents' joy in their new-born child, or with the intention of wishing her a happy life.

Joyce ♀, formerly ♂
Apparently from the Norman male name Josce (Middle English Josse), which in turn is from Jodocus, a Latinized form of a Breton name,

Iodoc, meaning 'lord', borne by a 7th-century Breton saint. The name was in use among Breton followers of William the Conqueror. However, although this was fairly common as a male given name in the Middle Ages, it had virtually died out by the 14th century. There is some evidence of its use as a female name in the 17th and 18th centuries, perhaps as a variant of ◊Joy. It was strongly revived in the 19th century under the influence of popular fiction. It is borne by characters in Mrs Henry Wood's East Lynne (1861) and Edna Lyall's In the Golden Days (1885). Modern use may well have been influenced also by the common Irish surname derived from the medieval Norman male name. See also ◊Joss.

Judah ♂
Biblical name (said to mean 'praised' in Hebrew), borne by the fourth son of Jacob (Genesis 29:35), who gave his name to one of the twelve tribes of Israel and to one of its two kingdoms.

Judd ♂
Medieval pet form of ◊Jordan, now restored to use as a given name from the derived surname.

Jude ♂
Short form of Judas, itself a Greek form of ◊Judah. This form is occasionally used in the New Testament and elsewhere to distinguish the apostle Jude (Judas Thaddaeus), to whom one of the Epistles in the New Testament is attributed, from the traitor Judas Iscariot. The name is also borne by the central character in Thomas Hardy's gloomy novel Jude the Obscure (1895). More recently it received some support from the Lennon and McCartney song 'Hey Jude' (1968).

Judith ♀
Biblical name, meaning 'Jewess' or 'woman from Judea', borne by a

Jewish heroine whose story is recorded in the Book of Judith in the Apocrypha. Judith is portrayed as a beautiful widow who delivers her people from the invading Assyrians by gaining the confidence of their commander, Holofernes, and cutting off his head while he is asleep; without their commander, the Assyrians are duly routed. The name is also borne by one of the Hittite wives of Esau (Genesis 26:34). This has been a perennially popular Jewish name. In the English-speaking world it was taken up among Nonconformists in the 18th century, and has enjoyed great popularity in the 20th century. It was in occasional use among Gentiles before this: for example, it was borne by a niece of William the Conqueror.
Pet forms: **Judy**, **Judi**, **Judie**.

Judy ♀
Pet form of ◊**Judith**. This was the name adopted by the singer and film star Judy Garland (1922–69, original name Frances Gumm).
Variants: **Judi**, **Judie**.

Jules ♂, now sometimes also ♀
French form of ◊**Julius**. It is a very common given name in France and is occasionally used in the English-speaking world, where it is also fairly common as an informal pet form of ◊**Julian** and ◊**Julie**.

Julia ♀
Feminine form of the old Roman family name ◊**Julius**. A woman called Julia is mentioned in Paul's Epistle to the Romans (Romans 16:15), and the name was borne by numerous early saints. Its frequency increased with the vogue for classical names in the 18th century, and it continues to enjoy considerable popularity, although the recent introduction of ◊**Julie** to the English-speaking world has reduced this somewhat.

Julian ♂, occasionally ♀
From the common Late Latin name

Juliānus, a derivative of ◊**Julius**. In classical times *Juliānus* was a name borne not only by various minor early saints, but also by the Roman emperor Julian 'the Apostate', who attempted to return the Roman Empire from institutionalized Christianity to paganism. For many centuries the English name *Julian* was borne by women as well as men, for example by the Blessed Julian of Norwich (*c.*1342–after 1413). The differentiation in form between *Julian* and ◊**Gillian** did not develop until the 16th century. *Julian* is still occasionally used as a female name.
Variant: ◊**Jolyon** ♂

Juliana ♀
Latin feminine form of *Juliānus* (see ◊**Julian**), which was revived in England in the 18th century and has been used occasionally ever since.

Julianne ♀
Modern combination of the given names ◊**Julie** and ◊**Anne**, perhaps sometimes intended as a form of ◊**Juliana**.

Julie ♀
French form of ◊**Julia**. This was imported to the English-speaking world in the 1920s, and for some reason has become enormously popular. Its popularity was increased in the 1960s by the fame of the actresses Julie Harris (b. 1925), Julie Andrews (b. 1934 as Julia Wells), and Julie Christie (b. 1940).

Juliet ♀
Anglicized form of French *Juliette* or Italian *Giulietta*, diminutive forms of ◊**Julia**. The name is most famous as that of the 'star-crossed' heroine of Shakespeare's tragedy *Romeo and Juliet*.

Julitta ♀
Of uncertain origin, probably a Late Latin form of ◊**Judith**, influenced by

◊**Julia**. This was the name borne by the mother of the infant saint Quiricus; she was martyred with him at Tarsus in 304.

Julius ♂

Roman family name, of obscure derivation, borne most notably by Gaius Julius Caesar (?102–44 BC). It was in use among the early Christians, and was the name of an early and influential pope (337–52), as well as of a later pope (1443–1513) who attempted to combat the corruption of the Renaissance papacy.

June ♀

The most successful and enduring of the names coined in the early 20th century from the names of months of the year (cf. ◊**April** and ◊**May**).

Juniper ♀

From the name of the plant (derived in the Middle Ages from Late Latin *iunipērus*, of uncertain origin). The term is also used in the Authorized Version of the Old Testament as a translation of Hebrew *rothem*, a substantial desert shrub whose wood was used in the building of the temple of Solomon. This is not a particularly common given name; there may have been some influence from ◊**Jennifer**

(the surname *Juniper* is in part derived from *Jennifer*).

Justin ♂

English form of the Latin name *Justīnus*, a derivative of ◊**Justus**. The name was borne by various early saints, notably a 2nd-century Christian apologist and a (possibly spurious) boy martyr of the 3rd century. As an English name, *Justin* has enjoyed considerable popularity in the second part of the 20th century.

Justina ♀

Feminine form of ◊**Justin**, from Latin *Justīna*. This was the name of an early virgin martyr executed at Padua under Diocletian.

Justine ♀

Feminine form of ◊**Justin**, from a French version of ◊**Justina**. Its popularity in Britain since the 1960s was partly due to the influence of Lawrence Durrell's novel of this name.

Justus ♂

Latin name meaning 'just' or 'fair'. Because of its transparently well-omened meaning, it has been used occasionally as a given name in several countries, including Germany and the Netherlands.

KAILEY KALE KALEY KANE KARA KAREN KA
RIN KARL KATARINA KATE KATELYN KATE
RINA KATH KATHA KATHARINE KATHERI
NE KATHERYN KATHLEEN KATHRYN KAT
HRYN KATHY KATIE KATLYN KATRINA KA
TRINE KATY KATYA KAY KAYE KAYLA KAYL

Kailey ♀
Variant spelling of ◊Kayley.
Variants: **Kaily, Kailee, Kaileigh.**

Kale ♂
Mainly North American: of uncertain
origin, perhaps an Anglicized form of
the Irish Gaelic name ◊Cathal. It may
have been invented as a masculine
equivalent of the currently popular
◊Kayley and its variants.

Kaley ♀
Variant spelling of ◊Kayley.
Variants: **Kalie, Kalee, Kaleigh.**

Kane ♂
Irish: Anglicized form of the
traditional Gaelic name *Cathán*,
meaning 'little battler', a derivative of
cath 'battle'.

Kara ♀
Variant spelling of ◊Cara.

Karen ♀
Danish form of ◊Katherine, first
introduced to the English-speaking
world by Scandinavian settlers in
America. It has been used in Britain
only since the 1950s, but has become
very popular.

Karin ♀
Swedish form of ◊Katherine, found as
a less common variant of ◊Karen in
America and Britain.

Karl ♂
German and Scandinavian form of
◊Charles. See also ◊Carl.

Katarina ♀
Swedish form of ◊Katherine, also
occasionally used in the English-
speaking world.

Kate ♀
Short form of ◊Katherine (or any of its
variant spellings), reflecting the
French pronunciation with -*t*- for -*th*-,
which was also usual in medieval
England. This short form has been
continuously popular since the Middle
Ages. It was used by Shakespeare for
two important characters: the
daughter of the King of France who is
wooed and won by King Henry V, and
the 'shrew' in *The Taming of the
Shrew*.

Katelyn ♀
Elaboration of ◊Kate with the suffix
-*lyn* (see ◊Lynn), or a respelling of
◊Caitlín.

Katerina ♀
Russian popular form of ◊Katherine,
also occasionally used in the English-
speaking world.

Kath ♀
Modern short form of ◊Katherine and
its variants.

Katha ♀
Altered form of ◊Kathy or elaborated
form of ◊Kath, with the Latinate
feminine suffix -*a*.

Katharine ♀
Variant of ◊Katherine, associated by
folk etymology with Greek *katharos*
'pure'. This is the preferred spelling in
Germany and North America: it is the
one used, for example, in the name of
the film star Katharine Hepburn
(1907–).

Katherine ♀
English form of the name of a saint

martyred at Alexandria in 307. The story has it that she was condemned to be broken on the wheel for her Christian belief. However, the wheel miraculously fell apart, so she was beheaded instead. There were many elaborations on this story, which was one of the most popular in early Christian mythology, and she has been the object of a vast popular cult. The earliest sources that mention her are in Greek and give the name in the form *Aikaterinē*. The name is of unknown etymology; the suggestion that it may be derived from *Hēcatē*, the pagan goddess of magic and enchantment, is not convincing. From an early date, it was associated with the Greek adjective *katharos* 'pure'. This led to spellings with -*th*- and to a change in the middle vowel (see ◊**Katharine**). Several later saints also bore the name, including the mystic St Katherine of Siena (1347–80) who both led a contemplative life and played a role in the affairs of state of her day. *Katherine* is also a royal name: in England it was borne by the formidable and popular Katherine of Aragon (1485–1536), first wife of Henry VIII, as well as by the wives of Henry V and Charles II.
Variants: **Katharine**, **Catherine**, **Catharine**, **Kath(e)ryn**, **Cathryn**.
Short forms: ◊**Kate**, **Kath**, **Cath**.
Pet forms: **Kathy**, **Cathy**, **Katy**, **Katie**, **Kit(ty)**.

Katheryn ♀
Altered spelling of ◊**Katherine**, influenced by the productive name suffix -*yn*.

Kathleen ♀
Of Irish origin: traditional Anglicized form of Gaelic ◊**Caitlín**.
Variant: **Cathleen**.

Kathryn ♀
Simplified form of ◊**Katheryn**, now the most common version of ◊**Katherine** in the United States.

Kathy ♀
Pet form of ◊**Katherine** and its variants.

Katie ♀
Variant spelling of ◊**Katy**.

Katlyn ♀
Variant of ◊**Katelyn**.

Katrina ♀
Variant spelling of ◊**Catrina**.

Katrine ♀
German and Danish contracted form of *Katharine*, now also occasionally used in the English-speaking world.

Katy ♀
Pet form of ◊**Katherine** and its many variants.

Katya ♀
Russian pet form of *Yekaterina* 'Katherine', now sometimes used as a given name in the English-speaking world.

Kay ♀ ♂
Pet form of any of the various names beginning with the letter *K*- (cf. ◊**Dee** and ◊**Jay**), most notably ◊**Katherine** and its many variants. As a male name it may also in part represent the name of the Arthurian knight Sir Kay, although he is not a particularly attractive character. His name is probably a Celticized form of Latin *Gaius*, an ancient Roman given name of uncertain derivation. As a female name it was famous as that of the actress Kay Kendall (1926–59; original name Justine McCarthy).

Kaye ♀
Variant spelling of ◊**Kay** as a female name.

Kayla ♀
Altered form of ◊**Kayley**, a recent coinage now enjoying a considerable vogue in North America.
Variant: **Kaylah**.

Kayley ♀
Of recent origin and uncertain

derivation, occurring in a remarkably large number of different spellings. It is probably a transferred use of the Irish surname *Kayley*, an Anglicized form of Gaelic *Ó Caollaidhe* 'descendant of Caollaidhe'. The latter is an ancient (male) personal name derived from *caol* 'slender'. Its adoption as a modern given name has probably also been influenced by the popularity of ◊**Keeley**, ◊**Kelly**, and ◊**Kylie**, not to mention ◊**Cally**.
Variants: **Kayly, Kayli(e), Kaylee, Kayleigh, Kail(e)y, Kailee, Kaileigh, Kaley, Kalie, Kalee, Kaleigh, Cayleigh, Caileigh, Caleigh.**

Kean ♂
Irish: Anglicized form of the Gaelic name ◊**Cian**.
Variant: **Keane**.

Keegan ♂
Transferred use of the Irish surname, an Anglicized form of Gaelic *Mac Aodhagáin*, a patronymic from the personal name *Aodhagán*, double diminutive of *Aodh* (see ◊**Aidan**).

Keeley ♀
Of recent origin and uncertain etymology, possibly an alteration of ◊**Keelin** to fit in with the pattern of female names ending in *-(e)y* or *-ie*. The Irish surname *Keeley* is a variant of ◊**Kayley**.
Variants: **Keely, Keelie, Keeleigh,** ◊**Keighley**.

Keelin ♀
Irish: Anglicized form of the Gaelic name *Caoilfhionn*, derived from *caol* 'slender' + *fionn* 'white'.

Keenan ♂
Transferred used of the Irish surname, Gaelic *Ó Cianáin* 'descendant of Cianán'. The latter is a personal name representing a diminutive of ◊**Cian**.

Keighley ♀
Fanciful respelling of ◊**Keeley**, inspired by the Yorkshire town of *Keighley*,

which is, however, pronounced '*keeth*-lee'.

Keir ♂
Transferred use of the Scottish surname, in origin a variant of ◊**Kerr**. The name has sometimes been chosen in honour of the trade unionist and first Labour MP, James Keir Hardie (1856–1915), whose mother's maiden name was Keir.

Keith ♂
Transferred use of a Scottish surname, originally a local name derived from lands so called in East Lothian, probably from a Celtic (Brythonic) word meaning 'wood'. The principal family bearing this surname were hereditary Earls Marischal of Scotland from 1455 to 1715. This is one of a number of Scottish aristocratic surnames that have become well established since the 19th century as male given names throughout the English-speaking world, not just in Scotland. Others include ◊**Bruce**, ◊**Douglas**, and ◊**Graham**.

Kelan ♂
Irish: Anglicized form of Gaelic *Caolán* originally a byname representing a diminutive form of *caol* 'slender'.

Kellen ♂
Of uncertain derivation, perhaps an altered form of ◊**Kelan**, or from the Scottish surname *McKellen* (Gaelic *Mac Ailein* 'son of Alan' or *Mac Cailein* 'son of Colin').

Kelly ♀ ♂
As a male name, this is an Anglicized form of Irish Gaelic *Ceallach*, a traditional name derived from *ceall* 'monastery', 'church'. It is now more commonly used as a female name, especially in Australia, but also elsewhere in the English-speaking world. This use probably derives from the Irish surname (Gaelic *Ó Ceallaigh* 'descendant of Ceallach'); cf. the

similar recent use of ◊**Casey** and
◊**Cassidy** as female given names.
Variants: **Kelley**, **Kellie** ♀

Kelsey ♂ ♀
Transferred use of the surname, which
is from an Old English masculine
personal name *Cēolsige*, derived from
cēol 'ship' + *sige* 'victory'. Its use as a
female given name may have been
influenced by names such as ◊**Elsie**.
Variant: **Kelsie**.

Kelvin ♂
Modern given name, first used in the
1920s. It is taken from a Scottish river
which runs through Glasgow into the
Clyde (cf. ◊**Clyde**). Its choice as a
given name may also have been
influenced by names such as ◊**Kevin**
and ◊**Melvin** and the fame of the
scientist Lord Kelvin (1824–1907).

Kemp ♂
Transferred use of the surname, which
originated in the Middle Ages as an
occupational name or nickname from
Middle English *kempe* 'athlete',
'wrestler' (from Old English *kempa*
'warrior', 'champion').

Ken ♂
Short form of ◊**Kenneth**, or
occasionally of various other male
names with this first syllable.

Kendall ♂ ♀
Transferred use of the surname, which
is at least in part a local name, either
from *Kendal* in Cumbria (formerly the
county town of Westmorland), so
named because it stands in the valley
of the river *Kent*, or from *Kendale* in
Driffield, Humberside, where the first
element is Old Norse *keld* 'spring'.
The surname may in some cases be
derived from the Welsh personal name
Cynddelw, which is of uncertain
origin, perhaps from an Old Celtic
element meaning 'high', 'exalted' +
delw 'image', 'effigy'.
Variants: **Kendal**, **Kendel(l)**, **Kendle**.

Kendra ♀
Recently coined name, probably as a
feminine form of ◊**Kendrick**, currently
enjoying a vogue in North America.

Kendrick ♂
In modern use a transferred use of the
surname, the origins of which are
complex. The source in many cases is
the Old Welsh personal name
Cynwrig. This is of uncertain
derivation: it may be composed of
elements meaning 'high', 'exalted' +
'hill' or 'summit'. The Scottish
surname *Ken(d)rick* is a shortened
form of *MacKen(d)rick* (Gaelic *Mac
Eanraig* 'son of Henry'); Scottish
bearers are descended from a certain
Henry MacNaughton, and the
(Mac)Ken(d)ricks are a sept of Clan
MacNaughton. As an English
surname, *Ken(d)rick* is derived, at
least in part, from the Middle English
given name *Cenric*, in which two Old
English personal names have fallen
together: *Cēnerīc* (from *cēne* 'keen' +
rīc 'power') and *Cynerīc* (from *cyne*
'royal' + *rīc* 'power'). *Cenric* survived
as a Christian name into the 17th
century.
Variant: **Kenrick**.

Kenelm ♂
From an Old English personal name
derived from *cēne* 'keen', 'bold' +
helm 'helmet', 'protection'. The name
was popular in England during the
Middle Ages, when a shadowy 9th-
century Mercian prince of this name
was widely revered as a saint and
martyr, although his death seems to
have been rather the result of personal
and political motives. It has remained
in occasional use ever since, especially
in the Digby family, where it tended
to alternate with ◊**Everard**. The most
famous Sir Kenelm Digby (1603–65)
was noted as a writer, scientist,
adventurer, diplomat, and lover.

Kennard ♂
Transferred use of a surname, derived
from a Middle English personal name

in which several earlier names have fallen together. The first element is either *cēne* 'keen' or *cyne* 'royal'; the second is either *weard* 'guardian' or *heard* 'hardy', 'brave', 'strong'.

Kennedy ♂ ♀
Anglicized form of Irish Gaelic *Cinnéidigh*, a traditional name derived from *ceann* 'head' + *éidigh* 'ugly'. In recent years it has sometimes been used as a given name in the English-speaking world in honour of the assassinated American president John F. Kennedy (1917–63) and his brother Robert (1925–68). Use as a female name is well established, although not frequent.

Kenneth ♂
Scottish: Anglicized form of two different Gaelic names, *Cinaed* and *Cainnech*. The former seems to have been originally a personal name meaning 'born of fire' and was the Gaelic name of Kenneth mac Alpin (d. 858), first king of the united Picts and Scots. The latter is a byname meaning 'handsome', and survives today in Scotland as the common Gaelic name *Coinneach* (cf. ◊**Mackenzie**). In the 20th century *Kenneth* has enjoyed great popularity as a given name well beyond the boundaries of Scotland.
Short form: **Ken**.
Pet form: **Kenny**.

Kenrick ♂
Simplified spelling of ◊**Kendrick**.

Kent ♂
Transferred use of the surname, in origin a local name from the English county. This is probably named with a Celtic word meaning 'border'. Use as a given name is of recent origin, but it is now quite popular. It may in part be seen as a short form of ◊**Kenton**.

Kenton ♂
Transferred use of the surname, in origin a local name from any of various places so called. The one in Devon gets its name from the British

river name *Kenn* + Old English *tūn* 'enclosure', 'settlement'; the one in north-west London is from the Old English personal name *Cēna* 'keen' + *tūn*; the one in Northumberland is from Old English *cyne-* 'royal' + *tūn*; and that in Staffordshire is probably from the personal name *Cēna* 'keen' or *Cyna* 'royal' + *tūn*.

Keren ♀
Shortened form of the Biblical name *Keren-happuch*, borne by the third of Job's daughters (Job 42:14). The name meant 'horn of eye-paint' in Hebrew.

Kerena ♀
Latinate elaboration of ◊**Keren**

Kermit ♂
Of Irish and Manx origin, from the Gaelic surname form *Mac Dhiarmaid* 'son of Diarmad' (see ◊**Dermot**). The name was borne by a son of the American president Theodore Roosevelt, and more recently by a frog puppet on Jim Henson's *Muppet Show*.

Kerr ♂
Transferred use of the surname, which is a northern English local name for someone who lived by a patch of wet ground overgrown with brushwood (Old Norse *kjarr*).

Kerry ♀ ♂
Of recent, Australian, origin, probably from the name of the Irish county. It is now becoming relatively common in Britain as well as Australia, especially as a female name.
Variants: **Kerrie**, **Kerri**, **Keri** (all ♀) See also ◊**Ceri**.

Kester ♂
Medieval Scottish form of ◊**Christopher**, occasionally revived as a modern given name.

Kestrel ♀
One of the rarer female names derived from vocabulary words denoting birds that have come into use in the 20th century. The word itself derives from

Old French *cresserelle*, apparently a derivative of *cressele* 'rattle'.

Keturah ♀
Biblical name (meaning 'incense' in Hebrew), borne by the wife Abraham married after Sarah's death (Genesis 25:1). The name is occasionally chosen in the English-speaking world by parents in search of an unusual name.

Kevin ♂
Of Irish origin: Anglicized form of the Gaelic name *Caoimhín*, originally a byname representing a diminutive of *caomh* 'comely', 'beloved'. This was the name of a 7th-century saint who is one of the patrons of Dublin.

Kezia ♀
Biblical name, borne by one of Job's daughters, born to him towards the end of his life, after his prosperity had been restored (Job 42:14). It represents the Hebrew word for the cassia tree (the English name of which is derived, via Latin and Greek, from Hebrew or a related Semitic source).
Variant: **Keziah**.
Pet forms: **Kizzie**, **Kizzy**.

Kiera ♀
Recently coined feminine form of ◊**Kieran**; cf. ◊**Ciara**.

Kieran ♂
Irish: Anglicized form of Gaelic ◊**Ciarán**.
Variants: **Kyran**; **Kieron** (borne, for example, by the Irish actor Kieron Moore, b. 1925).

Killian ♂
Irish: Anglicized form of Gaelic ◊**Cillian**. This name was borne by various early Irish saints, including the 7th-century author of a 'Life of St Bridget', and missionaries to Artois and Franconia.
Variant: **Kilian**.

Kim ♀ ♂
Originally a short form of ◊**Kimberley**, now established as an independent

given name. The hero of Rudyard Kipling's novel *Kim* (1901) bore the name as a short form of *Kimball* (a surname used as a given name). In recent years, as a female name it has been borne by a number of well-known people, including the film stars Kim Novak (b. 1933) and Kim Bassinger (b. 1953).

Kimberley ♀ ♂
The immediate source of the given name is the town in South Africa, the scene of fighting during the Boer War, which brought it to public notice at the end of the 19th century. The town was named after a certain Lord Kimberley, whose ancestors derived their surname from one of the places in England called Kimberley. The first part of the placename derives from various Old English personal names; the second (from Old English *lēah*) means 'wood' or 'clearing'.
Variants: **Kimberly** (the more common North American spelling), **Kimberli(e)**, **Kimberlee**, **Kimberleigh** (all ♀)

King ♂
From the vocabulary word for a male monarch, bestowed, especially in America, with a hint of the notion that the bearer would have kingly qualities; cf. ◊**Duke** and ◊**Earl**. In some cases it may be a transferred use of the surname (originally a nickname or an occupational name given to someone who was employed in a royal household). Its frequency has increased recently as a Black name, no doubt partly in honour of the civil rights leader Martin Luther King (1929–68).

Kingsley ♂ ♀
Transferred use of the surname, originally a local name derived from various places (in Cheshire, Hampshire, Staffordshire) named in Old English as *Cyningeslēah* 'king's wood'. It is not clear what was the initial impulse towards its use as a given name; the usual pattern in such

cases is for a mother's maiden name to be chosen as a given name, but in this case the choice may have been made in honour of the author Charles Kingsley (1819–75).
Variants: **Kingsly**, **Kingslie**.

Kirk ♂
Transferred use of the surname, originally a northern English and Scottish local name for someone who lived near a church (from Old Norse *kirkja*). Recent use has probably been influenced to some extent by the film actor Kirk Douglas, born in 1916 as Issur Danielovich Demsky.

Kirsten ♀
Danish and Norwegian form of ◊**Christine**, now well established also in the English-speaking world.

Kirstie ♀
Scottish pet form of ◊**Kirstin**, now used as an independent given name throughout the English-speaking world.

Kirstin ♀
Scottish vernacular form of ◊**Christine**, now also used outside Scotland.

Kirsty ♀
Variant spelling of ◊**Kirstie**.

Kit ♂ ♀
Pet form of ◊**Christopher**; also of ◊**Katherine** and its variants.

Kitty ♀
Pet form of ◊**Katherine**.

Kizzie ♀
Pet form of ◊**Kezia**.
Variant: **Kizzy**.

Krista ♀
Variant spelling of ◊**Christa**.

Kristeen ♀
Fanciful respelling of ◊**Christine**.
Variants: **Kristene**, **Kristine**.

Kristen ♂
Danish form of ◊**Christian**.

Kristene ♀
Fanciful respelling of ◊**Christine**.

Kristie ♀
Variant of the female name ◊**Christie**, under the influence of the Scottish form ◊**Kirstie**.

Kristina ♀
Swedish and Czech form of ◊**Christina**.

Kristine ♀
Variant spelling of ◊**Christine**, under the influence of ◊**Kristina**.

Kristy ♀
Variant spelling of ◊**Kristie**.

Kyla ♀
Recently coined name, created as a feminine form of ◊**Kyle** or else a variant of ◊**Kylie**.

Kyle ♂ ♀
Scottish: from a topographic term denoting a narrow strait or channel, from Gaelic *caol* 'narrow'. In part it is a transferred use of the surname, a local name from the region in Ayrshire named with this word.

Kylie ♀
Of Australian origin, said to represent an Aboriginal term for the boomerang. However, it seems more likely that the name is an invention, influenced by ◊**Kyle** and ◊**Kelly**. It is extremely popular in Australia and, in part due to the Australian actress Kylie Minogue (b. 1969), it has also acquired some currency in Britain and elsewhere.
Variants: **Kyley**, **Kylee**, **Kyleigh**.

Kyra ♀
Apparently a variant spelling of *Cyra*, feminine form of ◊**Cyrus**, or else a feminine name formed directly from ◊**Kyran**.

Kyran ♂
Variant spelling of ◊**Kieran**.

LACEY LACHLAN LAETITIA LAILA LALAGE L
AMBERT LAMONT LANA LANCE LANCELO
T LANDON LANE LANNA LARA LARAINE L
ARCH LARISSA LARK LARRY LASSARINA LA
TASHA LATISHA LAURA LAUREL LAURELLE
LAUREN LAURENCE LAURETTA LAURIE LAV

Lacey ♀ ♂
Transferred use of the surname,
originally a Norman baronial name
from *Lassy*, Calvados. The Lacey
family was powerful in Ireland during
the early Middle Ages.
Variant: **Lacy**.

Lachlan ♂
Scottish (Gaelic *Lachlann*, earlier
Lochlann): said to refer originally to a
migrant from Norway, the 'land of the
lochs'. It is normally used only in
families that have some connection
with the Highlands of Scotland.

Laetitia ♀
Original Latin form of ◊**Lettice**,
occasionally used as a given name in
the English-speaking world.

Laila ♀
Variant spelling of ◊**Leila**.

Lalage ♀
Classical name, pronounced '*lal*-a-
dgee' or '*lal*-a-ghee'. It was used by
Horace in his *Odes* as the name of his
beloved of the moment. This was a
literary pseudonym derived from
Greek *lalagein* 'to chatter' or 'babble'.
It has enjoyed a modest popularity
among classically educated parents
since the 19th century. It is the name
of the narrator in E. Arnot Robertson's
Ordinary Families (1933) and it also
occurs in John Fowles's *The French
Lieutenant's Woman* (1969).
Pet forms: **Lally**, **Lallie**.

Lambert ♂
Transferred use of the surname, which
is from an Old French given name of
Germanic origin, from *land* 'land',

'territory' + *beorht* 'famous'. This was
introduced to Britain by the Normans,
but its frequency in Britain in the
later Middle Ages was mainly due to
its popularity among immigrants from
the Low Countries (who came to
England in connection with the cloth
trade). St Lambert of Maastricht was a
7th-century saint who aided St
Willibrord in his evangelical work.

Lamont ♂
Mainly U.S.: transferred use of the
Irish and Scottish surname, derived
from the medieval given name
Lagman, from Old Norse *Logmaðr*,
from *log* 'law' + *maðr* 'man'. The
final *t* of the surname is not
etymological, but in the medieval
period *d* and *t* were added or dropped
capriciously at the ends of words after
n (for the reverse process, cf.
◊**Rosalyn**).

Lana ♀
Especially North American: of
uncertain origin. If not simply an
invention, it may have been devised as
a feminine equivalent of ◊**Alan** (of
which it is an anagram), or a
shortened form of ◊**Alana**. It seems to
have been first used by the film
actress Lana Turner (b. 1920), whose
original name was *Julia*.

Lance ♂
Old French form of the Germanic
personal name *Lanzo*, a short form of
various compound names with the
first element *land* 'land', 'territory' (cf.
e.g. ◊**Lambert**), but associated from an
early date with Old French *lance*,
'lance' (the weapon, from Latin

lancea). The modern use as a given name most probably arose as a transferred use of the surname derived from the medieval given name, although it is also commonly taken as a short form of ◊**Lancelot**.

Lancelot ♂

The name borne by one of King Arthur's best and most valued knights, who eventually betrayed his trust by becoming the lover of Queen Guinevere. The name is of uncertain origin. It is probably, like other Arthurian names, of Celtic derivation, but has been heavily distorted by mediation through French sources.

Landon ♂

Mainly U.S.: transferred use of the surname, in origin a local name from any of various places in England called *Langdon*, from Old English *lang* 'long' + *dūn* 'hill'.

Lane ♂, occasionally ♀

Mainly U.S.: apparently a transferred use of the surname, in origin a local name for someone who lived in or by a lane (Old English *lane*, originally denoting a narrow pathway between hedges or banks).

Lanna ♀

Shortened form of ◊**Alanna**.

Lara ♀

Russian short form of ◊**Larissa**, introduced in the early 20th century to the English-speaking world. Here it became popular in particular as the name of one of the principal characters in Boris Pasternak's novel *Dr Zhivago* (1957), which was made into a popular Hollywood film in 1965. The name is associated with a musical theme, 'Lara's theme', from the film score by Maurice Jarre.

Laraine ♀

Mainly U.S., especially as a Black name: of uncertain origin, perhaps a variant spelling of ◊**Lorraine** or derived from the French phrase *la reine* 'the queen' (cf. ◊**Raine**).
Variants: **Lareine**, **Lareina**.

Larch ♀

Mainly U.S.: from the name of the tree (adopted in the 16th century from German *larche*, ultimately from Latin *larix*).

Larissa ♀

Of uncertain origin. It is the name of a Greek martyr venerated in the Eastern Church, and may perhaps be derived from the ancient Thessalian town of Larissa.

Lark ♀

Mainly North American and Australian: from the name of the bird (Old English *lāwerce*). This is one of a small set of female given names derived from vocabulary words denoting birds, which achieved some currency in the mid-20th century. The lark is traditionally associated with early rising and cheerfulness, and is noted for its sweet song.

Larry ♂

Pet form of ◊**Laurence** or ◊**Lawrence**.

Lassarina ♂

Irish: Anglicized form of the Gaelic name *Lasairíona*, derived from *lasair* 'flame' + *fíon* 'wine'.

Latasha ♀

Mainly U.S., especially as a Black name: a recent coinage, blending ◊**Latisha** and ◊**Natasha**.

Latisha ♀

Mainly U.S., especially as a Black name: a recent coinage, probably a respelling of ◊**Laetitia**.

Laura ♀

Feminine form of the Late Latin male name *Laurus* 'Laurel'. St Laura was a 9th-century Spanish nun who met her death in a cauldron of molten lead. Laura is also the name of the woman addressed in the love poetry of the Italian poet Petrarch (Francesco

Petrarca, 1304–74), and it owes much of its subsequent popularity to this. There have been various speculations about her identity, but it has not been established with any certainty. He first met her in 1327 while living in Avignon, and she died of the plague in 1348. The current popularity of the given name in the English-speaking world dates from the 19th century, when it was probably imported from Italy.

Laurel ♀
19th-century adoption of the vocabulary word for the tree (Middle English *lorel*, a dissimilated form of Old French *lorer*), probably influenced by ◊**Laura**. It may have been taken as a pet form of the latter.

Laurelle ♀
Elaborated form of ◊**Laurel**.

Lauren ♀
Apparently modelled on ◊**Laurence**, this was first used, or at any rate first brought to public attention, by the film actress Lauren Bacall (born Betty Jean Perske in 1924), famous for her partnership with Humphrey Bogart. They appeared together in several films, especially *To Have and Have Not* (1943) and *The Big Sleep* (1946). See also ◊**Loren**.

Laurence ♂
From a French form of Latin *Laurentius* 'man from Laurentum'. *Laurentum* was a town in Latium, which may have got its name from Latin *laurus* 'laurel', although it is more probably of pre-Roman origin. The given name was popular in the Middle Ages, under the influence of a 3rd-century saint who was one of the seven deacons of Rome. He was martyred in 258. The legend is that, having been required to hand over the Church's treasures to the civil authorities, he assembled the poor and sick and presented them. For this act of Christian defiance, he was roasted

to death on a gridiron. In England the name is also associated with St Laurence of Canterbury (d. 619). A more recent influence has been the actor Sir Laurence Olivier (1907–89). See also ◊**Lawrence**.
Pet form: **Larry**.

Lauretta ♀
Italian diminutive form of ◊**Laura**, also sometimes used in the English-speaking world.

Laurie ♀ ♂
Pet form of ◊**Laura**, ◊**Laurel**, and ◊**Laurence**.

Lavender ♀
From the vocabulary word denoting the herb with sweet-smelling flowers (Old French *lavendre*, from Late Latin *lavendula*).

Lavinia ♀
Name, according to Roman mythology, of the wife of Aeneas, and thus the mother of the Roman people. Legend had it that she gave her name to the Latin town of *Lavinium*, but in fact she was almost certainly invented to explain the placename, which is of pre-Roman origin. She was said to be the daughter of King Latinus, who was similarly invented to account for the name of *Latium*.

Lawrence ♂
Anglicized spelling of ◊**Laurence**. This is the usual spelling of the surname, and is now becoming increasingly common as a given name, especially in North America.
Pet form: **Larry**.

Layla ♀
Variant of ◊**Leila**.

Laz ♂
Modern informal pet form of ◊**Larry** (cf. *Baz* from *Barry* and *Gaz* from *Gary*).

Lea ♀
Variant spelling of ◊**Leah** or ◊**Lia**, or possibly sometimes a shortened form

of ◊**Azalea**. Occasionally it is a variant of the female name ◊**Lee**, from an alternative form of the surname, pronounced as a single syllable.

Leaf ♂
From the vocabulary word for the part of a plant (Old English *lēaf*). This was one of the names taken from the world of nature in the 1960s under 'hippy' influence, and it has not been enduringly popular. Choice as a given name may have been influenced by the Scandinavian name *Leif*, from Old Norse *Leifr*, meaning 'heir'.

Leah ♀
Biblical name (meaning 'languid' in Hebrew), borne by the elder sister of Rachel (Genesis 29:23). Jacob served her father Laban for seven years in return for the hand of Rachel, but was deceived into marrying Leah first. He was then given Rachel as well, but had to labour seven more years afterwards. The name is mainly Jewish, although it also enjoyed some popularity among the Puritans in the 17th century.

Leander ♂
Latin form of the Greek name *Leandros*, derived from *leōn* 'lion' + *anēr* 'man' (genitive *andros*). In Greek legend, Leander swam across the Hellespont every night to visit his beloved Hero and back again every morning; he was eventually drowned during a storm. In Christian times, the name was borne by a 6th-century saint, the brother of Sts Fulgentius, Isidore, and Florentina. He was a leading ecclesiastical figure of his day, a friend of Gregory the Great, and became archbishop of Seville. In modern times, the name has occasionally been used as an elaboration of the male name ◊**Lee**.

Leanne ♀
Modern combination of ◊**Lee** and ◊**Anne**, or else a respelling of ◊**Liane**. *Variant*: **Leanna**.

Leda ♀
Name borne in classical mythology by a queen of Sparta, who was ravished by Zeus in the shape of a swan. She gave birth to two eggs which, when hatched, revealed the two sets of twins: Castor and Pollux, and Helen and Hermione.

Lee ♂ ♀
Transferred use of the surname, in origin a local name from any of numerous places so called from Old English *lēah* 'wood', 'clearing'. It is especially popular now in the United States, where it is sometimes chosen in honour of the great Confederate general Robert E. Lee (1807–70). It is also popular in Canada.

Leesa ♀
Respelled version of ◊**Lisa**, influenced by ◊**Lee**.

Leigh ♂ ♀
Variant of ◊**Lee**, from an alternative spelling of the surname. Use as a female name may have been influenced by the British actress Vivien Leigh (1913–67), born Vivien Hartly.

Leighton ♂
Transferred use of the surname, in origin a local name from any of several places named with Old English *lēac* 'leek' + *tūn* 'enclosure', 'settlement', for example Leighton Buzzard in Bedfordshire.

Leila ♀
Of Arabic origin, now fairly common in the English-speaking world, having been used as a name for an oriental beauty by both Byron, in *The Giaour* (1813) and *Don Juan* (1819–24), and by Lord Lytton for the heroine of his novel *Leila* (1838). In Arabic it means 'night', apparently alluding to a dark complexion.
Variants: **Laila**, **Layla**, **Lila**.

Leland ♂
Mainly U.S.: transferred use of the

surname, in origin a local name for someone who lived by a patch of fallow land, from Middle English *lay*, *ley* 'fallow' + *land* 'land'. The surname is well established in the United States. It was borne by the humorous writer Charles Leland (1824–1903), author of *The Breitmann Ballads*, and it is also the name of a town in Mississippi.

Len ♂
Short form of ◊**Leonard**, and possibly also of the rarer given name ◊**Lennox**. In the case of the British trade union leader Len Murray (b. 1922) it represents a short form of ◊**Lionel**.
Pet form: **Lenny**.

Lena ♀
Abstracted from various names ending in these syllables, such as *Helena* and *Magdalena*. In America it is famous as the name of the singer Lena Horne (1917–91).

Lenda ♀
20th-century coinage, an arbitrary alteration of ◊**Linda**.

Lennard ♂
Variant spelling of ◊**Leonard**, perhaps in part a transferred use of the surname, which was derived from the given name in the Middle Ages.

Lennox ♂
Transferred use of the Scottish surname, which is also the name of an earldom. It originated as a local name from a district north of Glasgow formerly known as *The Levenach*. This was the first name of the British composer Sir Lennox Berkeley (1903–89).

Lenny ♂
Pet form of ◊**Len**.
Variant: **Lennie**.

Lenora ♀
Originally a contracted form of ◊**Leonora**, although sometimes chosen as an expanded version of ◊**Lena**.

Leo ♂
From a Late Latin personal name, meaning 'lion', which was borne by a large number of early Christian saints, most notably Pope Leo the Great (?390–461).
Variant: **Leon** (taken from the oblique case).

Leona ♀
Latinate feminine form of ◊**Leo**.

Leonard ♂
From an Old French personal name of Germanic origin, derived from *leon* 'lion' + *hard* 'hardy', 'brave', 'strong'. This was the name of a 5th-century Frankish saint, the patron of peasants and horses. Although it was introduced into Britain by the Normans, *Leonard* was not a particularly common name during the Middle Ages. It was revived in the 19th century and became very popular.
Variant: **Lennard**.
Short form: **Len**.
Pet forms: **Lenny**, **Lennie**.

Léonie ♀
French: from Latin *Leonia*, feminine form of *Leonius*, derived from *leo* 'lion'. It is now also widely used (normally without the accent) in the English-speaking world.

Leonora ♀
Shortened form of ◊**Eleonora**.

Leopold ♂
From an Old French name of Germanic (Frankish) origin, from *liut* 'people' + *bold* 'bold', 'brave'. The first element was altered by association with Latin *leo* 'lion'. A name of this origin may have been introduced into Britain by the Normans, but if so it did not survive long. It was reintroduced from the Continent towards the end of the 19th century in honour of Leopold, King of the Belgians (1790–1865), the uncle of Queen Victoria, to whom he was an

influential adviser in her youth: she named one of her sons after him.

Leroy ♂

Now considered a typical Black American given name, but formerly also extensively borne by White Americans. It is from a French nickname meaning 'the king', but it is not entirely clear why this particular form should have become such a popular given name in English.

Les ♂

Short form of ◊**Leslie**.

Lesley ♀ ♂

Originally a variant of ◊**Leslie**, but now specialized in Britain as the usual female form. Its first recorded use as a female name is in a poem by Robert Burns.

Leslie ♂ ♀

Transferred use of the Scottish surname derived from the lands of *Lesslyn* in Aberdeenshire (a placename perhaps named in Gaelic as *leas cuilinn* 'garden of hollies'). Surnames and clan names have been used as given names more readily and from an earlier date in Scotland than elsewhere, and this is the name of an ancient family, who in the 14th and 15th centuries were close associates of the Scottish royal house of Stewart and who have held the earldom of Rothes since 1457. The British film actor Leslie Howard (1890–1943), who was of Hungarian origin, had a considerable influence on the popularity of the name, especially in the United States, where he appeared in *Gone with the Wind* (1939). A famous female bearer is the French film actress Leslie Caron (b. 1930).
Short form: **Les** ♂

Lester ♂

Transferred use of the surname, in origin a local name from the city of *Leicester*. The placename is recorded in the 10th century as *Ligora cæster*, representing a British name of obscure origin + the Old English term *cæster* 'Roman fort'.

Leticia ♀

Simplified spelling of ◊**Laetitia**.

Lettice ♀

From the medieval vernacular form of the Latin name ◊**Laetitia**. It was popular among the Victorians, but is now out of fashion.
Pet forms: **Letty**, **Lettie**.

Levi ♂

Biblical name (meaning 'associated' in Hebrew), given by Jacob's wife Leah to her third son as an expression of her hope, 'Now this time will my husband be joined unto me, because I have born him three sons: therefore was his name called Levi' (Genesis 29:34). The Levites (a Jewish priestly caste) are descended from Levi. In the New Testament, Levi is a byname of the apostle and evangelist Matthew. In modern times the name is mainly Jewish.

Levon ♂

U.S.: of unknown origin; possibly an unexplained variant of ◊**Levi**.

Lewie ♂

Respelling of ◊**Louis**, or a pet form of ◊**Lewis**.

Lewis ♂

Common English form, since the Middle Ages, of the French name ◊**Louis**. In modern use it is also in part a transferred use of the surname derived from this given name.
Pet form: **Lewie**.

Lex ♂

Shortened form of ◊**Alex**.

Lexine ♀

Elaboration of ◊**Lexy** with the addition of the feminine diminutive suffix -*ine*.

Lexy ♀

Pet form of ◊**Alexandra**, particularly common in Scotland.

Lia ♀
Italian: of uncertain derivation,
probably a short form of *Rosalia* (see
◊**Rosalie**).

Liam ♂
Irish: short form of *Uilliam*, Gaelic
form of ◊**William**. It is now generally
used as an independent given name.

Liane ♀
Of uncertain origin, probably a short
form of French *Éliane*, from Latin
Aeliāna, the name of an early martyr
at Amasea in Pontus. *Aeliānus* was an
old Roman family name, perhaps a
hypercorrected form of *Ēliānus* or
Hēliānus, from Greek *hēlios*.
Variant: **Lianne**.

Libby ♀
Pet form of ◊**Elizabeth**, based
originally on a child's unsuccessful
attempts to pronounce the name.

Lila ♀
Variant spelling of ◊**Leila**.

Lilac ♀
From the vocabulary word denoting
the shrub with large sprays of heavily
scented purple or white flowers. The
word is from French, which derived it
via Spanish from Arabic *līlak*, from
Persian *nīlak* 'bluish', a derivative of
nīl 'blue'.

Lilian ♀
Of uncertain origin, first recorded in
the late 16th century, and probably
derived from a nursery form of
◊**Elizabeth**. It is now sometimes
regarded as a derivative of the flower
name ◊**Lily**, but this was not used as a
given name in England until the 19th
century.
Variant: **Lillian**.

Lilith ♀
The name borne, according to
medieval tradition, by a wife of Adam
prior to Eve. She is said to have been
turned into an ugly demon for refusing
to obey him. *Lilith* occurs in the Bible
as a vocabulary word meaning 'night

monster' or 'screech owl' (Isaiah
34:14), and in Jewish folklore is the
name of an ugly demon. In spite of its
unpleasant connotations, it has
occasionally been used as a given
name in the 20th century, perhaps in
part being taken as an elaborated form
of ◊**Lily**.

Lily ♀
From the vocabulary word for the
flower (via Old French, from Latin
lilium), regarded in Christian imagery
as a symbol of purity.
Variant: **Lillie** (borne, for example, by
the actress Lillie Langtry (1853–1929),
friend of King Edward VII).

Lincoln ♂
Transferred use of the surname, in
origin a local name from the name of
the city of Lincoln. This is found in
the 7th century as *Lindum colonia*,
representing a British name probably
meaning 'lake' (cf. Welsh *llyn*) + the
Latin defining term *colonia* 'colony',
'settlement'. As a given name it has
sometimes been bestowed in honour
of Abraham Lincoln (1809–65), 16th
president of the United States, who
led the Union to victory in the Civil
War and enforced the emancipation of
slaves.

Linda ♀
Of relatively recent origin and
uncertain etymology. It is first
recorded in the 19th century. It may
be a shortened form of ◊**Belinda**, an
adoption of Spanish *linda* 'pretty', or a
Latinate derivative of any of various
other Germanic female names ending
in *-lind* meaning 'weak', 'tender',
'soft'. It has become very popular in
the 20th century.
Pet forms: **Lindie**, **Lindy**.

Linden ♀
Ostensibly from the vocabulary word
denoting the lime tree (originally the
adjectival form, derived from Old
English *linde*). However, the given

name is of recent, probably 20th-century, origin and it is more likely that this is simply an elaboration of ◊**Linda**, along the lines of ◊**Lauren** from ◊**Laura**.

Lindie ♀
Pet form of ◊**Linda**.

Lindon ♂
Variant spelling of ◊**Lyndon**.

Lindsay ♀ ♂
Transferred use of the Scottish surname, originally borne by Sir Walter de Lindesay, one of the retainers of King David I of Scotland (1084–1153), who took the name to Scotland from Lindsey in Lincolnshire. This place was named in Old English as the 'wetland (Old English *ey*) belonging to Lincoln'. It was at first used as a male name, and this is still the case in Scotland, but elsewhere it is now nearly always used for girls.
Variants: **Lindsey**, **Lins(e)y**, **Lynsey**, **Linzi**.

Lindy ♀
Pet form of ◊**Linda**.

Linford ♂
Transferred use of the surname, a local name from any of various places, most of which are named with Old English *līn* 'flax' or *lind* 'lime tree' + *ford* 'ford'. In the case of Great and Little Linford in Berkshire, the first element is Old English *hlyn* 'maple'. As a given name it is associated in particular with the British athlete Linford Christie.

Linnet ♀
Simplified spelling of ◊**Linnette**, strongly influenced in popularity by the vocabulary word for the small bird (Old French *linotte*, a derivative of *lin* 'flax', on the seeds of which it feeds).

Linnette ♀
Variant spelling of ◊**Lynette**.

Linsey ♀
Simplified spelling of *Lindsey* (see ◊**Lindsay**).
Variant: **Linsy**.

Linton ♂
Transferred use of the surname, originally a local name from any of numerous places in England so called. Most get the name from Old English *līn* 'flax', 'cotton' or *lind* 'lime tree' + *tūn* 'enclosure', 'settlement'.

Linus ♂
Latin form of the Greek name *Linos*, which is of uncertain origin. In Greek mythology, Linus is a famous musician who taught music to Hercules; it is also the name of an infant son of Apollo who was exposed to die on a mountainside in Argos. The name may have been invented to explain the obscure refrain, *'ailinon'*, of the so-called 'Linus song', traditionally sung at harvest time in Argos. In the Christian era, *Linus* was the name of the second pope, St Peter's successor, who was martyred in *c*.76. He has been tentatively identified with the Linus to whom Paul sends greetings in 2 Timothy 4:21. Nowadays, the given name is associated with a character in the popular *Peanuts* strip cartoon series, a little boy inseparable from his security blanket.

Linzi ♀
Fanciful respelling of ◊**Lindsay**.

Liona ♀
Altered form of ◊**Leona**, influenced by ◊**Lionel**.

Lionel ♂
From a medieval diminutive of the Old French name *Léon* (see ◊**Leo**) or the Middle English nickname *Lion*.

Lis ♀
Variant spelling of ◊**Liz**. See also ◊**Lys**.

Lisa ♀
Variant of ◊**Liza**, influenced by French *Lise* and German *Liese*.

Lisbet ♀
Pet form of ◊**Elizabeth**.

Lisette ♀
French diminutive form of *Lise*, which is itself a shortened form of ◊**Elisabeth**.

Lisha ♀
Modern coinage, a shortened and respelled form of names such as ◊**Delicia** and ◊**Felicia**, on the model of *Trisha* from ◊**Patricia**.

Lissa ♀
Short form of ◊**Melissa**. See also ◊**Lyssa**.

Livia ♀
In modern use often taken as a short form of ◊**Olivia**, but originally a distinct name, a feminine form of the Roman family name *Livius*. This is of uncertain derivation, perhaps connected with *lividus* 'bluish'.

Liz ♀
The most common of all the various short forms of ◊**Elizabeth**.

Liza ♀
Shortened form of ◊**Eliza**.
Variant: **Lisa**.

Lizzie ♀
Pet form of ◊**Liz**, with the diminutive suffix *-ie*.
Variant: **Lizzy**.

Lleu ♂
Welsh: traditional name, meaning 'bright, shining', cognate with the name of the Celtic god known in Old Irish as *Lugh*, in Gaulish as *Lugus*. This name was borne in the *Mabinogi* by Lleu Llaw Gyffes 'Lleu Skilful Hand', the son of Aranrhod. It has been revived in modern times.

Llew ♂
Welsh: traditional name meaning 'lion'. It is also used as a short form of ◊**Llewelyn**.

Llewelyn ♂
Very popular traditional Welsh name:

an altered form (influenced by the vocabulary word *llew* 'lion') of *Llywelyn*, an ancient name of uncertain derivation. It probably goes back to the Old Celtic name *Lugobelinos*, the first element of which is *Lugu-* (the name of a god; see ◊**Lleu**); the second is a name-forming element found also in names such as *Cunobelinus* (*Cymbeline*). In historical times the name was borne in particular by Llywelyn ap Iorwerth (1173–1240) and his grandson Llywelyn ap Gruffydd (d. 1282), Welsh princes who for a time united their countrymen in North Wales and led opposition to the power of the Norman barons in South Wales and the Marches.

Lloyd ♂
Transferred use of the Welsh surname, originally a nickname meaning 'grey(-haired)' (Welsh *llwyd*). See also ◊**Floyd**.

Logan ♂
Transferred use of the Scottish surname, in origin a local name from a place so called in Ayrshire.

Lois ♀
New Testament: name, of unknown origin, borne by the grandmother of the Timothy to whom St Paul wrote two epistles (see 2 Timothy 1:5). Both Timothy and his mother Eunice bore common Greek names, but *Lois* remains unexplained.

Lola ♀
Spanish pet form (originally a nursery form) of ◊**Dolores**, now established as an independent given name in the English-speaking world. It owes some of its popularity to the fame of Lola Montez (1818–1861), stage name adopted by Marie Gilbert, an Irish dancer and courtesan who had affairs with Liszt, Dumas, and others. From 1846–8 she so captivated the elderly Ludwig I of Bavaria that she became the virtual ruler of the country, precipitating riots, a constitutional

crisis, and the abdication of the king. She arrived in New York in 1851, and spent the last years of her life working to help prostitutes.

Lolicia ♀
Mainly U.S.: elaborated form of ◊**Lola**, with the addition of a suffix derived from names such as ◊**Delicia**.

Lolita ♀
Spanish diminutive form of ◊**Lola**. This was once quite common as a given name in its own right in America, with its large Hispanic population, but has since been overshadowed by its association with Vladimir Nabokov's novel *Lolita* (1955). The Lolita of the title is the pubescent object of the narrator's desires, and the name is now used as a generic term for any under-age sex kitten.

Lonnie ♂
Of uncertain origin, possibly an Anglicized or pet form of the Spanish name *Alonso* or a variant of ◊**Lenny**. It is chiefly associated in Britain with the skiffle singer Lonnie Donegan, famous in the 1950s and 1960s.

Lora ♀
German form of ◊**Laura**, occasionally also used in the English-speaking world.

Lorcan ♂
Irish: Anglicized form of the Gaelic name *Lorcán*, from a diminutive of Gaelic *lorc* 'fierce' (or possibly 'dumb'). This was borne by St Lorcán Ó Tuathail (1128–80), archbishop of Dublin, known in English as Laurence O'Toole.

Loreen ♀
Elaboration of ◊**Lora**, with the addition of the suffix -*een* (originally an Irish diminutive, Gaelic -*ín*).
Variant: **Lorene**.

Lorelle ♀
Elaboration of ◊**Lora**, with the addition

of the suffix -*elle* (originally a French feminine diminutive).

Loren ♀, occasionally ♂
Variant spelling of ◊**Lauren**.

Lorena ♀
Latinate elaboration of the female name ◊**Loren**.

Lorene ♀
Variant spelling of ◊**Loreen**.

Loreto ♀
Religious name borne by Roman Catholics, referring to the town in central Italy to which in the 13th century the Holy House of the Virgin is supposed to have been miraculously transported from Nazareth by angels.

Loretta ♀
Variant of ◊**Lauretta**, normally borne by Roman Catholics, among whom it is associated with ◊**Loreto**.

Lori ♀
Pet form of ◊**Lorraine** or variant of ◊**Laurie**.

Lorin ♂
Mainly U.S.: variant spelling of the male name ◊**Loren**.
Variant: **Lorrin**.

Lorinda ♀
Elaboration of ◊**Lora**, with the addition of the productive feminine suffix -*inda* (cf. e.g. ◊**Belinda**, ◊**Clarinda**, ◊**Lucinda**).

Lorna ♀
Invented by R. D. Blackmore for the heroine of his novel *Lorna Doone* (1869), child captive of the outlawed Doones on Exmoor, who is eventually discovered to be in reality Lady Lorna Dugal, daughter of the Earl of Dugal. Blackmore seems to have derived the name from the Scottish placename *Lorn(e)* (Gaelic *Latharna*), a territory in Argyll. The given name is now popular in Scotland.

Lorne ♂
Especially Canadian: of uncertain derivation, presumably from the

territory of *Lorne* in Argyll (cf. ◊**Lorna**). One of the earliest bearers was the Canadian actor Lorne Greene (b. 1915), and the given name is now also fairly common in Scotland.

Lorraine ♀
Transferred use of the surname, in origin denoting a migrant from the province of *Lorraine* in eastern France. This derives its name from Latin *Lotharingia* 'territory of the people of Lothar'. The latter is a Germanic personal name derived from *hlud* 'fame' + *heri*, *hari* 'army'. *Lorraine* began to be used as a female given name in Scotland in the 19th century, and has recently become enormously popular, for reasons which are not clear.
Variants: **Loraine**, **Lorane**.

Lorri ♀
Variant spelling of ◊**Lori**.

Lorrin ♂
Mainly U.S.: variant spelling of the male name ◊**Loren**.

Lottie ♀
Pet form of ◊**Charlotte**. It was common in the 19th century, but is much less used at the present time.
Variant: **Lotty**.

Lou ♂ ♀
Short form of ◊**Louis** or, less commonly, ◊**Louise**.

Louella ♀
Modern coinage from the first syllable of ◊**Louise** + the productive suffix *-ella* (an Italian or Latinate feminine diminutive; cf. ◊**Ella**). It is particularly associated with the Hollywood gossip columnist Louella Parsons (1880–1972).
Variant: **Luella**.

Louie ♂
Variant spelling of ◊**Lewie**.

Louis ♂
An extremely common French name, of Germanic (Frankish) origin, from *hlud* 'fame' + *wīg* 'warrior'. It was very common in French royal and noble families. Louis I (778–840) was the son of Charlemagne, who ruled both as King of France and Holy Roman Emperor. Altogether, the name was borne by sixteen kings of France up to the French Revolution, in which Louis XVI perished. Louis XIV, 'the Sun King' (1638–1715), reigned for seventy-two years (1643–1715), presiding in the middle part of his reign over a period of unparalleled French power and prosperity. In modern times *Louis* is also found in the English-speaking world (usually pronounced '*loo*-ee'). In Britain the Anglicized form ◊**Lewis** is rather more common, whereas in America the reverse is true.
Short form: **Lou**.

Louisa ♀
Latinate feminine form of ◊**Louis**, commonly used as an English given name since the 18th century.

Louise ♀
French feminine form of ◊**Louis**, introduced to England in the 17th century.
Short form: **Lou**.

Lourdes ♀
Religious name borne by Roman Catholics, referring to the place in southern France where a shrine was established after a young peasant girl, Bernadette Soubirous, had visions of the Virgin Mary and uncovered a healing spring in 1858. In recent times, Lourdes has become a major centre for pilgrimage, especially by people suffering from various illnesses or physical handicaps.

Lovell ♂
Transferred use of the surname, which originated in the Middle Ages from the Old (Norman) French nickname *Louvel* 'wolf-cub', a diminutive of *lou* 'wolf'.

Lowell ♂

Mainly U.S.: transferred use of the surname of a well-known New England family, whose members included the poet Robert Lowell (1917–77). The surname is a variant of ◊Lovell.

Loyal ♂

Mainly U.S.: name derived from the modern English adjective (from Old French *leial*, from Latin *legalis* 'legal').

Luana ♀

First used in King Vidor's 1932 film *The Bird of Paradise* as the name of a Polynesian maiden, and taken up since. It is apparently an arbitrary combination of the syllables *Lu-* and *-ana*.
Variants: **Luanna, Luanne**.

Lucas ♂

In part a learned form of ◊Luke, in part a transferred use of the surname derived from it in the Middle Ages. The Latin form *Lucas* was often used in the Middle Ages in written documents in place of the spoken vernacular form *Luke*, hence the common surname. It is also the spelling preferred in the Authorized Version of the New Testament, which has had some influence on its selection as a given name.

Lucetta ♀

Fanciful elaboration of ◊Lucia or ◊Lucy, formed with the productive suffix *-etta*, originally an Italian feminine diminutive suffix. The name is found in Shakespeare, where it is borne by Julia's waiting woman in *Two Gentlemen of Verona*, but it is not much used in Italy and was unusual in England before the 19th century.

Lucia ♀

Feminine form of the old Roman given name *Lucius*, which is probably a derivative of Latin *lux* 'light'. The female name is common in Italy and elsewhere, and is found as a learned, Latinate doublet of *Lucy* in England. St Lucia of Syracuse, who was martyred in 304, was a very popular saint in the Middle Ages; she is often represented in medieval art as blinded and with her eyes on a platter, but the tradition that she had her eyes put out is probably based on nothing more than the association between light and eyes.

Lucilla ♀

Latin pet form of ◊Lucia, with the diminutive feminine suffix *-illa*. This name was borne by various minor early saints, including one martyred at Rome in *c*.258.

Lucille ♀

French form of ◊Lucilla, used also in the English-speaking world, especially in the southern United States. A well-known bearer of the name was the American comedy actress Lucille Ball (1910–89).

Lucinda ♀

Derivative of ◊Lucia, with the addition of the productive suffix *-inda*. The formation is first found in Cervantes's *Don Quixote* (1605), but was not much in use in the 17th century except as a literary name. It enjoyed considerable popularity in England in the 18th century, and has been in use ever since.

Lucretia ♀

Feminine form of the Roman family name *Lucretius*, which is of unknown derivation. In Roman legend, this is the name of a Roman maiden of the 5th century BC who killed herself after being raped by the King of Rome; the resulting scandal led to the end of the monarchy. It was also borne by a Spanish martyr who perished under Diocletian, but is now chiefly remembered as the name of Lucretia Borgia (1480–1519), regarded in legend as a demon poisoner who had incestuous relations with her father, Pope Alexander VI, and her brother

Cesare. Although these allegations cannot now be disproved, history records her, after her marriage in 1501 to Alfonso d'Este, Duke of Ferrara, as being in reality a beautiful, intelligent, and fair-minded woman, and a generous patron of the arts.

Lucy ♀

From Old French *Lucie*, the vernacular form of ◊**Lucia**. It is sometimes assumed that *Lucy* is a pet form of ◊**Lucinda**, but there is no etymological justification for this assumption. It was in fairly widespread use in the Middle Ages, and increased greatly in popularity in the 18th century.

Ludmila ♀

Russian and Czech: from a Slavonic personal name derived from *lud* 'people', 'tribe' (a borrowing from Germanic *liut*) + *mil* 'grace', 'favour'. St Ludmila (d. 921) was a duchess of Bohemia and grandmother of St Wenceslas; she was murdered on the orders of her mother-in-law and came to be regarded as a martyr.
Variant: **Ludmilla** (in the English-speaking world).

Ludovic ♂

From Latin *Ludovicus*, the form used in medieval documents to represent the Germanic name *Hludwig* (see ◊**Louis**). In the west of Scotland it came to be used as an Anglicized form of the Gaelic name *Maol Dòmhnaich* 'devotee of the Lord', probably because both contain the same succession of sounds: *l-d-o-v-c(h)*.
Short form: **Ludo**.

Luella ♀

Variant spelling of ◊**Louella**.

Luke ♂

Middle English vernacular form of ◊**Lucas**, Latin form of the post-classical Greek name *Loukas* 'man from Lucania'. This owes its perennial popularity throughout Christian Europe to the fact that, from the 2nd century onwards, the third gospel in the New Testament has been ascribed to the Lucas or Luke mentioned at various places in Acts and in the Epistles. Little is known about him beyond the facts that he was a doctor, a Gentile, and a friend and convert of St Paul.

Lulu ♀

Pet form, originally a reduplicated nursery form, of *Luise*, the German form of ◊**Louise**. It is now also used in the English-speaking world, both as a pet form of *Louise* and as an independent given name.

Luther ♂

Mainly North American: from the German surname, which is from a Germanic personal name derived from *liut* 'people' + *heri*, *hari* 'army'. It is commonly bestowed among evangelical Protestants, in honour of the ecclesiastical reformer and theologian Martin Luther (1483–1546). In recent times it has also been bestowed in honour of the assassinated civil rights leader Martin Luther King (1929–68).

Lyall ♂

Transferred use of the Scottish surname, which is probably derived from the Old Norse personal name *Liulfr*, of which the first element is obscure. The second is clearly Old Norse *úlfr* 'wolf'. See also ◊**Lyle**.

Lydia ♀

Of Greek origin, meaning 'woman from Lydia', an area of Asia Minor. The name is borne in the Bible by a woman of Thyatira who was converted by St Paul and who entertained him in her house (Acts 16:14–15, 40). It has enjoyed steady popularity in the English-speaking world since the 17th century.

Lyle ♂

Transferred use of the mainly Scottish surname, in origin a local name for someone who came 'from the island' (Anglo-Norman *de l'isle*). (The island in question would in many cases have been an area of higher, dry ground in a marsh or fen, rather than in a sea or river.) There may have been some confusion with ◊**Lyall**.

Lyn ♀
Variant spelling of ◊**Lynn**.

Lynda ♀
Variant spelling of ◊**Linda**.

Lyndon ♂
Transferred use of the surname, in origin a local name from a place in the former county of Rutland (now part of Leicestershire), so called from Old English *lind* 'lime tree' + *dūn* 'hill'. In the United States, use as a given name has been influenced by the American president Lyndon Baines Johnson (1908–73).
Variant: **Lindon**.

Lynette ♀
In modern use a derivative of ◊**Lynn**, formed with the French feminine diminutive suffix *-ette*. However, this is not the origin for the name as used in Tennyson's *Idylls of the King* (1859–85), through which it first came to public attention. There, it

represents an altered form of some Celtic original; cf. Welsh ◊**Eluned**.
Variants: **Lynnette, Lin(n)ette, Linnet**.

Lynn ♀
Of uncertain origin: possibly an altered short form of ◊**Linda**, or a derivative of the French name *Line*, which originated as a short form of various female names ending in this syllable, for example *Caroline*. The element *-lyn(n)* has been a productive suffix of English female given names since at least the middle of the 20th century. *Lynn* itself has enjoyed considerable popularity in recent times.

Lynsey ♀
Variant spelling of ◊**Lindsay**.

Lys ♀
Variant spelling of ◊**Liz**, apparently inspired by medieval French *(fleur de) lys* 'lily'.

Lysette ♀
Variant spelling of ◊**Lisette**.

Lyssa ♀
Short form of ◊**Alyssa**. In form it coincides with the name, in Greek mythology, of the personification of madness or frenzy. See also ◊**Lissa**.

MAB MABEL MABELLE MABLE MACKENZIE
MADDIE MADDIAON MADDY MADELAI
NE MADELINE MADELINE MADELYN MA
DGE MADISON MADLYN MADOLINE MA
DONNA MAE MAEVE MAGDALEN MAGGI
E MAGNUS MAIDIE MAIR MAIRE MAIREA

M

Mab ♀
Short form of ◊**Mabel**. See also ◊**Maeve**.

Mabel ♀
Originally a nickname from the Old French vocabulary word *amabel*, *amable* 'lovely' (related to modern English *amiable* 'friendly', 'good-humoured'). The initial vowel began to be lost as early as the 12th century (the same woman is referred to as both *Mabilia* and *Amabilia* in a document of 1185), but a short vowel in the resulting first syllable was standard, giving a rhyme with *babble*, until the 19th century, when people began to pronounce the name to rhyme with *table*.

Mabelle ♀
Elaborated form of ◊**Mabel**, under the influence of the French phrase *ma belle* 'my beautiful one'.

Mable ♀
Variant spelling of ◊**Mabel**.

Mackenzie ♂ ♀
Mainly North American: transferred use of the Scottish surname, which is from Gaelic *Mac Coinnich*, a patronymic from *Coinneach* 'comely'. The *z* of the surname represents the medieval letter yogh, pronounced as a 'y' glide. In North America this is more commonly a female name than a male one.
Variants: **Makenzie, Makensie** ♀

Maddie ♀
Variant spelling of ◊**Maddy**.

Maddison ♂ ♀
Variant spelling of ◊**Madison**.

Maddy ♀
Pet form of ◊**Madeleine** and its variants. In the United States it is also used as a pet form of the modern female name ◊**Madison**.
Variant: **Maddie**

Madelaine ♀
Variant spelling of ◊**Madeleine**.

Madeleine ♀
The French form of the byname of a character in the New Testament, Mary *Magdalene* 'Mary of Magdala'. Magdala was a village on Lake Galilee, a few miles north of Tiberias. The woman 'which had been healed of evil spirits and infirmities' (Luke 8:2) was given this name in the Bible to distinguish her from other bearers of the very common name ◊**Mary**. It was widely accepted in Christian folk belief that she was the same person as the repentant sinner who washed Christ's feet with her tears in the previous chapter (Luke 7), but there is no support in the text for this identification.
Variants: **Madelaine, Madeline, Mad(e)lyn, Madoline**; ◊**Magdalen**.
Pet forms: **Maddy, Maddie**.

Madeline ♀
Variant of ◊**Madeleine**, common especially in Ireland.

Madelyn ♀
Variant of ◊**Madeleine**, influenced by the productive name suffix *-lyn* (see ◊**Lynn**).

Madge ♀

Pet form of ◊**Margaret**, a palatalized version of *Mag(g)* (see ◊**Maggie**).

Madison ♀ ♂

Mainly U.S.: transferred use of the surname, in origin a metronymic from the medieval woman's given name *Madde*, a pet form of ◊**Madeleine** (cf. ◊**Maddy**) or ◊**Maud**. Use as a given name seems to have been influenced by the statesman James Madison (1751–1836), who was president during the War of 1812 and took part in drafting the U.S. constitution and Bill of Rights. It is currently enjoying something of a vogue as a female name.

Variant: **Maddison**.
Pet forms: **Maddy, Maddie** ♀

Madlyn ♀

Contracted spelling of ◊**Madelyn**.

Madoline ♀

Variant of *Madeline* (see ◊**Madeleine**).

Madonna ♀

From an Italian title of the Virgin Mary (literally 'my lady'), applied to countless Renaissance paintings of a beautiful young woman (with and without an infant), representing the mother of Christ. Its use as a given name is a fairly recent phenomenon, arising among Americans of Italian descent. In the 1980s, the name became particularly well known as a result of the fame of the American pop star Madonna Ciccone (b. 1959).

Mae ♀

Variant spelling of ◊**May**, possibly influenced by ◊**Maeve**. It has been most notably borne by the American film actress Mae West (b. 1892), whose prominent bust led to her name being given, by members of the RAF, to a type of inflatable life jacket used in the Second World War. This spelling is now no longer much used.

Maeve ♀

Irish: Anglicized form of Gaelic *Meadhbh* (earlier *Medb*), an ancient name meaning 'intoxicating', 'she who makes drunk'. It is borne by the Queen of Connacht in the Irish epic *Táin Bó Cuailnge*. In this, Meadhbh leads a raid on Ulster in order to seize the Brown Bull of Cooley, but she is repulsed single-handed by the hero Cú Chulainn. Shakespeare's Queen Mab, 'the fairy's midwife' (*Romeo and Juliet* I. iv. 53), owes her name, if nothing else, to the legendary Queen of Connacht.

Variants: **Mave, Meave**.

Magdalen ♀

English vernacular form of ◊**Madeleine**, the usual form of the given name in the Middle Ages.

Maggie ♀

Pet form of ◊**Margaret**. In the Middle Ages the short form *Mag(g)* was common, as a result of the early loss in pronunciation of the English preconsonantal *r*. This is not now used as a given name, but has given rise to the surname *Maggs*.

Magnus ♂

Originally a Latin byname meaning 'great', this was first extracted from the name of *Charlemagne* (recorded in Latin chronicles as *Carolus Magnus* 'Charles the Great') and used as a given name by the Scandinavians. It was borne by seven medieval kings of Norway, including Magnus I (1024–47), known as Magnus the Good, and Magnus VI (1238–80), known as Magnus the Law Mender. There are several early Scandinavian saints called Magnus, including an earl of Orkney (d. 1116), to whom Kirkwall cathedral is dedicated. The name was imported to Scotland and Ireland during the Middle Ages.

Maidie ♀

From a pet form of the vocabulary word *maid* 'young woman' (Old English *mæg(den)*), originally used as an affectionate nickname.

Mair ♀
Welsh form of ◊**Mary**, derived from
Latin *Maria* via Old Welsh *Meir*. See
also ◊**Mari**.

Máire ♀
Irish Gaelic form of ◊**Mary**.

Mairéad ♀
Irish Gaelic form of ◊**Margaret**,
pronounced '*my-raid*' (in Munster) or
'*ma-raid*' (in Connacht). The name is
also used in Scotland, where it is
spelled **Mairead** or **Maighread**.

Màiri ♀
Scottish Gaelic form of ◊**Mary**.

Maisie ♀
Scottish: pet form derived from
Mairead, the Gaelic form of
◊**Margaret**, with the Scottish and
northern English diminutive suffix *-ie*.

Makenzie ♀
Simplified spelling of the female name
◊**Mackenzie**.
Variant: **Makensie**.

Malachy ♂
Irish: name of an Irish king who
defeated the Norse invaders in an
important battle. His Gaelic baptismal
name was *Maoileachlainn* 'devotee of
St Seachnall or Secundinus', but in
medieval sources telling of his life this
has already been altered to coincide
with that of the biblical prophet
generally known in English as
Malachi. Malachi was the last of the
twelve minor prophets of the Old
Testament; he foretold the coming of
Christ and his name means,
appropriately, 'my messenger' in
Hebrew.

Malcolm ♂
Anglicized form of the medieval
Gaelic name *Mael Coluim* 'devotee of
St Columba'. Columba, whose name
means 'dove' in Latin, was a 6th-
century monk of Irish origin who
played a leading part in the conversion
to Christianity of Scotland and
northern England; see also ◊**Calum**

and ◊**Colm**. He has always been one of
the most popular saints in Scotland,
but in the Middle Ages it was felt to
be presumptuous to give the names of
saints directly to children; instead
their blessing was invoked by
prefixing the name with *mael* 'devotee
of' or *gille* 'servant of'.

Mallory ♂ ♀
Especially North American:
transferred use of the surname, which
originated as a Norman French
nickname for an unfortunate person,
from Old French *malheure* 'unhappy'
or 'unlucky'. This is now well
established as a female name in North
America.
Variant: **Mallery**.

Malvina ♀
Semi-fictional name, based on Gaelic
mala mhìn 'smooth brow', invented
by James Macpherson (1736–96), the
Scottish antiquarian poet who
published works allegedly translated
from the ancient Gaelic bard Ossian.
The name became popular in
Scandinavia because of the admiration
of the Emperor Napoleon for the
Ossianic poems: he was godfather to
several of the children of his marshal
Jean Baptiste Bernadotte (who ruled
Norway and Sweden (1818–44) as Karl
XIV Johan) and imposed his own taste
in naming practices on them, hence
the frequency of Ossianic given names
in Scandinavia. *Las Malvinas* is the
Argentinian name for the Falkland
Islands, but it has no connection with
the Ossianic name, being derived from
the name of the French seaport St
Malo.

Mamie ♀
Short form of ◊**Margaret** or ◊**Mary**,
originating as a nursery form. It has
occasionally been used as an
independent given name, especially in
America, where it was the name by
which the wife of President
Eisenhower was usually known.

Manda ♀
Shortened form of ◊**Amanda**.

Mandy ♀ ♂
Pet form of ◊**Amanda**, now sometimes used as an independent given name.

Manfred ♂
From an old Germanic personal name, usually said to be from *man* 'man' + *fred, frid* 'peace'. However, it is more likely that the first element was *magin* 'strength' (the usual Norman form being *Mainfred*) or *manag* 'much'. This name was in use among the Normans, who introduced it to Britain. However, it did not become part of the common stock of English given names, and was reintroduced from Germany in the 19th century. It was a traditional name among the Hohenstaufens, and was borne by the last Hohenstaufen king of Sicily (1258–66), who died in battle against papal forces at Benevento. The name was also used by Byron for the central character in his poetic drama *Manfred* (1817), a brooding outcast, tormented by incestuous love for his half-sister.

Manley ♂
Transferred use of the surname, which in most cases originated as a local name from places in Devon and Cheshire, named in Old English as 'the common wood or clearing', from *(ge)mæn* 'common', 'shared' + *lēah* 'wood', 'clearing'. Its choice as a first name may well have been influenced by association with the vocabulary word *manly* and the hope that the qualities denoted by the adjective would be attributes of the bearer. The vocabulary word may also lie behind some cases of the surname, as a nickname for a 'manly' person.

Manny ♂
Pet form of ◊**Emmanuel**, found mainly as a Jewish name.

Mara ♀
Of biblical origin, from Hebrew *Mara* 'bitter', a name referred to by Naomi when she went back to Bethlehem because of the famine in the land of Moab and the deaths of her husband and two sons: 'call me not Naomi, call me Mara: for the Almighty hath dealt very bitterly with me' (Ruth 1:20).

Marc ♂
French form of ◊**Mark**, now also quite popular in the English-speaking world. It was given some currency in England in the 1960s by the pop singer Marc Bolan.

Marcel ♂
French: from the Latin name *Marcellus*, originally a diminutive of ◊**Marcus**. The name has always been popular in France as it was borne by a 3rd-century missionary to Gaul, martyred at Bourges with his companion Anastasius. It is now occasionally also used in the English-speaking world.

Marcella ♀
Feminine form of *Marcellus*; see ◊**Marcel**. St Marcella was a Roman noblewoman of the late 4th century who lodged St Jerome for three years.

Marcia ♀
Often used as a feminine equivalent of ◊**Mark**, but in fact a feminine form of *Marcius*, itself a derivative of ◊**Marcus**. One St Marcia is commemorated in a group with Felix, Luciolus, Fortunatus, and others; another with Zenais, Cyria, and Valeria; and a third with Ariston, Crescentian, Eutychian, Urban, Vitalis, Justus, Felicissimus, Felix, and Symphorosa. None is individually very famous.
Variant: **Marsha**.
Pet forms: **Marcie**, **Marcy**, **Marci** (mainly North American).

Marcus ♂
The original Latin form of ◊**Mark**, of unknown derivation; it may possibly be connected with *Mars*, the name of the Roman god of war, or the adjective

mas 'male', 'virile' (genitive *maris*). This was one of the very small number of Roman given names of the classical period. There were only about a dozen of these in general use, with perhaps another dozen confined to particular families. *Marcus* was rarely used as a given name in the English-speaking world until recent years, when it has been seized on by parents seeking to give a distinctive form to a common and popular name. As an American Black name it is sometimes bestowed in honour of the Black Consciousness leader Marcus Garvey (1887–1940).

Marea ♀
Altered spelling of ◊**Maria**.

Mared ♀
Welsh form of ◊**Margaret**, a simplified form of *Marged*.

Maretta ♀
Scottish: Anglicized form of *Mairead*, the Gaelic version of ◊**Margaret**. See also ◊**Marietta**.

Marga ♀
Short form of ◊**Margaret** or any of the large number of related names beginning with these two syllables.

Margaret ♀
An extremely common medieval given name, derived via Old French *Marguerite* and Latin *Margarīta* from Greek *Margarītēs*, from *margaron* 'pearl', a word ultimately of Hebrew origin. The name was always understood to mean 'pearl' throughout the Middle Ages. The first St Margaret was martyred at Antioch in Pisidia during the persecution instigated by the Emperor Diocletian in the early 4th century. However, there is some doubt about her name, as the same saint is venerated in the Orthodox Church as ◊**Marina**. There were several other saintly bearers of the name, including St Margaret of Scotland (d. 1093), wife of King Malcolm Canmore and daughter of Edmund Ironside of England. It was also the name of the wife of Henry VI of England, Margaret of Anjou (1430–82), and of Margaret Tudor (1489–1541), sister of Henry VIII, who married James IV of Scotland and ruled as regent there after his death. See also ◊**Margery**, ◊**Marjorie**.
Short forms: **Meg, Peg, Madge, Marge**.
Pet forms: ◊**Maggie, Meggie**, ◊**Peggy, Margie**, ◊**May**. See also ◊**Daisy**.

Margery ♀
The usual medieval vernacular form of ◊**Margaret** (now also commonly spelled ◊**Marjorie**). This form of the name is preserved in the nursery rhyme 'See-saw, Margery Daw'.

Margie ♀
Pet form of ◊**Margaret**, from the informal short form *Marge*.
Variants: **Marjie, Marjy, Marji**.

Margot ♀
French pet form of ◊**Marguerite**, now used as an independent given name. In England it is still usually pronounced in the French way, but in Eastern Europe the final consonant is sounded, and this has had some influence in America.

Marguerite ♀
French form of ◊**Margaret**, also used in the English-speaking world, where its use has been reinforced by the fact that the name was adopted in the 19th century for a garden flower, a large cultivated variety of daisy. *Margaret* was earlier used in English as a dialect word denoting the ox-eye daisy, and the French equivalent was borrowed into English just in time to catch the vogue for deriving female given names from vocabulary words denoting flowers. See also ◊**Daisy**.

Mari ♀
Welsh form of ◊**Mary**; see also ◊**Mair**.

Maria ♀
Latin form of ◊**Mary**. In the English-speaking world it is a learned revival

dating from the 18th century, pronounced both 'ma-*ree*-a' and, more traditionally, 'ma-*rye*-a'. The Latin name *Maria* arose as a back-formation from the early Christian female name *Mariam*. This was taken as an accusative case, with the usual Latin feminine accusative ending -*am*. In fact, however, it is an indeclinable Aramaic alternative form of the Hebrew name ◊**Miriam**.

Mariah ♀

Elaborated spelling of ◊**Maria**, influenced by the many female names of Hebrew origin ending in -*a* plus an optional final *h*.

Mariamne ♀

The form of ◊**Miriam** used by the Jewish historian Flavius Josephus, writing in Latin in the 1st century BC, as the name of the wife of King Herod. On the basis of this evidence, it has been thought by some to be closer to the original form of the name actually borne by the Virgin Mary, and has therefore been bestowed in her honour.

Marian ♀

Originally a medieval variant spelling of ◊**Marion**. However, in the 18th century, when combined names began to come into fashion, it was sometimes understood as a combination of ◊**Mary** and ◊**Ann**.

Marianne ♀

Extended spelling of ◊**Marian**, reinforcing the association of the second element with ◊**Ann(e)**. It also represents a French assimilated form of ◊**Mariamne**. *Marianne* is the name used for the symbolic figure of the French Republic.

Marie ♀

French form of ◊**Maria**. When first introduced to England in the Middle Ages, it was Anglicized in pronunciation and respelled ◊**Mary**. This French form was reintroduced into the English-speaking world as a separate name in the 19th century, and is still pronounced more or less in the French manner, although sometimes with the stress on the first syllable.

Mariella ♀

Italian diminutive form of ◊**Maria**, now sometimes used as an independent given name in the English-speaking world.

Marietta ♀

Italian diminutive form of ◊**Maria**, now quite often used as a given name in the English-speaking world. In Gaelic Scotland *Mar(i)etta* is quite commonly used as an Anglicized form of *Mairead*, the Gaelic form of ◊**Margaret**.

Marigold ♀

One of the older of the group of names that were adopted from words for flowers in the late 19th and early 20th centuries. The Old English name of the flower was *golde*, presumably from *gold* (the precious metal), in reference to its colour. At some time before the 14th century the flower became associated with the Virgin Mary, and its name was extended accordingly to *marigold*.

Marilee ♀

Modern coinage, a combination of ◊**Mary** and ◊**Lee**.

Marilene ♀

Modern coinage, a combination of the name ◊**Mary** with the productive suffix -*lene*, or else a variant of ◊**Marilyn**.

Marilyn ♀

20th-century elaboration of ◊**Mary**, with the addition of the productive suffix -*lyn* (see ◊**Lynn**). A major influence on the popularity of the name was the film star Marilyn Monroe (1926–62), originally named Norma-Jean Baker.
Variants: **Marilynn**, **Marylyn(n)**, ◊**Marilene**.

Marina ♀

From a Late Latin name, a feminine form of the family name *Marīnus*. This was in fact a derivative of *Marius*, a traditional name of uncertain derivation, but even during the early centuries AD it was widely assumed to be identical with the Latin adjective *marīnus* 'of the sea'. The early saints of this name are all of very doubtful historical authenticity.

Marion ♀

Originally a medieval French diminutive form of ◊**Marie**, introduced to Britain in the Middle Ages, and now completely Anglicized in pronunciation.

Marisa ♀

20th-century elaboration of ◊**Maria**, with the suffix *-isa* abstracted from such names as *Lisa* and *Louisa*.

Marissa ♀

Variant of ◊**Marisa**, with the suffix *-issa*, abstracted from names such as *Clarissa*.

Marjie ♀

Variant spelling of ◊**Margie**.
Variants: **Marjy**, **Marji**.

Marjorie ♀

The usual modern spelling of ◊**Margery**. It seems to have arisen as the result of folk etymological association of the name with that of the herb *marjoram* (cf. ◊**Rosemary**). This word is of uncertain origin; its Middle English and Old French form was *majorane*, without the first *-r-*.
Variant: **Marjory**.

Mark ♂

From the Latin name ◊**Marcus**, borne by the Evangelist, author of the second gospel in the New Testament, and by several other early and medieval saints. In Arthurian legend, King *Mark* is the aged ruler of Cornwall to whom Isolde is brought as a bride by Tristan; his name was presumably of Celtic origin, perhaps derived from the element *march* 'horse'. This was not a particularly common name in the Middle Ages.

Marlene ♀

Contracted form of Latin *Maria Magdalene* (see ◊**Madeleine**). The name is of German origin, but is now also widely used in the English-speaking world, normally in a pronunciation with two syllables (cf. ◊**Arlene** and ◊**Charlene**). Probably the first, and certainly the most famous, bearer of the name was the film star Marlene Dietrich (1901–92), who was christened Maria Magdalena von Losch. The name was further popularized in the 1940s by the wartime German song 'Lili Marlene', which was immensely popular among both German and British troops in North Africa.

Marlon ♂

Name apparently first brought to public attention by the American actor Marlon Brando (b. 1924). The name was borne also by his father. It is of uncertain origin, possibly derived from ◊**Marc** with the addition of the French diminutive suffix *-lon* (originally a combination of two separate suffixes, *-el* and *-on*). The actor's family is partly of French extraction.

Marmaduke ♂

Of uncertain derivation. It is generally held to be an Anglicized form of the Old Irish name *Mael-Maedóc* 'devotee of Maedóc'. The name *Maedóc* was borne by various early Irish saints, most notably a 6th-century abbot of Clonmore and a 7th-century bishop of Ferns. Mael-Maedóc Ó Morgair (1095–1148) was a reformer of the Church in Ireland and a friend of Bernard of Clairvaux. However, the modern Gaelic form (from *c*.1200) is *Maol-Maodhóg* (pronounced 'mul-may-og'), so that the name would have had to have been borrowed into English before this loss of the *d*.

Marmaduke has never been common except in a small area of North Yorkshire.
Short form: ◊**Duke**.

Marna ♀
Swedish vernacular form of ◊**Marina**, now occasionally also used in the English-speaking world.
Pet form: **Marnie** (well established as an independent given name in North America).

Marquis ♂
Mainly U.S.: taken from the vocabulary word denoting the rank of nobility (cf. ◊**Earl**, ◊**Prince**, ◊**King**). This derives from Old French *marchis*, i.e. 'lord of the marches (border districts)'. The spelling was later influenced by the Provençal and Spanish equivalents. Use as a given name may also have been influenced by the Scottish surname *McMarquis*, Gaelic *Mac Marcuis*, a patronymic from ◊**Marcus**.

Marsh ♂
Transferred use of the surname, in origin a local name for someone who lived on a patch of marshy ground, from Middle English *mersche* (Old English *mersc*). It is also used as an informal short form of ◊**Marshall**, and possibly also as a masculine equivalent of ◊**Marsha**, by back-formation.

Marsha ♀
Phonetic spelling of ◊**Marcia**, associated particularly with the American film star Marsha Hunt (b. 1917).

Marshall ♂
Transferred use of the surname, derived from a Norman French occupational term that originally denoted someone who looked after horses, ultimately from Germanic *marah* 'horse' + *scalc* 'servant'. By the time it became fixed as a surname it had the meaning 'shoeing smith'; later it came to denote an official whose

duties were to a large extent ceremonial. The surname is pronounced the same as the Latin name *Martial* (from Latin *Mars*, genitive *Martis*; cf. ◊**Martin**). This may have contributed something to its use as a given name.

Martha ♀
New Testament name, of Aramaic rather than Hebrew origin, meaning 'lady'. It was borne by the sister of Lazarus and Mary of Bethany (John 11:1). According to Luke 10:38, when Jesus visited the house of Mary and Martha, Mary sat at his feet, listening to him, while Martha 'was cumbered about much serving', so that she complained to Jesus, 'Lord, dost thou not care that my sister hath left me to serve alone?' For this reason, the name *Martha* has always been associated with hard domestic work, as opposed to the contemplative life.

Marti ♀
Short form of ◊**Martina** or ◊**Martine**. Its best-known bearer in Britain is the English comedienne Marti Caine (b. 1945).
Variants: **Martie**, **Marty**.

Martin ♂
English form of the Latin name *Martīnus*. This was probably originally derived from *Mars* (genitive *Martis*), the name of the Roman god of war (and earlier of fertility). *Martin* became very popular in the Middle Ages, especially on the Continent, as a result of the fame of St Martin of Tours. He was born the son of a Roman officer in Upper Pannonia (an outpost of the Roman Empire, now part of Hungary), and although he became a leading figure in the 4th-century Church, he is chiefly remembered now for having divided his cloak in two and given half to a beggar. The name was also borne by five popes, including one who defended Roman Catholic dogma against Eastern Orthodox theology. He

died after suffering imprisonment and privations in Naxos and public humiliation in Constantinople, and was promptly acclaimed a martyr by supporters of the Roman Church. Among Protestants, the name is sometimes bestowed in honour of the German theologian Martin Luther (1483–1546); *Martin* was used as a symbolic name for the Protestant Church in satires by both Dryden and Swift. A further influence may be its use as the given name of the civil-rights leader Martin Luther King (1929–68).
Variant: **Martyn**.
Pet form: **Marty**.

Martina ♀
Feminine form of the Latin name *Martīnus* (see ◊**Martin**). It was in use from an early period, being borne by a notorious poisoner mentioned by the historian Tacitus. The 3rd-century saint of the same name is of doubtful authenticity. Modern use of the name in the English-speaking world seems to be the result of German or Eastern European influence, as in the case of the tennis player Martina Navratilova (b. 1956), who was born in Czechoslovakia.

Martine ♀
French form of ◊**Martina**, also used in the English-speaking world.

Marty ♂ ♀
Short form of ◊**Martin** or of ◊**Martina** and ◊**Martine**. It has sometimes been used as an independent male name in the latter part of the 20th century, being associated particularly with the comedian Marty Feldman (1933–83), the 1960s pop singer Marty Wilde (b. 1938 as Reginald Smith), and the country-and-western singer Marty Robbins (b. 1926).

Martyn ♂
Variant spelling of ◊**Martin**.

Marvin ♂
Medieval variant of ◊**Mervyn**,

resulting from the regular Middle English change of -*er*- to -*ar*-. Modern use may represent a transferred use of the surname derived from this in the Middle Ages. It is very popular in the United States, where it is associated in particular with the American singer Marvin Gaye (1939–84).

Mary ♀
Originally a Middle English Anglicized form of French ◊**Marie**, from Latin ◊**Maria**. This is a New Testament form of ◊**Miriam**, which St Jerome derives from elements meaning 'drop of the sea' (Latin *stilla maris*, later altered to *stella maris* 'star of the sea'). *Mary* is the most popular and enduring of all female Christian names, being the name of the Virgin Mary, mother of Jesus Christ, who has been the subject of a cult from earliest times. Consequently, the name was extremely common among early Christians, several saints among them, and by the Middle Ages was well established in every country in Europe at every level of society. It has been enduringly popular ever since, its popularity having been almost completely undisturbed by the vagaries of fashion that affect other names. In the New Testament, *Mary* is also the name of several other women: Mary Magdalene (see ◊**Madeleine**); Mary the sister of Martha, who sat at Jesus's feet while Martha served (Luke 10:38–42; John 11:1–46; 12:1–9) and who came to be taken in Christian tradition as symbolizing the value of a contemplative life; the mother of St Mark (Colossians 4:10); and a Roman matron mentioned by St Paul (Romans 16:6).

Marylyn ♀
Variant spelling of ◊**Marilyn**.
Variant: **Marylynn**.

Mason ♂
Especially U.S.: transferred use of the surname, which originated in the early

Middle Ages as an occupational name for a worker in stone, Old French *maçon* (of Germanic origin, connected with Old English *macian* 'to make').

Masterman ♂
Transferred use of the surname, which originated in Scotland as a term denoting a retainer or servant: the 'man' of the 'master'. This was used in particular for the eldest sons of barons and the uncles of lords. As a given name it is principally known from the central character of Captain Frederick Marryat's novel *Masterman Ready* (1841).

Mathew ♂
Variant spelling of ◊**Matthew**.

Mathias ♂
Variant spelling of ◊**Matthias**.

Matilda ♀
Latinized form of a Germanic personal name derived from *maht*, *meht* 'might' + *hild* 'battle'. This was the name of an early German queen (895–968), wife of Henry the Fowler, who was noted for her piety and generosity. It was also the name of the wife of William the Conqueror and of the daughter of Henry I of England (see ◊**Maud**). The name was introduced into England by the Normans, and this Latinized form is the one that normally occurs in medieval records, while the vernacular form *Maud* was the one in everyday use. *Matilda* was revived in England as a learned form in the 18th century.
Variant: **Mathilda**.
Short form: **Tilda**.
Pet forms: **Mattie**, **Matty**; **Tilly**, **Tillie**.

Matt ♂
Short form of ◊**Matthew**.

Matthew ♂
English form of the name of the Christian evangelist, author of the first gospel in the New Testament. His name is a form of the Hebrew name *Mattathia*, meaning 'gift of

God', which is fairly common in the Old Testament, being rendered in the Authorized Version in a number of different forms: *Mattan(i)ah*, *Mattatha(h)*, *Mattithiah*, *Mattathias*, and so on. In the Authorized Version, the evangelist is regularly referred to as *Matthew*, while the apostle chosen to replace Judas Iscariot is distinguished as ◊**Matthias**. A related name from the same Hebrew roots, but reversed, is ◊**Jonathan**.
Variant: **Mathew**.
Short form: **Matt**.
Pet forms: **Mattie**, **Matty**.

Matthias ♂
New Testament Greek form of the Hebrew name *Mattathia* (see ◊**Matthew**), or rather of an Aramaic derivative. The Latin form of the name is *Matthaeus*. In English the form *Matthias* is used in the Authorized Version of the New Testament to distinguish the disciple who was chosen after the treachery of Judas to make up the twelve (Acts 1:23–26) from the evangelist *Matthew*. However, this distinction is not observed in other languages, where *Matthias* (or a version of it) is often a learned doublet existing alongside a vernacular derivative.
Variant: **Mathias**.

Mattie ♂ ♀
Pet form of ◊**Matthew** or ◊**Matilda**.
Variant: **Matty**.

Maud ♀
Medieval vernacular form of ◊**Matilda**. This form was characteristically Low German (i.e. including medieval Dutch and Flemish). The wife of William the Conqueror, who bore this name, was the daughter of Baldwin, Count of Flanders. In Flemish and Dutch the letter -*t*- was generally lost when it occurred between vowels, giving forms such as *Ma(h)auld*. *Maud* or *Matilda* was also the name of the daughter (1102–67) of Henry I of England; she was married early in life

to the Holy Roman Emperor Henry V, and later disputed the throne of England with her cousin Stephen. In 1128 she married Geoffrey, Count of Anjou. A medieval chronicler commented, 'she was a good woman, but she had little bliss with him'. The name *Maud* became quite common in England in the 19th century, when its popularity was influenced in part by Tennyson's poem *Maud*, published in 1855.

Maude ♀
Variant of ◊**Maud**, the usual spelling of the name in North America.

Maura ♀
Of Celtic origin. St Maura was a 5th-century martyr, of whom very little is known; her companion is variously named as *Britta* (of Celtic origin) and *Baya* (of Latin origin). In Ireland *Maura* is now commonly regarded as a form of ◊**Mary** (cf. ◊**Moira** and ◊**Maureen**).

Maureen ♀
Anglicized form of Irish Gaelic *Máirín*, a pet form of *Máire*. Among other influences, the name was popularized by the film actress Maureen O'Hara (b. 1920). See also ◊**Moreen**.
Variants: **Maurene**, **Maurine**.
Short form: **Mo**.

Maurice ♂
From the Late Latin name *Mauricius*, a derivative of *Maurus* (a byname meaning 'Moor', i.e. 'dark', 'swarthy'), borne by, among others, an early Byzantine emperor (c.539–602). It was introduced to Britain by the Normans, and was popular in the Middle English period, but was not widely adopted by the nobility, and became rare in the 17th century. It is now sometimes believed in Britain and America to be a mainly French name, perhaps because of the enormous popular influence of the French singer and film actor Maurice Chevalier

(1888–1972), who, in his public image at least, was the very epitome of Gallic charm. See also ◊**Morris**.
Short form: **Mo**.

Mave ♀
Variant spelling of ◊**Maeve**, also sometimes used as an informal short form of ◊**Mavis**.

Mavis ♀
Not found before the last decade of the 19th century. It is one of the small class of female given names taken from vocabulary words denoting birds. *Mavis* is another word for the song-thrush, first attested in Chaucer. It is from Old French, and probably ultimately of Breton origin.

Max ♂
Short form of ◊**Maximilian** and, perhaps now more commonly in the English-speaking world, of ◊**Maxwell**. It is also used as an independent given name.

Maxie ♂ ♀
Pet form of ◊**Max**, now more commonly used as an independent female given name.

Maximilian ♂
From the Latin name *Maximiliānus* (a diminutive of *Maximus* 'greatest'). This was borne by a 3rd-century saint numbered among the 'Fourteen Holy Helpers'. Although already existing, the name was reanalysed in the 15th century by the Emperor Friedrich III, who bestowed it on his first-born son (1459–1519), as a blend of the names *Maximus* and *Aemiliānus*, intending thereby to pay homage to the two classical Roman generals Q. Fabius Maximus 'Cunctator' and P. Cornelius Scipio Aemilianus. The name became traditional in the Habsburg family in Austria-Hungary and also in the royal house of Bavaria. It was borne by an ill-fated Austrian archduke (1832–67) who was set up as emperor of Mexico but later overthrown and shot.

Maxine ♀

Modern coinage, first recorded around 1930. It is a derivative of ◊**Max** by addition of the feminine ending -ine.

Maxwell ♂

Transferred use of the Scottish surname, in origin a local name from a minor place on the River Tweed, named as 'the stream (Old English well(a)) of Mack'. The latter is a form of ◊**Magnus**. Maxwell was the middle name of the newspaper tycoon William Maxwell Aitken, Lord Beaverbrook (1879–1964), who was born in Canada, and it has been used as a given name among his descendants. It is now also frequently taken as an expansion of ◊**Max**.

May ♀

Pet form of both ◊**Margaret** and ◊**Mary**. The popularity of this name, which was at its height in the early 20th century, has been reinforced by the fact that it fits into the series of month names with ◊**April** and ◊**June**, and also belongs to the group of flower names, being another word for the hawthorn, whose white flowers blossom in May. It has been out of fashion for a time.

Maya ♀

Latinate version of ◊**May** or a respelled form of the name of the Roman goddess *Māia*, influenced by the common English name *May*. The goddess Maia was one of the Pleiades, the daughters of Atlas and Pleione; she was the mother by Jupiter of Mercury. Her name seems to be derived from the root *māi-* 'great', seen also in Latin *māior* 'larger'. In the case of the American writer Maya Angelou (b. 1929), *Maya* is a nickname which she acquired in early childhood as a result of her younger brother's referring to her as 'mya sista'.

Maybelle ♀

Altered form of ◊**Mabel**, influenced by the independent names ◊**May** and ◊**Belle**.

Maynard ♂

Transferred use of the surname, which is derived from a Norman French given name of Germanic origin, from *magin* 'strength' + *hard* 'hardy', 'brave', 'strong'.

Meagan ♀

Recent variant spelling of ◊**Megan**. *Variant*: **Meaghan**.

Meave ♀

Variant of ◊**Maeve**.

Meg ♀

Short form of ◊**Margaret**, an alteration of the obsolete short form *Mag(g)* (as in ◊**Maggie**). Until recently *Meg* was a characteristically Scottish pet form, but it is now used more widely. Its popularity no doubt owes something to Meg March, one of the four sisters who are the main characters in Louisa M. Alcott's novel *Little Women* (1855).

Megan ♀

Welsh pet form of ◊**Meg**, nowadays generally used as an independent first name both within and beyond Wales, but nevertheless retaining a strong Welsh flavour.
Variants: **Meghan**, **Meag(h)an** (pseudo-Irish spellings much used in Australia and Canada).

Meggie ♀

Pet form of ◊**Meg** or of ◊**Megan**, as in the case of the central character of Colleen McCullough's novel *The Thorn Birds* (1977).

Meghan ♀

Recent variant spelling of ◊**Megan**.

Mehetabel ♀

Biblical name (meaning 'God makes happy' in Hebrew), borne by a character, 'the daughter of Matred, the daughter of Mezahab', who is mentioned in passing in a genealogy (Genesis 36:39). The name achieved

some currency among the Puritans in the 17th century. Nowadays, however, it is chiefly associated with the companion (a cat) of Archy, the cockroach in the poems of Don Marquis (1927).
Variant: **Mehitabel**.

Meical ♂
Welsh form of ◊**Michael**.
Short form: **Meic**.

Meilyr ♂
Welsh: traditional name derived from an Old Celtic name, *Maglorīx*, derived from *maglos* 'chief' + *rīx* 'ruler'.

Meinwen ♀
Welsh: modern coinage composed of the elements *main* 'slender' + *(g)wen*, feminine form of *gwyn* 'white', 'fair', 'blessed', 'holy'.

Meirion ♂
Welsh: traditional name, derived in the sub-Roman period from Latin *Mariānus* (a derivative of *Marius*; see ◊**Maria**).

Mel ♂ ♀
Short form of ◊**Melvin** or ◊**Melville**, or, in the case of the female name, of ◊**Melanie** or the several other female names beginning with this syllable.

Melanie ♀
From an Old French form of Latin *Melania*, a derivative of the feminine form, *melaina*, of the Greek adjective *melas* 'black', 'dark'. This was the name of two Roman saints of the 5th century, a grandmother and granddaughter. St Melania the Younger was a member of a rich patrician family. She led an austere and devout Christian life and, on inheriting her father's wealth, she emancipated her slaves, sold her property, and gave the proceeds to the poor. She also established several contemplative houses, including one on the Mount of Olives, to which she eventually retired. The name *Melanie* was introduced to England from

France in the Middle Ages, but died out again. It has been reintroduced and has become popular in the late 20th century.
Variants: **Melany**, ◊**Melony**.

Melinda ♀
Modern coinage, derived from the first syllable of names such as ◊**Melanie** and ◊**Melissa**, with the addition of the productive suffix *-inda* (cf. e.g. ◊**Lucinda**).

Melissa ♀
From the Greek word *melissa* 'bee'. It is the name of the good witch who releases Rogero from the power of the bad witch Alcina in Ariosto's narrative poem *Orlando Furioso* (1532). The name has recently increased considerably in popularity, together with other female names sharing the same first syllable.
Variant: **Melitta** (from an ancient Greek dialectal variant of the same word).

Melody ♀
Modern transferred use of the vocabulary word (Greek *melōdia* 'singing of songs', from *melos* 'song' + *aeidein* 'to sing'), chosen partly because of its pleasant associations and partly under the influence of other female names with the same first syllable.

Melony ♀
Variant of ◊**Melanie**, perhaps influenced by ◊**Melody**.
Variants: **Mellony**, **Mel(l)oney**.

Melville ♂
Mainly North American: transferred use of the Scottish surname, which originated as a Norman baronial name borne by the lords of a place in northern France called *Malleville* 'bad settlement', i.e. settlement on infertile land. The name was taken to Scotland as early as the 12th century and became an important surname there; use as a given name seems also to have originated in Scotland.

Melvin ♂

Very popular modern name of uncertain origin, probably a variant of the less common ◊**Melville**. The variant **Melvyn** is associated particularly with the film star Melvyn Douglas (1901–81).

Mercedes ♀

Spanish name associated with the cult of the Virgin Mary, from the liturgical title *Maria de las Mercedes* (literally, 'Mary of Mercies'; in English, 'Our Lady of Ransom'). Latin *mercēdes* (plural) originally meant 'wages' or 'ransom'. In Christian theology, Christ's sacrifice is regarded as a 'ransom for the sins of mankind', hence an 'act of ransom' was seen as identical with an 'act of mercy'. There are feasts in the Roman Catholic calendar on 10 August and 24 September to commemorate the Virgin under this name. As a given name, this is now occasionally used in England, and more commonly in the United States, but normally only by Roman Catholics. It is associated with the American film actress Mercedes McCambridge (b. 1918). A more materialistic association with the high-class German brand of car so named may also be having an influence on the continued use of the name in this increasingly secular age.

Mercia ♀

Latinate elaboration of ◊**Mercy**, coinciding in form with the name of the Anglo-Saxon kingdom of Mercia, which dominated England during the 8th century under its king, Offa.

Mercy ♀

From the vocabulary word denoting the quality of magnanimity, and in particular God's forgiveness of sinners, a quality much prized in Christian tradition. The word is derived from Latin *mercēs*, which originally meant 'wage' or 'reward' (see ◊**Mercedes**). The name was much favoured by the Puritans; Mercy is the companion of Christiana in the second part of John Bunyan's *Pilgrim's Progress* (1684). Subsequently, it fell out of use as a given name. In modern use, this is often an Anglicized form of *Mercedes*.

Meredith ♂ ♀

From the Old Welsh personal name *Maredudd*, later *Meredudd*. This is of uncertain origin; the second element is Welsh *iudd* 'lord'. In recent years the name has sometimes been given to girls, presumably being thought of as the formal form of ◊**Merry**.

Merfyn ♂

Welsh: traditional name derived from Old Welsh *mer*, probably meaning 'marrow' + *myn* 'eminent'. This name was borne by a shadowy 9th-century Welsh king.

Meriel ♀

Variant of ◊**Muriel**. Both forms are 19th-century revivals of an older Celtic name. Of the two forms, *Meriel* was never as popular as *Muriel*.

Merle ♀ ♂

Probably a contracted form of ◊**Meriel**, but also associated with the small class of female names derived from birds, since it is identical in form with Old French *merle* 'blackbird' (Latin *merula*). The name came to public notice in the 1930s with the actress Merle Oberon (1911–79); she was born Estelle Merle O'Brien Thompson. In Britain this is still normally a female name; in the United States it is more commonly borne by males.

Merlin ♂

Usual English form of the Welsh name *Myrddin*. The name is most famous as that of the legendary magician who guides the destiny of King Arthur. It is apparently composed of Old Celtic elements meaning 'sea' and 'hill' or 'fort', but it has been distorted by mediation through Old French sources, which associated the second element with the diminutive suffix *-lin*.

Variant: **Merlyn** (occasionally given to girls, as if containing the productive suffix of female names *-lyn*).

Merrill ♂
Transferred use of the surname, which was derived in the Middle Ages from the female name ◊**Meriel** or ◊**Muriel**.

Merrily ♀
Mainly U.S.: apparently a respelling of ◊**Marilee**, reshaped to coincide with the adverb derived from the adjective *merry*.

Merry ♀
Apparently an assimilated form of ◊**Mercy**. In Dickens's novel *Martin Chuzzlewit* (1844), Mr Pecksniff's daughters ◊**Charity** and *Mercy* are known as *Cherry* and *Merry*. Nowadays the name is usually bestowed because of its association with the adjective denoting a cheerful and jolly temperament (cf. ◊**Happy**). In the accent of Canada and the central and northern United States there is no difference in pronunciation between *Merry* and *Mary*.

Mervyn ♂
Anglicized form of Welsh ◊**Merfyn**, now widely popular both in and beyond Wales.
Variant: **Mervin**.
Short form: **Merv**.

Meryl ♀
Recent coinage, owing its current popularity to the fame of the American actress Meryl Streep (b. Mary Louise Streep in 1949). It has also been influenced in part by the ending *-yl* in names such as ◊**Cheryl**.

Meurig ♂
Welsh form of ◊**Maurice**, derived from Latin *Mauricius* via Old Welsh *Mouric*.

Mia ♀
Danish and Swedish pet form of ◊**Maria**. It is now also used in the English-speaking world, largely as a result of the fame of the actress Mia Farrow (b. 1945).

Micah ♂
Biblical name (meaning 'who is like Yahweh?' in Hebrew, and thus a doublet of ◊**Michael**). This was the name of a prophet, author of the book of the Bible that bears his name, and which dates from the late 8th century BC.

Michael ♂
English form of a common biblical name (meaning 'who is like God?') borne by one of the archangels, who is also regarded as a saint of the Catholic Church. In the Middle Ages, Michael was regarded as captain of the heavenly host (see Revelation 12:7–9), symbol of the Church Militant, and patron of soldiers. He was often depicted bearing a flaming sword. The name is also borne by a Persian prince and ally of Belshazzar mentioned in the Book of Daniel. See also ◊**Michal**.
Short forms: **Mike**, **Mick**.
Pet form: **Micky**.

Michaela ♀
Latinate feminine form of ◊**Michael**.

Michal ♀
Biblical name (meaning 'brook' in Hebrew) borne by a daughter of Saul who married King David. It is probably through confusion with this name that ◊**Michael** has occasionally been used as a female given name in the English-speaking world.

Michelle ♀
French feminine form of *Michel*, the French form of ◊**Michael**. This name is now also used extensively in the English-speaking world (partly influenced by a Beatles song with this name as its title).
Short forms: **Chelle**, ◊**Shell**.

Mick ♂
Short form of ◊**Michael**; now common

as a generic, and often derogatory, term for a Catholic Irishman.
Pet form: **Micky**. See also ◊**Mikki**.

Mickenzie ♀
Altered form of ◊**Mackenzie**, influenced by the name ◊**Mick**.

Mignonette ♀
Probably a direct use of the French nickname *mignonette* 'little darling', a feminine diminutive of *mignon* 'sweet', 'cute', 'dainty'. Alternatively, it may belong to the class of names derived from vocabulary words denoting flowers (the word in English is used for various species of *Reseda*).

Mihangel ♂
Older Welsh form of ◊**Michael**, representing a contraction of the phrase 'Michael the Archangel'.

Mike ♂
Usual short form of ◊**Michael**. It is also used as an independent given name, particularly in the United States.
Pet form: **Mikey**.

Mikki ♀
Feminine variant of *Micky* (see ◊**Mick**) or pet form of ◊**Michaela**, now sometimes used as an independent given name.
Variants: **Micki**, **Mickie**, **Mickey**.

Mildred ♀
19th-century revival of the Old English female personal name *Mildþrȳð*, derived from *mild* gentle + *þrȳð* 'strength'. This was the name of a 7th-century abbess, who had a less famous but equally saintly elder sister called *Mildburh* and a younger sister called *Mildgȳð*; all were daughters of a certain Queen Ermenburh. Their names illustrate clearly the Old English pattern of combining and recombining the same small group of name elements within a single family.

Miles ♂
Of Norman origin but uncertain derivation. Unlike most Norman names, it is, as far as can be ascertained, not derived from any known Old French or Germanic name element. It may be a greatly altered pet form of ◊**Michael**, which came to be associated with the Latin word *miles* 'soldier' because of the military attributes of the archangel Michael. However, the usual Latin form of the name in the Middle Ages was *Milo*. There is a common Slavonic name element *mil* 'grace', 'favour', with which it may possibly have some connection. The name has been modestly popular in England ever since the Norman Conquest. See also ◊**Milo** and ◊**Myles**.

Milla ♀
Shortened form of ◊**Camilla**.

Millicent ♀
From an Old French name, *Melisende*, of Germanic (Frankish) origin, from *amal* 'labour' + *swinth* 'strength'. This was the name of a daughter of Charlemagne. It was adopted by the Normans and introduced by them to Britain.

Millie ♀
Pet form of ◊**Millicent**, and also, less commonly, of names such as ◊**Mildred** and ◊**Camilla**.

Milo ♂
Latinized form of ◊**Miles**, regularly used in documents of the Middle Ages, and revived as a given name in the 19th century.

Milton ♂
Transferred use of the surname, in origin a local name from the numerous places so called, a large number of which get their name from Old English *mylentūn* 'settlement with a mill'. Others were originally named as 'the middle settlement (of three)', from Old English *middel* 'middle' + *tūn* 'settlement'. The surname is most famous as that of the poet John Milton (1608–74), and the

given name is sometimes bestowed in his honour.
Short form: **Milt**.

Mimi ♀
Italian pet form of ◊**Maria**, originally a nursery name. The heroine of Puccini's opera *La Bohème* (1896) announces 'They call me Mimi', and since that time the name has occasionally been used in the English-speaking world.

Minnie ♀
Pet form of ◊**Wilhelmina**, at its peak of popularity in the latter half of the 19th century, when several names were introduced into Britain from Germany in the wake of Queen Victoria's consort, Prince Albert of Saxe-Coburg-Gotha, whom she married in 1840. It has now largely fallen out of use, partly because German names in general became unacceptable in Britain during the First World War, partly perhaps also because of association with cartoon characters such as Minnie Mouse (in Walt Disney's animations) and Minnie the Minx (in the *Beano* 'children's comic').

Mirabelle ♀
French: from Latin *mīrābilis* 'wondrous', 'lovely' (a derivative of *mīrāri* 'to wonder at', 'admire'; cf. ◊**Miranda**). The same name is found in Italian in the form **Mirabella**. Both the French and Italian forms were quite common in the later Middle Ages. The form *Mirabel* is found occasionally in France and England as a male given name. By the 16th century, both forms were rare.
Variant: **Mirabella** (a Latinate form).

Miranda ♀
Invented by Shakespeare for the heroine of *The Tempest* (1611). It represents the feminine form of the Latin gerundive *mīrandus* 'admirable', 'lovely', from *mīrāri* 'to wonder at', 'admire'; cf. ◊**Amanda**.

Mireille ♀
French: apparently first used, in the Provençal form **Mireio**, as the title of a verse romance by the poet Frédéric Mistral (1830–1914). The name is probably a derivative of Provençal *mirar* 'to admire' (cf. ◊**Miranda**). The poet himself declared it to be a form of ◊**Miriam**, but this was apparently in order to overcome the objections of a priest to baptizing his god-daughter with a non-liturgical name. The name is now occasionally also used in the English-speaking world.

Miriam ♀
Biblical name: the Old Testament form of the Hebrew name *Maryam* (see ◊**Mary**). Of uncertain ultimate origin, this is first recorded as being borne by the elder sister of Moses (Exodus 15:20). Since the names of both Moses and his brother Aaron are probably of Egyptian origin, it is possible that this female name is too. It was enthusiastically taken up as a given name by the Israelites, and is still found mainly, but by no means exclusively, as a Jewish name.

Missy ♀
Modern coinage from a pet form of the vocabulary word *miss*, applied to a young girl (cf. ◊**Maidie**) and common as a pet name and form of address in the southern United States. The vocabulary word *miss* originated in Middle English as a short form of *mistress*.

Misty ♀
Modern coinage, apparently from the vocabulary word.

Mitchell ♂
Transferred use of the surname, itself derived from a common medieval form of ◊**Michael**, representing an Anglicized pronunciation of the French name *Michel*, introduced to Britain by the Normans.
Short form: **Mitch**.

Mo ♀ ♂

Short form of ◊**Maureen** and, less
commonly, of ◊**Maurice**.

Moira ♀

Anglicized form of Irish Gaelic *Máire*,
a form of ◊**Mary**). This is now a
popular name in its own right
throughout the English-speaking
world.
Variant: **Moyra**.

Molly ♀

Long-established pet form of ◊**Mary**,
representing an altered version of the
earlier pet form *Mally*. The name is
chiefly associated with Ireland,
although it is not known to be Gaelic.
It is at present somewhat out of
fashion.

Mona ♀

Anglicized form of the Gaelic name
Muadhnait, a feminine diminutive of
muadh 'noble'. It is no longer
restricted to people with Irish
connections, and has sometimes been
taken as connected with Greek *monos*
'single', 'only'.

Monica ♀

Of uncertain ultimate origin. This was
the name of the mother of St
Augustine, as transmitted to us by her
famous son. She was a citizen of
Carthage, so her name may well be of
Phoenician origin, but in the early
Middle Ages it was taken to be a
derivative of Latin *monēre* 'to warn',
'counsel', or 'advise', since it was as a
result of her guidance that her son
was converted to Christianity.

Monroe ♂

Transferred use of the Scottish
surname, usually spelled *Munro*. The
ancestors of the Scottish Munros are
said to have originally come from
Ireland, apparently from a settlement
by the River Roe in County Derry;
their name is therefore supposed to be
derived from Gaelic *bun Rotha*
'mouth of the Roe'. In the United
States the popularity of the given

name may have been influenced by
the fame of James Monroe
(1758–1831), fifth president of the
United States and propounder (in
1823) of the Monroe Doctrine,
asserting that European powers should
not seek to colonize in North or South
America and that the United States
would not intervene in European
affairs. A more recent influence could
have been the film star Marilyn
Monroe (1926–62), whose original
name was Norma-Jean Baker;
however, the name is not bestowed on
female children, so the influence of
her adopted surname does not appear
to have been significant.
Variants: **Monro**, **Munro(e)**.

Montague ♂

Transferred use of the surname,
originally a Norman baronial name
borne by the lords of Montaigu in La
Manche. (The placename is from Old
French *mont* 'hill' (Latin *mons*,
genitive *montis*) + *aigu* pointed (Latin
acūtus). A certain Drogo of Montaigu
is known to have accompanied
William the Conqueror in his invasion
of England in 1066, and *Montague*
thus became established as an
aristocratic British family name.

Montgomery ♂

Transferred use of the surname,
originally a Norman baronial name
from various places in Calvados. The
placename is derived from Old French
mont 'hill' + the Germanic personal
name *Gomeric* 'power of man'. It has
never been common as a given name,
although it was given additional
currency by the actor Montgomery
Clift (1920–66), and during and after
the Second World War by the British
field marshal, Bernard Montgomery
(1887–1976).

Montmorency ♂

Transferred use of the surname,
originally a Norman baronial name
from a place in Seine-et-Oise. The
placename is derived from Old French

mont 'hill' + the Gallo-Roman personal name *Maurentius*. The given name enjoyed a brief vogue in the 19th century, but is now regarded as affected and so hardly ever used.

Monty ♂
Short form of ◊**Montague** or of the much rarer ◊**Montgomery** and ◊**Montmorency**. It is now sometimes found as an independent given name. As a Jewish name, it was originally used as an approximate English equivalent of ◊**Moses**.

Mór ♀
Scottish and Irish Gaelic: from the vocabulary word *mór* 'large', 'great'. This was the commonest of all female given names in late medieval Ireland, and has continued in frequent use in both Scotland and Ireland to the present day.
Pet forms: ◊**Morag**, ◊**Moreen**.

Morag ♀
Scottish: Anglicized spelling of Gaelic *Mórag*, a pet form of ◊**Mór**. In the 20th century this name has become hugely popular in its own right in Scotland, and is also used elsewhere in the English-speaking world.

Moray ♂
Scottish: variant of ◊**Murray**, and the more usual spelling of the placename from which the surname is derived.

Moreen ♀
Irish: Anglicized form of Gaelic *Móirín*, a pet form of ◊**Mór**. It has now been to a large extent confused with ◊**Maureen**.

Morgan ♂ ♀
Welsh: traditional male name derived from Old Welsh *Morcant*. The first element is of uncertain derivation, the second represents the Old Celtic element *cant* 'circle', 'completion'. In recent years it has occasionally been used outside Wales as a female name, perhaps with conscious reference to

King Arthur's jealous stepsister Morgan le Fay.

Morley ♂
Transferred use of the surname, in origin a local name from any of the numerous places named with Old English *mōr* 'moor', 'marsh' + *lēah* 'wood', 'clearing'.

Morna ♀
Irish and Scottish: variant of ◊**Myrna**. This is the name borne by Fingal's mother in the Ossianic poems of James Macpherson (cf. ◊**Malvina**).

Morris ♂
Variant of ◊**Maurice**. The spelling *Morris* was quite common as a given name in the Middle Ages, but it fell out of use and was readopted in modern times, in part from the surname earlier derived from the given name.

Mortimer ♂
Transferred use of the surname, in origin a Norman baronial name borne by the lords of *Mortemer* in Normandy. The placename meant 'dead sea' in Old French, and probably referred to a stagnant marsh. It was not used as a given name until the 19th century.

Morton ♂
Transferred use of the surname, in origin a local name from any of the numerous places so called from Old English *mōrtūn* 'settlement by or on a moor'. It is also widely used as a Jewish name, having been adopted as an approximate English equivalent of ◊**Moses**.
Short form: **Mort**.

Morven ♀
This was the name of Fingal's kingdom in the Ossianic poems of James Macpherson. In reality it is a district in north Argyll, on the west coast of Scotland, properly *Morvern*, known in Gaelic as *a' Mhorbhairne* 'the big gap'. *Morven* could

alternatively be held to represent Gaelic *mór bheinn* 'big peak'.

Morwenna ♀

Cornish and Welsh: from an Old Celtic personal name derived from an element cognate with Welsh *morwyn* 'maiden'. It was borne by a somewhat obscure Cornish saint of the 5th century; churches in her honour have named several places in Cornwall. The name was revived in Wales in the mid-20th century as a result of nationalistic sentiment.

Moses ♂

Biblical name, the English form of the name of the patriarch (**Moshe** in Hebrew) who led the Israelites out of Egypt (Exodus 4). His name is thought to be of Egyptian origin, most probably from the same root as that found in the second element of names such as *Tutmosis* and *Rameses*, where it means 'born of (a certain god)'. Various Hebrew etymologies have been proposed, beginning with the biblical 'saved (from the water)' (Exodus 2:10), but none is convincing. It is now mainly a Jewish name, although until the mid-20th century it also enjoyed considerable popularity among Christians in England, especially among Puritans and Nonconformists.

Moss ♂

Transferred use of the surname derived from the usual medieval vernacular form of ◊**Moses**, or a revival of this form. In Wales it has in recent years also been used as a short form of ◊**Mostyn**.

Mostyn ♂

Welsh: from the name of a place in Clwyd, on the Dee estuary. The place in fact derives its name from Old English rather than Welsh elements: it appears in Domesday Book as *Mostone*, from Old English *mos* 'moss' + *tūn* 'enclosure', 'settlement'.

Moya ♀

Modern name of uncertain origin; it may be derived from ◊**Moyra**.

Moyra ♀

Variant spelling of ◊**Moira**.

Muir ♂

Transferred use of the Scottish surname, in origin a local name representing a Scottish dialect variant of *moor* 'rough grazing'.

Muireall ♀

Scottish Gaelic traditional name, pronounced '*moor*-all', apparently from Old Celtic words meaning 'sea' + 'bright'. It is often Anglicized as ◊**Muriel**.

Muireann ♀

Irish Gaelic traditional name, pronounced '*mwir*-an', apparently from *muir* 'sea' + *fionn* 'white', 'fair'. The spelling **Muirinn** is also used, and there has been considerable confusion with ◊**Maureen** and ◊**Moreen**.

Muiris ♂

Irish form of ◊**Maurice**. In part it also represents a contracted form of the Gaelic name *Muirgheas*, which is probably derived from *muir* 'sea' + *gus* 'vigour'.

Muirne ♀

Irish Gaelic traditional name, pronounced '*moor*-nya', originally a byname meaning 'beloved'.
Anglicized forms: **Myrna**, **Morna**.

Mungo ♂

Scottish: of uncertain derivation. It is recorded as the byname of St Kentigern, the 6th-century apostle of south-west Scotland and north-west England. Having been glossed in Latin by his biographer as *carissimus amicus* 'dearest friend', the name (in its Brythonic form *Munghu*) to represent later Welsh *fy nghi* 'my dog', i.e. 'my pet'.
Variant: **Munga** (Scottish Gaelic).

Munroe ♂
Variant spelling of ◊**Monroe**.
Variant: **Munro**.

Murdo ♂
Scottish: Anglicized spelling of the old Gaelic name *Muireadhach* (now *Murchadh*), apparently a derivative of *muir* 'sea'.
Variant: **Murdoch**.

Murgatroyd ♂
Transferred use of the Yorkshire surname, in origin a local name from an unidentified place named as 'the clearing (Yorkshire dialect *royd*) belonging to (a certain) Margaret'.

Muriel ♀
Of Celtic origin; see ◊**Muireall**. Forms of the name are found in Breton as well as in Scottish and Irish Gaelic, and in the Middle Ages it was in use even in the heart of England, having been introduced from various sources; the surname *Merrill* is derived from it. See also ◊**Meriel**.

Murray ♂
Transferred use of the Scottish surname, in origin a local name from the region now called *Moray*.
Variant: **Moray**.

Myfanwy ♀
Welsh: name composed of the Welsh affectionate prefix *my-* + *banwy*, a variant form of *banw*, related to *benyw* or *menyw* 'woman'. Its popularity dates only from relatively recent times, when specifically Welsh names have been sought as tokens of Welsh national identity.

Myles ♂
Variant spelling of ◊**Miles**.

Myra ♀
Invented in the 17th century by the poet Fulke Greville (1554–1628). It is impossible to guess what models he

had consciously or unconsciously in mind, but it has been variously conjectured that the name is an anagram of ◊**Mary**; that it is a simplified spelling of Latin *myrrha* 'myrrh', 'unguent'; and that it is connected with Latin *mīrāri* 'to admire' or 'wonder at' (cf. ◊**Miranda**).

Myriam ♀
Variant spelling of ◊**Miriam**. This is the usual spelling of the name in France.

Myrna ♀
Irish: Anglicized form of Gaelic ◊**Muirne**, now also used elsewhere in the English-speaking world. It is associated with the film star Myrna Loy (1905–).
Variant: **Morna**.

Myron ♂
From a classical Greek name, derived from Greek *myron* 'myrrh'. The name was borne by a famous sculptor of the 5th century BC. It was taken up with particular enthusiasm by the early Christians because they associated it with the gift of myrrh made by the three kings to the infant Christ, and because of the association of myrrh (as an embalming spice) with death and eternal life. The name was borne by various early saints, notably a 3rd-century martyr of Cyzicus and a 4th-century bishop of Crete. Their cult is greater in the Eastern Church than the Western.

Myrtle ♀
From the vocabulary word denoting the plant (Old French *myrtille*, Late Latin *myrtilla*, a diminutive of classical Latin *myrta*). This is one of the group of plant names that became popular as female given names in the late 19th century.

NADIA NADINE NAHUM NAN NANCY
NANETTE NAOMI NAT NATALIE NATALYA
NATASHA NATHALIE NATHAN NATHANI
EL NEA NED NEIL NELL NELSON NENA NE
RISSA NERYS NESA NESTA NETTA NETTIE N
EVILLE NEWTON NGAIO NGAIRE NIA NIA

Nadia ♀

French and English spelling of Russian *Nadya* (a pet form of *Nadezhda* 'hope'). This name has enjoyed a considerable vogue in the English-speaking world in the 20th century.

Nadine ♀

French elaboration of ◊**Nadia**. Many names of Russian origin became established in France and elsewhere in the early 20th century as a result of the popularity of the Ballet Russe, established in Paris by Diaghilev in 1909.

Nahum ♂

Biblical name (meaning 'comforter' in Hebrew), borne by a prophet of the 7th century BC. He was the author of the book of the Bible that bears his name, in which he prophesies the downfall of Nineveh, which fell in 612 BC. This is a well-established Jewish name, which was also popular among 17th-century Puritans in England. It was borne by the minor Restoration dramatist Nahum Tate (1652–1715), who rewrote Shakespeare's *King Lear* with a happy ending.

Nan ♀

Originally a pet form of ◊**Ann** (for the initial *N-*, cf. ◊**Ned**). It is now generally used as a short form of ◊**Nancy**.

Nancy ♀

Of uncertain origin. From the 18th century it is clearly used as a pet form of ◊**Ann** (cf. ◊**Nan**), but it may originally have been a similar formation deriving from the common medieval given name *Annis*, a vernacular form of ◊**Agnes**. Nowadays it is an independent name, and was especially popular in America between about 1920 and 1960.
Variants: **Nancie**, **Nanci**.
Short forms: **Nan**, **Nance**.

Nanette ♀

Elaboration of ◊**Nan**, with the addition of the French feminine diminutive suffix *-ette*.

Naomi ♀

Biblical name (meaning 'pleasantness' in Hebrew), borne by the wise mother-in-law of Ruth. The name has long been regarded as typically Jewish, but recently it has begun to come into more general use.

Nat ♂

Short form of ◊**Nathan** and ◊**Nathaniel**.

Natalie ♀

French form of ◊**Natalya**, adopted from Russian in the early 20th century, probably, like ◊**Nadine**, under the influence of Diaghilev's Ballet Russe, which was established in Paris in 1909. The name is now very common in France and in the English-speaking world, where it was borne by the actress Natalie Wood (1938–82). She was born Natasha Gurdin, in San Francisco. Her father was of Russian descent, her mother of French extraction.
Variant: **Nathalie**.

Natalya ♀

Russian: from the Late Latin name *Natália*, a derivative of Latin *natális (diēs)* 'birthday', especially Christ's birthday, i.e. Christmas (cf. ◊**Noël**). St Natalia was a Christian inhabitant of Nicomedia who is said to have given succour to the martyrs, including her husband Adrian, who suffered there in persecutions under Diocletian in 303. She is regarded as a Christian saint, although she was not herself martyred.

Natasha ♀
Russian: pet form of ◊**Natalya**, now widely adopted as an independent name in the English-speaking world and elsewhere. Like *Noëlle* and ◊**Noël**, it is sometimes given to girls born on or about Christmas Day.

Nathalie ♀
Variant spelling of ◊**Natalie**. The *th* is a mere elaboration in the French spelling and has not yet had any effect on the pronunciation.

Nathan ♂
Biblical name, meaning 'he (God) has given' in Hebrew (cf. ◊**Nathaniel**). This was the name of a prophet who had the courage to reproach King David for arranging the death in battle of Uriah the Hittite in order to get possession of the latter's wife Bathsheba (2 Samuel 12:1–15). It was also the name of one of David's own sons. In modern times this name has often been taken as a short form of ◊**Nathaniel** or of ◊**Jonathan**.

Nathaniel ♂
English form of a New Testament name, which is derived from the Greek form of a Hebrew name meaning 'God has given' (cf. ◊**Nathan**, which is sometimes taken as a short form of this name). It was borne by one of the less prominent of Christ's apostles (John 1:45; 21:2), who in fact is probably identical with ◊**Bartholomew**. The spelling used in the Authorized Version of the New Testament is **Nathanael**, but this has never been common as a given name in the English-speaking world.

Neal ♂
Variant spelling of ◊**Neil**.
Variant: **Neale**.

Ned ♂
Short form of ◊**Edward**, originating in the misdivision of phrases such as *mine Ed* (cf. ◊**Nan**). It was common in the Middle Ages and up to the 18th century, but in the 19th was almost entirely superseded in the role of short form by ◊**Ted**. It is now, however, enjoying a modest revival.

Neil ♂
Anglicized form of the enduringly popular Gaelic name **Niall**. Its derivation is disputed, and it may mean 'cloud', 'passionate', or perhaps 'champion'. It was adopted by the Scandinavians in the form *Njal* and soon became very popular among them. From the Middle Ages onwards, this name was found mainly in Ireland, the Highlands of Scotland, and the English-Scottish Border region. However, in the 20th century it has spread to enjoy great popularity in all parts of the English-speaking world.
Variants: **Neal(e)**. See also ◊**Nigel**.

Nell ♀
Medieval short form of ◊**Eleanor**, ◊**Ellen**, and ◊**Helen**; for the initial *N-*, cf. ◊**Ned**. It was the name by which Charles II's mistress Eleanor Gwyn (1650–87) was universally known to her contemporaries, and at about that time it also became established as an independent name.
Pet forms: **Nellie**, **Nelly**.

Nelson ♂
Transferred use of the surname, which originated in the Middle Ages as either a patronymic from ◊**Neil** or a metronymic from ◊**Nell**. Use as a given name probably began as a tribute to the British admiral Lord Nelson (1758–1805), the victor of the Battle of Trafalgar; cf. ◊**Horatio**. It is,

however, now much more common in the United States than in Britain, and in the 1930s became associated with the American film actor and singer Nelson Eddy (1901–67), remembered particularly for his romantic roles with Jeanette MacDonald.

Nena ♀
Variant spelling of ◊**Nina**.

Nerissa ♀
Of Shakespearian origin. It is the name of a minor character in *The Merchant of Venice*, Portia's waiting woman, who marries Gratiano. The name seems to be a Latinate elaboration of Greek *nērēis* 'sea sprite'.

Nerys ♀
Welsh: of uncertain derivation, perhaps intended to be from Welsh *nêr* 'lord', with the suffix *-ys* by analogy with other female names such as ◊**Dilys** and ◊**Gladys**. This was not used as a given name in the Middle Ages, and dates only from the recent Welsh cultural revival; this has been accompanied by a spate of modern coinages of Welsh names, enabling Welsh parents to give their children names reflecting their national identity.

Nessa ♀
Originally a short form of *Agnessa*, a Latinate form of ◊**Agnes**. In modern use in the English-speaking world it is more often a short form of ◊**Vanessa**, and is also used as an independent given name.
Pet form: **Nessie**.

Nesta ♀
Welsh: Latinized version of **Nest**, a Welsh pet form of ◊**Agnes**. Nesta was the name of the grandmother of the 12th-century chronicler Giraldus Cambrensis ('Gerald the Welshman').

Netta ♀
Apparently a Latinate variant of ◊**Nettie**, though in Gaelic-speaking

areas of Scotland it is more probably a feminine form of ◊**Neil**.

Nettie ♀
Pet form derived from various female names ending in the syllable *-nette*, for example ◊**Annette** and ◊**Jeannette**, with the diminutive suffix *-ie*. It had a brief vogue in the late 19th and early 20th centuries.

Neville ♂
Transferred use of the surname, in origin a Norman baronial name from any of several places in Normandy called *Néville* or *Neuville* 'new settlement'. First used as a given name in the early 17th century, and with increasing regularity from the second half of the 19th, it is now so firmly established as a given name that it has lost touch with its origin as a surname.

Newton ♂
Mainly U.S.: transferred use of the surname, in origin a local name from any of the very numerous places so called from Old English *nēowe* 'new' + *tūn* 'enclosure', 'settlement'. This is said to be the commonest of all English placenames. The most famous bearer of the surname is probably Sir Isaac Newton (1642–1727), the English scientist.
Short form: **Newt**.

Ngaio ♀
New Zealand name, pronounced 'nye-oh': apparently from the Maori word *ngaio* which, among other things, means 'clever'. *Ngai* is also a prefix meaning 'tribe' or 'clan'; the given name may have originated as a tribal name.

Ngaire ♀
New Zealand (Maori) name, pronounced 'nye-ree': of unknown origin. It is usually Anglicized as ◊**Nyree**. See also ◊**Ngaio**.

Nia ♀
Welsh form of ◊**Niamh**.

Niall ♂
Original Irish and Scottish Gaelic spelling of ◊Neil. It has been strongly revived among non-Gaelic speakers in the 20th century.

Niamh ♀
Irish Gaelic name, pronounced 'nee-uv', from a vocabulary word meaning 'brightness' or 'beauty'. It was borne in Irish mythology by the daughter of the sea god, who fell in love with the youthful Oisín, son of Finn MacCool, and carried him off over the sea to the land of perpetual youth, *Tír na nÓg*, where there is no sadness, no ageing, and no death. It is now a very popular given name in Ireland.

Nichol ♂
Variant of ◊Nicol.
Variant: **Nicholl**.

Nicholas ♂
English form of the post-classical Greek personal name *Nikolaos*, derived from *nikē* 'victory' + *laos* 'people'. The spelling with *-ch-* first occurred as early as the 12th century, and became firmly established at the time of the Reformation, although *Nicolas* is still occasionally found. St Nicholas was a 4th-century bishop of Myra in Lycia, about whom virtually nothing factual is known, although a vast body of legend grew up around him, and he became the patron saint of Greece and of Russia, as well as of children, sailors, merchants, and pawnbrokers. His feast-day is 6 December, and among the many roles which legend has assigned to him is that of bringer of Christmas presents, in the guise of 'Santa Claus' (an alteration of the Dutch form of his name, *Sinterklaas*).
Variants: **Nicolas, Nickolas**.
Short form: **Nick**.
Pet form: **Nicky**.

Nicholl ♂
Variant spelling of ◊Nichol.

Nick ♂
Short form of ◊Nicholas.
Variant: **Nik**.

Nickie ♀
Variant of the female name ◊Nicky.
Variant: **Nicki**.

Nickolas ♂
Variant spelling of ◊Nicholas, influenced by the short form ◊Nick.

Nicky ♂ ♀
Pet form of ◊Nicholas and of ◊Nicola.
Variants: **Nickie, Nicki, Nikki** ♀

Nico ♂ ♀
Modern short form of both ◊Nicholas and ◊Nicola.

Nicol ♂
Common medieval vernacular form of ◊Nicholas, current until a relatively late period in Scotland, and now being revived in more general use. Modern use as a given name may owe something to the character Bailie Nicol Jarvie in Sir Walter Scott's novel *Rob Roy*.
Variants: **Nicoll, Nichol(l)**.

Nicola ♀
Latinate feminine form of ◊Nicholas.
Pet forms: **Nicky, Nickie, Nicki, Nikki**.

Nicole ♀
French feminine form of ◊Nicholas, now increasingly common in the English-speaking world.

Nicolette ♀
French diminutive form of ◊Nicole, now also used as an independent given name in the English-speaking world.

Nicoll ♂
Variant spelling of ◊Nicol.

Nigel ♂
Anglicized form of the medieval name *Nigellus*, a Latinized version (ostensibly representing a diminutive of Latin *niger* 'black') of the vernacular *Ni(h)el*, i.e. ◊Neil. Although it is frequently found in medieval records, this form was

probably not used in everyday life before its revival by antiquarians such as Sir Walter Scott in the 19th century.

Nigella ♀

Latinate feminine form of ◊**Nigel**. Adoption as a given name may also have been encouraged by the fact that this is an alternative name (from its black seed) for the flower known as 'love-in-a-mist'.

Nik ♂

Modern variant spelling of ◊**Nick**.

Nikita ♀

Originally a Russian male name, from Greek *Anikētos* 'unconquered, unconquerable' (from *a-* 'not' + *nikān* 'to conquer'). This was the name of an early pope (c.152–160); he was a Syrian by descent and is particularly honoured in the Eastern Church. In recent years, however, the name has begun to be used in the English-speaking world as a female name, perhaps being taken as an elaboration of ◊**Nikki** with the feminine diminutive suffix *-ita*.

Nikki ♀

Pet form of ◊**Nicola**, now sometimes used as an independent given name.

Nina ♀

Russian name (originally a short form of names such as *Antonina*), now commonly also used in the English-speaking world.
Variant: **Nena**.

Ninette ♀

French diminutive form of ◊**Nina**. Like ◊**Nadine**, this was one of the names brought to the English-speaking world from Russian via French in the early 20th century.

Ninian ♂

Scottish and Irish: of uncertain origin. This was the name of a 5th-century British saint who was responsible for evangelizing the northern Britons and the Picts. His name first appears in the Latinized form *Ninianus* in the 8th century; this appears to be identical to the *Nynnyaw* recorded in the *Mabinogi*. The given name was used in his honour until at least the 16th century in Scotland and has recently been revived.

Nita ♀

Short form of various names that end in these syllables, as for example *Anita* and *Juanita*.

Noah ♂

English form of the name of the biblical character whose family was the only one saved from the great Flood ordained by God to destroy mankind because of its wickedness. The origin of the name is far from certain; in the Bible it is implied that it means 'rest' (Genesis 5:29, 'and he called his name Noah, saying, This same shall comfort us concerning our work and the toil of our hands, because of the ground which the Lord hath cursed'). One tradition indeed explains it as derived from the Hebrew root meaning 'to comfort' (see ◊**Nahum**) with the final consonant dropped.

Noam ♂

Modern Jewish name, from a Hebrew vocabulary word meaning 'delight', 'joy', 'pleasantness' (cf. ◊**Naomi**, from the same Hebrew root). Its most famous bearer is the American linguist Noam Chomsky (b. 1928).

Noble ♂

Mainly U.S.: name derived from the modern English adjective (via Old French from Latin *nobilis*). The idea behind it may have been to hint at high-born origin or to suggest qualities of character. In part there may be some influence from the surname, which arose in the Middle Ages as a descriptive nickname in the first sense.

Noël ♂ ♀

From Old French *noel, nael*

'Christmas', from Latin *natālis diēs (Domini)* 'birthday (of the Lord)'. The meaning is still relatively transparent, partly because the term occurs as a synonym for 'Christmas' in the refrain of well-known carols. The name is often given to children born at Christmas time.

Variants: **Noel**; **Noëlle**, **Noelle** (feminine forms).

Nola ♀
Probably a short form of the Gaelic name ◊**Fionnuala** (cf. ◊**Nuala**). It may alternatively have been created as a feminine form of ◊**Nolan**.

Nolan ♂
Transferred use of the Irish surname, Gaelic *Ó Nualláin* 'descendant of Nuallán'. The latter is an ancient Gaelic personal name, originally a byname representing a diminutive of *nuall* 'chariot-fighter', 'champion'.

Nolene ♀
Mainly Australian: name created as a feminine form of ◊**Nolan**.
Variant: **Noleen**.

Noll ♂
Pet form of ◊**Oliver**, frequent in the Middle Ages and occasionally revived in modern times. The initial consonant seems to derive from the misdivision of a vocative phrase; cf. ◊**Ned**.

Nona ♀
From the feminine form of the Latin ordinal *nonus* 'ninth', sometimes used as a given name in Victorian times for the ninth-born child in a family if it was a girl, or even for the ninth-born girl. At the present day, when few people have nine children, let alone nine daughters, it has passed into more general, if only occasional, use.

Nonie ♀
Pet form of ◊**Ione** or of ◊**Nora**, also used to a limited extent as an independent given name.

Nora ♀
Short form of names such as *Leonora* and *Honora*. *Nora* (Gaelic *Nóra*) was at one time regarded as a peculiarly Irish name; as such, it may be a derivative of ◊**Fionnuala**, due to confusion of *l* and *r* (cf. ◊**Molly** from ◊**Màire**).
Variant: **Norah**.

Norbert ♂
From an Old French name of Germanic (Frankish) origin, from *nord* 'north' + *berht* 'bright', 'famous'. The best-known bearer of this name was an 11th-century saint who founded an order of monks, known as Norbertians (also called Premonstratensians from their first home at Premontré near Laon). *Norbert* was one of several names of Germanic origin that were revived in Britain in the late 19th century, but it is now rather more common in North America than in Britain.

Noreen ♀
Anglicized form of the Irish Gaelic name *Nóirín*, a diminutive of *Nóra* (see ◊**Nora**).
Variants: **Norene**, **Norine**.

Norma ♀
Apparently invented by Felice Romani in his libretto for Bellini's opera of this name (first performed in 1832). It is identical in form with Latin *norma* 'rule', 'standard', but there is no evidence that this word was the actual source of the name. In recent times, it has come to be taken in England and the Scottish Highlands as a feminine equivalent of ◊**Norman**. An influence on the popularity of the compound *Norma-Jean* has been the film star Marilyn Monroe (1926–62), originally named Norma-Jean Baker.

Norman ♂
Of Germanic origin, from *nord* 'north' + *man* 'man', i.e. 'Norseman'. This name was in use in England before the Conquest, and was reinforced by its

use among the Norman invaders themselves. The Normans were the inhabitants of Normandy in northern France, whose name is a reference to the Vikings who took control of the region in the 9th century. In the 11th and 12th centuries they achieved remarkable conquests, including not only Britain but also Sicily, southern Italy, and Antioch.

Norris ♂
Transferred use of the surname, which is derived from Norman French *norreis* (in which the stem represents the Germanic element *nord* 'north'), originally a local designation for someone who had migrated from the north.

Norton ♂
Transferred use of the surname, in origin a local name from any of the numerous places so called from Old English *norð* 'north' + *tūn* 'enclosure', 'settlement'.

Nuala ♀
Irish: short form of the Gaelic name ◊**Fionnuala**. It is now in general use as an independent given name.

Nye ♂
Pet form of the Welsh name ◊**Aneirin**, representing the middle syllable of that name as commonly pronounced. The name is particularly associated with the Welsh Labour statesman Aneurin Bevan (1897–1960).

Nyree ♀
New Zealand: Anglicized spelling of a Maori name usually transcribed as ◊**Ngaire**. It is relatively common in New Zealand and has been taken up to some extent in Britain due to the fame of the New Zealand-born actress Nyree Dawn Porter (b. 1940).

OBADIAH OBERON OCTAVIA OCTAVIUS O
DETTE ODRA OLGA OLIVE OLIVER OLIVIA
OLLIE OLIVEN OMAR OONA OPAL OPALIN
EOPHELIA OPHRAH ORALIE ORAN OREN
ORSON ORVILLE OSBERT OSCAR OSWALD
OTIS OTTOLINE OWEN OBADIAH OBERO

Obadiah ♂

From a biblical name meaning
'servant of God' in Hebrew (cf. Arabic
Abdullah, which has the same
meaning). This was the name of a
prophet who gave his name to one of
the shorter books of the Bible, and of
two other minor biblical characters: a
porter in the temple (Nehemiah
12:25), and the man who introduced
King Ahab to the prophet Elijah
(1 Kings 18).

Oberon ♂

Variant spelling of ◊**Auberon**.

Octavia ♀

Of Latin origin, representing a
feminine form of ◊**Octavius**.

Octavius ♂

From the Roman family name, derived
from Latin *octāvus* 'eighth'. The name
was fairly frequently given to the
eighth child (or eighth son) in large
Victorian families. It is much less
common these days, when families
rarely extend to eight children, but is
occasionally selected for reasons of
family tradition or for some other
reason without regard to its original
meaning.

Odette ♀

French feminine diminutive form of
the Old French masculine name *Oda*,
which is of Germanic origin (derived
from a word meaning 'prosperity',
'fortune', or 'riches'). Although the
original male name has dropped out of
use, this feminine derivative has
survived.

Odile ♀

French: from the medieval Germanic
name *Odila* (a derivative of *od*
meaning 'prosperity', 'fortune',
'riches'). This was the name of an 8th-
century saint who founded a
Benedictine convent at what is now
Odilienburg in Alsace. She is the
patron saint of Alsace.

Ofra ♀

Variant spelling of ◊**Ophrah**.

Olga ♀

Russian name of Scandinavian origin,
originally derived from the Old Norse
adjective *heilagr* 'prosperous',
'successful'. It was imported by the
Scandinavian settlers who founded the
first Russian state in the 9th century.
St Olga of Kiev (d. 969) was a
Varangian noblewoman who was
baptized at Byzantium in about 957
and set about converting her people.
The name was introduced to the
English-speaking world in the late
19th century, but retains a
distinctively Russian flavour.

Olive ♀

One of the earliest and most
successful of the names coined during
the 19th century from vocabulary
words denoting plants, no doubt partly
because an olive branch has been a
symbol of peace since biblical times.
See also ◊**Olivia**.

Oliver ♂

From a French name, *Olivier*, recorded
as the name of one of Charlemagne's
paladins (retainers), the close
companion in arms of Roland in the

Chanson de Roland. Whereas Roland is headstrong and rash, Oliver is thoughtful and cautious. Ostensibly this name derives from Late Latin *olivārius* 'olive tree' (cf. ◊Olive), but Charlemagne's other paladins all bear solidly Germanic names, so it is more probably an altered form of a Germanic name, perhaps distantly connected with Old Norse *Óleifr* 'ancestral relic'.
Pet forms: Ollie, ◊Noll.

Olivia ♀

Latinate name, first used by Shakespeare for the rich heiress wooed by the duke in *Twelfth Night* (1599). Shakespeare may have taken it as a feminine form of ◊Oliver or he may have derived it from Latin *oliva* 'olive'. In the 1970s it came to be associated with the Australian pop singer and actress Olivia Newton-John (b. 1948).

Ollie ♂

Pet form of ◊Oliver, associated particularly with the comic film actor Oliver Hardy (1892–1957), the rotund partner of Stan Laurel.

Olwen ♀

Welsh: from *ôl* 'footprint', 'track' + *(g)wen* 'white', 'fair', 'blessed', 'holy'. A character of this name in Welsh legend had the magical property of causing flowers to spring up behind her wherever she went.

Omar ♂

Biblical name (apparently meaning 'talkative' in Hebrew) borne by a character mentioned in a genealogy (Genesis 36:11). It has been occasionally used from Puritan times down to the present day in America. More often, however, it is of Arabic origin, as in the case of the film actor and international bridge player Omar Sharif (b. 1926 in Egypt).

Oona ♀

Irish: Anglicized form of the Gaelic name *Úna* (see ◊Una).
Variant: Oonagh.

Opal ♀

One of the rarer female names created in the late 19th century from vocabulary words for gemstones. This is ultimately derived (via Latin and Greek) from an Indian language (cf. Sanskrit *upala* 'precious stone').

Opaline ♀

Comparatively recent coinage: an elaboration of ◊Opal with the addition of *-ine*, a productive suffix of female names (originally a French diminutive suffix).

Ophelia ♀

The name of a character in Shakespeare's *Hamlet*, the beautiful daughter of Polonius; she loves Hamlet, and eventually goes mad and drowns herself. In spite of the ill omen of this literary association, the name has enjoyed moderate popularity since the 19th century. It was first used by the Italian pastoral poet Jacopo Sannazzaro (1458–1530), who presumably intended it as a feminine form of the Greek name *Ōphelos* 'help'. Shakespeare seems to have borrowed the name from Sannazzaro, without considering whether it was an appropriate name for a play set in medieval Denmark.

Ophrah ♀ ♂

Hebrew name meaning 'fawn'. In the Old Testament it is borne by a man (1 Chronicles 4:14), but it is now more commonly used as a female name.
Variants: Ophra, Ofra.

Oralie ♀

Of uncertain origin, possibly an altered form of French *Aurélie* (see ◊Aurelia).
Variant: Oralee.

Oran ♂

Irish: Anglicized form of Gaelic

Odhrán, originally a diminutive of *odhar* 'dun', 'sallow'. The name was borne by various early saints, notably a 6th-century abbot of Meath who accompanied Columba to Scotland and is said to have been buried alive by the latter as a foundation sacrifice.

Oren ♂

Biblical name, apparently meaning 'pine tree' in Hebrew, mentioned in a genealogy (1 Chronicles 2:25). This name is in use in the United States in a number of different spellings. In some cases it may be a variant of the Irish name ◊**Oran**.
Variants: **Orren**, **Orin**, **Orrin**.

Orson ♂

From a Norman French nickname meaning 'bear-cub' (a diminutive of *ors* 'bear', Latin *ursus*). This was occasionally used as a given name in the Middle Ages, but in modern times it probably represents a transferred use of the surname derived from the medieval nickname. In the 20th century its most famous bearer has been the American actor and director Orson Welles (1915–85), who dropped his more prosaic first name, George, in favour of his middle name before embarking on a career in films.

Orville ♂

Though in appearance a surname of Norman baronial origin, this name was in fact invented (with the intention of evoking such associations) by the novelist Fanny Burney for the hero, Lord Orville, of her novel *Evelina* (1778).

Osbert ♂

From an Old English personal name derived from *ōs* 'god' + *beorht* 'bright', 'famous'. It is not now common, but earlier in the 20th century it enjoyed a modest vogue in Britain, being borne for example by the cartoonist Osbert Lancaster and the writer Osbert Sitwell.

Oscar ♂

Old Irish name, apparently from Gaelic *os* 'deer' + *cara* 'friend'. This is borne in the Fenian sagas by a grandson of Finn MacCool. It was resuscitated by the antiquarian poet James Macpherson (1736–96), author of the Ossian poems. It is now also a characteristically Scandinavian name; it was introduced there because Napoleon, an admirer of the works of Macpherson, imposed the name on his godson Oscar Bernadotte, who became King Oscar I of Sweden in 1844 (see also ◊**Malvina**). In more recent times it has been associated particularly with the Irish writer and wit Oscar Wilde (1854–1900), and with the annual awards for achievement in the film industry made by the American Academy of Motion Picture Arts and Sciences.

Oswald ♂

From an Old English personal name, derived from *ōs* 'god' + *weald* 'rule'. This was the name of two English saints. The first was a 7th-century king of Northumbria, who was killed in battle in 641. He was a Christian, a convert of St Aidan's, and his opponent, Penda, was a heathen, so his death was counted as a martyrdom by the Christian Church. The second St Oswald was a 10th-century bishop of Worcester and archbishop of York, of Danish parentage, who effected reforms in the English Church. The name more or less died out after the Middle Ages, but underwent a modest revival in the 19th century as part of the vogue for pre-Conquest English names.

Otis ♂

Especially U.S.: transferred use of the surname, in origin a patronymic derived from the genitive case of the medieval given name *Ote* or *Ode* (of Norman, and ultimately Germanic, origin; cf. ◊**Odette**). It came to be used as a given name in America in honour of the Revolutionary hero James Otis (1725–83); in modern times it has been bestowed in honour of the American soul singer Otis Redding (1941–67).

Ottoline ♀

French diminutive of *Ottilie*, a variant of ◊**Odile**. The name acquired some currency in the English-speaking world in the early 20th century, partly due to the influence of the literary hostess Lady Ottoline Morrell (1873–1938).

Owen ♂

Welsh: of uncertain origin. It may have derived in the sub-Roman period from the Latin name *Eugenius* (see ◊**Eugene**). Alternatively, it may represent an Old Celtic name meaning 'born of Esos'. *Esos* or *Aesos* was a god with a cult in Gaul.

PADDY PADRAIG PAIGE PAMELA PANDOR
A PANSY PARKER PAT PATIENCE PATRICIA
PATRICK PATRICK PATSY PATTY PAUL PAUL
A PAULETTE PAULINE PEARCE PEARL PEG P
EGGEN PEGGY PELHAM PEN PENELOPE PEN
INNAH PENN PENNY PERCE PERCIVAL PER

Paddy ♂

Pet form of ◊**Patrick**. The formation in
-*y* is in origin characteristic of
Lowland Scots, and this pet form
seems to have arisen in Ulster in the
17th century. Since the 19th century
it has come to function in English as a
generic nickname for an Irishman.

Pádraig ♂

Irish Gaelic form of ◊**Patrick**.

Paige ♀

Used regularly in North America, but
seldom elsewhere. It is evidently a
transferred use of the surname *Paige*, a
less common variant of *Page*,
originally an occupational name given
to someone who served as a page to a
great lord. It is not clear why this
should have been taken up in the 20th
century as a female given name. The
American film actress Janis Paige
(born in 1920 under the name Donna
Mae Jaden) may have something to do
with it. There are a number of
actresses and singers with the
surname *Page*, but they are unlikely
to have directly influenced the choice
of the given name in this spelling.
Variant: **Page**.

Pamela ♀

Invented by the Elizabethan pastoral
poet Sir Philip Sidney (1554–86), in
whose verse it is stressed on the
second syllable. There is no clue to
the sources that influenced Sidney in
this coinage. It was later taken up by
Samuel Richardson for the name of
the heroine of his novel *Pamela*
(1740). In Henry Fielding's *Joseph
Andrews* (1742), which started out as

a parody of *Pamela*, Fielding
comments that the name is 'very
strange'.
Variant: **Pamella** (a modern spelling).

Pandora ♀

Name borne in classical mythology by
the first woman on earth, created by
the fire god Hephaistos as a scourge
for men in general, in revenge for
Prometheus' act of stealing fire on
behalf of mankind. Pandora was given
as a wife to Prometheus' foolish
brother Epimetheus, along with a box
which she was forbidden to open.
Being endowed with great curiosity,
she nevertheless did open it, and
unleashed every type of hardship and
suffering on the world, Hope alone
being left inside the box. The name
itself is ironically derived from the
Greek words *pan* 'all', 'every' + *dōron*
'gift'.

Pansy ♀

19th-century coinage, from word
denoting the garden flower, which is
named from Old French *pensee*
'thought'. This was never particularly
popular, and is seldom chosen at all
now that the word *pansy* has acquired
a derogatory slang sense denoting an
effeminate man.

Parker ♂

Transferred use of the common
surname, in origin an occupational
name for a gamekeeper employed in a
medieval game park.

Pat ♂ ♀

Short form of both ◊**Patrick** and

◊**Patricia**.
Pet forms: **Patty**, **Pattie**, **Patti** ♀; ◊**Patsy**.

Patience ♀

From the vocabulary word denoting one of the Seven Christian Virtues. This name was a favourite with the Puritans, and survived better than many similar names, but now seems somewhat old-fashioned. The word is derived from Latin *pati* 'to suffer', and was associated by the early Christians with those who endured persecution and misfortune without complaint or loss of faith.

Patricia ♀

From Latin *Patricia*, feminine form of *Patricius*; see ◊**Patrick**.
Short forms: **Pat**, **Tricia**, **Trisha**.
Pet forms: **Patty**, **Pattie**, **Patti**.

Patrice ♂ ♀

Medieval French form of both the male and female Latin names *Patricius* (see ◊**Patrick**) and ◊**Patricia**. In modern French it is used only as a male name, but in the English-speaking world it is used occasionally also as a female name, apparently under the influence of names such as *Bernice*.

Patrick ♂

Name of the apostle and patron saint of Ireland (*c.*389–461), Gaelic *Pádraig*. He was a Christian Briton and a Roman citizen, who as a young man was captured and enslaved by raiders from Ireland. He escaped and went to Gaul before returning home to Britain. In about 419 he felt a call to do missionary work in Ireland. He studied for twelve years at Auxerre, and in 432 returned to Ireland. For the rest of his life it is difficult to distiguish fact from fiction. He apparently went to the court of the high kings at Tara and made some converts there, then travelled around Ireland making further converts until about 445, when he established his archiepiscopal see at Armagh. By the

time of his death almost the whole of Ireland is said to have been converted to Christianity. He is also credited with codifying the laws of Ireland. In his Latin autobiography, as well as in later tradition, his name appears as *Patricius* 'patrician' (i.e. belonging to the Roman senatorial or noble class), but this may actually represent a Latinized form of some lost Celtic (British) name.
Short form: ◊**Pat**.
Pet forms: ◊**Paddy**, ◊**Patsy**.

Patsy ♀ ♂

Pet form of ◊**Patricia** or ◊**Patrick**. It is generally a female name; as a male name it is almost completely restricted to Irish communities. Its popularity does not seem to have been seriously affected by its use in derogatory senses in the general vocabulary, in America meaning 'a dupe' and in Australia 'a homosexual'.

Patty ♀

Pet form of ◊**Patricia**.
Variants: **Pattie**, **Patti**.

Paul ♂

From Latin *Paulus*, a Roman family name, originally a nickname meaning 'small', used in the post-classical period as a given name. Pre-eminently this is the name of the saint who is generally regarded, with St Peter, as co-founder of the Christian Church. Born in Tarsus, and originally named *Saul*, he was both a Roman citizen and a Jew, and at first found employment as a minor official persecuting Christians. He was converted to Christianity by a vision of Christ while on the road to Damascus, and thereafter undertook extensive missionary journeys, converting people, especially Gentiles, to Christianity all over the eastern Mediterranean. His preaching aroused considerable official hostility, and eventually he was beheaded at Rome in about AD 65. He is the author of the fourteen epistles to churches and

individuals which form part of the
New Testament.

Paula ♀
Latin feminine form of ◊**Paul**, borne
by various minor early saints and
martyrs.

Paulette ♀
French diminutive feminine form of
◊**Paul**. It is widely used in the English-
speaking world, where, however, it is
a more recent importation than
◊**Pauline**.

Pauline ♀
French form of the Latin name
Paulīna (feminine of *Paulīnus*, a
derivative of the family name *Paulus*
'small') that has long been common
also in the English-speaking world,
where it is now established as the
most common female equivalent of
◊**Paul**.

Pearce ♂
Variant of ◊**Pierce**. It normally
represents a transferred use of the
English surname derived from the
given name in the Middle Ages. It has
been a popular name among Irish
nationalists since the rising of 1916,
led by the writer and educationist
Patrick Henry Pearce; he was executed
by the British and is regarded as a
martyr to the nationalist cause.

Pearl ♀
One of the group of names coined in
the 19th century from words for
precious and semi-precious stones. It
has a longer history as a Jewish name,
representing an Anglicized form of
Yiddish *Perle* (see also ◊**Peninnah**).

Peg ♀
Pet form of ◊**Margaret**, a variant of
◊**Meg**. The reason for the alternation
of *M*- and *P*-, which occurs also in
Molly/Polly, is not known; it has been
ascribed to Celtic influence, but this
particular alternation does not
correspond to any of the usual
mutational patterns in Celtic
languages.

Pegeen ♀
Anglicized form of Irish Gaelic *Peigín*,
a diminutive of *Peig*, the Gaelic form
of ◊**Peg**.

Peggy ♀
Pet form of ◊**Margaret**; see ◊**Peg**.
Variants: **Peggie**, **Peggi**.

Pelham ♂
Transferred use of the surname, in
origin a local name from a place in
Hertfordshire, so called from the Old
English personal name *Pēo(t)la* + *hām*
'homestead'. From 1715 a family
bearing this surname held the
dukedom of Newcastle.

Pen ♀
Short form of ◊**Penelope**, and
sometimes also of ◊**Peninnah**.

Penelope ♀
Name borne in Greek mythology by
the wife of Odysseus who sat
patiently awaiting his return for
twenty years, meanwhile, as a
supposed widow, fending off by
persuasion and guile a pressing horde
of suitors for her hand in marriage.
Her name would seem to derive from
Greek *pēnelops* 'duck', and play is
made with this word in the *Odyssey*.
However, this may obscure a more
complex origin, now no longer
recoverable.
Short form: **Pen**.
Pet form: **Penny**.

Peninnah ♀
Jewish traditional name, meaning
'coral' in Hebrew. It was borne in the
Bible by the co-wife (with Hannah) of
Elkanah, the father of Samuel. In
modern Hebrew it means 'pearl' and
has become a popular name, often
being substituted for Yiddish *Perle* and
English ◊**Pearl**.
Variants: **Peninna**, **Penina**.

Penn ♂
Mainly U.S.: transferred use of the

surname, for the most part originally a local name from any of various places named with the British element *pen* 'hill', which was adopted into Old English. In other cases it may have referred to someone who lived near a sheep pen (Old English *penn*). The given name is sometimes chosen in honour of the founder of Pennsylvania, the Quaker William Penn (1644–1718), who was born in London into a family of Gloucestershire origin.

Penny ♀
Pet form of ◊**Penelope**, now sometimes also used as an independent given name.

Perce ♂
Variant of ◊**Pierce** or informal short form of ◊**Percy**.

Percival ♂
From Old French versions of the Arthurian legend, where the name is spelled *Perceval*. According to Chrétien de Troyes (12th century) and Wolfram von Eschenbach (c.1170–1220), Perceval (German *Parzifal*) was the perfectly pure and innocent knight who alone could succeed in the quest for the Holy Grail (a cup or bowl with supernatural powers, which in medieval legend was identified with the chalice that had received Christ's blood at the Crucifixion). Later versions of the Grail legend assign this role to Sir Galahad. The name *Perceval* probably represents a drastic remodelling of the Celtic name *Peredur*, as if from Old French *perce(r)* 'pierce' + *val* 'valley'. This may well have been influenced by ◊**Percy**, which was similarly analysed as a compound of *perce(r)* 'pierce' + *haie* 'hedge'.

Percy ♂
Originally a transferred use of a famous surname, but long established as a given name, and now often erroneously taken as a pet or informal

form of ◊**Percival**. The surname originated as a Norman baronial name, borne by a family who had held a fief in Normandy called *Perci* (from Late Latin *Persiācum*, composed of the Gallo-Roman personal name *Persius* and the local suffix *-ācum*). As a given name it was taken up in the early 18th century in the Seymour family, which had intermarried with the Percy family. The poet Percy Bysshe Shelley (1792–1822) was also distantly connected with this family, and it was partly due to his influence that the given name became more widespread. It is at present out of fashion.

Perdita ♀
A Shakespearian coinage, borne by a character in *The Winter's Tale* (1610). The feminine form of Latin *perditus* 'lost', it has a clear reference to the events of the play, and this is explicitly commented on in the text. The name is now more closely associated in some people's minds with a (canine) character in Dodie Smith's *One Hundred and One Dalmatians* (1956), made into a film by Walt Disney.
Pet form: **Perdie**.

Peregrine ♂
From Latin *Peregrīnus* 'foreigner', 'stranger', a name borne by various early Christian saints, perhaps referring to the belief that men and women are merely sojourners upon the earth, their true home being in heaven. In modern times the name is rare, borne mostly by Roman Catholics, who choose it in honour of those saints.

Perry ♂
Pet form of ◊**Peregrine**, or transferred use of the surname *Perry*, in origin a local name for someone who lived by a pear tree (Old English *pirige*). In modern times, it has been borne by the American singer Perry Como

(b. 1912), whose name was originally Nick Perido.

Perse ♂
Variant of ◊Pierce.

Persis ♀
Of New Testament origin, from Greek *Persis*, originally an ethnic name meaning 'Persian woman'. This name is borne by a woman mentioned fleetingly by St Paul—'the beloved Persis, which laboured much in the Lord' (Romans 16:12)—and was taken up from there at the time of the Reformation.

Pet ♀
Short form of ◊Petula, in part influenced by the common affectionate term of address 'pet', derived from the vocabulary word for a tame animal kept for companionship.

Peta ♀
Modern feminine form of ◊Peter, not used before the 1930s.

Petal ♀
From the vocabulary word for the part of a flower, also used as a term of endearment.

Pete ♂
Short form of ◊Peter.

Peter ♂
English form of the name of the best-known of all Christ's apostles, traditionally regarded as the founder of the Christian Church. The name derives, via Latin, from Greek *petros* 'stone', 'rock'. This is used as a translation of the Aramaic byname *Cephas*, given to the apostle Simon son of Jona, to distinguish him from another of the same name (Simon Zelotes). 'When Jesus beheld him, he said, Thou art Simon the son of Jona: thou shalt be called Cephas, which is by interpretation, A stone' (John 1:42). According to Matthew 16:17–18, Christ says more explicitly, 'Blessed art thou, Simon Bar-jona . . . thou art

Peter, and upon this rock I will build my church'.
Short form: **Pete**.

Petra ♀
Feminine form of ◊Peter, representing a hypothetical Latin name *Petra*; *petra* is in fact the regular Late Latin word for 'stone' (Greek *petra*), of which *petrus* is a byform.

Petronel ♀
From Latin *Petronilla*, originally a feminine diminutive of the Roman family name *Petrōnius* (of uncertain derivation). The name *Petronilla* was borne by a 1st-century martyr, and early in the Christian era came to be connected with ◊Peter, so that in many legends surrounding her she is described as a companion or even the daughter of St Peter.

Petula ♀
Of uncertain origin, not used before the 20th century. It is possibly a Christian coinage intended to mean 'supplicant', 'postulant', from Late Latin *petulāre* 'to ask', or there may be some connection with the flower name *petunia*. Alternatively, it may be an elaboration of the vocabulary word *pet* used as a term of endearment, with the suffix *-ula* abstracted from names such as *Ursula*.
Short form: **Pet**.

Phil ♂ ♀
Short form of ◊Philip, ◊Phyllis, or of any of the various other male and female names beginning with the syllable *Phil-*.

Philip ♂
From the Greek name *Philippos*, meaning 'lover of horses', from *philein* 'to love' + *hippos* 'horse'. This was popular in the classical period and since. It was the name of the father of Alexander the Great. It was also the name of one of Christ's apostles, of a deacon ordained by the apostles after

the death of Christ, and of several other early saints.
Short forms: **Phil**, **Pip**.

Philippa ♀
Latin feminine form of ◊**Philip**. In England during the Middle Ages the vernacular name *Philip* was borne by women as well as men, but female bearers were distinguished in Latin records by this form. It was not, however, used as a regular given name until the 19th century.

Phillida ♀
Variant of ◊**Phyllis**, derived from the genitive case (Greek *Phyllidos*, Latin *Phyllidis*) with the addition of the Latin feminine ending -*a*.
Variant: **Phyllida**.

Phillip ♂
Variant spelling of ◊**Philip**, in part a reflection of the surname, which is usually spelled *Phillips*.

Philomena ♀
From the name of an obscure saint (probably of the 3rd century) with a local cult in Italy. In 1527 the bones of a young woman were discovered under the church altar at San Severino near Ancona, together with a Latin inscription declaring them to be the body of St Filomena. Her name seems to be a feminine form of Latin *Philomenus*, Greek *Philomenēs*, from *philein* 'to love' + *menos* 'strength'. The name became popular in the 19th century, as a result of the supposed discovery in 1802 of the relics of another St Philomena in the catacombs at Rome. All the excitement, however, resulted from the misinterpretation of the Latin inscription *Filumena pax tecum* 'peace be with you, beloved' (from Greek *philoumena* 'beloved').

Phineas ♂
Biblical name, borne by two minor characters. One was a grandson of Aaron, who preserved the purity of the race of Israel and deflected God's wrath by killing an Israelite who had taken a Midianite woman to wife (Numbers 25:6–15); the other, a son of the priest Eli, was killed in combat with the Philistines over the Ark of the Covenant (1 Samuel 1:3; 4:6–11). The name is spelled *Phinehas* in the Authorized Version, and has been taken to mean 'serpent's mouth' (i.e. 'oracle') in Hebrew, but this is an incorrect popular etymology. It is in fact derived from the Egyptian name *Panḥsj*, originally a byname meaning 'the Nubian' and used as a personal name in Ancient Egypt. *Phineas* was popular among the Puritans in the 17th century, and has been occasionally used since, especially in America.

Phoebe ♀
Latin form of the name of a Greek deity, *Phoibē* (from *phoibos* 'bright'), partly identified with Artemis, goddess of the moon and of hunting, sister of the sun god Apollo, who was also known as *Phoibos* (Latin *Phoebus*).

Phyllida ♀
Variant spelling of ◊**Phillida**.

Phyllis ♀
Name of a minor character in Greek mythology who killed herself for love and was transformed into an almond tree; the Greek word *phyllis* means 'foliage', so clearly her name doomed her from the start.

Piaras ♂
Irish Gaelic name, derived in the Middle Ages from Anglo-Norman ◊**Piers**. Piaras Feiritéar (1600–53) was a Kerry chieftain and poet. In the 20th century *Piaras* has been used as a Gaelic form of ◊**Pearce**.

Pierce ♀
English and Irish: variant of ◊**Piers**, in use in Ireland from the time of the Norman Conquest up to the present day. In many cases it may represent a transferred use of the English surname

derived from the given name in the Middle Ages.

Piers ♂

Regular medieval vernacular form of ◊**Peter** (from the Old French nominative case, as against the oblique *Pier*, modern *Pierre*). In the form *Pierce* it survived into the 18th century, although in part this may be a transferred use of the surname derived from the medieval given name. *Piers* was revived in the mid-20th century, perhaps partly under the influence of William Langland's great rambling medieval poem *Piers Plowman* (1367–86), in which the character of Piers symbolizes the virtues of hard work, honesty, and fairness.

Pip ♂

Contracted short form of ◊**Philip**, best known as the name of the main character in Charles Dickens's *Great Expectations* (1861), whose full name was Philip Pirrip.

Pippa ♀

Contracted pet form of ◊**Philippa**, now quite commonly used as an independent given name. It was popularized in the 19th century by Browning's narrative poem *Pippa Passes* (1841), in which the heroine is a child worker in an Italian silk-mill, whose innocent admiration of 'great' people is ironically juxtaposed with their sordid lives. The name is presumably supposed to be Italian, but is not in fact used in Italy.

Polly ♀

Variant of ◊**Molly**, now established as an independent given name. The reason for the interchange of *M*- and *P*- is not clear; cf. ◊**Peg**.
Short form: **Poll**.

Poppy ♀

From the word denoting the flower, Old English *popæg* (from Latin *papāver*). It has been used as a given name since the latter years of the 19th

century, and reached a peak of popularity in the 1920s.

Portia ♀

This is the name of two characters in the works of Shakespeare. The most celebrated of them is an heiress in *The Merchant of Venice* who, disguised as a man, shows herself to be a brilliant advocate and delivers a stirring speech on the quality of mercy. It is also the name of the wife of Brutus in *Julius Caesar*. The historical Brutus's wife was called *Porcia*, feminine form of the Roman family name *Porcius*, which is apparently a derivative of Latin *porcus* 'pig'.
Variant: **Porsha**.

Posy ♀

Pet form (originally a nursery version) of ◊**Josephine**. It has also been associated with the vocabulary word *posy* 'bunch of flowers' (originally a collection of verses, from *poesy* 'poetry'). It is occasionally used as an independent given name, fitting into the series of names associated with flowers that arose in the 19th century.

Preston ♂

Transferred use of the surname, in origin a local name from any of the numerous places in England named with Old English *prēost* 'priest' + *tūn* 'enclosure', 'settlement'.

Primrose ♀

One of the several female names taken from words for flowers in the late 19th century. The word is from Latin *prima rosa* 'first rose', although it does not in fact have any connection with the rose family.

Prince ♂

Originally a nickname from the royal title, Old French *prince* (Latin *princeps*). This word was introduced to Britain by the Normans. In the United States *Prince* is common as a Black name.

Priscilla ♀

Of New Testament origin: from a post-classical Latin personal name, a feminine diminutive of the Roman family name *Priscus* 'ancient'. *Priscilla* was the name of a woman with whom St Paul stayed at Corinth (Acts 18:3), referred to elsewhere as *Prisca*. The name was popular among the Puritans in the 17th century and again enjoyed a vogue in the 19th century.

Pet form: **Prissy**.

Pru ♀

Short form of ◊**Prudence** and ◊**Prunella**.

Variant: **Prue**.

Prudence ♀

Originally a medieval form of the Latin name *Prūdentia*, a feminine form of *Prūdentius*, from *prūdens* 'provident'. The Blessed Prudentia was a 15th-century abbess who founded a new convent at Como in Italy. Later, among the Puritans in 17th-century England, *Prudence* was associated with the vocabulary word for the quality name.

Short forms: **Prue**, **Pru**.

Prunella ♀

Latinate name, probably one of the names coined in the 19th century from vocabulary words for plants and flowers, in this case from a diminutive derived from Late Latin *pruna* 'plum'. The name has enjoyed a minor vogue in the latter part of the 20th century, being borne by two well-known English actresses, Prunella Scales and Prunella Gee.

Short forms: **Prue**, **Pru**.

Pryderi ♂

Welsh: traditional name, meaning 'caring for' (later 'anxiety'). It is borne in the *Mabinogi* by Pryderi, son of Pwyll, who makes several appearances in the narrative.

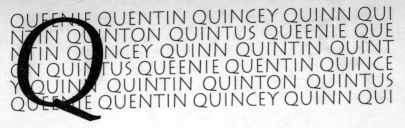
QUEENIE QUENTIN QUINCEY QUINN QUI
NTIN QUINTON QUINTUS QUEENIE QUE
NTIN QUINCEY QUINN QUINTIN QUINT
ON QUINTUS QUEENIE QUENTIN QUINCE
Y QUINN QUINTIN QUINTON QUINTUS
QUEENIE QUENTIN QUINCEY QUINN QUI

Queenie ♀

Pet form from the affectionate nickname *Queen*, with the addition of the diminutive suffix *-ie*. In the Victorian era it was sometimes used as an allusive pet form for ◊**Victoria**. The vocabulary word *queen* goes back to Old English *cwēn*, related to *cwene* 'woman', with a fanciful respelling.

Quentin ♂

From the Old French form of the Latin name *Quintīnus*, a derivative of the given name ◊**Quintus**. The name was borne by a 3rd-century saint who worked as a missionary in Gaul.
Variants: **Quintin, Quinton.**

Quincy ♂

Mainly U.S.: transferred use of the English surname, in origin a Norman baronial name borne by a family that held lands at *Cuinchy* in Pas-de-Calais, Normandy. The placename is derived from the Gallo-Roman personal name ◊**Quintus**. This was the surname of a prominent New England family in the colonial era. Josiah Quincy (1744–75) was a lawyer and Revolutionary patriot, a close friend of John Adams (1735–1826) who became second president of the United States (1797–1801). The latter's son, John Quincy Adams (1767–1848), also served as president (1825–9). He may have received his middle name in honour of his father's friend Josiah Quincy, or it may have been taken from the township of Quincy, Massachusetts, where he was born and where the Adams family had their seat.
Variant: **Quincey.**

Quinn ♂

Transferred use of the Irish surname, Gaelic *Ó Cuinn* 'descendant of Conn'. The latter is from a word meaning 'leader' or 'chief'. It may also sometimes be used as a short form of ◊**Quincy** or ◊**Quintin**.

Quintin ♂

Variant of ◊**Quentin**.

Quinton ♂

Variant of ◊**Quentin**, influenced by the surname so spelled. The surname is a local name from any of several places named with Old English *cwēn* 'queen' + *tūn* 'enclosure', 'settlement'.

Quintus ♂

An old Roman given name meaning 'fifth'. It has been used in the English-speaking world, mainly in the 19th century, for the fifth-born son or fifth-born child in a family (cf. ◊**Sextus**, ◊**Septimus**, ◊**Octavius**, and ◊**Nona.**

RABBIE RACHAEL RACHEL RACHELLE RAE
RAELENE RAFE RAINBOW RAINE RALPH R
AMSAY RAN RANALD RANDA RANDALL R
ANDOLF RANDY RANULF RAQUEL RASTUS
RAY RAYMOND RAYNER READ REANNA R
EARDEN REBA REBECCA REDMOND REENI

Rabbie ♂
Scottish: pet form of ◊**Robert**, from the short form *Rab, Rob*. It is now often associated with the poet Robert Burns (1759–96).

Rachael ♀
Variant of ◊**Rachel**, influenced by ◊**Michael**.

Rachel ♀
Biblical name (meaning 'ewe' in Hebrew), borne by the beloved wife of Jacob and mother (after long barrenness) of Joseph (Genesis 28–35) and of Benjamin, at whose birth she died. In the Middle Ages and later this was regarded as a characteristically Jewish name, but it is now also widely used among Gentiles.

Rachelle ♀
Elaborated form of ◊**Rachel**, as if from French, but actually a recent coinage in English.

Rae ♀
Mainly Australian: probably originally a short form of ◊**Rachel**, but now generally taken as a feminine form of ◊**Ray** or ◊**Raymond**, or simply a derivative of *ray* meaning 'sunbeam'. In some cases it may represent a transferred use of the Scottish surname *Rae*, originally either a short form of *MacRae* (from a Gaelic personal name meaning 'son of grace') or a nickname from the roebuck. It is often used in combinations such as *Rae Ellen* and *Mary Rae*.

Raelene ♀
Australian: fanciful coinage of recent origin, from ◊**Rae** + the productive feminine suffix *-lene*.

Rafe ♂
Spelling representation of the traditional pronunciation of the name ◊**Ralph**, a pronunciation now largely restricted to the upper classes in England.

Rainbow ♀
From the vocabulary word (from Old English *regn* 'rain' + *boga* 'bow', 'arch'). This is one of the names taken from the world of nature in the 1960s under the influence of the 'flower-power' movement. It has not proved enduringly popular.

Raine ♀
Of modern origin and uncertain derivation. It is possibly a respelling of the French vocabulary word *reine* 'queen' (cf. ◊**Regina**), or a transferred use of the surname *Raine* or *Rayne*. The surname is derived from a medieval given name, a short form of various Germanic compound names derived from *ra(g)in* 'advice', 'decision'. In modern times, this given name is borne by the Countess Spencer, daughter of the romantic novelist Barbara Cartland and stepmother of the Princess of Wales.

Ralph ♂
From a Norman French name, *Raulf*, a contracted form of the Germanic personal name *Radulf*, derived from *rād* 'counsel' + *wulf* 'wolf'. The spelling with *-ph* is due to classical influence in the 18th century.
Variants: **Ralf**, ◊**Rafe**.

Ramsay ♂

Transferred use of the Scottish surname, in origin a local name imported to Scotland from *Ramsey* in Huntingdonshire (so called from Old English *hramsa* 'wild garlic' + *ēg* 'island'). In the 12th century David, brother of King Alexander I of Scotland, was brought up at the English court, and acquired the earldoms of Huntingdon and Northampton. When he succeeded his brother as king, he took many of his retainers and associates with him to Scotland, and some of them took their surnames with them from places in eastern England. This explains why some famous Scottish surnames, such as *Ramsay*, *Lindsay*, *Graham*, etc., are derived from placenames in that part of England. Some of these surnames have in turn gone on to be used as given names.

Variant: **Ramsey**.

Ran ♂

Short form of the various names beginning with this syllable, as, for example, ◊**Randolf**, ◊**Ranald**, and ◊**Ranulf**.

Ranald ♂

Scottish: Anglicized form of the Gaelic name *Raghnall*, a borrowing of the Old Norse name *Rögnvaldr*, derived from *regin* 'advice', 'decision' + *valdr* 'ruler'.

Randa ♀

Modern coinage, probably a shortened form of ◊**Miranda**. See also ◊**Randy**.

Randall ♂

Common medieval vernacular form of ◊**Randolf**. This fell out of use, but before it did so gave rise to a surname. Modern use as a given name represents a transferred use of this surname.

Variants: **Randal**, **Randel(l)**, **Randle**.

Randolf ♂

From a Norman given name, Old Norse *Rannulfr*, derived from *rand* 'rim', 'shield' (or *hrafn* 'raven') + *úlfr* 'wolf'.

Variant: **Randolph**.

Randy ♂ ♀

Mainly North American and Australian: as a male name this originated as a pet form of ◊**Randall**, ◊**Randolf**, or ◊**Andrew**. As a female name it may have originated either as a transferred use of the male name or else as a pet form of ◊**Miranda** (cf. ◊**Randa**). It is now fairly commonly used as an independent name, mainly by men, in spite of the unfortunate connotations of the slang term *randy* 'lustful'.

Variants: **Randie**, **Randi** ♀

Ranulf ♂

Scottish: from an Old Norse personal name, *Reginulfr*, derived from *regin* 'advice', 'decision' + *úlfr* 'wolf'. This was introduced into Scotland by Scandinavian settlers in the early Middle Ages.

Raquel ♀

Spanish form of ◊**Rachel**, brought to public attention by the fame and good looks of the film actress Raquel Welch (b. 1940 as Raquel Tejada, in Chicago). Her father was Bolivian, her mother of English stock.

Variant: **Raquelle**.

Rastus ♂

Of New Testament origin, where it is a shortened form of the Latin name *Erastus* (Greek *Erastos*, from *erān* 'to love'). This was the name of the treasurer of Corinth converted to Christianity by St Paul (Romans 16:23). In the early 20th century *Rastus* came to be regarded as a typically Black name, for reasons which are unclear.

Ray ♂

Short form of ◊**Raymond**, now often used as an independent given name. In some instances it may represent a transferred use of the surname *Ray*, which for the most part originated as a nickname, from Old French *rei*, *roi* 'king' (cf. ◊**Roy** and ◊**Leroy**).

Raymond ♂

From an Old French name, *Raimund*, of Germanic origin, from *ragin* 'advice', 'decision' + *mund* 'protector'. This is of Old French origin was adopted by the Normans and introduced by them into England. Subsequently it dropped out of use, but was revived in the middle of the 19th century, together with several other given names of Old English and Norman origin.
Short form: ◊**Ray**.

Rayner ♂

Transferred use of the surname derived from a Norman personal name. This is of Old French origin (*Rainer*), from a Germanic (Frankish) personal name derived from *ragin* 'advice', 'decision' + *heri*, *hari* 'army'.

Read ♂

Transferred use of the English surname, which for the most part originated as a nickname for someone with red hair or a ruddy complexion (from Old English *rēad* 'red'; cf. ◊**Reid**). In other cases, it may have arisen as a local name, from Old English *hrēod* 'reeds' or *rēod* 'cleared land'.

Reanna ♀

Modern coinage, apparently an altered form of the Welsh name ◊**Rhiannon** influenced by the spelling of ◊**Deanna**.
Variant: **Reanne**.

Rearden ♂

Variant of ◊**Riordan**.

Reba ♀

Modern coinage, apparently derived from the first and last syllables of ◊**Rebecca**.

Rebecca ♀

Biblical, from the Latin form of the Hebrew name *Rebekah*, borne by the wife of Isaac, who was the mother of Esau and Jacob (Genesis 24–27). The Hebrew root occurs in the Bible only in the vocabulary word *marbek* 'cattle stall', and its connection with the name is doubtful. In any case, Rebecca was Aramean, and the name probably has a source in Aramaic. It has always been common as a Jewish name; in England and elsewhere it began to be used also by Christians at the time of the Reformation, when Old Testament names became popular. It was very common among the Puritans in the 17th century, and has enjoyed a tremendous vogue in England in the latter part of the 20th century, among people of many different creeds.
Short forms: **Becca**, **Beck**.
Pet form: **Becky**.

Redmond ♂

Irish: apparently an Anglicized form of the Gaelic name *Réamann*, itself a form of ◊**Raymond**. An alternative explanation derives it from an Old English personal name derived from *ræd* 'counsel' + *mund* 'protector'.

Reenie ♀

Respelling of ◊**Renée**, representing an Anglicized pronunciation of the name. It may also occasionally be a pet form of various names ending in the syllable -*reen*, such as ◊**Doreen** and ◊**Maureen**.

Rees ♂

Anglicized spelling of the Welsh name ◊**Rhys**, in some cases representing a transferred use of the surname so spelled, which is derived from the Welsh given name.
Variants: **Rees**, **Reece**.

Reg ♂

Short form of ◊**Reginald**, often preferred by bearers of that name for use in almost all situations, but rarely actually bestowed as a baptismal name.

Regan ♀

Apparently of Shakespearian origin. This is the name of one of the three daughters in *King Lear* (1605), a most unattractive character, who flatters her father into giving her half his kingdom and then turns him out into a raging storm at night. It is not known where Shakespeare got the name; he presumably believed it to be of Celtic origin. It can be identified with the Irish Gaelic word *ríogan* 'queen' (pronounced 'ree-gan'). Modern use has been reinforced by the Irish surname *Re(a)gan* (Gaelic *Ó Riagáin*).

Reggie ♂
Pet form of ◊**Reg**, common in the 19th and early 20th centuries, but now less so.

Regina ♀
From the Latin vocabulary word meaning 'queen'. It was occasionally used as a given name among the early Christians; a St Regina, probably of the 3rd century, was venerated as a virgin martyr at Autun from an early date. In modern use it is normally borne by Roman Catholics in allusion to the epithet *Rēgīna Coeli* 'Queen of Heaven', a cult title of the Virgin Mary since the 8th century.

Reginald ♂
Of Norman origin, derived from *Reginaldus*, a Latinized form of ◊**Reynold** influenced by Latin *rēgīna* 'queen'. The full form is now regarded as very formal, and bearers generally shorten it to ◊**Reg** in ordinary usage.

Reid ♂
Transferred use of Scottish and Northern English surname, in origin as a nickname for someone with red hair or a ruddy complexion (from Old English *rēad* 'red'; cf. ◊**Read**).

Reine ♀
French vernacular form of Latin *rēgīna* 'queen', probably arising for the most part as an affectionate nickname, but also perhaps with reference to the Virgin Mary, one of whose titles is 'Queen of Heaven'.

Rena ♀
Of recent origin, either an altered form of ◊**Renée**, or else a variant spelling of ◊**Rina**.

Renée ♀
French: from the Late Latin name *Renāta*, feminine of *Renātus* 'reborn', used by early Christians as a baptismal name celebrating spiritual rebirth in Christ. The name is also used in the English-speaking world, often without the accent and in a highly Anglicized pronunciation (cf. ◊**Reenie**).

Reuben ♂
Biblical name (said to mean 'behold, a son' in Hebrew), borne by one of the twelve sons of Jacob, and so the name of one of the twelve tribes of Israel. Genesis 29:32 explains it as follows: 'and Leah conceived, and bare a son, and she called his name Reuben: for she said, Surely the Lord hath looked upon my affliction: now therefore my husband will love me'. In Genesis 30:14–15, Reuben is depicted as a devoted son to his mother, but he incurred his father's wrath for seducing his concubine Bilhah and on his deathbed Jacob, rather than blessing him, cursed Reuben because of this incident (Genesis 49:4). Despite this, the name has enjoyed steady popularity as a Jewish name. Among Christians (chiefly Nonconformists) it was briefly in vogue after the Reformation and again in the 19th century, but is out of fashion at present.

Rex ♂
From the Latin vocabulary word meaning 'king'. This was not used as a personal name in Latin of the classical or Christian periods, and its adoption as a given name seems to have been a 19th-century innovation. Its popularity was increased by the fame of the British actor Rex Harrison (1908–90), who was christened Reginald Carey.

Rexanne ♀
Altered form of ◊Roxane or feminine equivalent of ◊Rex.

Reynard ♂
From an Old French name of Germanic (Frankish) origin, derived from *ragin* 'advice', 'decision' + *hard* 'hardy', 'brave', 'strong'. In French, *renard* has become the generic term for a fox, as a result of the popularity of medieval beast tales featuring *Re(y)nard le goupil* 'Reynard the Fox'. The name was adopted by the Normans and introduced by them to Britain.

Reynold ♂
From an Old French name, *Reinald*, *Reynaud*, of Germanic (Frankish) origin, derived from *ragin* 'advice', 'decision' + *wald* 'ruler'. This was adopted by the Normans and introduced by them into England. In modern use, the given name sometimes represents a transferred use of the surname derived from the Norman personal name.
Variant: ◊Reginald. See also ◊Ronald.

Rhea ♀
The name borne, according to Roman tradition, by the mother (Rhea Silvia) of Romulus and Remus, who grew up to be the founders of the city of Rome. It was also a title of the goddess Cybele, introduced to Rome from Phrygia. Its meaning is unknown. It is comparatively rarely used as a given name in the modern world.

Rheanna ♀
Altered form of the Welsh name ◊Rhiannon, influenced by the spelling of ◊Deanna.

Rhett ♂
Transferred use of a surname well established in South Carolina, an Anglicization of the Dutch surname *de Raedt* (from Middle Dutch *raet* 'advice'). This was brought to North America in 1694 by William Rhett (1666–1723). Robert Barnwell Rhett (1800–76) was a South Carolina congressman and senator, a noted secessionist. The name was used by Margaret Mitchell in *Gone with the Wind* (1936) for the character of the black sheep and charmer Rhett Butler. Like some of the other unusual names in that novel, it has attained a modest currency.

Rhetta ♀
Name coined as a feminine form of ◊Rhett.

Rhiannon ♀
Welsh: name borne in Celtic mythology by a minor deity associated with the moon, and in the *Mabinogi* by a daughter of Hyfeidd the Old. It is probably derived from the Old Celtic title *Rigantona* 'great queen'; it was not used as a given name before the 20th century.

Rhoda ♀
From the post-classical Greek name *Rhoda*, derived either from *rhodon* 'rose', or as an ethnic name meaning 'woman from Rhodes' (Greek *Rhodos*). In the New Testament Rhoda was a servant in the house of Mary the mother of John, where Peter went after his release from prison by an angel (Acts 12:13). In the Scottish Highlands *Rhoda* is used as a feminine form of ◊Roderick.

Rhodri ♂
Welsh: from an Old Welsh personal name derived from *rhod* 'wheel' + *rhi* 'ruler', borne by a 9th-century Welsh king.
Variant: **Rhodrhi**.

Rhona ♀
Of uncertain derivation, apparently originating in Scotland sometime around 1870. The spelling *Rona* is also found, and it is probable that the name was devised as a feminine form of ◊Ronald. It has also been suggested that it may be associated with the Hebridean island name *Rona* (cf. ◊Ailsa, ◊Iona, ◊Isla). In either case the

spelling would then have been altered by association with ◊**Rhoda**.

Rhonda ♀
Modern coinage, a blend of ◊**Rhoda** and ◊**Rhona**. It is now often taken to be a Welsh name derived from *rhon* 'pike', 'lance' (as in ◊**Rhonwen**) + *-da* 'good', as in ◊**Glenda**. The name is associated particularly with the red-haired American film actress Rhonda Fleming (b. 1922).

Rhonwen ♀
Welsh: traditional name derived either from *rhon* 'lance' + *(g)wen* 'white', 'fair', 'blessed', 'holy', or from *rhawn* 'hair' + *(g)wen*. It was used by medieval Welsh poets as a form of ◊**Rowena**, regarded as the progenitrix of the English nation, and is now fairly common in Wales.

Rhydderch ♂
Welsh: traditional name, originally a byname meaning 'reddish-brown'. This was a relatively common name in the Middle Ages and in Tudor times, when it gave rise to the surname *Prothero(e)* (Welsh *ap Rhydderch* 'son of Rhydderch'). It has recently been revived by parents proudly conscious of their Welsh roots and culture. See also ◊**Roderick**.

Rhys ♂
Welsh: traditional name meaning 'ardour'. The name was borne in the early Middle Ages by various rulers in south-west Wales, such as Rhys ap Tewdur (d. 1093) and Rhys ap Gruffudd (1132–97). See also ◊**Rees**.

Ria ♀
Short form of ◊**Maria**, of German origin but now also used occasionally in the English-speaking world.

Ricarda ♀
Latinate feminine form of ◊**Richard**.

Rich ♂
Short form of ◊**Richard**. There was a medieval given name *Rich(e)*, but it is connected only indirectly with the modern form. It represents a short form of several medieval names, including not only *Richard* but also other, rarer names of Old French (Germanic) origin with the same first element, as, for example, *Rich(i)er* 'power army' and *Richaud* 'power rule'.

Richard ♂
One of the most enduringly successful of the Old French personal names introduced into Britain by the Normans. It is of Germanic (Frankish) origin, derived from *rīc* 'power' + *hard* 'hardy', 'brave', 'strong'. It has enjoyed continuous popularity in England from the Conquest to the present day, influenced by the fact that it was borne by three kings of England, in particular Richard I (1157–99). He was king for only ten years (1189–99), most of which he spent in warfare abroad, taking part in the Third Crusade and costing the people of England considerable sums in taxes. Nevertheless, he achieved the status of a folk hero, and was never in England long enough to disappoint popular faith in his goodness and justice. He was also Duke of Aquitaine and Normandy and Count of Anjou, fiefs which he held at a time of maximum English expansion in France. His exploits as a leader of the Third Crusade earned him the nickname 'Coeur de Lion' or 'Lionheart' and a permanent place in popular imagination, in which he was even more firmly enshrined by Sir Walter Scott's novel *Ivanhoe* (1820).
Short forms: Rick, ◊**Dick**, ◊**Rich**.
Pet forms: **Ricky**, **Rickie**; **Dicky**, **Dickie**; ◊**Richie**.

Richelle ♀
Modern feminine form of ◊**Richard**, derived from the first syllable of that name + *-elle*, feminine diminutive suffix of French origin. It may also have been influenced by ◊**Rachelle** and ◊**Rochelle**.

Richie ♂

Pet form of ♂**Richard**. The suffix -ie
was originally characteristic of
Scotland and northern England, but
the name is now found elsewhere. In
some cases it represents a transferred
use of the surname derived from the
Scottish pet name.
Variant: **Ritchie** (probably also a
transferred use of the surname spelled
thus).

Rick ♂

Short form of ♂**Richard**.

Ricky ♂

Pet form of ♂**Richard**, also used as an
independent female given name.
Variants: **Rickie**; **Ricki**, **Rikki** ♀

Ridley ♂

Transferred use of the surname, in
origin a local name from any of
various places so named. Those in
Essex and Kent are from Old English
hrēod 'reeds' + *lēah* 'wood' or
'clearing'. The two in Cheshire and
Northumberland are from *rydde*
'cleared land' + *lēah*. The given name
may have been chosen in some cases
by ardent Protestants in honour of
Bishop Nicholas Ridley (?1500–55),
burnt at the stake for his
Protestantism under Mary Tudor.

Rikki ♀

Variant spelling of the female name
Ricky.

Riley ♂

In some cases a transferred use of the
English surname, a local name from a
place named with Old English *ryge*
'rye' + *lēah* 'clearing', 'meadow'.
There is one such place in Devon and
another in Lancashire. In other cases
it probably represents a re-spelling of
the Irish surname *Reilly*, which is
from an old Irish personal name,
Raghallach, of unknown origin.

Rina ♀

Short form of any of the various
female names ending in these

syllables, for example *Katerina* and
Carina.

Riordan ♂

Irish: Anglicized form of the Gaelic
name *Ríordán*, earlier *Ríogh-bhardán*,
from *ríogh* 'king' + *bardán*, a
diminutive of *bard* 'poet'.
Variant: **Rearden**.

Rita ♀

Originally a short form of *Margarita*,
the Spanish form of ♀**Margaret**, but
now commonly used as an
independent given name. It is
associated particularly with the
American film star Rita Hayworth
(1918–87).

Ritchie ♂

Variant spelling of ♂**Richie**.

River ♂

From the vocabulary word (Anglo-
Norman *river(e)*). This is one of the
names taken from the world of nature
in the 1960s under 'hippy' influence,
and it has not been enduringly
popular. Use as a given name may
have been influenced by the surname
Rivers, in origin a Norman baronial
name from various places in northern
France called *Rivières*.

Rob ♂

Short form of ♂**Robert**.

Robbie ♂

Pet form of ♂**Robert**.

Robert ♂

One of the many French names of
Germanic origin that were introduced
into Britain by the Normans, derived
from the nearly synonymous elements
hrod 'fame' + *berht* 'bright', 'famous'.
It had a native Old English
predecessor of similar form
(*Hreodbeorht*), which was supplanted
by the Norman name. It was the name
of two dukes of Normandy in the 11th
century: the father of William the
Conqueror (sometimes identified with
the legendary Robert the Devil), and
his eldest son. It was borne by three

kings of Scotland, notably Robert the Bruce (1274–1329), who freed Scotland from English domination. The altered short form *Bob* is very common, but *Hob* and *Dob*, which were common in the Middle Ages and gave rise to surnames, are extinct. See also ◊**Rupert**.

Short forms: **Bob, Rob**. Scottish: **Rob, Rab**.
Pet forms: **Bobby, Robbie,** ◊**Robin**. Scottish: **Robbie, Rabbie**.

Roberta ♀
Latinate feminine form of ◊**Robert**.

Robin ♂ ♀
Originally a pet form of ◊**Robert**, from the short form ◊**Rob** + the diminutive suffix -*in* (of Old French origin), but now nearly always used as an independent name. In recent years it has been increasingly used as a female name, partly under the influence of the vocabulary word for the bird.
Variant: **Robyn** ♀

Rochelle ♀
Of uncertain origin, probably a feminine diminutive form of the French male name *Roch* (from Germanic *hrok* 'rest'), borne by a 14th-century saint, patron of the sick. This female name is little used in France but common in North America. It may in part represent a respelling of ◊**Rachelle**.

Rocky ♂
Mainly U.S.: of recent origin, originally a nickname for a tough individual. The name came to public notice through the American heavyweight boxing champion Rocky Marciano (1923–69). He was of Italian extraction, and Anglicized his original name, *Rocco* (a cognate of French *Roch*; see ◊**Rochelle**), into a form that seems particularly appropriate for a fighter. It was later taken up in a series of films as the name of a boxer played by the muscular actor Sylvester Stallone, and it has also been adopted as a nickname among devotees of body-building.

Rod ♂
Short form of ◊**Roderick** and ◊**Rodney**.
Pet form: **Roddy**.

Roda ♀
Variant spelling of ◊**Rhoda**.

Roderick ♂
Of Germanic origin, from *hrōd* 'fame' + *rīc* 'power'. This name was introduced into England, in slightly different forms, first by Scandinavian settlers in the Danelaw and later by the Normans. However, it did not survive beyond the Middle English period. It owes its modern use to a poem by Sir Walter Scott, *The Vision of Don Roderick* (1811), where it is an Anglicized form of the cognate Spanish name *Rodrigo*, borne by the last Visigothic king of Spain, whose vision is the subject of the poem. It is now also very commonly used as an Anglicized form of two unrelated Celtic names: Scottish Gaelic *Ruairidh* (see ◊**Rory**) and Welsh ◊**Rhydderch**.

Rodge ♂
Informal short form of ◊**Roger**.

Rodger ♂
Variant spelling of ◊**Roger**, in part from the surname derived from the given name in the Middle Ages.

Rodney ♂
Originally a transferred use of the surname, but in independent use as a given name since the 18th century, when it was bestowed in honour of Admiral Lord Rodney (1719–92), who soundly defeated the French navy in 1759–60. The surname probably derives ultimately from a placename, but the location and etymology of this are uncertain. Stoke Rodney in Somerset is probably named from the surname: the manor was held by one Richard de *Rodene* in the early 14th century.

Roger ♂

From an Old French personal name,
Rog(i)er, of Germanic (Frankish)
origin, from *hrōd* 'fame' + *gār*, *gēr*
'spear'. This was adopted by the
Normans and introduced by them to
Britain, replacing the native Old
English form *Hrōðgār*. Roger, Count of
Sicily (*c.* 1031–1101), son of Tancred,
recovered Sicily from the Arabs. His
son, also called Roger, ruled Sicily as
king, presiding over a court noted for
its splendour and patronage of the
arts.
Variant: **Rodger**.

Róisín ♀

Irish Gaelic name, pronounced '*roe*-
sheen': pet form of *Rós*, the Gaelic
form of ◊**Rose**.
Variant: **Rosheen** (Anglicized spelling).

Roland ♂

From an Old French personal name of
Germanic (Frankish) origin, from *hrōd*
'fame' + *land* 'land', 'territory'. This
was adopted by the Normans and
introduced by them to Britain. In Old
French literature, it is borne by a
legendary Frankish hero, a vassal of
Charlemagne, whose exploits are
related in the *Chanson de Roland*.
The subject of the poem is Roland's
death at the Battle of Roncesvalles in
the Pyrenees in 778, while protecting
the rearguard of the Frankish army on
its retreat from Spain. Roland is
depicted in literature and legend as
headstrong and impulsive. His devoted
friendship with the prudent Oliver is
also legendary.
Variant: **Rowland**.
Pet forms: **Roly**, **Rowley**.

Rolf ♂

Contracted version of an old
Germanic personal name derived from
hrōd 'fame' + *wulf* 'wolf'. This is
found in Old Norse as *Hrólfr*. As an
English given name, it represents in
part the survival of a form imported
by the Normans, in part a much more
recent (19th-century) importation of

the modern German name. See also
◊**Rudolf**.

Rollo ♂

Latinized form of *Roul*, the Old
French version of ◊**Rolf**. This form
appears regularly in Latin documents
of the Middle Ages, but does not seem
to have been used in everyday
vernacular contexts. It is the form by
which the first Duke of Normandy
(*c.*860–932) is generally known. He
was a Viking who, with his followers,
settled at the mouth of the Seine and
raided Paris, Chartres, and elsewhere.
By the treaty of St Clair he received
the duchy of Normandy from Charles
III, on condition that he should
receive Christian baptism. Use of this
name in English families in modern
times seems to be a consciously
archaistic revival.

Roly ♂

Pet form of ◊**Roland**. See also
◊**Rowley**.

Ron ♂

Short form of ◊**Ronald**.
Pet form: **Ronnie**.

Rona ♀

Variant spelling of ◊**Rhona**.

Ronald ♂

From the Old Norse personal name
Rögnvaldr (see ◊**Ranald**). This name
was regularly used in the Middle Ages
in northern England and Scotland,
where Scandinavian influence was
strong. It is now widespread
throughout the English-speaking
world.
Short form: **Ron**.
Pet form: **Ronnie**.

Ronan ♂

Irish: from Gaelic *Rónán*, a
diminutive from *rón* 'seal' (the
animal). The name is recorded as
being borne by various early Celtic
saints, but there has been much
confusion in the transmission of their
names and most of them are also

reliably named as *Ruadhán* (see
◊**Rowan**). The most famous is a 5th-
century Irish saint who was
consecrated as a bishop by St Patrick
and subsequently worked as a
missionary in Cornwall and Brittany.

Ronnie ♂ ♀
Pet form of ◊**Ronald**, or sometimes of
◊**Veronica**.

Rory ♂
Anglicized form of the Gaelic name
Ruaidhrí, *Ruarí* (Irish) or *Ruairidh*,
Ruaraidh (Scottish). In Scotland this is
further Anglicized to ◊**Roderick**.

Ros ♀
Short form of ◊**Rosalind** and
◊**Rosamund**.

Rosa ♀
Latinate form of ◊**Rose**.

Rosaleen ♀
Variant of ◊**Rosalyn**, influenced by the
suffix -*een* (in origin the Irish Gaelic
diminutive -*ín*). 'Dark Rosaleen' was
the title of a poem by James Clarence
Mangan (1803–49), based on the
Gaelic poem *Róisín Dubh*; in it the
name is used as a figurative allusion
to the Irish nation.

Rosalie ♀
French form of the Latin name
Rosalia (a derivative of *rosa* 'rose'),
introduced to the English-speaking
world in the latter part of the 19th
century. St Rosalia was a 12th-century
Sicilian virgin, and is the patron of
Palermo.

Rosalind ♀
From an Old French personal name of
Germanic (Frankish) origin, from *hros*
'horse' + *lind* 'weak', 'tender', 'soft'. It
was adopted by the Normans and
introduced by them to Britain. In the
Middle Ages it was reanalysed by folk
etymology as if from Latin *rosa linda*
'lovely rose'. Its popularity as a given
name owes much to its use by
Edmund Spenser for the character of a
shepherdess in his pastoral poetry, and
by Shakespeare as the name of the
heroine in *As You Like It* (1599).

Rosaline ♀
Originally a variant of ◊**Rosalind**; cf.
◊**Rosalyn** and ◊**Rosaleen**. It is the
name of a minor character in
Shakespeare's *Love's Labour's Lost*
and is used for another, who does not
appear but is merely mentioned, in
Romeo and Juliet.

Rosalyn ♀
Altered form of ◊**Rosalind**. *Rosalin*
was a common medieval form, since
the letters *d* and *t* were often added or
dropped capriciously at the end of
words after *n*. The name has been
further influenced by the productive
suffix -*lyn* (see ◊**Lynn**).
Variants: **Rosalynn(e)**.

Rosamund ♀
From an Old French personal name of
Germanic (Frankish) origin, from *hros*
'horse' + *mund* 'protection'. This was
adopted by the Normans and
introduced by them to Britain. In the
later Middle Ages it was reanalysed by
folk etymology as if from Latin *rosa
munda* 'pure rose' or *rosa mundi* 'rose
of the world', titles given to the Virgin
Mary. The spelling **Rosamond** has
been common since the Middle Ages,
when scribes used *o* for *u*, to
distinguish it from *n* and *m*, all of
which consisted of very similar
downstrokes of the pen. 'Fair
Rosamond' (Rosamond Clifford) was a
legendary beauty who lived at
Woodstock in Oxfordshire in the 12th
century. She is said to have been the
mistress of King Henry II, and to have
been murdered by the queen, Eleanor
of Aquitaine, in 1176.

Rosanne ♀
Modern coinage, from a combination
of the names ◊**Rose** and ◊**Anne**,
probably influenced by the popularity
of the given name ◊**Roxane**.
Variants: **Roseanne**, **Rosanna**; **Rosannagh**
(a fanciful respelling).

Roscoe ♂

Transferred use of the surname, in
origin a local name from a place in
northern England named with Old
Norse *rá* 'roe deer' + *skógr* 'wood',
'copse'.

Rose ♀

Ostensibly from the vocabulary word
denoting the flower (Latin *rosa*).
However, the name was in use
throughout the Middle Ages, long
before any of the other female names
derived from flowers, which are
generally of 19th-century origin. In
part it may refer to the flower as a
symbol of the Virgin Mary, but it
seems more likely that it also has a
Germanic origin, probably as a short
form of various female names based
on *hros* 'horse' or *hrōd* 'fame'. The
Latinate form *Rohesia* is commonly
found in documents of the Middle
Ages. As well as being a name in its
own right, it is currently used as a
short form of ◊**Rosemary** and, less
often (because of their different
pronunciation), of other names
beginning *Ros-*, such as ◊**Rosalind** and
◊**Rosamund**.

Pet form: **Rosie**.

Roselle ♀

Modern coinage, a combination of the
given name ◊**Rose** with the productive
suffix *-elle* (originally a French
feminine diminutive suffix).

Rosemary ♀

19th-century coinage, from the name
of the herb (which is from Latin *ros
marīnus* 'sea dew'). It is often also
assumed to be a combination of the
names ◊**Rose** and ◊**Mary**.

Variant: **Rosemarie**.
Pet form: **Rosie**.

Rosetta ♀

Italian pet form of ◊**Rosa**, sometimes
also used in the English-speaking
world.

Rosheen ♀

Irish: Anglicized form of ◊**Róisín**.

Rosie ♀

Pet form of ◊**Rose** and ◊**Rosemary**. It
was first used in the 1860s and is now
well established as an independent
given name, particularly in the United
States.

Ross ♂

Either an adoption of the Gaelic
topographic term *ros* 'headland' (cf.
◊**Glen**, ◊**Kyle**) or a transferred use of
the Scottish surname, which is borne
by a large and ancient family whose
members have played a major role in
Scottish history.

Rowan ♂ ♀

As a male name this represents a
transferred use of the surname, which
is of Irish origin, being an Anglicized
form of the Gaelic byname *Ruadhán*
'little red one'. It was borne by a 6th-
century saint who founded the
monastery of Lothra. As a female
name it seems to be from the
vocabulary word (of Scandinavian
origin) denoting the tree, an attractive
sight with its clusters of bright red
berries.

Rowena ♀

Latinized form of a Saxon name of
uncertain form and derivation. It is
perhaps from Germanic *hrōd* 'fame' +
wynn 'joy'. It first occurs in the Latin
chronicles of Geoffrey of Monmouth
(12th century) as the name of a
daughter of the Saxon invader Hengist,
and was taken up by Sir Walter Scott
as the name of a Saxon woman, Lady
Rowena of Hargottstanstede, who
marries the eponymous hero of his
novel *Ivanhoe* (1819).

Rowland ♂

Variant of ◊**Roland**, or a transferred
use of the surname derived from that
given name in the Middle Ages.

Rowley ♂

Variant of ◊**Roly**, or transferred use of
the surname, a local name from any of
the various places in England named

with Old English *rūh* 'rough', 'overgrown' + *lēah* 'wood', 'clearing'.

Roxane ♀
From Latin *Roxana*, Greek *Roxanē*, recorded as the name of the wife of Alexander the Great. She was the daughter of Oxyartes the Bactrian, and her name is presumably of Persian origin; it is said to mean 'dawn'. In English literature it is the name of the heroine of a novel by Defoe (1724), a beautiful adventuress who, deserted by her husband, enjoys a glittering career as a courtesan, but eventually dies in a state of penitence, having been thrown into prison for debt.
Variants: **Roxanne**, **Roxanna**.

Roy ♂
Originally a Scottish name, representing an Anglicized spelling of the Gaelic nickname *Ruadh* 'red'. It has since spread to other parts of the English-speaking world, where it is often reanalysed as Old French *roy* 'king' (cf. ◊**Leroy**).

Royle ♂
Transferred use of the surname, in origin a local name from a place in Lancashire, so called from Old English *ryge* 'rye' + *hyll* 'hill'. It may have become popular as a given name because of association with the vocabulary word *royal* (cf. ◊**Noble** and ◊**King**).

Royston ♂
Transferred use of the surname, in origin a local name from a place in Hertfordshire, known in the Middle Ages as the 'settlement of Royce'. The latter is an obsolete variant of ◊**Rose**, from its Germanic form. Royston is now widely used as a given name especially among West Indians, although the reasons for its popularity in that community are not known.

Roz ♀
Variant spelling of ◊**Ros**, with the final consonant altered to represent the voiced sound of the names from which it derives.

Rozanne ♀
Variant of ◊**Rosanne** or *Roxanne* (see ◊**Roxane**).

Rube ♂ ♀
Informal short form of ◊**Reuben** and ◊**Ruby**.

Ruben ♂
Variant spelling of ◊**Reuben**.

Ruby ♀
From the vocabulary word for the gemstone (Latin *rubīnus*, from *rubeus* 'red'). The name was chiefly common in the late 19th century and up to the middle of the 20th. It is now out of fashion.

Rudolf ♂
From a Latinized version, *Rudolphus*, of the Germanic name *Hrōdwulf* (see ◊**Rolf**). It was introduced to the English-speaking world from Germany in the 19th century. *Rudolf* was a hereditary name among the Habsburgs, the Holy Roman Emperors and rulers of Austria, from the Emperor Rudolf I (1218–91) to the Archduke Rudolf, Crown Prince of Austria-Hungary, who died in mysterious circumstances at his country house at Meyerling in 1889. Rudolf Rassendyll was the central character of Anthony Hope's adventure stories *The Prisoner of Zenda* (1894) and *Rupert of Hentzau* (1898), in which he is an English gentleman who bears a great physical resemblance to the King of Ruritania, to whom he is distantly related. He successfully impersonates the king for reasons of state. In the 20th century the popularity of this name was further enhanced by the American silent-film actor Rudolph Valentino (1895–1926), born in Italy as Rodolpho di Valentina d'Antonguolla. However, it is at present out of fashion.
Variant: **Rudolph**.

Rudy ♂
Pet form of ◊**Rudolf**.

Rufus ♂
From a Latin nickname meaning 'red(-haired)', sometimes used in medieval documents as a translation of various surnames with the same sense. It began to be used as a given name in the 19th century.

Rupert ♂
Low German form of ◊**Robert**, first brought to England by Prince Rupert of the Rhine (1618–92), a dashing military leader who came to help his uncle, Charles I, in the Civil War.

Russ ♂
Short form of ◊**Russell**, now also used as an independent given name. In some cases it may represent a transferred use of the surname *Russ*, from Old French *rous* 'red'.

Russell ♂
Transferred use of the common surname, originally from the Old French nickname *Rousel* 'little red one' (a diminutive of *rous* 'red', from Latin *russus*). Use as a given name may have been inspired by the philosopher Bertrand Russell (1872–1970), who was noted for his liberal agnostic views and his passionate championship of causes such as pacifism (in the First World War), free love, and nuclear disarmament. He was the grandson of the Victorian statesman Lord John Russell (1792–1878).

Rusty ♂ ♀
Nickname for someone with reddish-brown hair, a derivative of modern English *rust* (Old English *rust*).

Ruth ♀
Biblical name (of uncertain derivation) of a Moabite woman who left her own people to remain with her mother-in-law Naomi, and afterwards became the wife of Boaz and an ancestress of David. Her story is told in the book of the Bible that bears her name. It was popular among the Puritans, partly because of its association with the English vocabulary word *ruth* meaning 'compassion'. It has always been popular as a Jewish name, but is now also widespread among people of many different cultures and creeds. *Pet form*: **Ruthi**.

Ryan ♂ ♀
From the Irish surname, Gaelic Ó Riain 'descendant of Rian'. The latter is an ancient Gaelic personal name of uncertain origin, probably a derivative of *rí* 'king'. *Ryan* is associated with the film actor Ryan O'Neal (b. 1941). It is also now well established in North America as a female given name.

SABINA SABRINA SACHEVERELL SADHBH S
ADIE ST JOHN SAL SALLY SALOME SAM SA
MANTHA SAMMY SAMSON SAMUEL SAN
DFORD SANDRA SANDY SANFORD SAPPH
IRE SARA SARAH SASHA SASKIA SAUL SAU
NDRA SAVANNAH SAWNEY SCARLETT SC

Sabina ♀

From the Latin name *Sabīna* 'Sabine woman'. The Sabines were an ancient Italic race whose territory was early taken over by the Romans. According to tradition, the Romans made a raid on the Sabines and carried off a number of their women, but when the Sabines came for revenge the women succeeded in making peace between the two groups. The name *Sabina* was borne by three minor early Christian saints, in particular a Roman maiden martyred in about 127.

Sabrina ♀

From the name of a character in Celtic legend, who supposedly gave her name to the River Severn. In fact this is one of the most ancient of all British river names, and its true origins are obscure. Legend, as preserved by Geoffrey of Monmouth, had it that Sabrina was the illegitimate daughter of a Welsh king called Locrine, and was drowned in the river on the orders of the king's wife Gwendolen. The river name is found in the form *Sabrina* in the Latin writings of Tacitus, Gildas, and Bede. Geoffrey of Monmouth comments that in Welsh the name is *Habren* (modern Welsh *Hafren*). The name of the legendary character is almost certainly derived from that of the river, rather than vice versa.

Sacheverell ♂

Transferred use of the surname, apparently originally a baronial name of Norman origin (from an unidentified place in Normandy believed to have been called *Saute-Chevreuil*, meaning 'roebuck leap'). It was made familiar as a given name by the writer Sacheverell Sitwell (1897–1985), who was named in honour of his ancestor William Sacheverell (1638–91), a minor Whig statesman.
Pet form: **Sachie**.

Sadhbh ♀

Irish Gaelic traditional name, pronounced *'syve'*. It is said to be from an obsolete Irish word meaning 'sweet'. It was a common female given name during the Middle Ages and has recently been revived. It is sometimes Anglicized as ◊**Sally**.

Sadie ♀

Originally a pet form of ◊**Sarah**, but now generally considered as an independent name. The exact formation is not clear: probably a nursery form.

St John ♂

Name expressing devotion to St John, generally pronounced *'sin-jen'*; it has been in use in the English-speaking world, mainly among Roman Catholics, from the last two decades of the 19th century up to the present day.

Sal ♀

Short form of ◊**Sally**.

Sally ♀

In origin a pet form of ◊**Sarah**, but in the 20th century normally considered as an independent name. It is frequently used as the first element in combinations such as *Sally-Anne* and

Sally-Jane. In Ireland it sometimes represents an Anglicization of ◊**Sadhbh**.
Short form: **Sal**.

Salome ♀

Greek form of an unrecorded Aramaic name, related to the Hebrew word *shalom* 'peace'. It was common at the time of Christ, and was borne by one of the women who were at his tomb and witnessed the Resurrection (Mark 16:1–8). This would normally have led to its common use as a Christian name, and it is indeed found as such in medieval times. However, according to the Jewish historian Josephus, it was also the name of King Herod's stepdaughter, the daughter of Queen Herodias. In the Bible, a daughter of Herodias, generally identified as this Salome, danced for Herod and so pleased him that he offered to give her anything she wanted. Prompted by her mother, she asked for (and got) the head of John the Baptist, who was in one of Herod's prisons (Mark 6:17–28). This story so gripped medieval imagination that the name Salome became more or less taboo until the end of the 19th century, when Oscar Wilde wrote a play about her and some unconventional souls began to choose the name for their daughters.

Sam ♂ ♀

Short form of ◊**Samuel** (or less frequently of ◊**Samson**), and of ◊**Samantha**.

Samantha ♀

Of problematic and much debated origin. It arose in the southern states of America in the 18th century, possibly as a combination of *Sam* (from ◊**Samuel**) + a newly coined feminine suffix *-antha* (perhaps suggested by ◊**Anthea**).

Sammy ♀ ♂

Pet form of **Samantha**, or much less frequently of ◊**Samuel** or ◊**Samson**.
Variants: **Sammie**, **Sammi** (female).

Samson ♂

Biblical name (Hebrew *Shimshon*, probably derived from *shemesh* 'sun'), borne by a Jewish champion and judge famous for his prodigious strength. He was betrayed by his mistress, Delilah, and enslaved and blinded by the Philistines; nevertheless, he was able to bring the pillars of the temple of the Philistines crashing down in a final suicidal act of strength (Judges 13–16). This famous story provided the theme for Milton's poetic drama *Samson Agonistes* (1671), which is modelled on ancient Greek tragedy. In the Middle Ages the popularity of the given name was increased in Celtic areas by the fame of a 6th-century Celtic saint who bore it, probably as a classicized form of some ancient Celtic name. He was a Welsh monk who did missionary work in Cornwall and afterwards established a monastery at Dol in Brittany.
Variant: **Sampson** (usually a transferred use of the surname, derived from the given name in the Middle Ages).

Samuel ♂

Biblical name (Hebrew *Shemuel*), possibly meaning 'He (God) has hearkened' (presumably to the prayers of a mother for a son). It may also be understood as a contracted form of Hebrew *sha'ulme'el* meaning 'asked of God'. In the case of Samuel the son of Hannah, this would be more in keeping with his mother's statement 'Because I have asked him of the Lord' (1 Samuel 1:20). Living in the 11th century BC, Samuel was a Hebrew judge and prophet of the greatest historical importance, who established the Hebrew monarchy, anointing as King both Saul and, later, David. In the Authorized Version two books of the Old Testament are named after him, although in Roman Catholic and Orthodox versions of the Bible they are known as the first and second Book of Kings. The story of Samuel being called by God while still a child serving in the house of Eli the priest (1 Samuel 3) is of great vividness and has moved countless generations. In England and America the name was particularly popular among the 17th-century Puritans and among Nonconformists from the 17th to the 19th century.

Sandford ♂
Mainly U.S.: transferred use of the surname (see ◊**Sanford**).

Sandra ♀
Short form of *Alessandra*, the Italian form of ◊**Alexandra**. A major influence in establishing this as a common given name in the English-speaking world was George Meredith's novel *Sandra Belloni* (1886), originally published as *Emilia in England* (1864); the heroine, Emilia Sandra Belloni, is a beautiful, passionate young singer.

Sandy ♂ ♀
Pet form, originally Scottish, of ◊**Alexander** and ◊**Alexandra**, now sometimes used as an independent given name. It is also used as a nickname for someone with a crop of 'sandy' (light reddish-brown) hair.
Variant: **Sandie** (female).

Sanford ♂
Mainly U.S.: transferred use of the surname, in origin a local name from any of numerous places in England called *Sandford*, from Old English *sand* 'sand' + *ford* 'ford'. Use as a given name honours Peleg Sanford, an early governor (1680–3) of Rhode Island.
Variant: **Sandford**.

Sapphire ♀
From the word for the gemstone (via Old French and Latin from Greek *sappheiros*, probably ultimately of Semitic origin). The Greek term seems to have originally denoted lapis lazuli, but was later transferred to the transparent blue stone. As a given name this is typically bestowed on a girl with deep blue eyes.

Sara ♀
Variant of ◊**Sarah**. This is the form used in the Greek of the New Testament (Hebrews 11:11).

Sarah ♀
Biblical name, borne by the wife of Abraham and mother of Isaac. According to the Book of Genesis, she was originally called *Sarai* (possibly meaning 'contentious' in Hebrew), but had her name changed by God to the more auspicious *Sarah* 'princess' in token of a greater blessing (Genesis 17:15, 'And God said unto Abraham, As for Sarai thy wife, thou shalt not call her name Sarai, but Sarah shall her name be').
Variants: **Sara**, ◊**Zara**.
Pet forms: ◊**Sally**, ◊**Sadie**.

Sasha ♂ ♀
English spelling of a Russian pet form of ◊**Alexander** and ◊**Alexandra**. It has been used in the English-speaking world as an independent name, introduced in the 20th century via France. Use as a female name in the English-speaking world is encouraged by the characteristically feminine -*a* ending.

Saskia ♀
Dutch: of uncertain derivation. The name has been in use since the Middle Ages, and was borne, for example, by the wife of the artist Rembrandt. It may be derived from Germanic *sachs* 'Saxon'.

Saul ♂
Biblical name (from a Hebrew word meaning 'asked for' or 'prayed for'), borne by one of the first kings of Israel. It was also the name of St Paul before his conversion to Christianity (Acts 9:4). It enjoyed some popularity among the Puritans, but is now once again mainly a Jewish name.

Saundra ♀

Scottish variant of ◊**Sandra**, reflecting the same development in pronunciation as is shown by surnames such as *Saunders* and *Saunderson*, originally from short forms of ◊**Alexander**.

Savannah ♀

Mainly U.S.: apparently from the name of cities in Georgia and South Carolina. Both are on the Savannah River, ostensibly named with the word for a treeless plain (derived via Spanish from a native South American word). However, the river name may be an adaptation of some other name existing prior to European settlement. The given name may be taken directly from the vocabulary word, more under the influence of its sound than its meaning. In this case, it could be regarded as no more than a fanciful elaboration of ◊**Anna** or ◊**Hannah**.
Variant: **Savanna**.

Sawney ♂

Scottish variant of ◊**Sandy**, resulting from a pronunciation which is also reflected in the surname *Saunders*. The name declined in popularity after the 18th century, no doubt adversely affected by the use of *Sawney* as a vocabulary word for a simpleton.

Scarlett ♀

Name popularized by the central character in the novel *Gone With the Wind* (1936) by Margaret Mitchell, later made into a famous film. The characters in the novel bear a variety of unusual given names, which had a remarkable influence on naming practices throughout the English-speaking world in the 20th century. According to the novel, the name of the central character was Katie Scarlett O'Hara (the middle name representing her grandmother's maiden surname), but she was always known as Scarlett. The surname *Scarlett* is in origin an occupational name for a dyer or for a seller of rich,

bright fabrics, from Old French *escarlate* 'scarlet cloth' (Late Latin *scarlāta*, of uncertain, probably Semitic, derivation).
Variant: **Scarlet**.

Scott ♂

Although this was in use as a personal name both before and after the Norman Conquest, modern use in most cases almost certainly represents a transferred use of the surname. This originated as a byname for someone from Scotland or, within Scotland itself, a member of the Gaelic-speaking people who originally came from Ireland. The given name is now often chosen by parents conscious of their Scottish ancestry and heritage, but it is also used more widely.

Séamas ♂

Modern Irish Gaelic form of ◊**James**, pronounced '*shay*-mus'.

Séamus ♂

Earlier Irish Gaelic form of ◊**James**; cf. ◊**Séamas**. This is also used without the accent as a partially anglicized form of the name.

Seán ♂

Irish Gaelic form of ◊**John**, pronounced '*shawn*'. It was derived in the early Middle Ages from Anglo-Norman *Jehan*. The name has always been common in Ireland, but is now also being increasingly chosen (usually without the accent) by parents who have no Irish connections. One influence on its popularity has been the actor Sean Connery (born 1929), of James Bond fame.

Sebastian ♂

From Latin *Sebastiānus*, the name of a 3rd-century saint, a Roman soldier martyred by the arrows of his fellow officers. His sufferings were a favourite subject for medieval artists. The name means 'man from Sebastē', a town in Asia Minor so called from Greek *sebastos* 'august', 'venerable',

used as a translation of the Latin imperial title *Augustus*.
Short forms: **Seb**.

Selena ♀
Variant of ◊**Selina**.

Selima ♀
Of uncertain origin. Its first known occurrence is in a poem by Thomas Gray (1716–71), recording the death of Horace Walpole's cat Selima, 'drowned in a tub of gold fishes'. The metre shows that the name was stressed on the first syllable, but there is no clue as to its derivation. Gray (or Walpole) was possibly influenced by the Arabic name *Selim* 'peace'.

Selina ♀
Of uncertain origin. It is first found in the 17th century, and it may be an altered form of *Selena* (Greek *Selēnē*), the name of a goddess of the moon, or of *Celina* (Latin *Caelīna*), a derivative of ◊**Celia**. The name suddenly became more popular in Britain in the 1980s, partly perhaps due to the television newsreader Selina Scott.

Selma ♀
Of uncertain origin, probably a contracted form of ◊**Selima**. It has also been occasionally used in Germany and Scandinavia, probably because it occurs as the name of Ossian's castle in Macpherson's ballads.

Selwyn ♂
Transferred use of the surname, which is of disputed origin. There was a given name *Selewyn* in use in the Middle Ages, which probably represents a survival of an unrecorded Old English name derived from *sēle* 'prosperity' or *sele* 'hall' + *wine* 'friend'. Alternatively, the surname may be Norman, derived from *Seluein*, an Old French form of the Latin name *Silvānus* (from *silva* 'wood'; cf. ◊**Silas**).
Variant: **Selwin**.

Senga ♀
Scottish: common in the north-east of Scotland, this name is popularly supposed to represent ◊**Agnes** spelled backwards (which it undeniably does). However, it is more likely to have originated from the Gaelic vocabulary word *seang* 'slender'.

Seònaid ♀
Scottish Gaelic form of ◊**Janet**, pronounced '*shaw*-natch'.
Variants: **Shona** (Anglicized), **Seona** (semi-Anglicized).

Septimus ♂
From a Late Latin name derived from Latin *septimus* 'seventh'. It was fairly commonly used in large Victorian families for the seventh son or a male seventh child, but is now rare.

Seraphina ♀
Latinate derivative of Hebrew *seraphim* 'burning ones', the name of an order of angels (Isaiah 6:2). It was borne by a rather shadowy saint who was martyred at the beginning of the 5th century in Italy, Spain, or Armenia.
Variant: **Serafina**.

Serena ♀
From a Latin name, representing the feminine form of the adjective *serēnus* 'calm', 'serene'. It was borne by an early Christian saint, about whom little is known. In her *Life* she is described as wife of the Emperor Domitian (AD 51–96), but there is no mention of her in any of the historical sources that deal with this period.

Seth ♂
Biblical name (from a Hebrew word meaning 'appointed', 'placed'), borne by the third son of Adam, who was born after the murder of Abel (Genesis 4:25, 'And Adam knew his wife again; and she bare a son, and called his name Seth: For God, said she, hath appointed me another seed instead of Abel, whom Cain slew'). It was popular among the Puritans (particularly for children born after the death of an elder sibling), and has been

occasionally used since. By the 20th
century it had become rare. It was
used for the darkly passionate rural
character Seth Starkadder in Stella
Gibbons's comic novel *Cold Comfort
Farm* (1932).

Seumas ♂
Scottish Gaelic form of ◊**James**,
pronounced '*shee*-mas'; it is also an
older Irish Gaelic form (cf. ◊**Séamas**).

Seumus ♂
Older Irish Gaelic form of ◊**James** (see
◊**Séamas**).

Sextus ♂
Traditional Latin given name,
meaning 'sixth'. It was taken up in
England during the Victorian period,
often for a sixth son or a sixth child,
but it is now little used.

Seymour ♂
Transferred use of the surname,
originally a Norman baronial name
from *Saint-Maur* in Normandy. This
place was so called from the
dedication of its church to St *Maurus*
(cf. ◊**Maurice**).

Shae ♀
Modern variant of the female name
◊**Shea**.

Shalene ♀
Modern variant of ◊**Charlene**.

Shamus ♂
Anglicized spelling of Irish Gaelic
◊**Séamus**, occasionally used in Ireland,
but now rare.

Shan ♀
Short form of ◊**Shantelle**.

Shane ♂ ♀
Anglicized form of Irish Gaelic ◊**Seán**,
representing a Northern Irish
pronunciation of the name. In recent
years it has also been used as a female
name.

Shanee ♀
Anglicized form of Welsh *Siani* (see).
◊**Siân**).

Shanelle ♀
Recent coinage, apparently a respelled
elaboration of ◊**Chanel**.

Shanna ♀
Recent coinage, apparently an altered,
more obviously feminine form of
◊**Shannon**.

Shannagh ♀
Variant of ◊**Shannah** or a transferred
use of the Irish surname *Shannagh*,
Gaelic *Ó Seanaigh* 'descendant of
Seanach'. The latter is a Gaelic
personal name derived from *sean* 'old',
'wise'.

Shannah ♀
Variant of ◊**Shanna** or a short form of
Sho-shannah, the Hebrew form of
◊**Susanna**.

Shannon ♀ ♂
From the name of a river in Ireland. It
is not clear why it has become so
popular as a given name, but cf.
◊**Clodagh**. In part it may also be a
transferred use of the Irish surname,
Gaelic *Ó Seanáin* 'descendant of
Seanán'. The latter is a diminutive of
Seán. Shannon is not found as a
traditional given name in Ireland
itself.

Shantelle ♀
Recent coinage, apparently a respelled
elaboration of ◊**Chantal**.

Shari ♀
Anglicized spelling of *Sári*, the
Hungarian form of ◊**Sarah**.

Sharlene ♀
Variant spelling of ◊**Charlene**.

Sharman ♂ ♀
As a male name this represents a
transferred use of the surname, a
variant of ◊**Sherman**. As a female
name it is an altered form of
◊**Charmaine**.

Sharon ♀
20th-century coinage, from a biblical
placename. The derivation is from the
phrase 'I am the rose of Sharon, and

the lily of the valleys' (Song of Solomon 2:1). The plant name 'rose of Sharon' is used for a shrub of the genus *Hypericum*, with yellow flowers, and for a species of hibiscus, with purple flowers. *Rosasharn* (Rose of Sharon) is the name of one of the characters in John Steinbeck's novel *The Grapes of Wrath* (1936).
Variant: **Sharron**.

Sharona ♀
Latinate elaborated form of ◊**Sharon**, now quite often used in the English-speaking world.

Sharonda ♀
Elaboration of ◊**Sharon**, with the suffix -*da* abstracted from names such as ◊**Glenda** and ◊**Linda**.

Sharron ♀
Variant spelling of ◊**Sharon**.

Shaughan ♂
Variant spelling of ◊**Shaun**, probably influenced by ◊**Vaughan**.
Variant: **Shaughn**.

Shaun ♂ ♀
Anglicized spelling of Irish Gaelic ◊**Seán**. In Canada it is also found as a girl's name.

Shauna ♀
Name invented as a feminine form of ◊**Shaun**.

Shaw ♂
Transferred use of the surname, in origin a local name meaning 'wood', 'copse' (Old English *sceaga*, Old Norse *skógr*).

Shawn ♂ ♀
Anglicized spelling of Irish Gaelic ◊**Seán**, used mainly in North America. In Canada it is also found as a girl's name.

Shawna ♀
Recently coined feminine form of ◊**Shawn**.

Shay ♀
Variant spelling of ◊**Shea** as a female name.
Variant: **Shaye**.

Shayla ♀
Recent coinage, apparently a variant of ◊**Sheila**.

Shayna ♀
Modern name, either taken from a Yiddish name derived from German *Schön(e)* 'beautiful', or else a variant of ◊**Sheena**.

Shea ♂ ♀
Transferred use of the Irish surname, Gaelic *Ó Séaghdha* 'descendant of Séaghdha'. The latter is a traditional name of uncertain derivation, perhaps meaning 'hawk-like', i.e. 'fine', 'goodly'.
Variants: **Shay, Shaye, Shae** (female).

Sheela ♀
Variant spelling of ◊**Sheila**.
Variants: **Sheelah, Sheelagh**.

Sheena ♀
Anglicized spelling of *Sìne*, the Scottish Gaelic form of ◊**Jane**.

Sheila ♀
Anglicized spelling of *Síle*, the Irish Gaelic form of ◊**Cecily**. This name has become so common and widespread that it is hardly felt to be Irish any longer. In Australia since the 19th century it has been a slang generic term for any woman.
Variants: **Sheela, Sheelah, She(e)lagh**.

Shelagh ♀
Variant of ◊**Sheila**. The final consonants in the written form seem to have been added to give a Gaelic feel to the name. There is no etymological justification for them.
Variant: **Sheelagh**.

Shelby ♀ ♂
Mainly U.S.: transferred use of the surname (now more common in America than Britain). This has the form of a northern English local name,

but no place bearing it has been identified. The chief inspiration for its use as a given name seems to be Isaac Shelby (1750–1826), Revolutionary commander and first governor of Kentucky.

Sheldon ♂

Transferred use of the surname, which originated as a local name from any of the various places so called. Examples occur in Derbyshire, Devon, and the West Midlands. The placename has a variety of different origins.

Shell ♀

Generally, this is a shortened form of ◊**Michelle**, respelled by association with the vocabulary word. In some cases it may be a shortened form of ◊**Shelley**.

Shelley ♀, occasionally ♂

Transferred use of the surname, the most famous bearer of which was the English Romantic poet Percy Bysshe Shelley (1792–1822). The surname is in origin a local name from one of the various places (in Essex, Suffolk, and Yorkshire) named in Old English as the 'wood (or clearing) on (or near) a slope (or ledge)'. The name is now almost exclusively female, in part perhaps as a result of association with ◊**Shirley** (the actress Shelley Winters was born in 1922 as Shirley Schrift), and in part due to the characteristically feminine ending -(e)y.

Sheree ♀

Respelled form of ◊**Cherie**.

Sheridan ♂ ♀

Transferred use of the surname made famous by the Irish playwright Richard Brinsley Sheridan (1751–1816). The surname is from Gaelic Ó Sirideáin 'descendant of Sirideán'. The latter is a personal name of uncertain origin, possibly connected with sirim 'to seek'. This is now occasionally also used as a female name. In the United States the

inspiration is probably the Unionist commander General Philip Henry Sheridan (1831–88)

Sherman ♂

Transferred use of the surname, which is an occupational name for someone who trimmed the nap of woollen cloth after it had been woven, from Old English scēara 'shears' + mann 'man'. In the United States it is sometimes bestowed in honour of the Civil War general William Tecumseh Sherman (1820–71).

Sherry ♀

Probably in origin a respelled form of ◊**Cherie**, but now associated with the fortified wine, earlier sherry wine, so named from the port of Jérez in southern Spain.
Variants: **Sherrie**, **Sherri**.

Sheryl ♀

Variant of ◊**Cheryl**.

Shevaun ♀

Anglicized form of Irish Gaelic ◊**Siobhán**.

Shilla ♀

Modern coinage, apparently an altered form of ◊**Sheila**.

Shireen ♀

Variant of ◊**Shirin**, by association with the productive suffix -een, abstracted from names such as ◊**Maureen** and ◊**Doreen**.

Shirin ♀

Muslim name of Persian or Arabic origin, now beginning to be used quite widely in the English-speaking world.
Variants: **Shirrin**, **Shireen**.

Shirley ♀, formerly ♂

Transferred use of the surname, in origin a local name from any of the various places (in the West Midlands, Derbyshire, Hampshire, and Surrey) named in Old English from scīr 'county', 'shire' or scīr 'bright' + lēah 'wood', 'clearing'. It was given by Charlotte Brontë to the heroine of her novel *Shirley* (1849). According to the novel, her parents had selected the name in prospect of a male child and used it regardless. *Shirley* had earlier been used as a male name (Charlotte Brontë refers to it as a 'masculine cognomen'), but this literary influence fixed it firmly as a female name. It was strongly reinforced during the 1930s and 1940s by the popularity of the child film star Shirley Temple (b. 1928).

Sholto ♂

Scottish: apparently an Anglicized form of a Gaelic name, *Sìoltach*, originally a byname meaning 'sower', i.e. 'fruitful' or 'seed-bearing'. This name is traditional in the Douglas family.

Shona ♀

Scottish: Anglicized form of Gaelic *Seonag* or *Seònaid*, Gaelic versions of ◊Joan and ◊Janet respectively. In America it is pronounced identically with ◊Shauna, and may be used as a variant spelling of that name. It has also become popular as a Black name, probably in part because is is spelled the same as the name of a central African people. Cf. ◊Zula for a similar formation.

Shula ♀

As a Jewish name this is a short form of ◊Shulamit. It has been adopted by non-Jews in the English-speaking world as an independent given name.

Shulamit ♀

Hebrew name meaning 'peacefulness', a derivative of *shalom* 'peace'. The name occurs as a personification in the Song of Solomon (6:13): 'Return, return, O Shulamite; return, return, that we may look upon thee'. It is a popular modern Hebrew name.
Variants: **Shulamith**, **Shulamite**.

Siân ♀

Welsh form of ◊Jane, derived from Anglo-Norman form *Jeanne*. In the

English-speaking world it is sometimes used without the accent.
Pet form: **Siani**.

Sibyl ♀

Variant spelling of ◊Sybil. Even in classical times there was confusion between the two vowels in this word.
Variants: **Sibylla** (Latinate); **Sibilla**; **Sibella** (by association with the Italian feminine diminutive suffix *-ella*).

Sidney ♂, occasionally ♀

Transferred use of the surname, which is usually said to be a Norman baronial name from *Saint-Denis* in France. However, at least in the case of the family of the poet and soldier Sir Philip Sidney (1554–86), it appears to have a more humble origin, being derived from lands in Surrey named as the 'wide meadow' (Old English *sīdan* 'wide' (dative case) + *ēg* 'island in a river', 'riverside meadow'). The popularity of the male name increased considerably in the 19th century, probably due to Sidney Carton, hero of Dickens's novel *A Tale of Two Cities* (1859). As a female name it is perhaps in part a contracted form of ◊Sidony, and coincidentally represents a metathesized form of ◊Sindy, but this use is quite rare.
Variant: **Sydney**.
Short form: **Sid**.

Sidony ♀

From Latin *Sidōnia*, feminine of *Sidōnius*, in origin an ethnic name meaning 'man from Sidon' (the city in Phoenicia). This came to be associated with the Greek word *sindon* 'winding sheet'. Two saints called Sidonius are venerated in the Catholic Church: Sidonius Apollinaris, a 4th-century bishop of Clermont, and a 7th-century Irish monk who was the first abbot of the monastery of Saint-Saëns (which is named with a much altered form of his name). *Sidonius* was not used as a given name in the later Middle Ages, but the feminine form was comparatively popular and has continued in occasional use ever since.

Variant: **Sidonie**.

Sierra ♀

Mainly U.S.: apparently from the vocabulary word referring to a mountain range (Spanish, from Latin *serra* 'saw', referring to the toothed appearance). The reasons for its adoption and popularity are not clear, but this was among the top one hundred female given names being bestowed in the United States in 1989. Cf. ◊**Savannah**.

Sigrid ♀

From an Old Norse female personal name derived from *sigr* 'victory' + *fríðr* 'fair', 'beautiful'.

Silas ♂

Of New Testament origin: Greek name, a short form of *Silouanus* (Latin *Silvānus*, a derivative of *silva* 'wood'). This name was borne by a companion of St Paul, who is also mentioned in the Bible in the full form of his name. The Eastern Church recognizes two separate saints, Silas and Silvanus, but honours both on the same day (20 July).

Síle ♀

Irish Gaelic form of ◊**Cecily**, pronounced '*shee*-la', derived in the early Middle Ages from the Anglo-Norman form *Cecile*.

Anglicized forms: ◊**Sheila**, **Sheela(h)**, **She(e)lagh**, **Shayla**, **Shilla**.

Silver ♀ ♂

From the name of the precious metal (Old English *siolfor*). It is sometimes given to babies born with very fair hair. It is also occasionally also used as a pet form of the names ◊**Silvestra** and ◊**Silvester**.

Silvester ♂

From a Latin name, meaning 'of the woods'. It was borne by various early saints, most notably by the first pope to govern a Church free from

persecution (314–35). His feast is on 31 December, and in various parts of Europe the New Year is celebrated under his name. The name has been continuously, if modestly, used from the Middle Ages to the present day.

Variant: **Sylvester**.

Silvestra ♀

Latin feminine form of ◊**Silvester**.

Silvia ♀

From Roman legend. Rhea *Silvia* was, according to Roman tradition, the mother of the twins Romulus and Remus, who founded Rome. Her name probably represents a reworking, by association with Latin *silva* 'wood', of some pre-Roman form. It was borne by a 6th-century saint, mother of Gregory the Great, and has always been relatively popular in Italy. Shakespeare used it as a typically Italian name in *Two Gentlemen of Verona*. It is now well established as an independent name in the English-speaking world.

Variant: **Sylvia**.

Sim ♂

Short form of ◊**Simon**, now rare, but more common in the Middle Ages, when it gave rise to the surnames *Simms* and *Simpson*.

Simeon ♂

Biblical name, from a Hebrew word meaning 'hearkening'. It is borne by several Old and New Testament characters, rendered in the Authorized Version variously as *Shimeon*, *Simeon*, and ◊**Simon**. In the New Testament, it is the spelling used for the man who blessed the infant Christ (Luke 2:25).

Simmie ♂

Pet form of ◊**Simon**, used mainly in Scotland.

Simon ♂

Usual English form of ◊**Simeon**, borne in the New Testament by various characters: two apostles, a brother of

Jesus, a Pharisee, a leper, a tanner, a sorcerer (who offered money for the gifts of the Holy Ghost, giving rise to the term *simony*), and the man who carried Jesus's cross to the Crucifixion.

Simone ♀
French feminine form of ◊**Simon**, now also quite commonly used in the English-speaking world.

Sinclair ♂
Transferred use of the Scottish surname, in origin a Norman baronial name borne by a family that held a manor in northern France called *Saint-Clair*, probably Saint-Clair-sur-Elle in La Manche. It is an extremely common Scottish surname: the Norman family received the earldoms of Caithness and Orkney. They merged with the Norse- and Gaelic-speaking inhabitants of their domains to form one of the most powerful of the Scottish Highland families. The name of the novelist Sinclair Lewis (1885–1951) may have had some influence on the choice of this as a 20th-century given name.

Sinda ♀
Variant of ◊**Sindy**.

Sindy ♀
Variant spelling of ◊**Cindy** that came into use in about 1950 and is most common in America.

Síne ♀
Irish Gaelic form of ◊**Jane**, pronounced 'shee-na', derived from Anglo-Norman *Jeanne*.
Variant: **Sheena** (Anglicized).

Sinéad ♀
Irish Gaelic form of ◊**Janet**, pronounced 'shin-*aid*', derived from the French form *Jeannette*. In the English-speaking world it is usually written without the accent, as in the case of the actress Sinead Cusack (b. 1948).

Siobhán ♀
Irish Gaelic form of ◊**Jane**, pronounced 'shiv-*awn*' or '*shoo*-an', derived from the Anglo-Norman form *Jehanne*. It became widely known in the English-speaking world, written without the accent, through the actress Siobhan McKenna (1923–86).
Variants: **Shevaun**, **Chevonne** (Anglicized).

Siôn ♂
Welsh form of ◊**John**, derived from Anglo-Norman *Jean*.

Sioned ♀
Welsh form of ◊**Janet**.

Sissy ♀
Pet form of ◊**Cicely** that came into use about 1890 but largely disappeared again after about 1920. In recent years it has undergone something of a revival.
Variants: **Sissey**, **Sissie**.

Skipper ♂
Originally a nickname from the vocabulary word *skipper* 'boss' (originally denoting a ship's captain, from Middle Dutch *schipper*), or else representing an agent derivative of *skip* 'to leap or bound' (probably of Scandinavian origin). It is now sometimes used as an independent given name in the United States.
Short forms: **Skip**, **Skipp**.

Sky ♀ ♂
From the vocabulary word (from Old Norse *ský* 'cloud'). This was one of the names taken from the world of nature (cf. ◊**Rainbow**, ◊**Leaf**, ◊**River**) during the 1960s under the influence of the hippy and flower-power movements. It continues to enjoy a modest popularity.

Skye ♀
Elaborated spelling of ◊**Sky**, influenced by the name of the island of *Skye* in the Hebrides. Cf. ◊**Ailsa**, ◊**Isla**, ◊**Iona**, and ◊**Rona**. The island is called *an t-Eilean Sgitheanach* in Gaelic, earlier

Scí, probably from a root meaning 'to cut' (cf. Gaelic *scian* 'knife'), referring presumably to the distinctively sharp, serrated outline of the Cuillin Mountains on the island.

Sly ♂ ♀
Mainly U.S.: recent coinage. The reasons for its adoption as a given name are not clear. In the case of the American actor Sylvester Stallone, it is used as a contracted pet form of his given name. As a female name it may have originated as a pet form of ◊**Selina**. The fact that it coincides in form with the vocabulary word *sly* meaning 'cunning' or 'devious' does not seem to have inhibited its current use as a given name.

Sofia ♀
Variant spelling of ◊**Sophia**.

Sofie ♀
Variant spelling of ◊**Sophie**.

Solomon ♂
Biblical name (Hebrew *Shlomo*, derived from *shalom* 'peace'), borne by one of the great kings of Israel, son of David and Bathsheba, who was legendary for his wisdom (2 Samuel 12–24; 1 Kings 1–11; 2 Chronicles 1–9). The books of Proverbs and Ecclesiastes were ascribed to him, and the Song of Solomon, otherwise known as the Song of Songs, bears his name. It has been sporadically used among Gentiles since the Middle Ages, but is still mainly a Jewish name.

Somerled ♂
Scottish (Highland): from the Old Norse personal name *Sumarlíðr*, probably originally a byname meaning 'summer traveller'. This was the name of the founder of the powerful and widespread Clan Macdonald, Lords of the Isles from the 12th to the 15th century, and it is still occasionally bestowed on members of clan Macdonald and its septs.
Variants: **Summerlad** (altered by folk

etymology); **Somhairle** (Gaelic form, also used in Ireland; Anglicized as **Sorley**).

Sondra ♀
Of recent origin, apparently an altered form of ◊**Sandra**.

Sonia ♀
Variant spelling of ◊**Sonya**.

Sonya ♀
Russian pet form of *Sofya* (see ◊**Sophia**), popular as a given name in its own right in Britain and elsewhere since the 1920s.

Soo ♀
Recent coinage, a fanciful variant spelling of ◊**Sue**.

Sophia ♀
From the Greek word meaning 'wisdom'. The Eastern cult of St Sophia arose as a result of misinterpretation of the phrase *Hagia Sophia* 'holy wisdom' as if it meant 'St Sophia'. The name became popular in England in the 17th and 18th centuries. The heroine of Fielding's novel *Tom Jones* (1749) is called Sophia Weston. In recent years, its popularity has been further increased by the fame of the Italian film actress Sophia Loren (b. 1934).
Variant: **Sofia**.

Sophie ♀
French form of ◊**Sophia**. In the English-speaking world, where it has been popular since the 18th century, it is often taken as a pet form of that name.
Variants: **Sofie**, **Sophy**.

Sorcha ♀
Irish and Scottish Gaelic name, pronounced 'sorr-a-ha'. It is derived from a Celtic word meaning 'brightness'. In Ireland it has long been considered a Gaelic form of ◊**Sarah**, and Anglicized as *Sarah* and *Sally*, but this is based on no more than a slight phonetic similarity.

Sorley ♂
Scottish (Highland) and Irish: Anglicized form of the Gaelic name *Somhairle* (pronounced '*sorr*-lee'). See ◊**Somerled**.

Sorrel ♀
From the vocabulary word for the plant (Old French *surele*, apparently a derivative of *sur* 'sour' (of Germanic origin), alluding to the acid taste of its leaves).
Variants: **Sorrell**, **Sorell**, **Sorel**.

Spencer ♂
Transferred use of the surname, in origin an occupational name for a 'dispenser' of supplies in a manor house. This is the name of a great English noble family, traditionally supposed to be descended from someone who performed this function in the royal household. Its popularity as a given name was influenced in the mid-20th century by the American film actor Spencer Tracy (1900–67).

Spike ♂
Normally a nickname, but occasionally used as a given name in recent years, due to the influence of the bandleader Spike Jones (1911–65) and the comedian Spike Milligan (b. 1918). As a nickname it usually refers to an unruly tuft or 'spike' of hair.

Stacey ♀ ♂
Of uncertain derivation, probably a transferred use of the surname, itself derived in the Middle Ages from a diminutive of *Stace*, a short form of ◊**Eustace**. It is not clear why this name should have become so common in the 1970s and 1980s as a female (occasionally male) given name.
Variants: **Stacy**, **Stacie**, **Staci**.

Stafford ♂
Transferred use of the surname, in origin a local name from any of various places so called from Old English *stæd* 'landing place' + *ford* 'ford', most notably the county town of Staffordshire. This was the surname of the family that held the dukedom of Buckingham in the 15th and 16th centuries.

Stan ♂
Short form of ◊**Stanley**.

Stanley ♂
Transferred use of the surname, in origin a local name from any of numerous places (in Derbys., Durham, Gloucs., Staffs., Wilts., and Yorks.) so called from Old English *stān* 'stone' + *lēah* 'wood', 'clearing'. This is well established as a given name, and has been widely used as such since the 1880s. It had been in occasional use earlier. Its popularity seems to have stemmed at least in part from the fame of the explorer Sir Henry Morton Stanley (1841–1904), who was born in Wales as John Rowlands but later took the name of his adoptive father, a New Orleans cotton dealer.
Short form: **Stan**.

Star ♀
Modern name, a vernacular equivalent of ◊**Stella**.
Variant: **Starr**.

Steff ♀
Short form of ◊**Stephanie**.
Pet forms: **Steffie**, **Steffy**.

Steffany ♀
Respelled form of ◊**Stephanie**.

Stella ♀
From Latin *stella* 'star'. This was not used as a given name before the 16th century, when Sir Philip Sidney seems to have been the first to use it (as a name deliberately far removed from the prosaic range of everyday names) in the sonnets addressed by Astrophel to his lady, Stella.

Steph ♀
Short form of ◊**Stephanie**.

Stephan ♂
Variant of ◊**Stephen**, preserving the vowels of the Greek name.

Stephanie ♀

From French *Stéphanie*, vernacular
form of Latin *Stephania*, a variant of
Stephana, which was in use among
early Christians as a feminine form of
Stephanus (see ◊**Stephen**).
Variant: **Steffany**.
Short form: **Steff**.
Pet forms: **Steffie, Steffy, Stevie**.

Stephen ♂

Usual English spelling of the name of
the first Christian martyr (Acts 6–7),
whose feast is accordingly celebrated
next after Christ's own (26 December).
His name is derived from the Greek
word *stephanos* 'garland', 'crown'.
Variants: **Steven, Stephan**.
Short form: **Steve**.
Pet form: **Stevie**.

Sterling ♂

Transferred use of the surname, a
variant of ◊**Stirling**. As a given name,
however, it is likely to have been
chosen because of its association with
the vocabulary word occurring in such
phrases as 'sterling qualities' and
'sterling worth'. This is derived from
the Middle English word *sterr-ling*
'little star': some Norman coins had a
little star on them. A 20th-century
influence on the name has been the
American film actor Sterling Hayden
(1916–86).

Steve ♂

Short form of ◊**Stephen** and ◊**Steven**,
associated with the American film
star Steve McQueen (1930–80), noted
for his 'tough-guy' roles.

Steven ♂

Variant of ◊**Stephen**, reflecting the
normal pronunciation of the name in
the English-speaking world.

Stevie ♂ ♀

Pet form of ◊**Stephen** and of
◊**Stephanie**. A well-known female
bearer was the poet Stevie Smith
(1902–71), whose baptismal name was
Florence Margaret Smith.

Stewart ♂

Variant of ◊**Stuart**, less common as a
given name, although more common
as a surname.

Stirling ♂

Transferred use of the surname, in
origin a local name from the town in
Scotland. The placename is of
uncertain derivation, perhaps from
Old Welsh *ystre Velyn* 'dwelling of
Melyn'.

Storm ♀

Apparently a 20th-century coinage,
although it may have been in use
slightly earlier. The name is
presumably derived from the
vocabulary word, adopted by admirers
of *Sturm und Drang*.

Stuart ♂

From the French version of the
surname *Stewart*. This form was
introduced to Scotland in the 16th
century by Mary Stuart, Queen of
Scots, who was brought up in France.
The surname originated as an
occupational or status name for
someone who served as a *steward* in a
manor or royal household. The
Scottish royal family of this name are
traditionally supposed to be descended
from a family who were hereditary
stewards in Brittany before the
Conquest. Use as a given name
originated in Scotland, but is now
widespread throughout the English-
speaking world.
Variant: **Stewart**.
Short forms: **Stu, Stew**.

Sue ♀

Short form of ◊**Susan** and, less
commonly, of ◊**Susanna** and ◊**Suzanne**.
Variants: **Su, Soo**.

Sukie ♀

Pet form of ◊**Susan**, very common in
the 18th century, but now rare.
Variant: **Sukey**.

Summer ♀

Mainly U.S.: from the vocabulary

word for the season (Old English *sumor*), used in modern times as a given name because of its pleasant associations. Nevertheless, the name ◊**Autumn** is now more common.

Summerlad ♂

Scottish: variant spelling of ◊**Somerled**, being taken by folk etymology as derived from the words *summer* and *lad*.

Susan ♀

English vernacular form of ◊**Susanna**, always the most common of this group of names. A 20th-century influence has been the American film star Susan Hayward (1918–75).
Variant: **Suzan**.
Short form: **Sue, Su, Soo**.
Pet forms: **Susie, Suzie, Suzy, Sukie, Sukey**.

Susanna ♀

New Testament form (Luke 8:3) of the Hebrew name *Shoshana* (from *shoshan* 'lily', which in modern Hebrew also means 'rose').
Variant: **Susana**.

Susannah ♀

Variant of ◊**Susanna**. This is the form of the name used in the Old Testament. The tale of Susannah, wife of Joachim, and the elders who falsely accused her of adultery, is to be found in the apocryphal book that bears her name, and was popular in the Middle Ages and later.
Variant: **Suzanna**.

Susie ♀

Pet form of ◊**Susan** and, less commonly, of ◊**Susanna(h)** and ◊**Suzanne**.
Variants: **Suzie, Suzy**.

Suzanne ♀

French form of ◊**Susanna**, now also used in the English-speaking world.

Suzette ♀

French pet form of ◊**Suzanne**, now also used in the English-speaking world.

Suzie ♀

Variant spelling of ◊**Susie**.
Variant: **Suzy**.

Sybil ♀

From the name (Greek *Sibylla* or *Sybilla*, with confusion over the vowels from an early period) of a class of ancient prophetesses inspired by Apollo. According to medieval theology, they were pagans denied the knowledge of Christ but blessed by God with some insight into things to come and accordingly admitted to heaven. It was thus regarded as a respectable name to be borne by Christians.
Variants: **Sybilla** (Latinate), **Sybille** (from French). See also ◊**Sibyl**.

Sydney ♂, occasionally ♀

Variant spelling of ◊**Sidney**. It was a medieval practice to write *y* for *i*, for greater clarity since *i* was easily confused with other letters.

Sylvester ♂

Variant spelling of ◊**Silvester**.

Sylvestra ♀

Variant spelling of ◊**Silvestra**.

Sylvia ♀

Variant spelling of ◊**Silvia**. It is now rather more common than the plain form.

Sylvie ♀

French form of ◊**Silvia**, now also used in the English-speaking world.

TABITHA TACEY TACITA TAD TADHG TALF
RYN TALIA TALIESIN TALITHA TALULLA TA
LYA TAM TAMARA TAMMY TAMSIN TANI
A TANNER TANSY TANYA TARA TARLACH
TARQUIN TARRA TASHA TATIANA TAWN
Y TAYLOR TEAGUE TEAL TEARLACH TED TE

Tabitha ♀

Aramaic name, meaning 'doe' or 'roe',
borne in the New Testament by a
woman who was restored to life by St
Peter (Acts 9:36–41). In the biblical
account this form of the name is given
together with its Greek equivalent,
◊Dorcas. It was one of the names
much favoured by Puritans and
Disssenters from the 17th to the 19th
centuries, and is still occasionally
used.
Pet form: **Tabby** (obsolete).

Tacey ♀

As a medieval given name this is
derived from the Latin imperative *tace*
'be silent', regarded as a suitable
admonition to women. As a modern
name, it is a pet form of ◊**Tacita** or
perhaps derived from ◊**Tracy**.

Tacita ♀

From Latin *Tacita*, feminine form of
the Roman family name *Tacitus*,
originally a byname meaning 'silent'.

Tad ♂

Normally an Anglicized form of
Gaelic ◊**Tadhg**, but sometimes a short
form of ◊**Thaddeus**. It is fairly
commonly used as an independent
given name, especially in America.

Tadhg ♂

Gaelic traditional name, pronounced
'tie' in Irish Gaelic, 'toog' in Scottish
Gaelic. It was originally a byname
meaning 'poet', 'philosopher', and was
a very common given name in Ireland
throughout the Middle Ages.
Anglicized forms: **Tad, Teague, Teigue**.

Talfryn ♂

Welsh: modern given name, originally
a local name, from Welsh *tal* 'high',
'end of' + a mutated form of *bryn*
'hill'.

Talia ♀

Variant spelling of ◊**Talya** and ◊**Thalia**.

Taliesin ♂

Welsh: from *tâl* 'brow' + *iesin*
'shining'. This was the name of a
legendary 6th-century Welsh poet, and
has been revived in recent times.

Talitha ♀

Of New Testament origin: from an
Aramaic word meaning 'little girl'.
Jesus raised a child from the dead with
the words 'Talitha cumi; which is,
being interpreted, Damsel, I say unto
thee, arise' (Mark 5:41).

Talulla ♀

Irish: Anglicized form of the Gaelic
name *Tuilelaith*, pronounced 'til-a-la',
derived from words meaning
'abundance' and 'lady' or 'princess'.
This name was borne by at least two
Irish saints of the 8th and 9th
centuries. The spelling **Tallulah** was
made famous by the American actress
Tallulah Bankhead (1903–68), who
inherited the name from her
grandmother.

Talya ♀

Shortened form of ◊**Natalya**.
Variant: **Talia** (see also ◊**Thalia**).

Tam ♂

Scottish short form of ◊**Thomas**.

Tamara ♀

Russian: probably derived from the

Hebrew name *Tamar*, from a vocabulary word meaning 'date palm', with the addition of the feminine suffix *-a*. The name Tamar is borne in the Bible by two female characters: the daughter-in-law of Judah, who is involved in a somewhat seamy story of sexual intrigue (Genesis 38), and a daughter of King David (2 Samuel 13), the full sister of Absalom, who is raped by her half-brother Amnon, for which Absalom kills him. It is rather surprising, therefore, that it should have given rise to such a popular given name. However, Absalom himself later has a daughter named Tamar, who is referred to as 'a woman of a fair countenance' (2 Samuel 14:27), and the name may derive its popularity from this reference. The name is now also used in the English-speaking world.

Tammy ♀
Pet form of ◊**Tamara** and ◊**Tamsin**.

Tamsin ♀
Contracted form of Latinate *Thomasina*, a feminine form of ◊**Thomas**. This was relatively common throughout Britain in the Middle Ages, but confined to Cornwall immediately before its recent revival.

Tania ♀
Variant spelling of ◊**Tanya**.

Tanner ♂
Transferred use of the common surname, in origin an occupational name for someone who treated animal skins to form leather (via Old English and Old French from a Late Latin word apparently derived from a Celtic name for the oak, whose bark was used in the process).

Tansy ♀
From the vocabulary word for the flower (Old French *tanesie*, derived from Greek *athanasia* 'immortal'). It has enjoyed some popularity as a given name in the 20th century.

Tanya ♀
Russian pet form of ◊**Tatiana**, now quite commonly used as an independent given name in the English-speaking world.
Variant: **Tania**.

Tara ♀
From the name (meaning 'hill') of a place in Meath, seat of the high kings of Ireland. It has been used as a female given name in America since around 1940, probably as a result of the success of the film *Gone with the Wind*, in which the estate of this name has great emotional significance. In Britain it was not much used before the 1960s. Its popularity then was influenced by the character Tara King in the television series *The Avengers*.
Variant: **Tarra**.

Tárlach ♂
Irish Gaelic name, pronounced 'tor-lah': a modern shortened form of the traditional name *Toirdhealbhach*, apparently originally a byname meaning 'instigator', from *toirdhealbh* 'prompting'. The belief that this is a derivative of the name of the Norse god of thunder, Þorr, is probably no more than folk etymology.

Tarquin ♂
The name borne by two early kings of Rome, Tarquinius Priscus 'the Old' (616–578 BC) and Tarquinius Superbus 'the Proud' (534–510 BC). It is of uncertain, probably Etruscan, origin; many of the most ancient Roman institutions and the vocabulary associated with them, as well as many Roman family names, were borrowed from the Etruscans. The name is now occasionally used in the English-speaking world.

Tarra ♀
Variant of ◊**Tara**.

Tasha ♀
Shortened form of ◊**Natasha**.

Tatiana ♀

Russian: of early Christian origin. This was the name of various early saints honoured particularly in the Eastern Church. In origin it is a feminine form of Latin *Tatiānus*, a derivative of *Tatius*, a Roman family name of obscure origin. Titus Tatius was, according to tradition, a king of the Sabines who later shared with Romulus the rule over a united population of Sabines and Latins. The name is now also used in the English-speaking world, though not so commonly as the pet form ◊**Tanya**.

Tawny ♀

From the vocabulary word denoting a light brown hair colour (Anglo-Norman *tauné*, Old French *tané* 'tanned'). This is probably a modern name created on the lines of examples such as ◊**Ginger** and ◊**Sandy**. However, it may also be a transferred use of the surname *Tawney*, which is a Norman baronial name from one of two places in Normandy: *Saint-Aubin-du-Thenney* or *Saint-Jean-du-Thenney*.
Variant: **Tawney**.

Taylor ♂ ♀

Transferred use of the surname, in origin an occupational name for a tailor (Anglo-Norman *taillour*, a derivative of *taillier* 'to cut', Late Latin *tāleāre*). Use as a given name was influenced by the U.S. president Zachary Taylor (1784–1850), hero of the Mexican War. It is now well established as a female name in North America; it was one of the top hundred female names bestowed in 1989. This may have been inspired by the film actress Elizabeth Taylor (b. 1932).

Teague ♂

Irish: Anglicized form of Gaelic ◊**Tadhg**.
Variant: **Teigue**.

Teal ♀

One of the female names taken from birds in the past couple of decades. The teal is a kind of small duck; its name is attested in English since the 14th century and is probably connected with Middle Low German *tēlink*, Middle Dutch *tēling*.
Variant: **Teale**.

Teàrlach ♂

Scottish Gaelic, pronounced 'tchar-lah': a modern shortened form of the ancient Gaelic name *Toirdhealbhach*; see ◊**Tárlach**.

Ted ♂

Short form of ◊**Edward**.
Pet form: **Teddy**.

Teddy ♂ ♀

Now generally used as a pet form of ◊**Edward**, although it was originally used of ◊**Theodore**. Teddy bears were so named from the American president Theodore Roosevelt (1858–1919). Occasionally it is also used as a female name, in part as a pet form of ◊**Edwina**.

Tegwen ♀

Welsh: modern coinage from *teg* 'lovely' + *(g)wen*, feminine form of *gwyn* 'white', 'fair', 'blessed', 'holy'.

Teigue ♂

Irish: Anglicized form of Gaelic ◊**Tadhg**.

Tel ♂

Altered short form of ◊**Terry** or ◊**Terence**, of recent origin. For the substitution of *-l* for *-r*, cf. ◊**Hal**.

Teleri ♀

Welsh: extension of the name ◊**Eleri**, with the addition of the honorific prefix *ty-* 'your'. Teleri, daughter of Peul, is mentioned in the *Mabinogi*.

Terence ♂

From the Latin name *Terentius*, which is of uncertain origin. It was borne by the Roman playwright Marcus Terentius Afer (who was a former slave, and took his name from his master, Publius Terentius Lucanus),

and later by various minor early Christian saints. Nowadays ◊**Terry** is often taken as a pet form of *Terence*, although it was originally an independent name. In Ireland *Terence* is used as an Anglicized form of the Gaelic name *Toirdhealbhach* (see ◊**Tárlach**).
Variants: **Terrance**, **Terrence**.
Short form: **Tel**. See also ◊**Terry**.

Teresa ♀
Italian and Spanish form of ◊**Theresa**. In the English-speaking world the name is often chosen in this spelling by Roman Catholics, with particular reference to the Spanish saint, Teresa of Ávila (Teresa Cepeda de Ahumada, 1515–82).

Terrance ♂
The most common U.S. spelling of ◊**Terence**.

Terrell ♂
Transferred use of the surname, a variant of ◊**Tyrrell**.

Terrence ♂
Variant spelling of ◊**Terence**.

Terri ♀
Mid 20th-century coinage, originating either as a pet form of ◊**Theresa** or as a feminine spelling of ◊**Terry**. It is now well established as an independent given name, particularly in North America.

Terry ♂
As a medieval given name this is a Norman form of the French name *Thierri*, from Germanic *Theodoric*, from *þeud* 'people', 'race' + *rīc* 'power', 'ruler'. This was adopted by the Normans and introduced by them to Britain. In modern English use it seems at first to have been a transferred use of the surname derived from the medieval given name, and later to have been taken as a pet form of ◊**Terence**.
Short form: **Tel**.

Terryl ♀
Modern coinage, apparently an elaboration of ◊**Terri** with the suffix -*yl* seen in names such as ◊**Cheryl**.

Tess ♀
Short form of ◊**Tessa**.

Tessa ♀
Now generally considered to be a pet form of ◊**Theresa**, although often used independently. However, the formation is not clear, and it may be of distinct origin. Literary contexts of the late 19th century show that the name was thought of as Italian, although it is in fact unknown in Italy.
Short form: **Tess**.

Tessie ♀
Pet form of ◊**Tessa**.
Variant: **Tessy**.

Tetty ♀
Pet form of ◊**Elizabeth**, common in the 18th century (when it was used, for example, by Samuel Johnson's wife) but now rare or obsolete.
Variant: **Tettie**.

Tex ♂
Mainly U.S.: in origin a nickname for someone from *Texas*. The name of the state derives from an Indian tribal name, meaning 'friends', recorded as early as 1541 in the form *Teyas* and subsequently transmitted through Spanish sources.

Thaddeus ♂
Latin form of a New Testament name, the byname used to refer to one of Christ's lesser-known apostles, whose given name was *Lebbaeus* (Matthew 10:3). It is of uncertain origin, possibly derived via Aramaic from the Greek name *Theodōros* 'gift of God' or *Theodotos* 'given by God'.
Short forms: **Thad**, ◊**Tad**.

Thalia ♀
Name borne in classical mythology by the Muse of comedy; it is derived from Greek *thallein* 'to flourish', and

has occasionally been chosen in recent years by parents in the English-speaking world in search of novelty.
Variant: **Talia** (see also ◊**Talya**).

Thea ♀
Shortened form of ◊**Dorothea**.

Thecla ♀
Contracted form of the Greek name *Theokleia*, derived from *theos* 'God' + *kleia* 'glory'. The name was borne by a 1st-century saint (the first female martyr), who was particularly popular in the Middle Ages because of the lurid details of her suffering recorded in the apocryphal 'Acts of Paul and Thecla'.

Theda ♀
Latinate short form of the various old Germanic female personal names derived from *þeud* 'people', 'race'. It enjoyed a brief popularity in the United States from about 1915 to 1925, due to the popularity of the silent-film actress Theda Bara (1890–1955), the original 'vamp'. Her original name was Theodosia Goodman.

Thelma ♀
First used by the novelist Marie Corelli for the heroine of her novel *Thelma* (1887). She was supposed to be Norwegian, but it is not a traditional Scandinavian name. Greek *thelēma* (neuter) means 'wish' or '(act of) will', and the name could perhaps be interpreted as a contracted form of this.

Theo ♂
Short form of ◊**Theodore** and, less commonly, of ◊**Theobald**.

Theobald ♂
From an Old French name of Germanic (Frankish) origin, derived from *þeud* 'people', 'race' + *bald* 'bold', 'brave'. The first element was altered under the influence of Greek

theos 'god'. This name was adopted by the Normans and introduced by them to Britain.
Short form: **Theo**.

Theodora ♀
Feminine form of ◊**Theodore**, borne most notably by a 9th-century empress of Byzantium, the wife of Theophilus the Iconoclast. It has frequently been used as an English given name. It means 'gift of God'; the elements are the same as those of ◊**Dorothea**, but in reverse order.

Theodore ♂
From the French form of the Greek name *Theodōros*, derived from *theos* 'god' + *dōron* 'gift'. The name was popular among early Christians and was borne by several saints.
Short forms: **Theo**, **Ted**.
Pet form: **Teddy**.

Theodosia ♀
Greek name derived from *theos* 'god' + *dōsis* 'giving'. It was borne by several early saints venerated in the Eastern Church, and is only very occasionally used in the English-speaking world today.

Thera ♀
Of uncertain derivation: it could represent a shortened form of ◊**Theresa**, or be derived from the name of the Greek island of *Thēra*.

Theresa ♀
Of problematic origin. The name seems to have been first used in Spain and Portugal, and, according to tradition, was the name of the wife of St Paulinus of Nola, who spent most of his life in Spain; she was said to have originated (and to have derived her name) from the Greek island of *Thēra*. However, this story is neither factually nor etymologically confirmed.
Variants: **Teresa**, **Treeza**.
Pet forms: ◊**Terri**, ◊**Tessa**.

219 TIMOTHY

Thirzah ♀
Variant of ◊**Tirzah**.
Variant: **Thirza**.

Thomas ♂
New Testament name, borne by one
of Christ's twelve apostles, referred to
as 'Thomas, called Didymus' (John
11:16; 20:24). *Didymos* is the Greek
word for 'twin', and the name is the
Greek form of an Aramaic byname
meaning 'twin'. The given name has
always been popular throughout
Christendom, in part because St
Thomas's doubts have made him seem
a very human character.
Short forms: **Tom**. Scottish: **Tam**.
Pet form: **Tommy**.

Tia ♀
Recent coinage, apparently originating
as a short form of the various given
names ending in *-tia*, as for example
◊**Laetitia** and ◊**Lucretia**.

Tiana ♀
Recent coinage, apparently an
elaborated form of ◊**Tia** or a shortened
form of ◊**Christiana**.

Tiara ♀
Recent coinage, apparently from the
vocabulary word for a woman's
jewelled headdress (via Latin, from
Greek *tiara(s)*, originally denoting a
kind of conical cap worn by the
ancient Persians). Cf. ◊**Tierra**.

Tiernan ♂
Irish: Anglicized form of the Gaelic
given name *Tiarnán* or *Tighearnán*, a
diminutive of *tighearna* 'lord'.

Tierney ♂ ♀
Transferred use of the Irish surname,
Gaelic *Ó Tighearnaigh* 'descendant of
Tighearnach'. The latter is a derivative
of *tighearna* 'lord'. Tighearnach was
the name of a 6th-century saint who
served as abbot of Clones and later as
bishop of Clogher. This is now well
established in North America as a
female name, at least in part due to

the influence of the film actress Gene
Tierney (1920–91).

Tierra ♀
Recent coinage, of uncertain
derivation, ostensibly from Spanish
tierra 'land', 'earth' (Latin *terra*), but
cf. ◊**Tiara**.

Tiffany ♀
Usual medieval English form of the
Greek name *Theophania* 'Epiphany',
from *theos* 'god' + *phainein* 'to
appear'. This was once a relatively
common name, given particularly to
girls born on the feast of the Epiphany
(6 January), and it gave rise to an
English surname. As a given name, it
fell into disuse until revived in the
20th century under the influence of
the famous New York jewellers,
Tiffany's, and the film, starring
Audrey Hepburn, *Breakfast at
Tiffany's* (1961). In 1982 this was
recorded as the most popular Black
female name in America.

Tilda ♀
Shortened form of ◊**Matilda**.

Tilly ♀
Pet form of ◊**Matilda**, much used from
the Middle Ages to the late 19th
century, when it also came to be used
as an independent given name. It is
rare in either use nowadays.
Variant: **Tillie**.

Tim ♂
Short form of ◊**Timothy**, also used in
Ireland as an Anglicized form of
◊**Tadhg**.
Pet form: **Timmy** (normally used only
for young boys).

Timothy ♂
English form of the Greek name
Timotheos, from *tīmē* 'honour' +
theos 'god'. This was the name of a
companion of St Paul; according to
tradition, he was stoned to death for
denouncing the worship of Diana. It
was not used in England before the
Reformation.

Short form: **Tim**.
Pet form: **Timmy**.

Tina ♀
Shortened form of ◊**Christina** and other female names ending in *-tina*; now often used as an independent given name.

Tirion ♀
Welsh: modern given name, from the vocabulary word meaning 'kind', 'gentle'.

Tirzah ♀
Biblical name, meaning 'pleasantness' or 'delight' in Hebrew, borne by a minor character mentioned in a genealogy (Numbers 26:33). It is also a biblical placename.
Variants: **Tirza**, **Thirzah**, **Thirza**.

Tita ♀
Either a short form of names ending in these two syllables, as for example *Martita*, or a feminine form of ◊**Titus**.

Titty ♀
Pet form of ◊**Laetitia**, which has now become obsolete because of its unfortunate coincidence in form with the slang word for a female breast.

Titus ♂
From an old Roman given name, of unknown origin. It was borne by a companion of St Paul who became the first bishop of Crete, and also by the Roman emperor who destroyed Jerusalem in AD 70. It is not commonly used as a given name in the English-speaking world.

Tobias ♂
Biblical name: Greek form of Hebrew *Tobiah* 'God is good'. This name is borne by several characters in the Bible (appearing in the Authorized Version also as *Tobijah*), but in the Middle Ages it was principally associated with the tale of 'Tobias and the Angel'. According to the Book of Tobit in the Apocrypha, Tobias, the son of Tobit, a rich and righteous Jew of Nineveh, was lucky enough to acquire the services of the archangel Raphael as a travelling companion on a journey to Ecbatana. He returned wealthy, married, and with a cure for his father's blindness. A historical St Tobias was martyred (*c*.315) at Sebaste in Armenia, together with Carterius, Styriacus, Eudoxius, Agapius, and five others.

Toby ♂
English vernacular form of ◊**Tobias**.

Todd ♂
Transferred use of the surname, which was originally a nickname from an English dialect word meaning 'fox'.

Tom ♂
Short form of ◊**Thomas**, in use since the Middle Ages, and recorded as an independent name since the 18th century.

Tommy ♂
Pet form of ◊**Thomas**.

Toni ♀
Feminine form of ◊**Tony**, in part used as a pet form of ◊**Antonia** but more commonly as an independent given name.

Tonia ♀
Shortened form of ◊**Antonia**, now quite widely used as an independent given name.

Tony ♂, occasionally ♀
Shortened form of ◊**Anthony**, now sometimes used as an independent given name.

Tonya ♀
Variant of ◊**Tonia**.

Topaz ♀
One of the rarer examples of the class of modern female names taken from vocabulary words denoting gemstones. The topaz gets its name via French and Latin from Greek; it is probably ultimately of Oriental origin. In the Middle Ages this was sometimes used as a male name, representing a form of ◊**Tobias**.

Torquil ♂

Scottish: Anglicized form of the
traditional Gaelic name *Torcall*,
originally a borrowing of the Old
Norse personal name Þorketill,
composed of the name of the god Þorr
+ *ketill* '(sacrificial) cauldron'.

Tory ♀

Pet form of ◊**Victoria**.

Tottie ♀

Pet form of ◊**Charlotte**, a rhyming
variant of ◊**Lottie**. The name was most
common in the 18th and 19th
centuries, like ◊**Tetty**.
Variant: **Totty**.

Tracy ♀, formerly ♂

Transferred use of the surname, in
origin a Norman baronial name from
places in France called *Tracy*, from the
Gallo-Roman personal name *Thracius*
+ the local suffix *-ācum*. In former
times, *Tracy* was occasionally used as
a male given name, as were the
surnames of other English noble
families. Later, it was also used as a
female name, generally being taken as
a pet form of ◊**Theresa**. In recent
years, it has become an immensely
popular female name. A strong
influence was the character of Tracy
Lord, played by Grace Kelly in the
film *High Society* (1956).
Variants: **Tracey**, **Tracie** (female).

Trahaearn ♂

Welsh: traditional name composed of
the intensive prefix *tra-* + *haearn*
'iron'.

Travis ♂

Transferred use of the surname, in
origin a Norman French occupational
name (from *traverser* 'to cross') for
someone who collected a toll from
users of a bridge or a particular stretch
of road. It is now regularly used as a
given name, especially in America and
Australia.

Treena ♀

Variant spelling of ◊**Trina**.

Treeza ♀

Modern contracted spelling of
◊**Theresa**.

Trefor ♂

Welsh variant of ◊**Trevor**.

Tremaine ♂

Transferred use of the Cornish
surname, in origin a local name from
any of several places named with
Cornish *tre* 'homestead', 'settlement'
+ *men* 'stone'.

Trent ♂

Especially U.S.: from the name of the
river that flows through the British
Midlands (cf. ◊**Clyde**), or a transferred
use of the surname derived from it.
The river name is of British origin: it
may be composed of elements
meaning 'through', 'across' and
'travel', 'journey', or it may mean
'traveller' or 'trespasser', a reference to
frequent flooding. The given name
may also in some cases be used as a
short form of ◊**Trenton**.

Trenton ♂

Mainly U.S.: from the name of the
city in New Jersey, the site of a
decisive defeat of the British (1776) by
Washington during the American
Revolution. The city was founded in
the late 17th century by a group of
English Quakers under the leadership
of a certain William Trent. It was
originally *Trent's Town*, reduced
within half a century to *Trenton*.

Trevelyan ♂

Transferred use of the Cornish
surname, in origin a local name from
a place mentioned in the Domesday
Book as *Trevelien*, i.e. 'homestead or
settlement (Cornish *tref*) of Elian'. The
latter is an ancient Celtic personal
name of obscure origin (cf. ◊**Elvis**).

Trevor ♂

Transferred use of the Welsh surname,
in origin a local name from any of the
very many places in Wales called
Trefor, from *tref* 'settlement' + *fôr*,

mutated form of *mawr* 'large'. In the mid-20th century it enjoyed considerable popularity in the English-speaking world among people with no connection with Wales, for example the actor Trevor Howard (1916–88), who was born in Kent.
Variant: **Trefor**.
Short form: **Trev**.

Tricia ♀
Shortened form of ◊**Patricia**.
Variant: **Trisha**.

Trina ♀
Shortened form of ◊**Katrina**.
Variant: **Treena**.

Triona ♀
Shortened form of ◊**Catriona**.

Trisha ♀
Variant spelling of ◊**Tricia**.

Trista ♀
Name invented as a feminine form of ◊**Tristan**.

Tristan ♂
From Celtic legend, the name borne by a hero of medieval romance. There are many different versions of the immensely popular tragic story of Tristan and his love for Isolde. Generally, they agree that Tristan was an envoy sent by King Mark of Cornwall to bring back his bride, the Irish princess Isolde. Unfortunately, Tristan and Isolde fall in love with each other, having accidentally drunk the love potion intended for King Mark's wedding night. Tristan eventually leaves Cornwall to fight for King Howel of Brittany. Wounded in battle, he sends for Isolde. She arrives too late, and dies of grief beside his bier. The name *Tristan* is of unknown derivation, though it may be connected with Pictish *Drostan*; it has been altered from an irrecoverable original as a result of transmission through Old French sources that insisted on associating it with Latin

tristis 'sad', a reference to the young knight's tragic fate.
Variant: **Trystan** (mainly Welsh).

Tristram ♂
Variant of ◊**Tristan**. Both forms of the name occur in medieval and later versions of the legend. In Laurence Sterne's comic novel *Tristram Shandy* (1759–67), the name is bestowed on the narrator through a misunderstanding and is regarded by his father as a great misfortune. Since the name originally intended for him was *Trismegistus*, the degree of misfortune may be taken as somewhat exaggerated.
Variants: **Tristam**, **Trystram**.

Trixie ♀
Pet name derived from ◊**Beatrix**.
Variant: **Trixi**.

Troy ♂ ♀
Probably originally a transferred use of the surname, which is derived from *Troyes* in France. Nowadays, however, the given name is principally associated with the ancient city of Troy in Asia Minor, whose fate has been a central topic in epic poetry from Homer onwards. The story tells how Troy was sacked by the Greeks after a siege of ten years; according to classical legend, a few Trojan survivors got away to found Rome (and, according to medieval legend, another group founded Britain).

Trudi ♀
German (especially Swiss) pet form of the various female names ending in *-trud(e)*, from Germanic *þrūþ* 'strength'.
Variants: **Trudie**, **Trudy**.

Truman ♂
Mainly U.S.: transferred use of the surname, in origin a nickname from Old English *trēowe* 'true', 'trusty' + *mann* 'man'. Use as a given name was boosted by the fame of Harry S. Truman (1884–1972), president of the United States (1945–52), although it

was in occasional use before he became president.
Variant: **Trueman**.

Trystan ♂
Variant (mainly Welsh) of ◊**Tristan**.

Tucker ♂
Transferred use of the surname, in origin an occupational name for a fuller (from Old English *tūcian* 'to torment').

Tudur ♂
Welsh: traditional name derived from the Old Celtic form *Teutorix*, composed of elements meaning 'people' or 'tribe' and 'ruler' or 'king'. It has often been described as a Welsh form of ◊**Theodore**, but there is in fact no connection between them. Rather, the Welsh name is ultimately cognate with the Germanic name *Theodoric* (see ◊**Terry**).
Variants: **Tudyr** (an earlier spelling); **Tudor** (an Anglicized spelling).

Turlough ♂
Irish: Anglicized form of Gaelic *Toirdhealbhach* (see ◊**Tárlach**).

Ty ♂
Mainly U.S.: short form of ◊**Tyler** and ◊**Tyrone**.

Tybalt ♂
The usual medieval form of ◊**Theobald**, rarely used nowadays. It occurs in Shakespeare's *Romeo and Juliet* as the name of a brash young man who is killed in a brawl.

Tyler ♂
Mainly North American: transferred use of the surname, in origin an occupational name for a tiler (an agent derivative of Old English *tigele* 'tile', from Latin *tēgula* 'covering'). John Tyler (1790–1862) was the tenth president of the United States.

Tyrrell ♂
Mainly U.S.: transferred use of the surname, which is common in Ireland, but of uncertain derivation. It may have originated as a nickname for a stubborn person, from Old French *tirel*, used of an animal which pulls on the reins, a derivative of *tirer* 'to pull'.
Variant: **Tyrell**.

Tyrone ♂
Mainly U.S.: from the name of a county in Northern Ireland and a town in Pennsylvania. Its use as a given name seems to be due to the influence of the two film actors (father and son) called Tyrone Power, especially the younger one (1913–58).

Tyson ♂
Mainly U.S.: transferred use of the surname, which is of dual origin. In part it is a metronymic from the medieval woman's given name *Dye*, pet form of *Dionysia*, and in part it is a nickname for a hot-tempered person, from Old French *tison* 'firebrand'. As a given name it is often taken as an expanded form or patronymic from ◊**Ty**.

UILLEAM UISDEAN ULICK ULTAN ULYSSES
UNA UNITY URIAH URIEL URIEN URSULA
UILLEAM UISDEAN ULICK ULTAN ULYSSES
UNA UNITY URIAH URIEL URIEN URSULA
UILLEAM UISDEAN ULICK ULTAN ULYSSES
UNA UNITY URIAH URIEL URIEN URSULA

Uilleam ♂

Scottish Gaelic form of ◊**William**.

Ùisdean ♂

Scottish Gaelic: traditional name, originally a borrowing of the Old Norse personal name *Eysteinn*, which is from *ei*, *ey* 'always', 'for ever' + *steinn* 'stone'.

Ulick ♂

Irish: Anglicized form of Gaelic *Uilleac* or *Uilleag*. This name probably derives from Old Norse *Hugleikr*, from *hugr* 'heart', 'mind', 'spirit' + *leikr* 'play', 'sport'. Alternatively, it may be a diminutive derived from a short form of *Uilleam*, a Gaelic form of ◊**William** (cf. ◊**Liam**).

Ultan ♂

Irish: Anglicized form of the Gaelic name *Ultán*, a diminutive form of the ethnic name *Ultach* 'Ulsterman'.

Ulysses ♂

Latin form of the Greek name *Odysseus*, borne by the famous wanderer of Homer's *Odyssey*. The name is of uncertain derivation (it was associated by the Greeks themselves with the verb *odyssesthai* 'to hate'). Moreover, it is not clear why the Latin form should be so altered; mediation through Etruscan has been one suggestion. As an English given name it has occasionally been used in the 19th and 20th centuries, especially in America (like other names of classical origin such as ◊**Homer** and ◊**Virgil**). It was the name of the 18th president of the United States, Ulysses S. Grant (1822–85). It has also been used in Ireland as a classicizing form of ◊**Ulick**.

Una ♀

Anglicized form of Irish Gaelic *Úna*, a traditional name of uncertain derivation. It is identical in form with the vocabulary word *úna* 'hunger', 'famine', but is more likely to be connected with *uan* 'lamb'. The Anglicized form is sometimes taken to be from the feminine of Latin *unus* 'one'. It is the name used by Spenser for the lady of the Red Cross Knight in *The Faerie Queene*: he probably had Latin rather than Irish in mind, even though he worked in Ireland for a while.
Variants: **Oona**, **Oonagh**.

Unity ♀

From the vocabulary word for the quality (Latin *unitās*, a derivative of *unus* 'one'). It achieved some currency among the Puritans, but has been mainly used in Ireland as a kind of Anglicized extended form of ◊**Una**.

Uriah ♂

Biblical name (from Hebrew, meaning 'God is light'), borne by a Hittite warrior treacherously disposed of by King David after he had made Uriah's wife Bathsheba pregnant (2 Samuel 11). The Greek form *Urias* occurs in the New Testament (Matthew 1:6). The name was popular in the 19th century, but is now most closely associated with the character of the obsequious Uriah Heep in Dickens's *David Copperfield* (1850) and has consequently undergone a sharp decline in popularity.

Uriel ♂

Biblical name derived from Hebrew *uri* 'light' + *el* 'God', and so a doublet of ◊**Uriah**. It is borne by two minor characters mentioned in genealogies (1 Chronicles 6:24; 2 Chronicles 13:2).

Urien ♂

Welsh: name borne by a character in the *Mabinogi*, Urien of Rheged. He is probably identical with the historical figure Urien who fought against the Northumbrians in the 6th century. The name is of uncertain origin: it may be derived from the Old Celtic elements *ōrbo* 'privileged' + *gen* 'birth'.

Ursula ♀

From the Latin name *Ursula*, a diminutive of *ursa* '(she-)bear'. This was the name of a 4th-century saint martyred at Cologne with a number of companions, traditionally said to have been eleven thousand, but more probably just eleven, the exaggeration being due to a misreading of a diacritic mark in an early manuscript. A more recent, secular influence has been the film actress Ursula Andress (b. 1936 in Switzerland).

VAL VALDA VALENE VALENTINE VALERIE V
ALETTA VAN VANESSA VAUGHAN VELMA
VENESSA VENETIA VERA VERE VERENA VE
RGIL VERINA VERITY VERNA VERNON VER
ONA VERONICA VESSA VESTA VI VIC VICKY
VICTOR VICTORIA VIKKI VINCE VINCENT

Val ♀, occasionally ♂
Short form of ◊**Valerie**, and sometimes also of ◊**Valentine**.

Valda ♀
20th-century coinage, an elaboration of the female name ◊**Val** with the suffix -*da*, extracted from names such as ◊**Glenda** and ◊**Linda**.

Valene ♀
20th-century coinage, an elaboration of the female name ◊**Val** with the productive feminine suffix -*ene*.

Valentine ♂, occasionally ♀
English form of the Latin name *Valentīnus*, a derivative of *valens* 'healthy', 'strong'. This was the name of a Roman martyr of the 3rd century, whose feast is celebrated on 14 February. This was the date of a pagan fertility festival marking the first stirrings of spring, which has survived in an attenuated form under the patronage of the saint.
Short form: **Val**.

Valerie ♀
From the French form of the Latin name *Valēria*, feminine *Valērius*, an old Roman family name apparently derived from *valēre* 'to be healthy', 'be strong'. The name owes its popularity in France to the cult of a 3rd-century saint said to have been converted by Martial of Limoges.
Short form: **Val**.

Valetta ♀
20th-century coinage, an elaboration of the female name ◊**Val** with the ending -*etta*, originally an Italian feminine diminutive suffix. *Valetta* or

Valletta is (apparently coincidentally) the name of the capital of Malta.

Van ♂
Short form of ◊**Ivan** or ◊**Evan**, as in the case of the American film actor Van Heflin (1910–71), born Emmett Evan Heflin and the Irish folk singer Van Morrison (b. 1945).

Vanessa ♀
Name invented by Jonathan Swift (1667–1745) for his friend Esther Vanhomrigh. It seems to have been derived from the first syllable of her (Dutch) surname, with the addition of the suffix -*essa* (perhaps influenced by the first syllable of her given name). The name has been quite popular in the 20th century, being borne for example by the actress Vanessa Redgrave (b. 1937).
Short form: **Nessa**.

Vaughan ♂
Transferred use of the Welsh surname, in origin a nickname from the mutated form (*fychan* in Welsh orthography) of the Welsh adjective *bychan* 'small'.
Variant: **Vaughn**.

Velma ♀
Of modern origin and uncertain derivation, possibly based on ◊**Selma** or ◊**Thelma**.

Venessa ♀
A modern altered form of ◊**Vanessa**.

Venetia ♀
Of uncertain origin, used occasionally since the late Middle Ages. In form

the name coincides with that of the region of northern Italy.

Vera ♀
Russian name, meaning 'faith', introduced to Britain at the beginning of the 20th century. It coincides in form with the feminine form of the Latin adjective *vērus* 'true'.

Vere ♂
Transferred use of the surname, in origin a Norman baronial name, from any of the numerous places in northern France so called from Gaulish *ver(n)* 'alder'.

Verena ♀
Characteristically Swiss name, first borne by a 3rd-century saint who lived as a hermit near Zurich. She is said to have come originally from Thebes in Egypt, and the origin of her name is now obscure. This name is now also used in the English-speaking world, where it is taken as an elaboration of ◊Vera.
Variant: **Verina**.

Vergil ♂
Variant spelling of ◊Virgil.

Verina ♀
Variant spelling of ◊Verena.

Verity ♀
From the archaic abstract noun meaning 'truth' (via Old French from Latin *vēritās*, a derivative of *vērus* 'true'; cf. ◊Vera). It was a popular Puritan name, and is still occasionally used in the English-speaking world.

Verna ♀
Name coined in the latter part of the 19th century, perhaps as a contracted form of ◊Verena or ◊Verona, or as a feminine form of ◊Vernon.

Vernon ♂
Transferred use of the surname, in origin a Norman baronial name from any of various places so called from Gaulish elements meaning 'place of alders' (cf. ◊Vere).

Verona ♀
Of uncertain origin. It seems to have come into use towards the end of the 19th century, and may either represent a shortened form of ◊Veronica or be taken from the name of the Italian city. It became more widely known from Sinclair Lewis's novel *Babbitt* (1923), in which it is borne by the daughter of the eponymous hero.

Veronica ♀
Latin form of ◊Berenice, influenced from an early date by association with the Church Latin phrase *vera icon* 'true image', of which this form is an anagram. The legend of the saint who wiped Christ's face on the way to Calvary and found an image of his face imprinted on the towel seems to have been invented to account for this derivation.
Pet form: **Ronnie**.

Vessa ♀
Modern creation, a contracted form of ◊Vanessa or an assimilated form of ◊Vesta.

Vesta ♀
From the Latin name of the Roman goddess of the hearth, cognate with that of a Greek goddess with similar functions, *Hestia*, but of uncertain derivation. It is only rarely used as a given name in the English-speaking world, but was borne as a stage name by the Victorian music-hall artiste Vesta Tilley (1864–1952). In some cases it may represent a simplified form of ◊Silvestra.

Vi ♀
Short form of ◊Violet.

Vic ♂
Short form of ◊Victor.

Vicky ♀
Pet form of ◊Victoria.
Variants: **Vickie, Vicki, Vikki**.

Victor ♂
From a Late Latin personal name

meaning 'conqueror'. This was popular among early Christians as a reference to Christ's victory over death and sin, and was borne by several saints. A 20th-century influence on the choice of the name has been the actor Victor Mature (b. 1915).
Short form: **Vic**.

Victoria ♀
Feminine form of the Latin name *Victōrius* (a derivative of ◊**Victor**), also perhaps a direct use of Latin *victōria* 'victory'. It was little known in England until the accession in 1837 of Queen Victoria (1819–1901), who got it from her German mother, Mary Louise Victoria of Saxe-Coburg. It did not begin to be a popular name among commoners in Britain until the 1940s, reaching a peak in the 1970s.
Pet forms: **Vicky, Vickie, Vicki, Vikki**.

Vikki ♀
Respelled form of ◊**Vicky**.

Vince ♂
Short form of ◊**Vincent**, in use at least from the 17th century, and probably earlier, since it has given rise to a surname.

Vincent ♂
From the Old French form of the Latin name *Vincens* 'conquering' (genitive *Vincentis*). This name was borne by various early saints particularly associated with France, most notably the 5th-century St Vincent of Lérins.
Short form: **Vince**.

Viola ♀
From Latin *viōla* 'violet'. The name is relatively common in Italy and was used by Shakespeare in *Twelfth Night*, where most of the characters have Italianate names. Its modern use in English has been influenced by the vocabulary word denoting the somewhat larger flower (a single-coloured pansy).

Violet ♀
From the name of the flower (Old French *violette*, Late Latin *violetta*, a diminutive of *viōla*). This was one of the earliest flower names to become popular in Britain, being well established before the middle of the 19th century, but it is now somewhat out of favour.
Short form: **Vi**.

Virgil ♂
Mainly U.S.: usual English form of the name of the most celebrated of Roman poets, Publius Vergilius Maro (70–19 BC). The correct Latin spelling is *Vergilius*, but it was early altered to *Virgilius* by association with *virgo* 'maiden' or *virga* 'stick'. Today the name is almost always given with direct reference to the poet, but medieval instances may have been intended to honour instead a 6th-century bishop of Arles or an 8th-century Irish monk who evangelized Carinthia and became archbishop of Salzburg, both of whom also bore the name. In the case of the later saint, it was a classicized form of the Gaelic name *Fearghal* (see ◊**Fergal**).
Variant: **Vergil**.

Virginia ♀
From the feminine form of Latin *Virginius* (more correctly *Verginius*; cf. ◊**Virgil**), a Roman family name. It was borne by a Roman maiden killed, according to legend, by her own father to spare her the attentions of an importunate suitor. It was not used as a given name in the Middle Ages. It was bestowed on the first American child of English parentage, born at Roanoke in August 1587, and has since become very popular. Both child and province were named in honour of Elizabeth I, the 'Virgin Queen'. Among modern influences on the choice of the name has been the actress Virginia McKenna (b. 1931).
Pet form: **Ginny**. See also ◊**Ginger**.

Vita ♀
19th-century coinage, either directly

from Latin *vita* 'life', or else as a feminine form of the male name *Vitus*. It has been borne most notably by the English writer Vita Sackville-West (1892–1962), in whose case it was a pet form of the given name *Victoria*.

Viv ♀ ♂

Short form of ◊**Vivian** and ◊**Vivien**.

Vivi ♀

Pet form of the female names ◊**Vivien** and ◊**Vivian**.

Vivian ♂, occasionally ♀

From an Old French form of the Latin name *Viviānus* (probably a derivative of *vivus* 'alive'). The name was borne by a 5th-century bishop of Saintes in western France, remembered for protecting his people during the invasion of the Visigoths.
Variants: **Vivien**, **Vyvyan**.
Short forms: **Viv**; **Vi**, **Vivi** (♀).

Vivien ♀, formerly ♂

Originally a male name, and generally taken as a variant of ◊**Vivian**. This spelling was quite common in Old French. It owes its popularity as a female name in the English-speaking world to Tennyson's *Merlin and Vivien* (1859). This name, from Arthurian legend, may represent an altered form of a Celtic name (perhaps a cognate of the Irish Gaelic name *Bé Bhinn* 'white lady', pronounced 'bay-veen'). The actress Vivien Leigh (1913–67) was christened *Vivian*.
Short forms: **Vi**, **Viv**, **Vivi**.

Vivienne ♀

French feminine form of ◊**Vivien**, popular also in the English-speaking world as an unambiguously female form of the name.

Vyvyan ♂

Fanciful respelling of the male name ◊**Vivian**.

WADE WALDO WALLACE WALLY WALTER
WANDA WARD WARNER WARREN WARW
ICK WASHINGTON WAT WATKIN WAYNE
WEBSTER WENDA WENDELL WENDY WESL
EY WESTON WHILTIERNA WHITLEY WHIT
NEY WILBERFORCE WILBUR WILFRID WILH

Wade ♂

Transferred use of the surname, in
origin either a local name from the
medieval vocabulary word *wade* 'ford'
(old English *(ge)wæd*), or else from a
medieval given name representing a
survival of Old English *Wada*, a
derivative of *wadan* 'to go', borne,
according to legend, by a great
sea-giant.

Waldo ♂

From a Latinate short form of various
old Germanic personal names derived
from *wald* 'rule'. This gave rise in the
Middle Ages to a surname, borne
notably by Peter Waldo, a 12th-
century merchant of Lyons, who
founded a reformist sect known as the
Waldensians, which in the 16th
century took part in the Reformation
movement. In America the name is
particularly associated with the poet
and essayist Ralph Waldo Emerson
(1803–82), whose father was a
Lutheran clergyman.

Wallace ♂

Transferred use of the surname, in
origin an ethnic byname from Old
French *waleis* 'foreign', used by the
Normans to denote members of
various Celtic races in areas where
they were in the minority: Welshmen
in the Welsh marches, Bretons in East
Anglia, and surviving Britons in the
Strathclyde region. The given name
seems to have been first used in
Scotland, being bestowed in honour of
the Scottish patriot William Wallace
(?1272–1305).

Wally ♂

Pet form of ◊**Walter** or, less
commonly, of ◊**Wallace**. It has dropped
almost completely out of fashion,
especially since the advent in the 20th
century of the slang term *wally*,
denoting a stupid or incompetent
person.

Walter ♂

From an Old French personal name of
Germanic (Frankish) origin, derived
from *wald* 'rule' + *heri*, *hari* 'army'.
This was adopted by the Normans and
introduced by them to England,
superseding the native Old English
form, *Wealdhere*. It was a very
popular name in medieval England,
normally pronounced 'Water'.
Short forms: **Wat**, **Walt**.

Wanda ♀

Of uncertain origin. Attempts have
been made to derive it from various
Germanic and Slavonic roots. It was
certainly in use in Poland in the 19th
century, and is found in Polish folk
tales as the name of a princess. The
derivation may well be from the
ethnic term *Wend* (see ◊**Wendell**). The
name was introduced to the English-
speaking world by Ouida (Marie
Louise de la Ramée), who used it for
the heroine of her novel *Wanda*
(1883).

Ward ♂

Transferred use of the surname,
originally an occupational name from
Old English *weard* 'guardian',
'watchman'.

Warner ♂

Transferred use of the surname, which is from a medieval given name introduced to Britain by the Normans. It is of Germanic origin, from *war(in)* 'guard' + *heri*, *hari* 'army'.

Warren ♂

Transferred use of the surname, which is of Norman origin, derived partly from a place in Normandy called *La Varenne* 'the game park' and partly from a Germanic personal name based on the element *war(in)* 'guard'. In America it has sometimes been bestowed in honour of General Joseph Warren, the first hero of the American Revolution, who was killed at Bunker Hill (1775). Among modern influences on the choice of the name has been the film actor Warren Beatty (b. 1937).

Warwick ♂

Transferred use of the surname, in origin a local name from the town in the West Midlands. The placename is probably from Old English *wær*, *wer* 'weir', 'dam' + *wīc* 'dairy farm'.

Washington ♂

Especially U.S.: transferred use of the surname of the first president of the United States, George Washington (1732–99), whose family came originally from Northamptonshire in England. They had been established in Virginia since 1656. The surname in this case is derived from the village of Washington in Co. Durham (now Tyne and Wear), so called from Old English *Wassingtūn* 'settlement associated with Wassa'.

Wat ♂

The usual medieval short form of ◊**Walter**, now occasionally revived.

Watkin ♂

Either a revival of the medieval given name (a pet form of ◊**Walter** (see ◊**Wat**), with the diminutive suffix *-kin*), or a transferred use of the surname derived from it.

Wayne ♂

Transferred use of the surname, in origin an occupational name for a carter or cartwright, from Old English *wægen* 'cart', 'waggon'. It was adopted as a given name in the second half of the 20th century, mainly as a result of the popularity of the American film actor John Wayne (1907–82), who was born Marion Michael Morrison; his screen name was chosen in honour of the American Revolutionary general Anthony Wayne (1745–96).

Webster ♂

Transferred use of the surname, in origin an occupational name for a weaver, Old English *webbestre* (a derivative of *webb* 'web'). The *-estre* suffix was originally feminine, but by the Middle English period the gender distinction had been lost. Use as a given name in America no doubt owes something to the politician and orator Daniel Webster (1782–1852) and the lexicographer Noah Webster (1758–1843).

Wenda ♀

Recent coinage, an altered form of ◊**Wendy** (cf. *Jenna* from *Jenny*). There has probably also been some influence by ◊**Wanda**. In the early Middle Ages a female name of this form was in occasional use on the Continent as a short form of various female names containing as their first element the ethnic name of the Wends (cf. ◊**Wendell**).

Wendell ♂

Especially U.S.: from the surname derived in the Middle Ages from the Continental Germanic personal name *Wendel*, in origin an ethnic name for a *Wend*, a member of the Slavonic people living in the area between the Elbe and the Oder, who were overrun by Germanic migrants in the 12th century. It has been adopted as a given name as a result of the fame of the American writer Oliver Wendell Holmes (1809–94) and his jurist son, also Oliver Wendell Holmes (1841–1935), members of a leading New England family.

Wendy ♀

Invented by J. M. Barrie for the 'little mother' in his play *Peter Pan* (1904). He took it from the nickname *Fwendy-Wendy* (i.e. 'friend') used for him by a child acquaintance, Margaret Henley. It achieved great popularity in its short lifespan, but is now out of fashion.

Variant: **Wendi**.

Wesley ♂

From the surname of the founder of the Methodist Church, John Wesley (1703–91), and his brother Charles (1707–88), who was also influential in the movement. Their family must have come originally from one or other of the various places in England called *Westley*, the 'western wood, clearing, or meadow'. The given name was at first confined to members of the Methodist Church, but is now widely used without reference to its religious connotations.

Short form: **Wes**.

Weston ♂

Transferred use of the surname, in origin a local name from any of the very many places in England named in Old English as 'the western enclosure', from *west* 'west' + *tūn* 'enclosure', 'settlement'.

Whiltierna ♀

Irish: Anglicized form of the Gaelic name *Faoiltiarna*, derived from *faol* 'wolf' + *tighearna* 'lord'.

Whitley ♀

Mainly U.S.: transferred use of the surname, a local name from any of various places in England named with Old English *hwīt* 'white' + *lēah* 'wood', 'clearing'. Use as a female given name may have been influenced by the adoption of ◊**Whitney** for the same purpose.

Whitney ♀ ♂

Mainly North American: transferred use of the surname, in origin a local name from any of various places in England named with the Middle English phrase *atten whiten ey* 'by the white island'. In the 1980s its popularity as a female name was increased by the fame of the American singer Whitney Houston.

Wilberforce ♂

Transferred use of the surname, in origin a local name from *Wilberfoss* in North Yorkshire, so called from the Old English female personal name *Wilburg* (see ◊**Wilbur**) + Old English *foss* 'ditch' (Latin *fossa*). It was taken up as a given name in honour of the anti-slavery campaigner William Wilberforce (1759–1833). It is now sometimes taken as an extended form of *Wilbur*.

Wilbur ♂

Mainly North American: transferred use of a comparatively rare surname, which is probably derived from a medieval female given name composed of Old English *will* 'will', 'desire' + *burh* 'fortress'.

Wilfrid ♂

From an Old English personal name, derived from *wil* 'will', 'desire' + *frīð* 'peace'. This was borne by two Anglo-Saxon saints: there is some doubt about the exact form of the name of the more famous, who played a leading role at the Council of Whitby (664); it may have been *Walfrid*, 'stranger peace'. Wilfrid the Younger was an 8th-century bishop of York. The name was not used in the later Middle Ages, but was revived in the 19th century, and enjoyed great popularity then and in the first part of the 20th century.

Variant: **Wilfred**.
Short form: **Wilf**.

Wilhelmina ♀

Feminine version of *Wilhelm*, the

German form of ◊**William**, formed
with the Latinate suffix -*ina*. This
name was introduced to the English-
speaking world from Germany in the
19th century. It is now very rarely
used.
Pet forms: **Minnie**.

Will ♂
Short form of ◊**William**, in use since
the early Middle Ages, when it was
occasionally used also for various
other given names of Germanic origin
containing the first element *wil* 'will',
'desire'.

Willa ♀
Name recently coined as a feminine
form of ◊**William**, by appending the
characteristically feminine ending -*a*
to the short form ◊**Will**.

Willard ♂
Especially U.S.: transferred use of the
surname, which is probably derived
from the Old English personal name
Wilheard, from *wil* 'will', 'desire' +
heard 'hardy', 'brave', 'strong'.

William ♂
Probably the most successful of all the
Old French names of Germanic origin
that were introduced to England by
the Normans. It is derived from
Germanic *wil* 'will', 'desire' + *helm*
'helmet', 'protection'. The fact that it
was borne by the Conqueror himself
does not seem to have inhibited its
favour with the 'conquered'
population: in the first century after
the Conquest it was the commonest
male name of all, and not only among
the Normans. In the later Middle Ages
it was overtaken by ◊**John**, but
continued to run second to that name
until the 20th century, when the
picture became more fragmented.
Short forms: **Will**, ◊**Bill**.
Pet forms: **Willy**, **Willie**, **Billy**.

Willoughby ♂
Transferred use of the surname, in
origin a local name from any of
various places in northern England so

called from Old English *welig* 'willow'
+ Old Norse *býr* 'settlement'.

Willow ♀
From the name of the tree (Old
English *welig*), noted for its grace and
the pliancy of its wood.

Willy ♂
Pet form of ◊**William**.

Wilma ♀
Contracted form of ◊**Wilhelmina**,
which has retained rather more
currency (especially in America) than
the full form of the name.

Wilmer ♂
From an Old English personal name,
derived from *wil* 'will', 'desire' + *mær*
'famous'. This died out in the Middle
Ages, but gave rise to a surname
before it did so. The modern given
name is probably a transferred use of
that surname, perhaps adopted in
particular as a masculine form of
◊**Wilma**.

Wilmette ♀
Especially U.S.: a recent coinage,
elaborated from ◊**Wilma** by means of
the productive ending -*ette* (originally
a French feminine diminutive suffix).

Wilmot ♂ ♀
Transferred use of the surname, which
is derived from a medieval pet form
(with the Old French diminutive
suffix -*ot*) of ◊**William**.

Win ♀
Short form of ◊**Winifred**.

Windsor ♂
Transferred use of the surname, which
is derived from a place in Berkshire,
originally named in Old English as
Windels-ōra 'landing place with a
windlass'. It is the site of a castle that
is in regular use as a residence of the
royal family. Use as a given name
dates from the mid-19th century and
was reinforced by its adoption in 1917
as the surname of the British royal
family (from their residence at

Windsor). It was felt necessary to replace the German name *Wettin*, which had been introduced by Queen Victoria's husband Albert, in deference to anti-German feeling during the First World War.

Winifred ♀

Anglicized form of the Welsh female personal name *Gwenfrewi*, derived from *gwen* 'white', 'fair', 'blessed', 'holy' + *frewi* 'reconciliation'. This was borne by a 7th-century Welsh saint around whom a large body of legends grew up. The form of the name has been altered by association with Old English *wynn* 'joy' + *frið* 'peace'.
Short form: **Win**.
Pet form: **Winnie**.

Winnie ♀

Pet form of ◊**Winifred** and of ◊**Winston**.

Winona ♀

Mainly North American: from a Sioux female name, said to be reserved normally for a first-born daughter.

Winston ♂

Although there was an Old English personal name, *Wynnstan*, from *wynn* 'joy' + *stān* 'stone', which would have had this form if it had survived, the modern given name is a transferred use of the surname, a local name from *Winston* in Gloucestershire. Use as a given name originated in the Churchill family: the first Winston Churchill (b. 1620) was baptized with the surname of his mother's family. The name has continued in the family ever since, and has been widely adopted in honour of the statesman Winston Spencer Churchill (1874–1965).

Winthrop ♂

Especially U.S.: from the surname of a leading American pioneering family. John Winthrop (1588–1649) was governor of Massachusetts Bay Colony from 1629, and played a major role in shaping the political institutions of New England. His son (1606–76) and grandson (1638–1707), who bore the same name, were also colonial governors. Their family probably came originally from one of the places in England called *Winthorpe* (named in Old English as the 'village of Wynna'.

Winton ♂

Transferred use of the surname, in origin a local name from any of the various places so called. One in Cumbria gets its name from Old English *winn* 'pasture' + *tūn* 'enclosure', 'settlement'; another in the same county is from *wiðig* 'willow' + *tūn*; the one in North Yorkshire is from the Old English personal name *Wina* + *tūn*.

Woodrow ♂

Transferred use of the surname, in origin a local name for someone who lived in a row of houses by a wood. Use as a given name was inspired by the American president (Thomas) Woodrow Wilson (1856–1924).

Woody ♂

Mainly U.S.: pet form of ◊**Woodrow**, or in some cases perhaps a nickname bestowed because of some imagined similarity to the cartoon character Woody Woodpecker. It has been borne by the American folk singer Woody (Woodrow Wilson) Guthrie (1912–67) and the 1940s band leader Woody (Woodrow Charles) Herman (b. 1913). The American humorist Woody Allen was born Allen Stewart Konigsberg in 1935.

Wyatt ♂

Transferred use of the surname, derived from a medieval given name representing a Norman French alteration of the Old English personal name *Wīgheard*, from *wīg* 'war' + *heard* 'hardy', 'brave', 'strong'.

Wyn ♂

Welsh: originally a byname from the Welsh vocabulary word *(g)wyn* 'white', 'fair', 'blessed', 'holy'. The name is found in this form from the early Middle Ages. It is at present extremely popular in Wales.

Wyndham ♂

Transferred use of the surname, which is derived from a contracted form of the name of *Wymondham* in Norfolk, originally named in Old English as the 'homestead of Wigmund'. John Wyndham was the pseudonym of the British science-fiction writer John Wyndham Parkes Lucas Beynon Harris (1903–63), creator of the Midwich cuckoos.

Wynne ♂ ♀

Probably a transferred use of the surname, which is derived from the Old and Middle English personal name *Wine*.

Variant: **Wynn**. See also ◊**Wyn** and ◊**Win**.

Wystan ♂

From an Old English personal name derived from *wīg* 'battle' + *stān* 'stone'. St Wistan was a 9th-century prince of Mercia, murdered by his nephew Bertulf. The modern given name is rare, being best known as that of the poet Wystan Hugh Auden (1907–73).

XANTHE XAVIER XAVIERA XENIA XANTH
E XAVIER XAVIERA XENIA XANTHE XAVIE
R XAVIERA XENIA XANTHE XAVIER XAVIE
RA XENIA XANTHE XAVIER XAVIERA XENI
A XANTHE XAVIER XAVIERA XENIA XANT
HE XAVIER XAVIERA XENIA XANTHE XAVI

Xanthe ♀

From the feminine form of the Greek
adjective *xanthos* 'yellow', 'bright'.
The name was borne by various minor
figures in classical mythology and is
occasionally chosen by parents in
search of an unusual given name for a
daughter.

Xavier ♂

From the surname of the Spanish
soldier–saint Francis Xavier (1506–52),
one of the founding members of the
Society of Jesus (the Jesuits). He was
born on the ancestral estate at Xavier
(now Javier) in Navarre, which in the
early Middle Ages was an independent
Basque kingdom. *Xavier* probably
represents a Hispanicized form of the
Basque placename *Etcheberria* 'the
new house'. (Spanish *x* was
pronounced in the Middle Ages as 'sh',
now as 'h'.) The given name is used
almost exclusively by Roman
Catholics.

Xaviera ♀

Name created as a feminine form of
▷**Xavier**.

Xenia ♀

Comparatively rare given name,
coined from the Greek vocabulary
word *xenia* 'hospitality', a derivative
of *xenos* 'stranger', 'foreigner'.

YASMIN YNYR YOLANDE YORATH YORICK
YORK YSANNE YSEULT YVES YVETTE YVON
NE YASMIN YNYR YOLANDE YORATH YOR
ICK YORK YSANNE YSEULT YVES YVETTE YV
ONNE YASMIN YNYR YOLANDE YORATH
YORICK YORK YSANNE YSEULT YVES YVETT

Yasmin ♀
Variant of ◊**Jasmine**, representing a 'learned' re-creation of the Persian form.

Ynyr ♂
Welsh: traditional name of uncertain derivation, probably from the Latin name *Honōrius* (a derivative of *honor* 'renown'). There is a passing reference in the *Mabinogi* to 'the battle between the two Ynyrs'.

Yolande ♀
Of uncertain origin. It is found in Old French in this form, and may be ultimately of Germanic origin, but if so it has been altered beyond recognition. It is also sometimes identified with the name of St *Jolenta* (d. 1298), daughter of the king of Hungary.
Variant: **Yolanda** (Latinate).

Yorath ♂
Anglicized form of the Welsh personal name ◊**Iorwerth** or, in some cases, a transferred use of the surname derived from it.

Yorick ♂
The name of the (defunct) court jester in Shakespeare's *Hamlet*. This is a respelling of *Jorck*, a Danish form of ◊**George**.

York ♂
Transferred use of the surname, which originated as a local name from the city in north-eastern England. The placename was originally *Eburacon*, a derivative of a Welsh word meaning 'yew'. The Anglo-Saxon settlers changed this to Old English *Eofor-wīc* 'boar farm', which in Old Norse became *Iorvík* or *Iork*. There has probably also been some influence from ◊**Yorick**.

Ysanne ♀
Recent coinage, a blend of the first syllable of ◊**Yseult** + the given name *Anne*.

Yseult ♀
Medieval French form of ◊**Isolde**, still occasionally used as a given name in the English-speaking world.

Yves ♂
French: from a Germanic personal name representing a short form of various compound names containing the element *iv* 'yew'. The final -*s* is the mark of the Old French nominative case. The name was introduced to Britain from France at the time of the Norman Conquest, and again in the 20th century. See also ◊**Ivo**.

Yvette ♀
French feminine diminutive form of ◊**Yves**, now also used in the English-speaking world.

Yvonne ♀
Yvon; form based on the Old French oblique case (cf. ◊**Ivon**) now also French feminine diminutive form of ◊**Yves** (or simply a feminine widely used in the English-speaking world).

ZACHARY ZACH ZANE ZANNA ZARA ZAYL
IE ZEB ZEBEDEE ZEBULUN ZED ZEKE ZELAH
ZELDA ZELMA ZENA ZEPH ZEPHYRINE ZET
A ZILAH ZINA ZIPPORAH ZITA ZOE ZOLA
ZULA ZACHARY ZACH ZANE ZANNA ZAR
A ZAYLIE ZEB ZEBEDEE ZEBULUN ZED ZEKE

Zachary ♂

English vernacular form of the New Testament Greek name *Zacharias*, a form of Hebrew *Zechariah* 'God has remembered'. This was the name of the father of John the Baptist, who underwent a temporary period of dumbness for his lack of faith (Luke 1), and of a more obscure figure, Zacharias son of Barachias, who was slain 'between the temple and the altar' (Matthew 23:35; Luke 11:51). Like many biblical names, it is now out of fashion, although in the United States it is familiar as the name of a 19th-century president, Zachary Taylor.

Zack ♂

Mainly North American: short form of ◊Zachary.

Zane ♂

Transferred use of a surname of uncertain origin. It came to prominence as the given name of the American writer Zane Grey (1875–1939), a descendant of the Ebenezer Zane who founded *Zaneville* in Ohio.

Zanna ♀

Modern coinage, apparently a shortened form of *Suzanna*.

Zara ♀

Of uncertain origin. It is sometimes said to be of Arabic origin, from *zahr* 'flower', but is more probably a respelled form of ◊Sara. It was given by Princess Anne and Mark Philips to their second child (b. 1981), which aroused considerable comment at the time as it was a departure from the traditional patterns of royal nomenclature.

Zaylie ♀

Of uncertain origin, perhaps a respelling of the rare French name *Zélie*, an altered form of *Célie*, the French version of ◊Celia.

Zeb ♂

Especially U.S.: short form of ◊Zebedee and ◊Zebulun.

Zebedee ♂

Name borne in the New Testament by the father of the apostles James and John, who was with his sons mending fishing nets when they were called by Christ (Matthew 4:21; Mark 1:20). This is from a Greek form of the Hebrew name that appears in the Old Testament as *Zebadiah* or *Zabdi* 'gift of Jehovah'.

Zebulun ♂

Biblical name, borne by the sixth son of Leah and Jacob. The name may mean 'exaltation', although Leah derives it from another meaning of the Hebrew root *zabal*, namely 'to dwell': 'now will my husband dwell with me, because I have born him six sons' (Genesis 30:20). It appears in the New Testament (Matthew 4:13) in the form *Zabulon*.
Variant: **Zebulon**.

Zed ♂

Especially U.S.: short form of the much rarer full name **Zedekiah**. This name, meaning 'justice of Yahweh' in Hebrew, is borne in the Bible by three separate characters.

Zeke ♂
Especially U.S.: shortened form of
◊**Ezekiel**.

Zelah ♀
Biblical name (meaning 'side' in
Hebrew), borne by one of the fourteen
cities of the tribe of Benjamin (Joshua
18:28). It is far from clear why it
should have come to be used, albeit
rarely, as a female given name in the
English-speaking world. It may simply
be a variant of ◊**Zillah** under the
influence of the placename. However,
for evidence that biblical placenames
did yield English given names, cf.
◊**Ebenezer**.

Zelda ♀
Modern name of uncertain origin,
possibly a short form of ◊**Griselda**. It
came to prominence in the 1920s as
the name of the wife of the American
writer F. Scott Fitzgerald (1896–1940).

Zelma ♀
Modern coinage, an altered form of
◊**Selma**.

Zena ♀
Of uncertain origin, probably a variant
spelling of ◊**Zina**.

Zeph ♂
Especially U.S: short form of the
much rarer full name **Zephaniah**. This
name, meaning 'hidden by God' in
Hebrew, was borne by one of the
minor biblical prophets, author of the
book of the Bible that bears his name.

Zephyrine ♀
From French *Zéphyrine*, an elaborated
name derived from Latin *Zephyrus*,
Greek *Zephyros* 'west wind'. St
Zephyrinus was pope 199–217, but
there is no equivalent female saint, so
it is rather surprising that this name
should have survived only in a female
form.

Zeta ♀
Of uncertain origin, probably a variant
spelling of ◊**Zita**. It also coincides in
form with the name of the letter of

the Greek alphabet equivalent to
English *z* (but not the last letter of the
Greek alphabet).

Zillah ♀
Biblical name (from a Hebrew word
meaning 'shade'), borne by one of the
two wives of Lamech (Genesis 4:19).
The name was taken up in the first
place by the Puritans, and again by
fundamentalist Christian groups in
the 19th century, partly because
Zillah is only the third woman to be
mentioned by name in the Bible, and
her name was therefore prominent to
readers of the Book of Genesis.

Zina ♀
Russian short form of **Zinaida** (from
Greek *Zēnais*, a derivative of the
name of the god *Zeus*), the name of an
obscure saint venerated in the Eastern
Church. It is also a Russian short form
of the rarer given name *Zinovia* (from
Greek *Zēnobia*, a compound of *Zeus*
+ *bios* 'life'). Its adoption as a given
name in the English-speaking world
probably owes something to its
resemblance to the popular female
given name ◊**Tina**.

Zipporah ♀
Jewish: common female form of the
rare Hebrew male name *Zippor*, from
Hebrew *zippor* 'bird'. The female
name is borne in the Bible by the wife
of Moses (Exodus 18:2–4).

Zita ♀
From the name of a 13th-century saint
from Lucca in Tuscany, who led an
uneventful life as a domestic servant;
she was canonized in 1696, and is
regarded as the patroness of domestic
servants. Her name was probably a
nickname from the medieval Tuscan
dialect word *zit(t)a* 'girl', although
efforts have been made to link it with
Greek *zētein* 'to seek'.

Zoë ♀
From a Greek name meaning 'life'.
This was already in use in Rome
towards the end of the classical period

(at first as an affectionate nickname), and was popular with the early Christians, who bestowed it with reference to their hopes of eternal life. It was borne by martyrs of the 2nd and 3rd centuries, but was taken up as an English given name only in the 19th century.

Variant: **Zoe**.

Zola ♀

Apparently a late 20th-century creation, formed from the first syllable of ◊**Zoë** with the ending *-la*, common in female names. It coincides in form with the surname of the French novelist Émile Zola (1840–1902), who was of Italian descent, but it is unlikely that he had any influence on the popularity of the name.

Zula ♀

Modern coinage derived from the tribal name of the Zulus. The Zulu people of Southern Africa formed a powerful warrior nation under their leader Chaka in the 19th century, and controlled an extensive empire. In 1838, under the leadership of their ruler Dingaan, they ambushed and slaughtered a group of some five hundred Boers. Not surprisingly, this given name is chosen mainly by Black people proud of their African origins.